COFFIN HILL

VOLUME 2

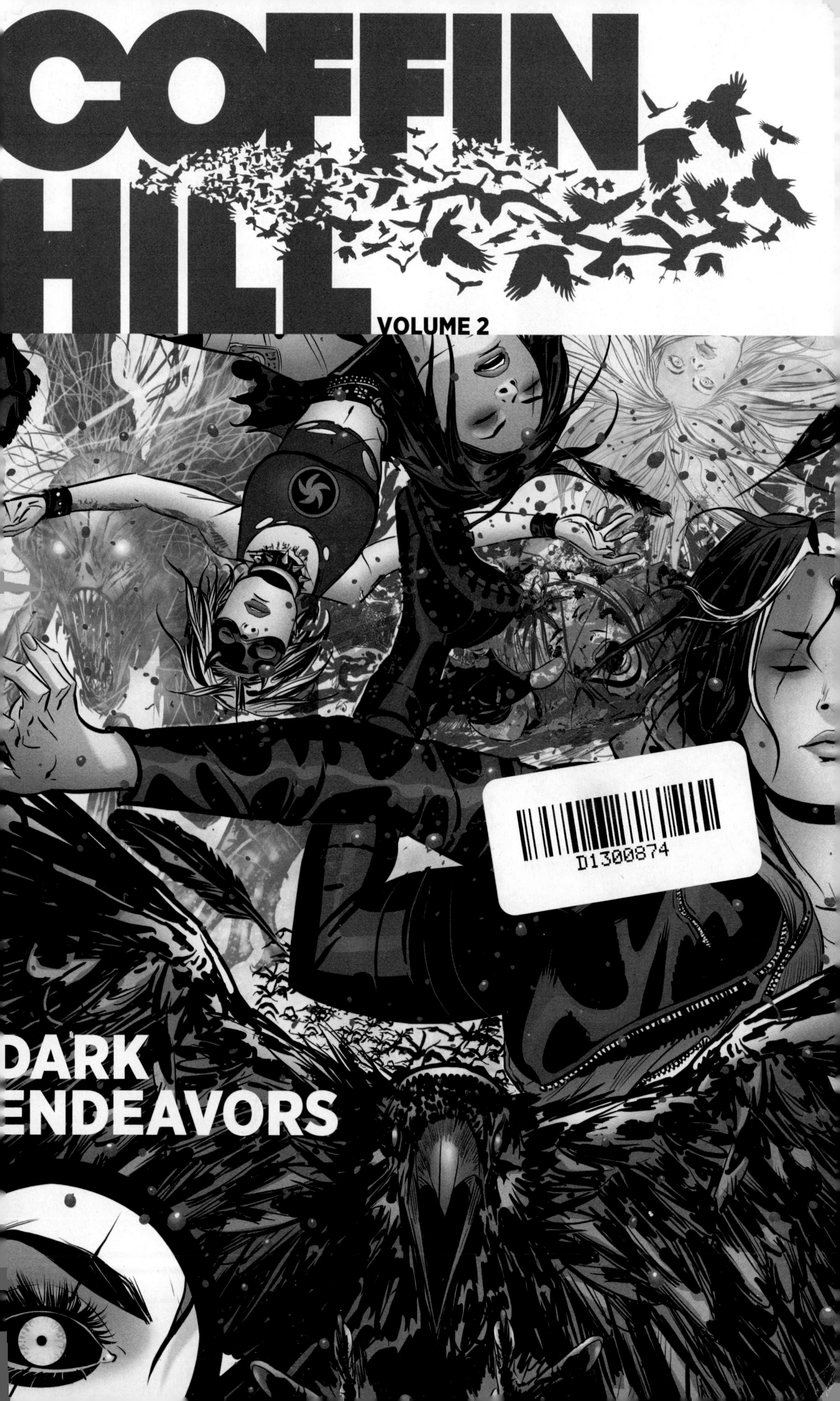
DARK
ENDEAVORS

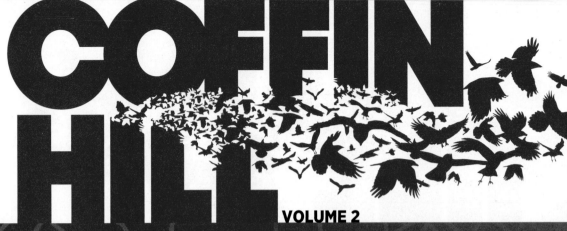

COFFIN HILL

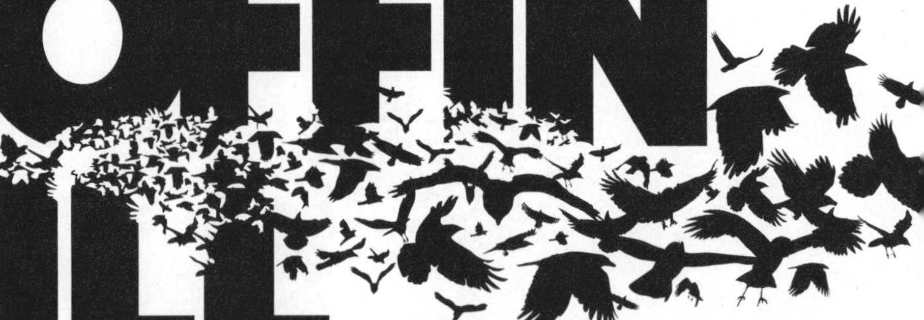

VOLUME 2

DARK ENDEAVORS

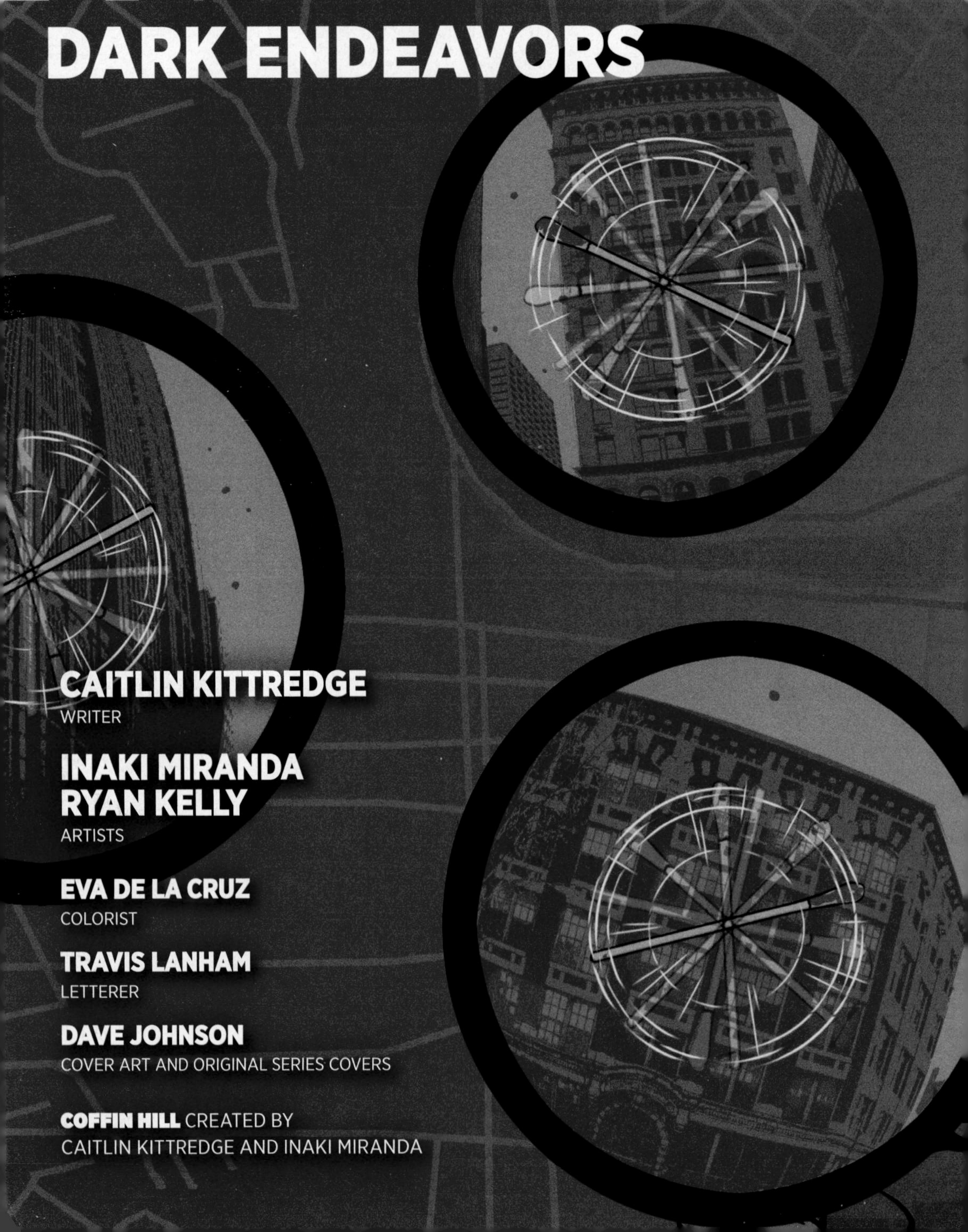

CAITLIN KITTREDGE
WRITER

INAKI MIRANDA
RYAN KELLY
ARTISTS

EVA DE LA CRUZ
COLORIST

TRAVIS LANHAM
LETTERER

DAVE JOHNSON
COVER ART AND ORIGINAL SERIES COVERS

COFFIN HILL CREATED BY
CAITLIN KITTREDGE AND INAKI MIRANDA

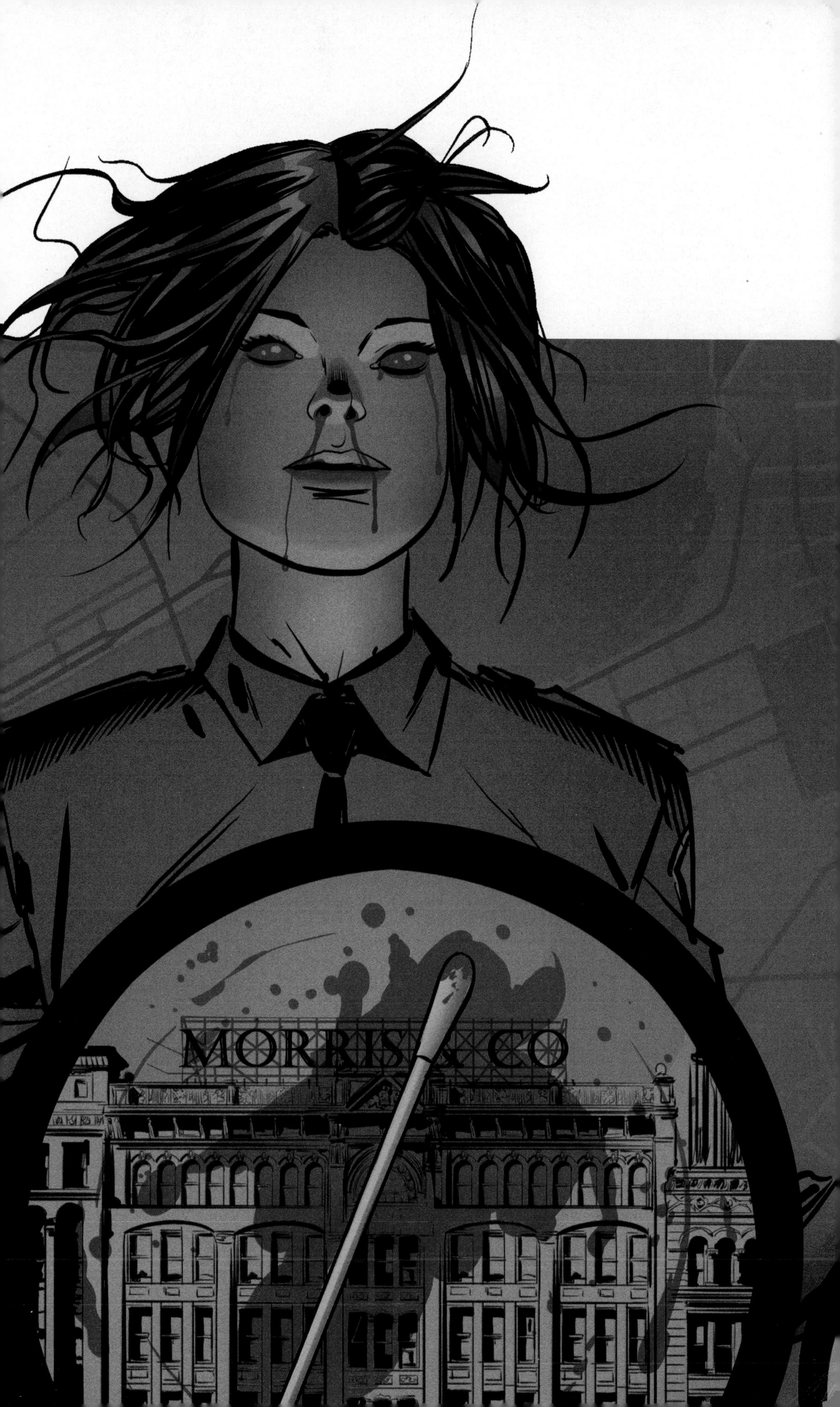
MORRIS & CO

SHELLY BOND
EXECUTIVE EDITOR – VERTIGO AND EDITOR – ORIGINAL SERIES

ROWENA YOW
ASSOCIATE EDITOR – ORIGINAL SERIES

SARA MILLER
ASSISTANT EDITOR – ORIGINAL SERIES

PETER HAMBOUSSI
EDITOR

ROBBIN BROSTERMAN
DESIGN DIRECTOR – BOOKS

CURTIS KING JR.
PUBLICATION DESIGN

HANK KANALZ
SENIOR VP – VERTIGO AND INTEGRATED PUBLISHING

DIANE NELSON
PRESIDENT

DAN DIDIO AND **JIM LEE**
CO-PUBLISHERS

GEOFF JOHNS
CHIEF CREATIVE OFFICER

AMIT DESAI
SENIOR VP – MARKETING & FRANCHISE MANAGEMENT

AMY GENKINS
SENIOR VP – BUSINESS AND LEGAL AFFAIRS

NAIRI GARDINER
SENIOR VP – FINANCE

JEFF BOISON
VP – PUBLISHING PLANNING

MARK CHIARELLO
VP – ART DIRECTION AND DESIGN

JOHN CUNNINGHAM
VP – MARKETING

TERRI CUNNINGHAM
VP – EDITORIAL ADMINISTRATION

LARRY GANEM
VP – TALENT RELATIONS AND SERVICES

ALISON GILL
SENIOR VP – MANUFACTURING AND OPERATIONS

JAY KOGAN
VP – BUSINESS AND LEGAL AFFAIRS, PUBLISHING

JACK MAHAN
VP – BUSINESS AFFAIRS, TALENT

NICK NAPOLITANO
VP – MANUFACTURING ADMINISTRATION

SUE POHJA
VP – BOOK SALES

FRED RUIZ
VP – MANUFACTURING OPERATIONS

COURTNEY SIMMONS
SENIOR VP – PUBLICITY

BOB WAYNE
SENIOR VP – SALES

LOGO DESIGN BY STEVE COOK

COFFIN HILL VOLUME 2: DARK ENDEAVORS

PUBLISHED BY DC COMICS. COMPILATION COPYRIGHT © 2015
CAITLIN KITTREDGE AND INAKI MIRANDA. ALL RIGHTS RESERVED.

DC COMICS, 1700 BROADWAY, NEW YORK, NY 10019
A WARNER BROS. ENTERTAINMENT COMPANY
PRINTED IN THE USA. FIRST PRINTING.
ISBN: 978-1-4012-5084-3

Library of Congress Cataloging-in-Publication Data

Kittredge, Caitlin, author.
  Coffin Hill. Volume 2, Dark Endeavors / Caitlin Kittredge, writer ; Inaki Miranda,
illustrator.
      pages cm
   ISBN 978-1-4012-5084-3 (paperback)
  1. Graphic novels. I. Miranda, Inaki, illustrator. II. Title. III. Title: Dark Endeavors.
PN6728.C597K59 2015
741.5'973--dc23
                               2014034198

SUSTAINABLE
FORESTRY
INITIATIVE

Certified Chain of Custody
20% Certified Forest Content,
80% Certified Sourcing
www.sfiprogram.org
SFI-01042
APPLIES TO TEXT STOCK ONLY

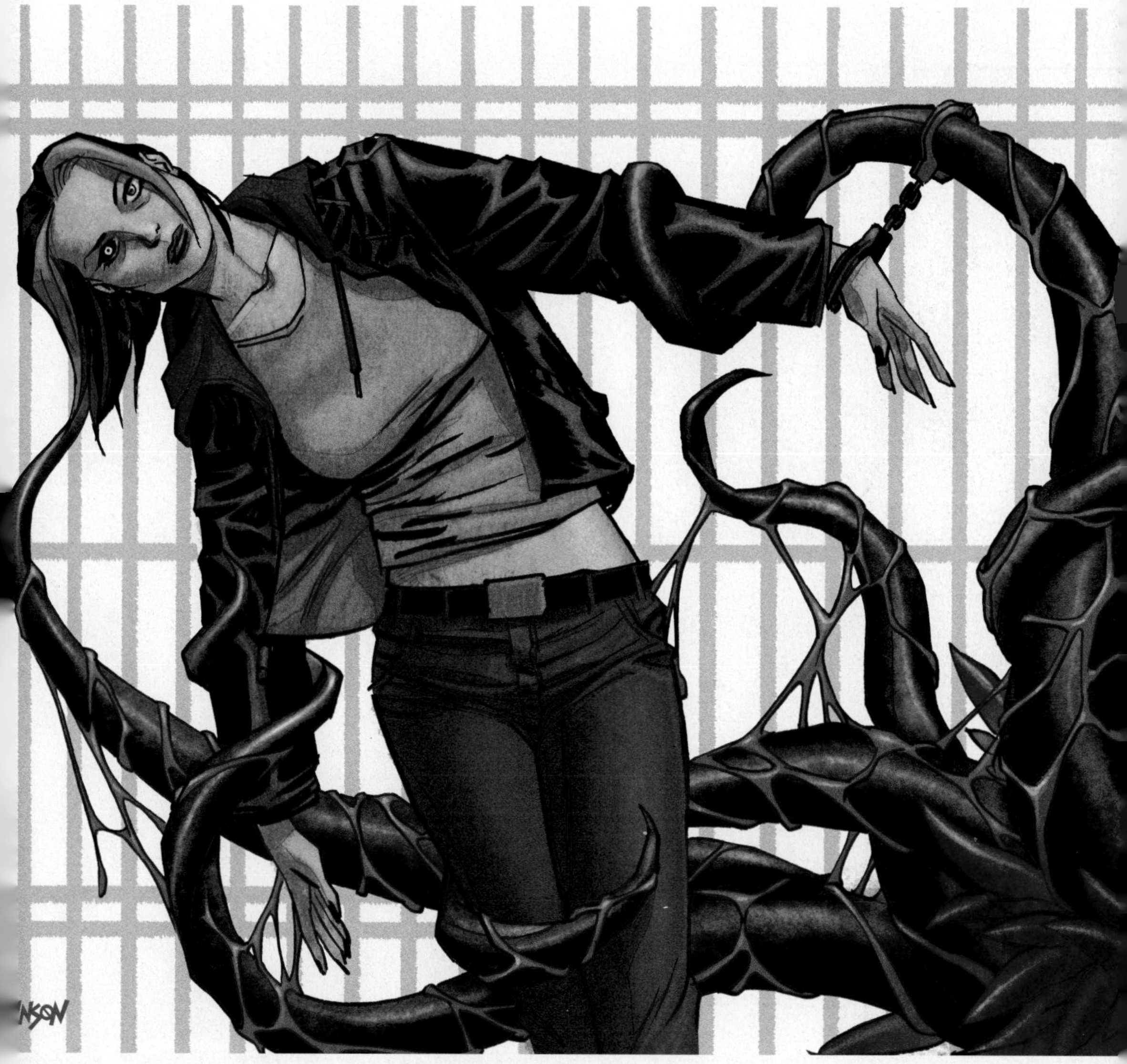

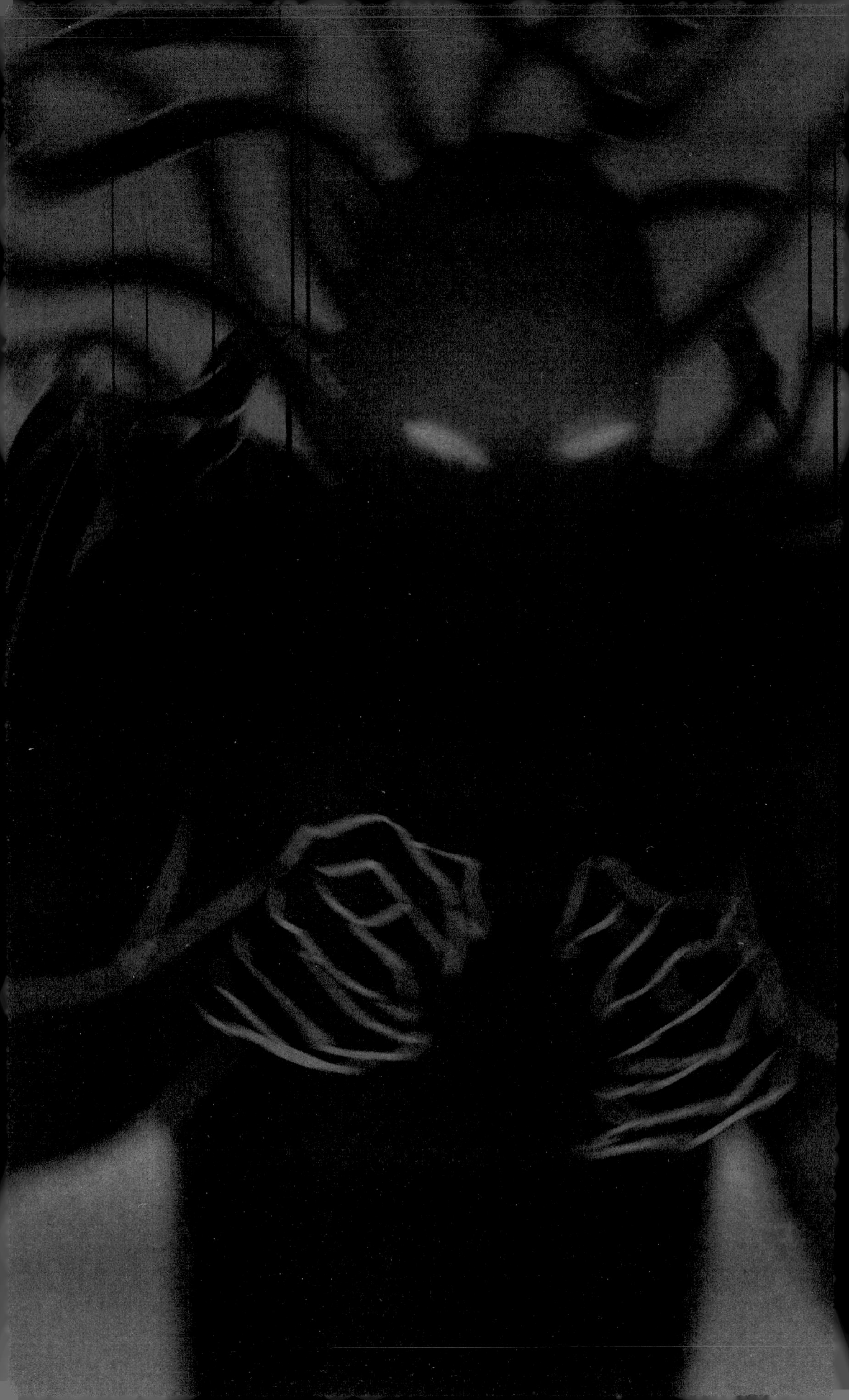

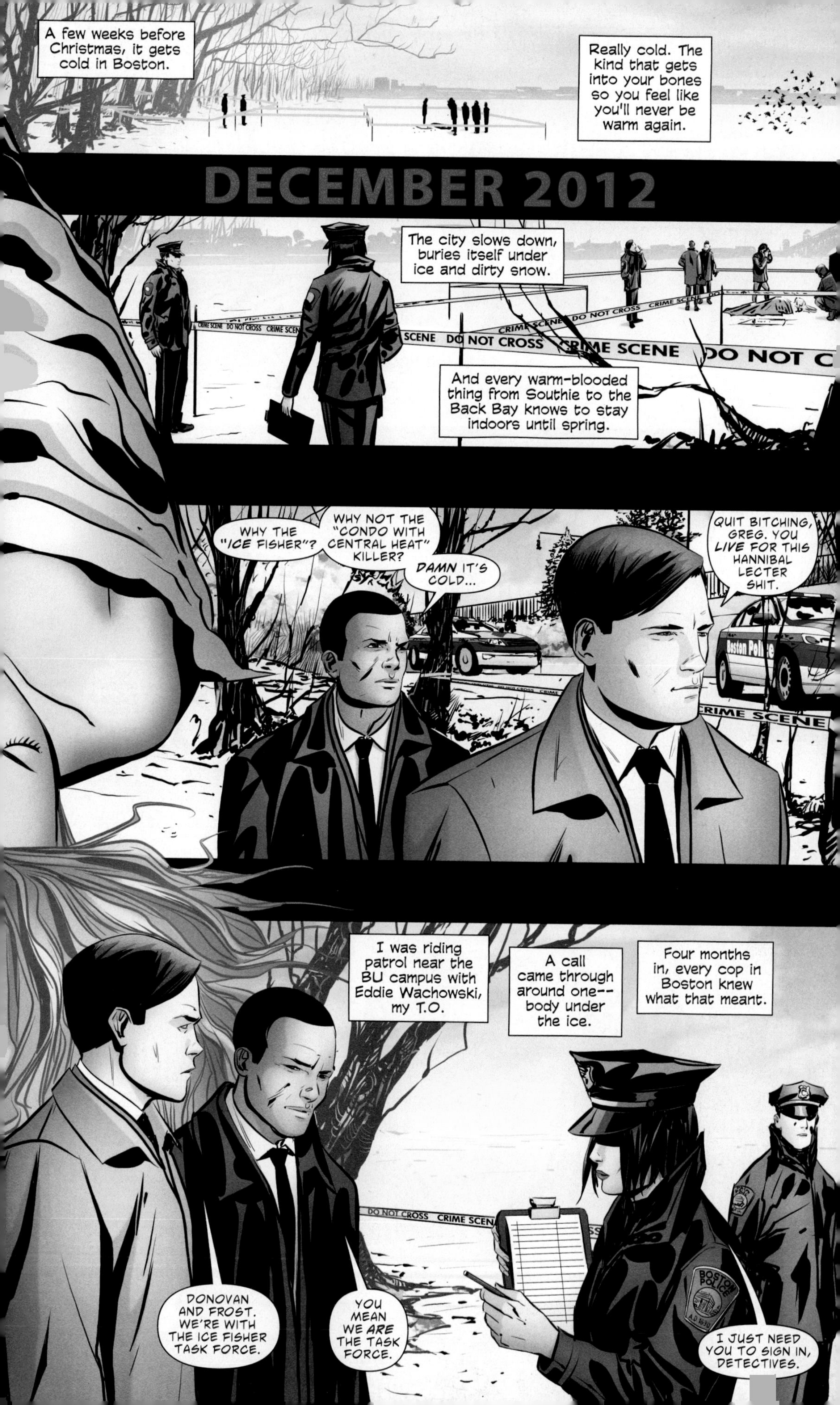
A few weeks before Christmas, it gets cold in Boston.
Really cold. The kind that gets into your bones so you feel like you'll never be warm again.
DECEMBER 2012
The city slows down, buries itself under ice and dirty snow.
CRIME SCENE DO NOT CROSS CRIME SCENE
And every warm-blooded thing from Southie to the Back Bay knows to stay indoors until spring.
WHY THE "ICE FISHER"?
WHY NOT THE "CONDO WITH CENTRAL HEAT" KILLER?
DAMN IT'S COLD...
QUIT BITCHING, GREG. YOU LIVE FOR THIS HANNIBAL LECTER SHIT.
I was riding patrol near the BU campus with Eddie Wachowski, my T.O.
A call came through around one-- body under the ice.
Four months in, every cop in Boston knew what that meant.
DONOVAN AND FROST. WE'RE WITH THE ICE FISHER TASK FORCE.
YOU MEAN WE ARE THE TASK FORCE.
I JUST NEED YOU TO SIGN IN, DETECTIVES.

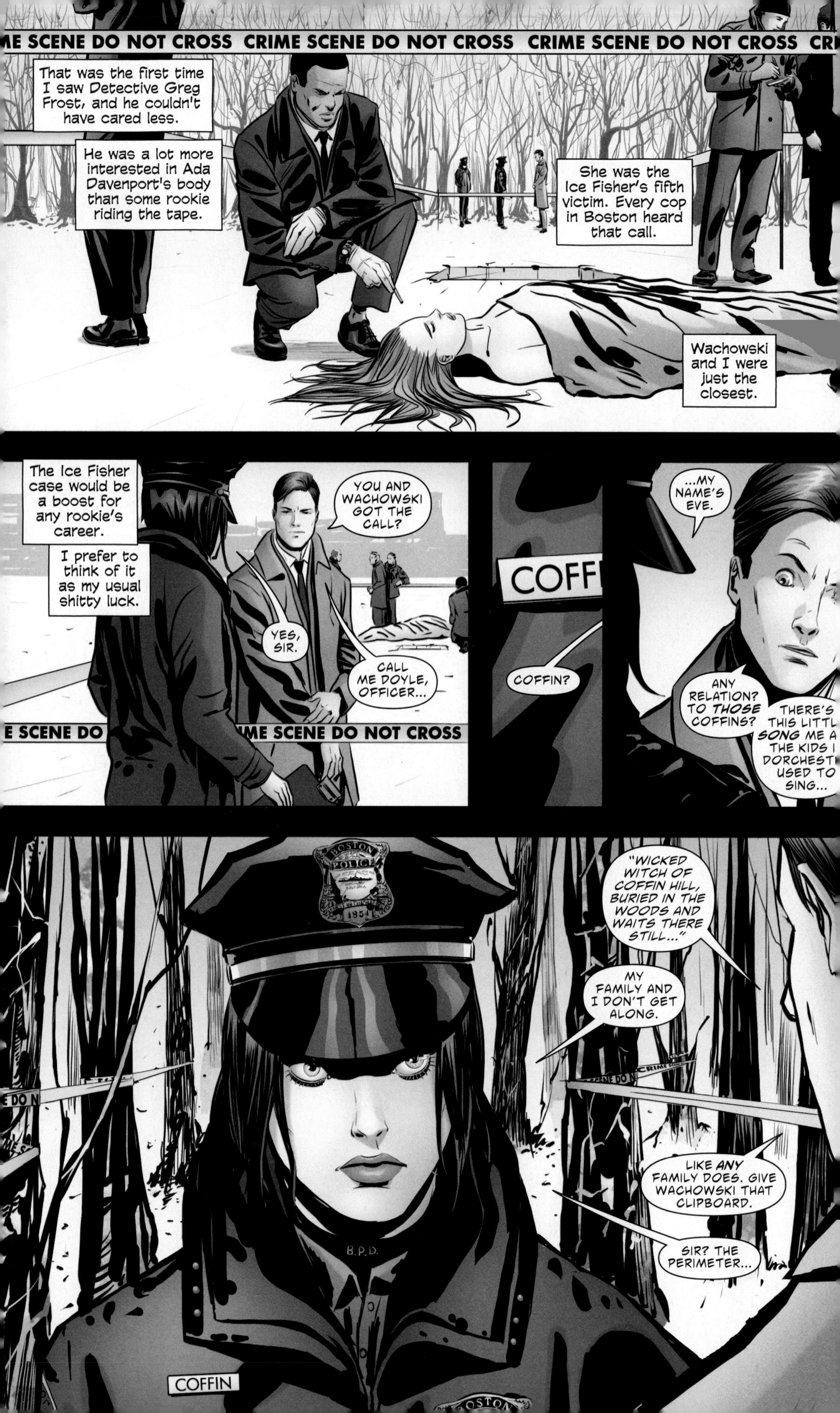
CRIME SCENE DO NOT CROSS CRIME SCENE DO NOT CROSS CRIME SCENE DO NOT CROSS
That was the first time I saw Detective Greg Frost, and he couldn't have cared less.
He was a lot more interested in Ada Davenport's body than some rookie riding the tape.
She was the Ice Fisher's fifth victim. Every cop in Boston heard that call.
Wachowski and I were just the closest.
The Ice Fisher case would be a boost for any rookie's career.
I prefer to think of it as my usual shitty luck.
YOU AND WACHOWSKI GOT THE CALL?
YES, SIR.
CALL ME DOYLE, OFFICER...
COFFIN?
...MY NAME'S EVE.
ANY RELATION? TO THOSE COFFINS?
"WICKED WITCH OF COFFIN HILL, BURIED IN THE WOODS AND WAITS THERE STILL..."
MY FAMILY AND I DON'T GET ALONG.
LIKE ANY FAMILY DOES. GIVE WACHOWSKI THAT CLIPBOARD.
SIR? THE PERIMETER...
COFFIN

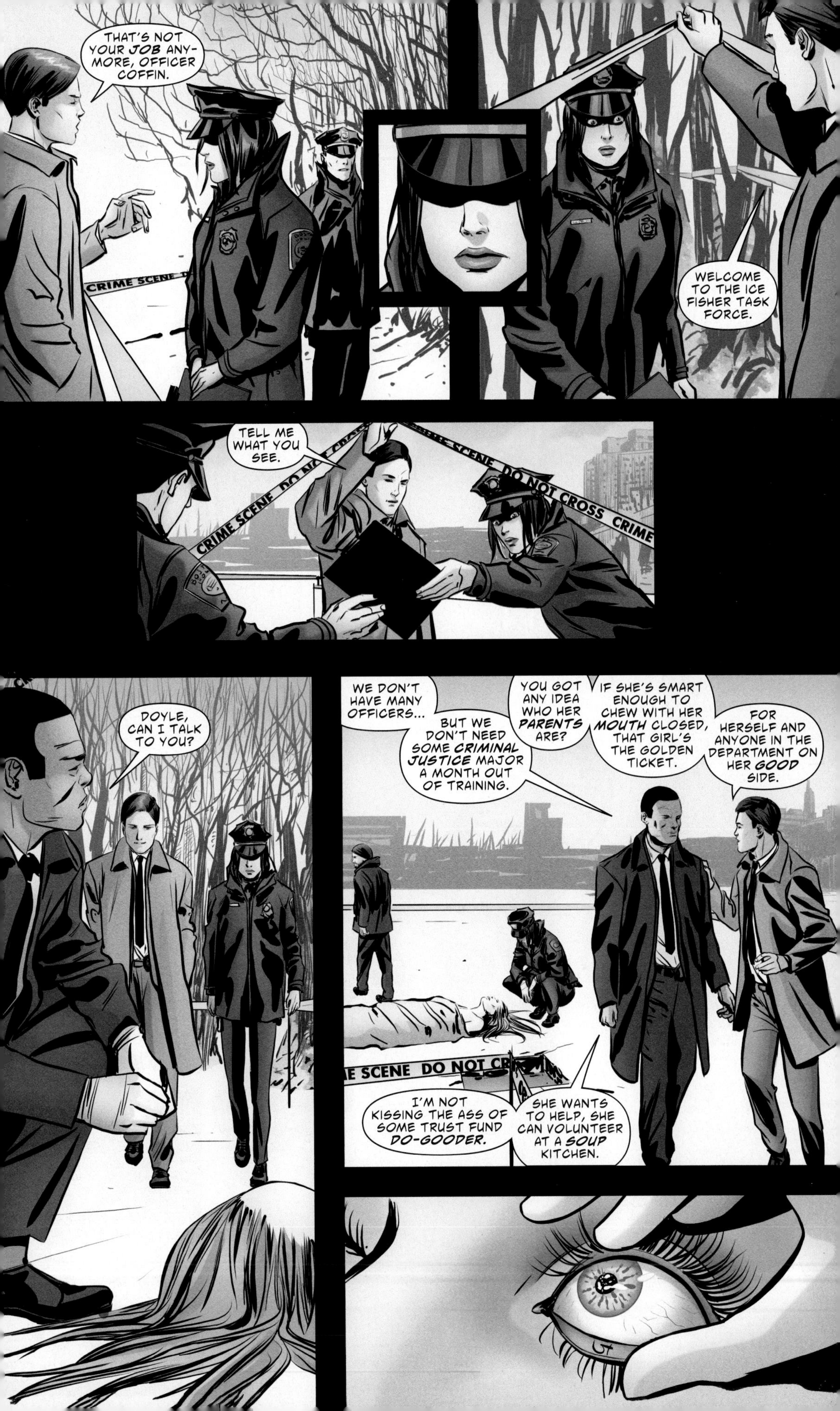
THAT'S NOT YOUR JOB ANYMORE, OFFICER COFFIN.
WELCOME TO THE ICE FISHER TASK FORCE.
TELL ME WHAT YOU SEE.
CRIME SCENE DO NOT CROSS CRIME
DOYLE, CAN I TALK TO YOU?
WE DON'T HAVE MANY OFFICERS...
BUT WE DON'T NEED SOME CRIMINAL JUSTICE MAJOR A MONTH OUT OF TRAINING.
YOU GOT ANY IDEA WHO HER PARENTS ARE?
IF SHE'S SMART ENOUGH TO CHEW WITH HER MOUTH CLOSED, THAT GIRL'S THE GOLDEN TICKET.
FOR HERSELF AND ANYONE IN THE DEPARTMENT ON HER GOOD SIDE.
I'M NOT KISSING THE ASS OF SOME TRUST FUND DO-GOODER.
SHE WANTS TO HELP, SHE CAN VOLUNTEER AT A SOUP KITCHEN.

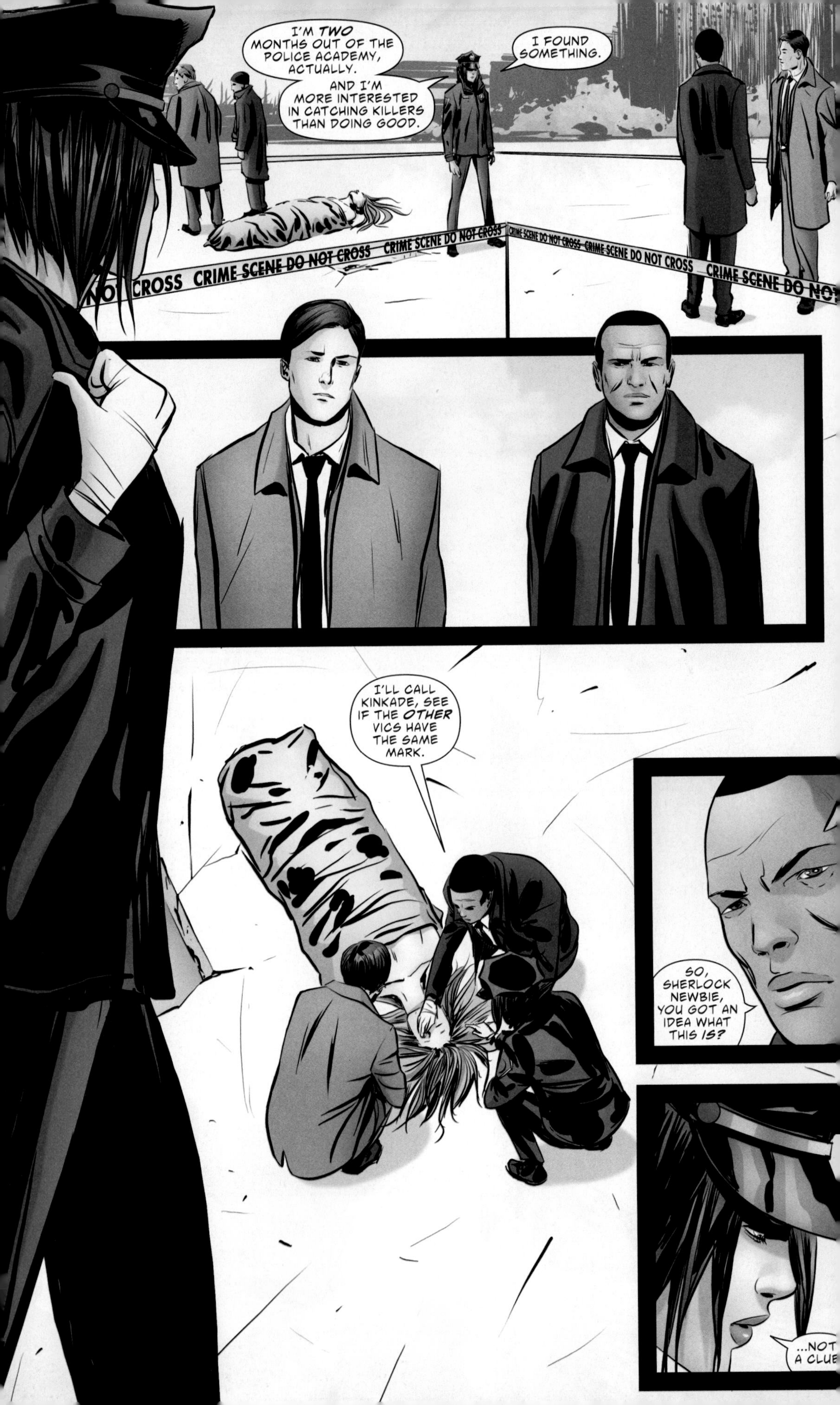
I'M TWO MONTHS OUT OF THE POLICE ACADEMY, ACTUALLY.
AND I'M MORE INTERESTED IN CATCHING KILLERS THAN DOING GOOD.
I FOUND SOMETHING.
CRIME SCENE DO NOT CROSS
I'LL CALL KINKADE, SEE IF THE OTHER VICS HAVE THE SAME MARK.
SO, SHERLOCK NEWBIE, YOU GOT AN IDEA WHAT THIS IS?
...NOT A CLUE

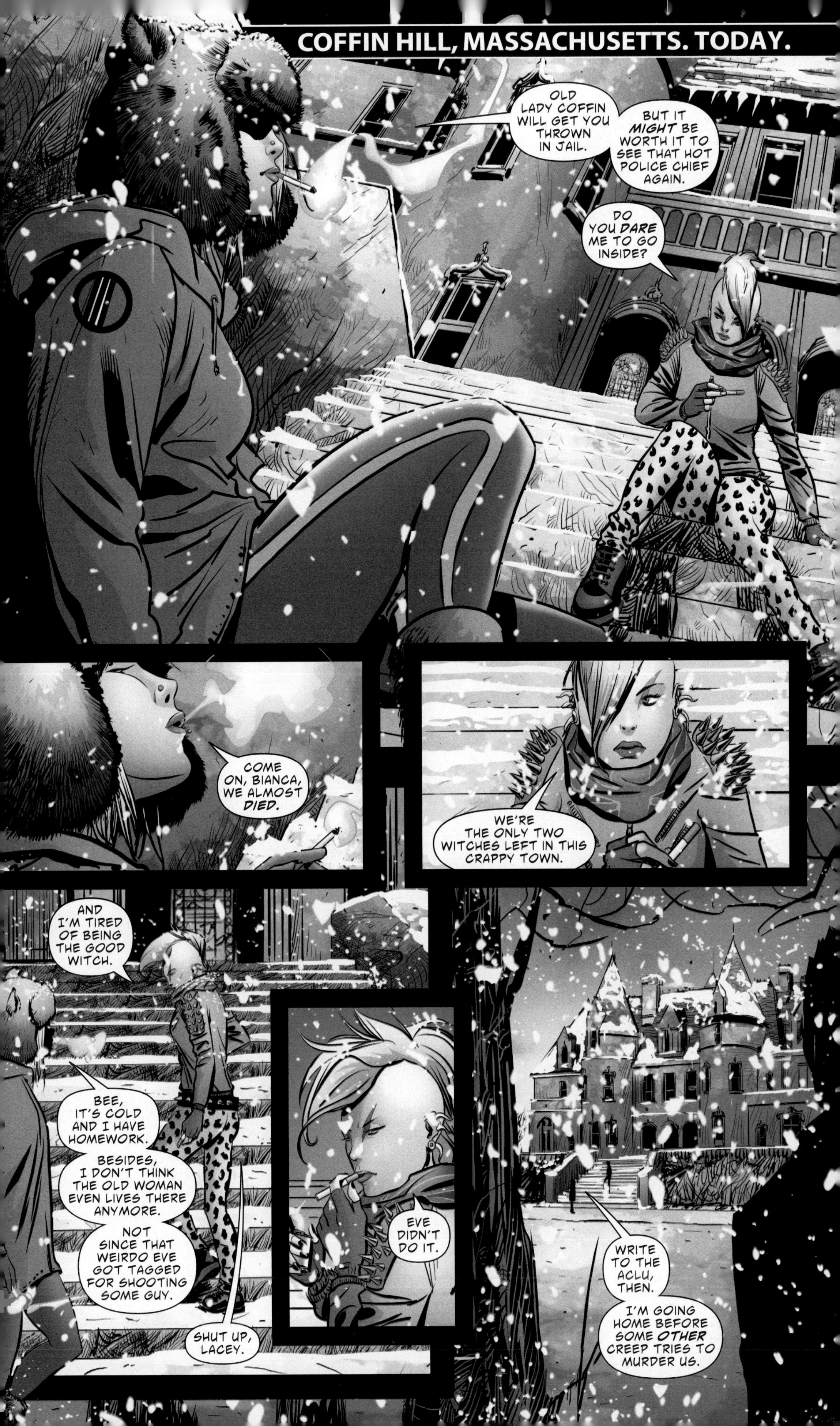

COFFIN HILL, MASSACHUSETTS. TODAY.
OLD LADY COFFIN WILL GET YOU THROWN IN JAIL.
BUT IT MIGHT BE WORTH IT TO SEE THAT HOT POLICE CHIEF AGAIN.
DO YOU DARE ME TO GO INSIDE?
COME ON, BIANCA, WE ALMOST DIED.
WE'RE THE ONLY TWO WITCHES LEFT IN THIS CRAPPY TOWN.
AND I'M TIRED OF BEING THE GOOD WITCH.
BEE, IT'S COLD AND I HAVE HOMEWORK.
BESIDES, I DON'T THINK THE OLD WOMAN EVEN LIVES THERE ANYMORE.
NOT SINCE THAT WEIRDO EVE GOT TAGGED FOR SHOOTING SOME GUY.
SHUT UP, LACEY.
EVE DIDN'T DO IT.
WRITE TO THE ACLU, THEN.
I'M GOING HOME BEFORE SOME OTHER CREEP TRIES TO MURDER US.

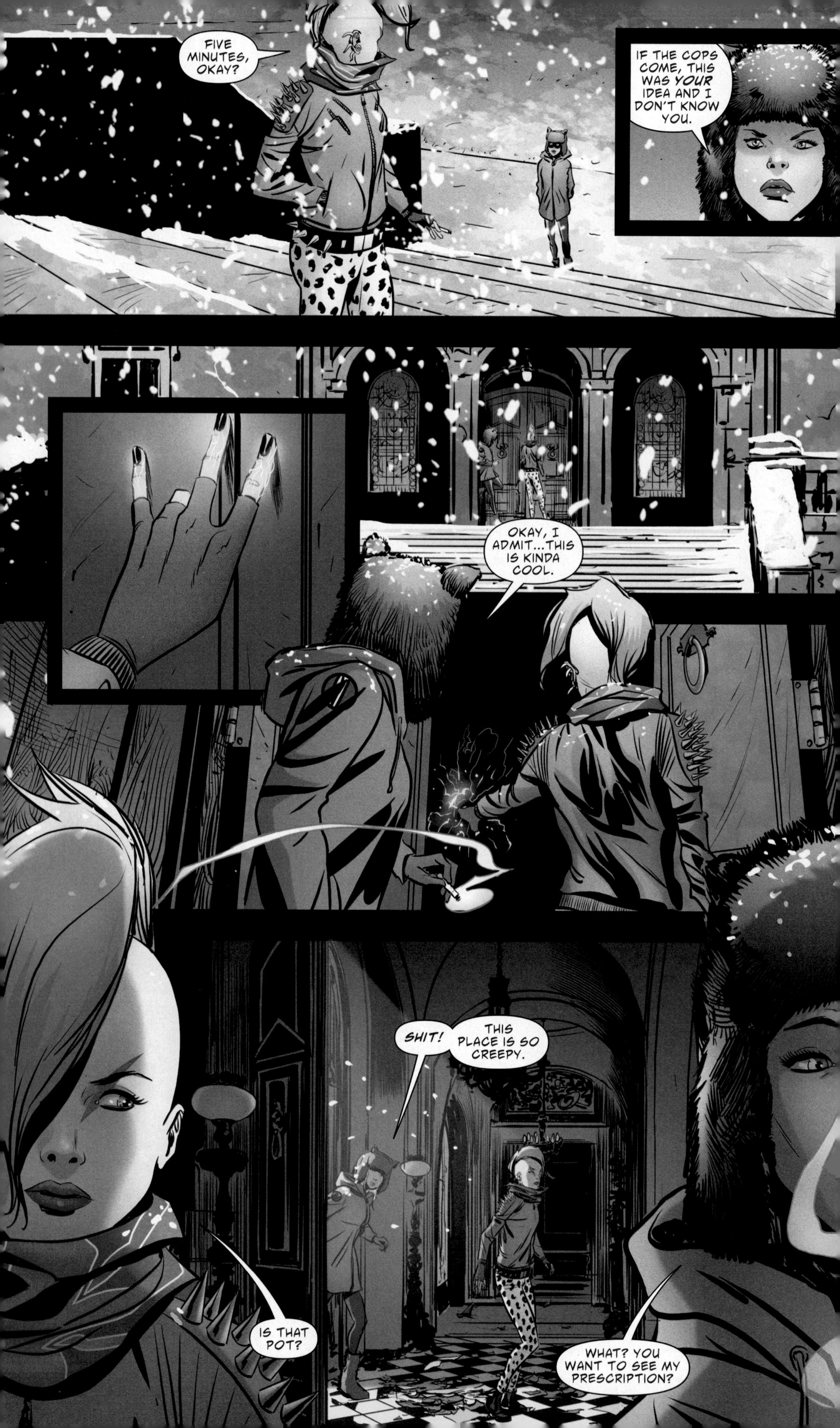
FIVE MINUTES, OKAY?
IF THE COPS COME, THIS WAS YOUR IDEA AND I DON'T KNOW YOU.
OKAY, I ADMIT...THIS IS KINDA COOL.
SHIT!
THIS PLACE IS SO CREEPY.
IS THAT POT?
WHAT? YOU WANT TO SEE MY PRESCRIPTION?

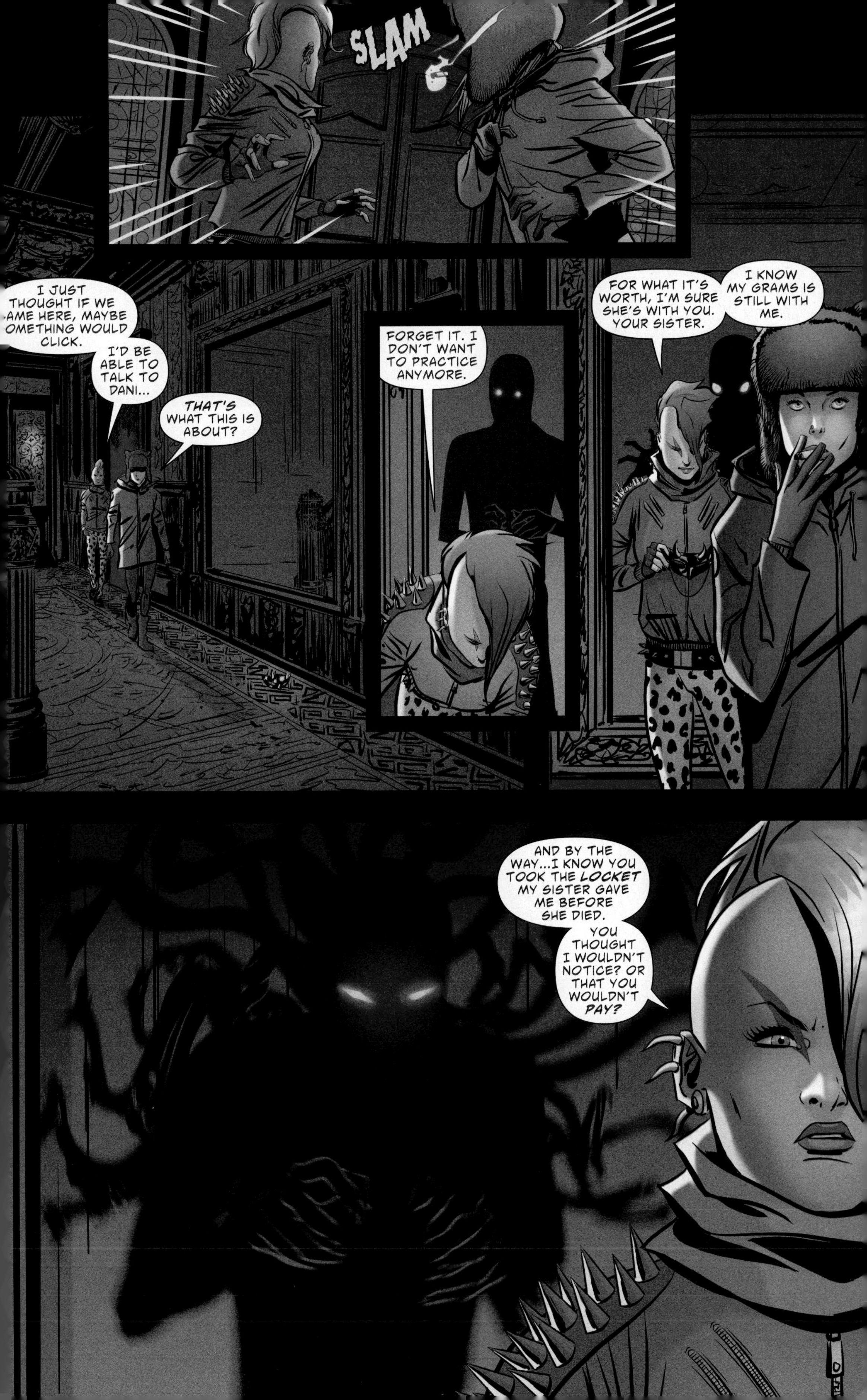
SLAM
I JUST THOUGHT IF WE AME HERE, MAYBE OMETHING WOULD CLICK.
I'D BE ABLE TO TALK TO DANI...
THAT'S WHAT THIS IS ABOUT?
FORGET IT. I DON'T WANT TO PRACTICE ANYMORE.
FOR WHAT IT'S WORTH, I'M SURE SHE'S WITH YOU. YOUR SISTER.
I KNOW MY GRAMS IS STILL WITH ME.
AND BY THE WAY...I KNOW YOU TOOK THE LOCKET MY SISTER GAVE ME BEFORE SHE DIED.
YOU THOUGHT I WOULDN'T NOTICE? OR THAT YOU WOULDN'T PAY?

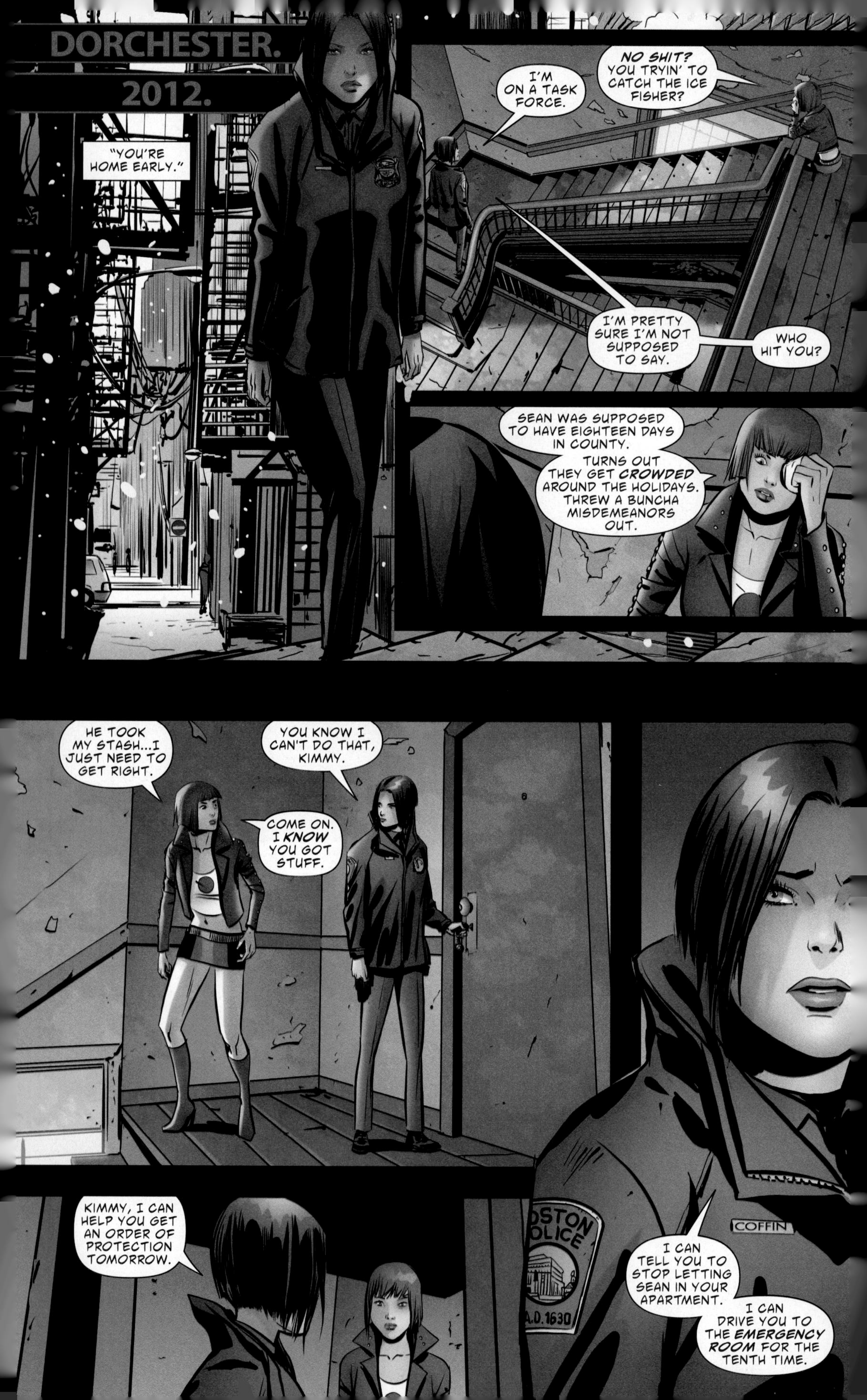
DORCHESTER.
2012.
"YOU'RE HOME EARLY."
I'M ON A TASK FORCE.
NO SHIT? YOU TRYIN' TO CATCH THE ICE FISHER?
I'M PRETTY SURE I'M NOT SUPPOSED TO SAY.
WHO HIT YOU?
SEAN WAS SUPPOSED TO HAVE EIGHTEEN DAYS IN COUNTY.
TURNS OUT THEY GET CROWDED AROUND THE HOLIDAYS. THREW A BUNCHA MISDEMEANORS OUT.
HE TOOK MY STASH...I JUST NEED TO GET RIGHT.
YOU KNOW I CAN'T DO THAT, KIMMY.
COME ON. I KNOW YOU GOT STUFF.
KIMMY, I CAN HELP YOU GET AN ORDER OF PROTECTION TOMORROW.
COFFIN
I CAN TELL YOU TO STOP LETTING SEAN IN YOUR APARTMENT.
I CAN DRIVE YOU TO THE EMERGENCY ROOM FOR THE TENTH TIME.

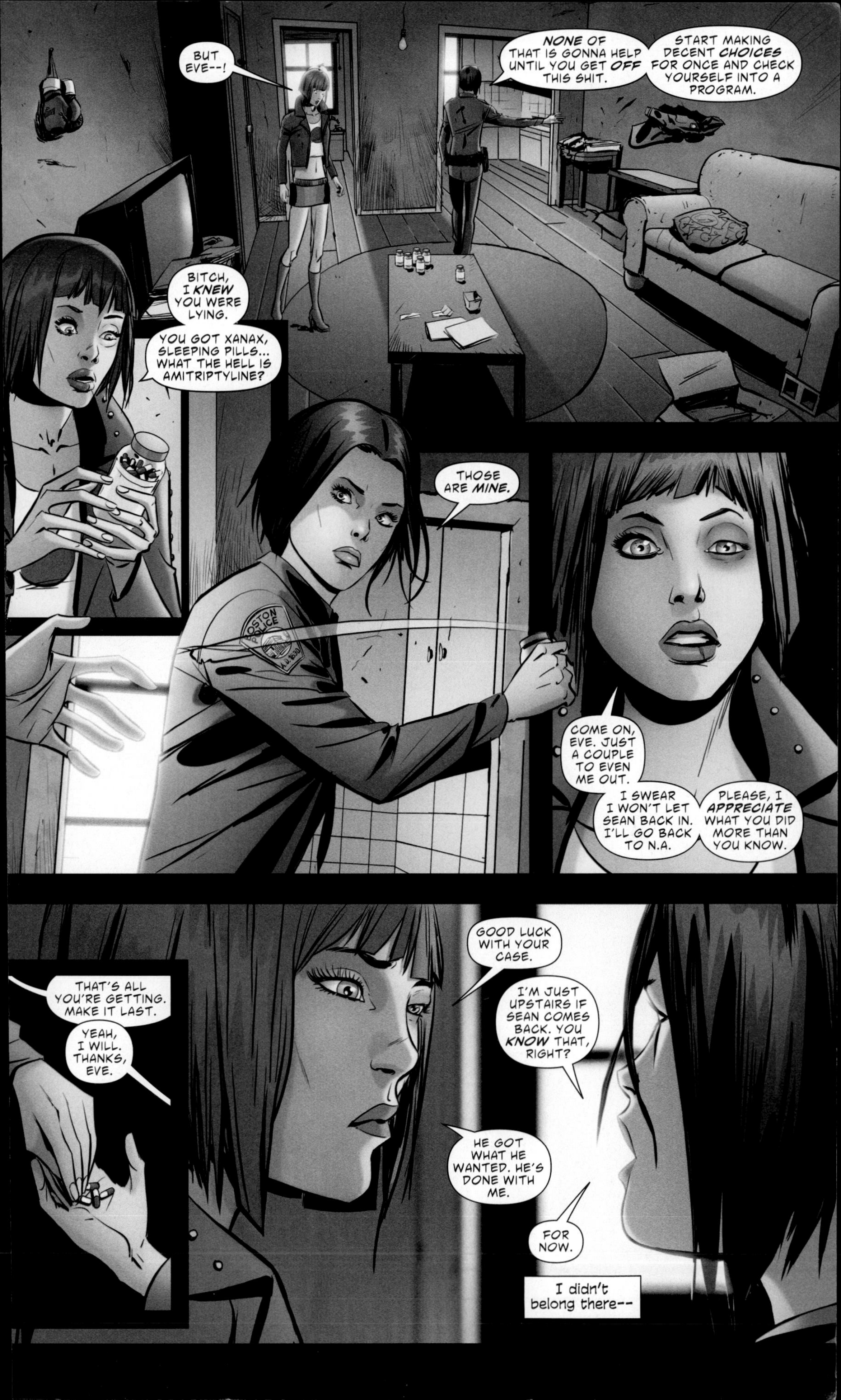
BUT EVE--!
NONE OF THAT IS GONNA HELP UNTIL YOU GET OFF THIS SHIT.
START MAKING DECENT CHOICES FOR ONCE AND CHECK YOURSELF INTO A PROGRAM.
BITCH, I KNEW YOU WERE LYING.
YOU GOT XANAX, SLEEPING PILLS... WHAT THE HELL IS AMITRIPTYLINE?
THOSE ARE MINE.
COME ON, EVE. JUST A COUPLE TO EVEN ME OUT.
I SWEAR I WON'T LET SEAN BACK IN. I'LL GO BACK TO N.A.
PLEASE, I APPRECIATE WHAT YOU DID MORE THAN YOU KNOW.
THAT'S ALL YOU'RE GETTING. MAKE IT LAST.
YEAH, I WILL. THANKS, EVE.
GOOD LUCK WITH YOUR CASE.
I'M JUST UPSTAIRS IF SEAN COMES BACK. YOU KNOW THAT, RIGHT?
HE GOT WHAT HE WANTED. HE'S DONE WITH ME.
FOR NOW.
I didn't belong there--

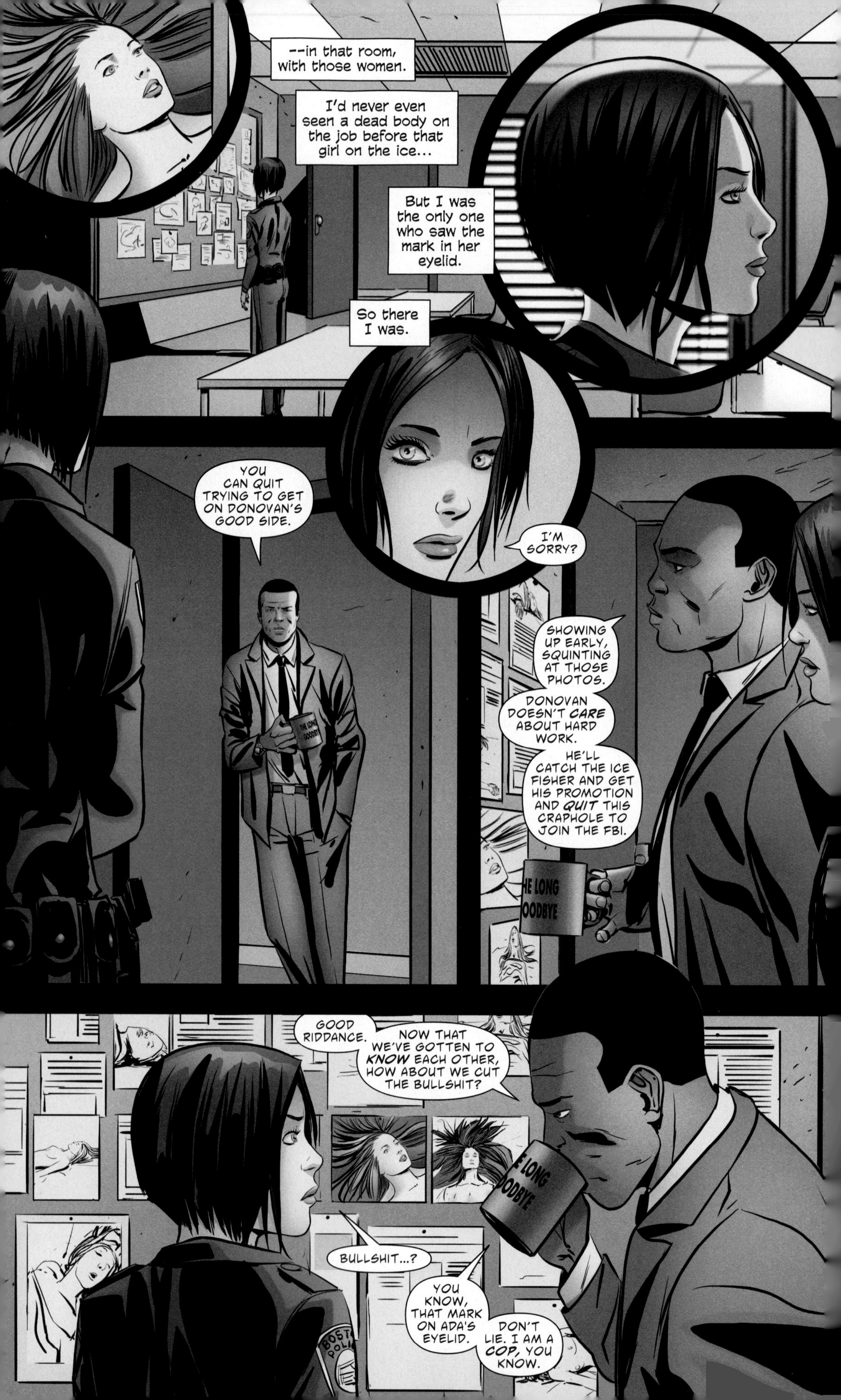
--in that room, with those women.
I'd never even seen a dead body on the job before that girl on the ice...
But I was the only one who saw the mark in her eyelid.
So there I was.
YOU CAN QUIT TRYING TO GET ON DONOVAN'S GOOD SIDE.
I'M SORRY?
SHOWING UP EARLY, SQUINTING AT THOSE PHOTOS.
DONOVAN DOESN'T CARE ABOUT HARD WORK.
HE'LL CATCH THE ICE FISHER AND GET HIS PROMOTION AND QUIT THIS CRAPHOLE TO JOIN THE FBI.
THE LONG GOODBYE
GOOD RIDDANCE.
NOW THAT WE'VE GOTTEN TO KNOW EACH OTHER, HOW ABOUT WE CUT THE BULLSHIT?
BULLSHIT...?
YOU KNOW, THAT MARK ON ADA'S EYELID.
DON'T LIE. I AM A COP, YOU KNOW.

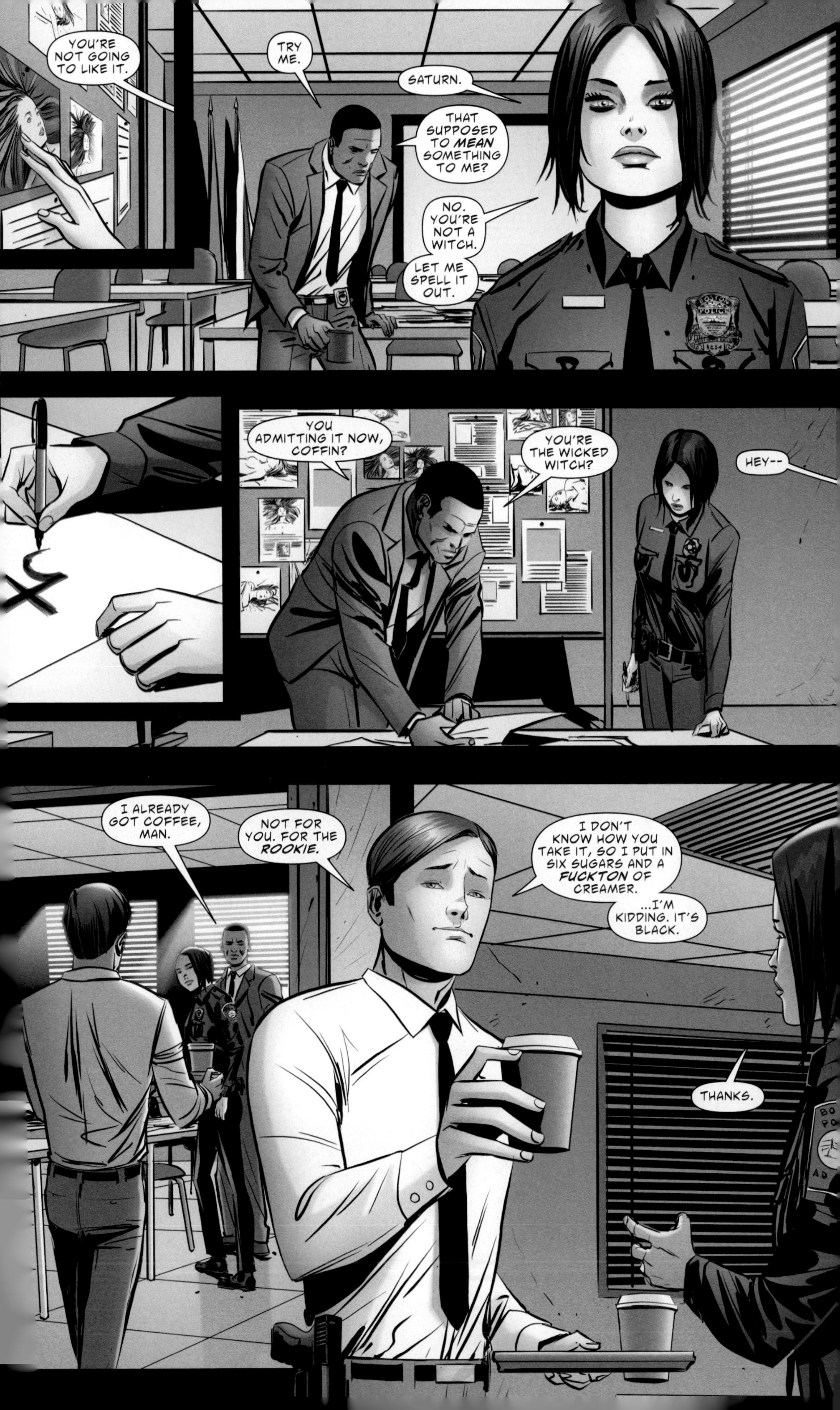

YOU'RE NOT GOING TO LIKE IT.
TRY ME.
SATURN.
THAT SUPPOSED TO *MEAN* SOMETHING TO ME?
NO. YOU'RE NOT A WITCH.
LET ME SPELL IT OUT.
YOU ADMITTING IT NOW, COFFIN?
YOU'RE THE WICKED WITCH?
HEY--
I ALREADY GOT COFFEE, MAN.
NOT FOR YOU. FOR THE *ROOKIE.*
I DON'T KNOW HOW YOU TAKE IT, SO I PUT IN SIX SUGARS AND A *FUCKTON* OF CREAMER.
...I'M KIDDING. IT'S BLACK.
THANKS.

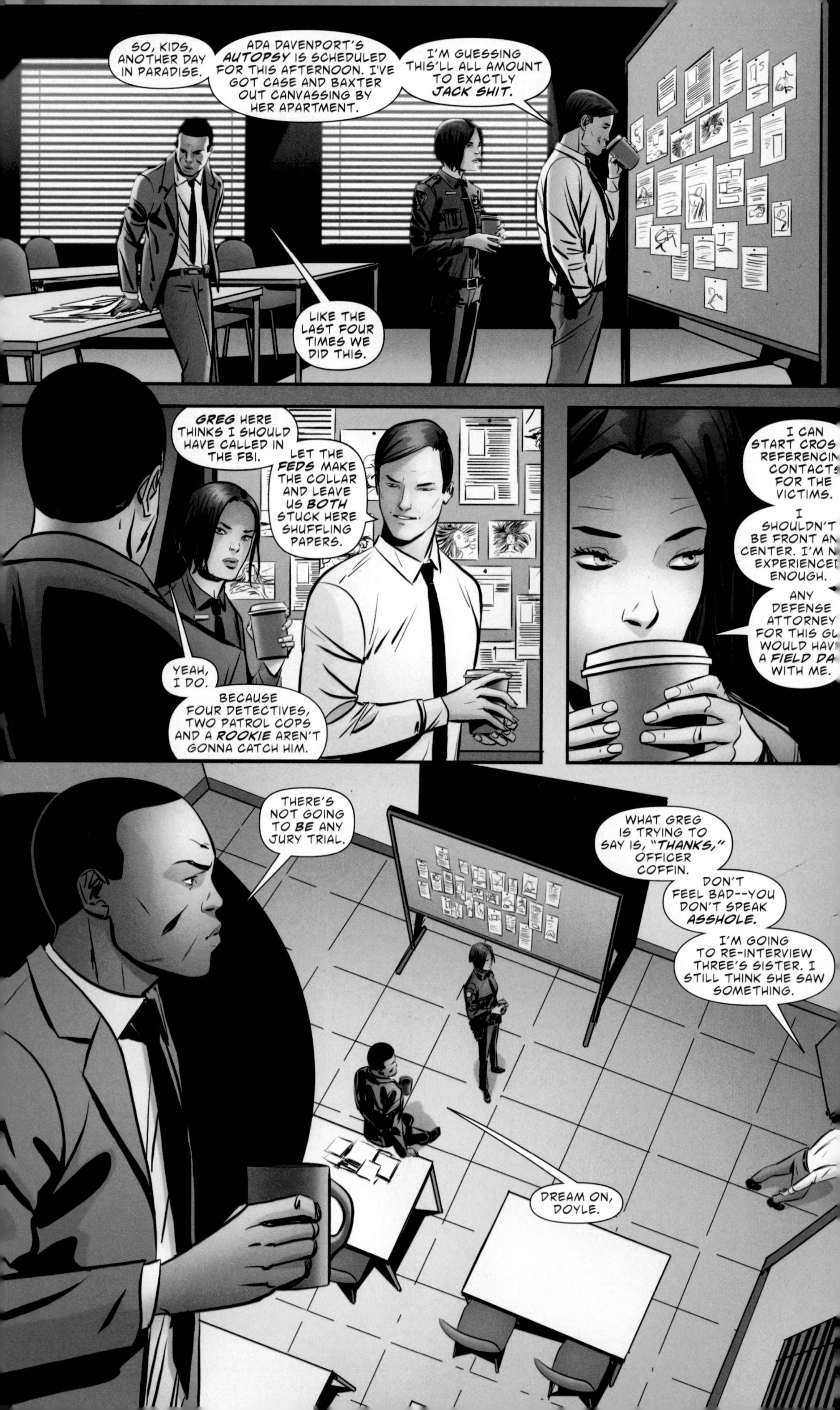
SO, KIDS, ANOTHER DAY IN PARADISE.
ADA DAVENPORT'S AUTOPSY IS SCHEDULED FOR THIS AFTERNOON. I'VE GOT CASE AND BAXTER OUT CANVASSING BY HER APARTMENT.
I'M GUESSING THIS'LL ALL AMOUNT TO EXACTLY JACK SHIT.
LIKE THE LAST FOUR TIMES WE DID THIS.
GREG HERE THINKS I SHOULD HAVE CALLED IN THE FBI.
LET THE FEDS MAKE THE COLLAR AND LEAVE US BOTH STUCK HERE SHUFFLING PAPERS.
YEAH, I DO.
BECAUSE FOUR DETECTIVES, TWO PATROL COPS AND A ROOKIE AREN'T GONNA CATCH HIM.
I CAN START CROS REFERENCIN CONTACT FOR THE VICTIMS.
I SHOULDN'T BE FRONT AN CENTER. I'M N EXPERIENCE ENOUGH.
ANY DEFENSE ATTORNEY FOR THIS GU WOULD HAV A FIELD DA WITH ME.
THERE'S NOT GOING TO BE ANY JURY TRIAL.
WHAT GREG IS TRYING TO SAY IS, "THANKS," OFFICER COFFIN.
DON'T FEEL BAD--YOU DON'T SPEAK ASSHOLE.
I'M GOING TO RE-INTERVIEW THREE'S SISTER. I STILL THINK SHE SAW SOMETHING.
DREAM ON, DOYLE.

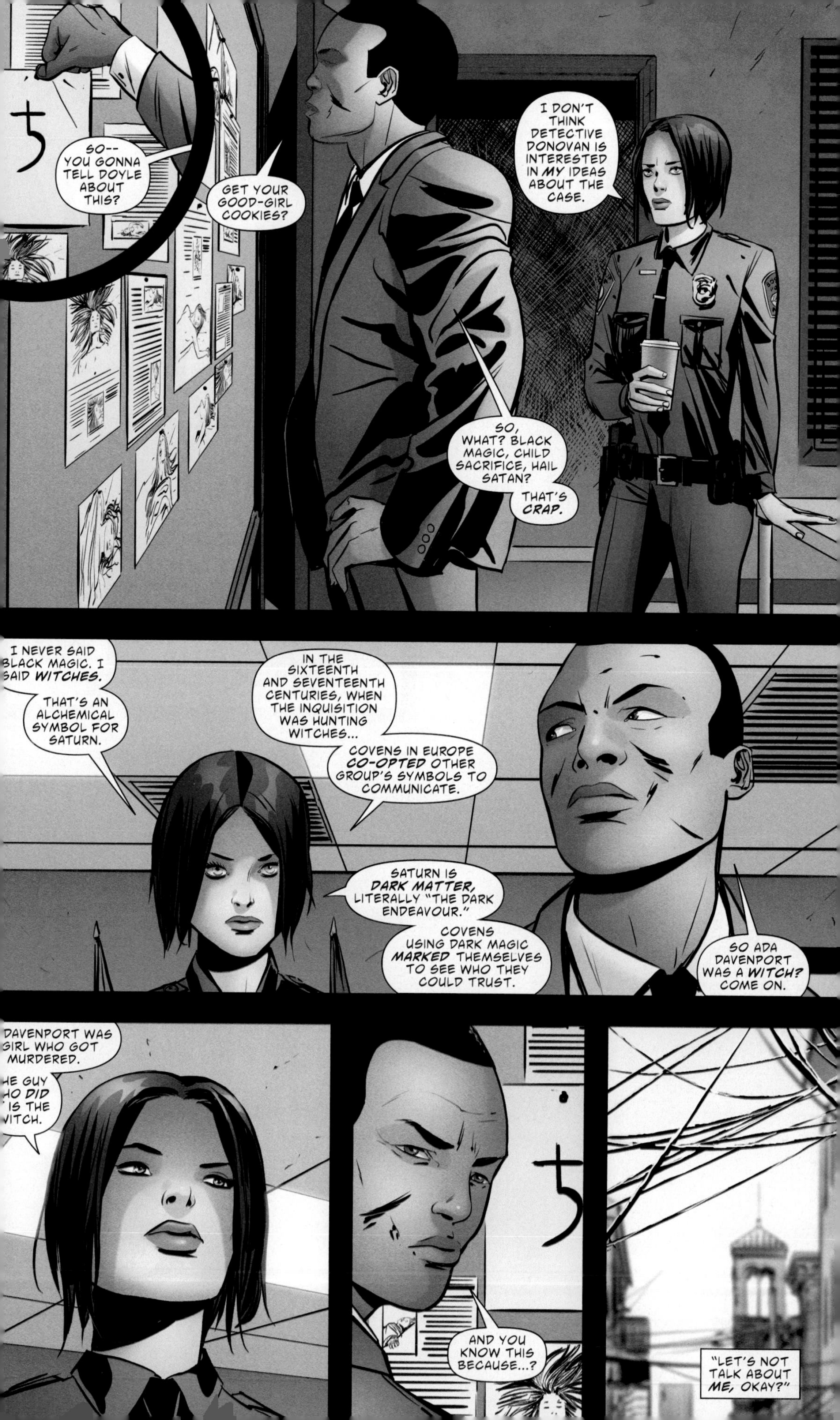
SO-- YOU GONNA TELL DOYLE ABOUT THIS?
GET YOUR GOOD-GIRL COOKIES?
I DON'T THINK DETECTIVE DONOVAN IS INTERESTED IN *MY* IDEAS ABOUT THE CASE.
SO, WHAT? BLACK MAGIC, CHILD SACRIFICE, HAIL SATAN?
THAT'S *CRAP.*
I NEVER SAID BLACK MAGIC. I SAID *WITCHES.*
THAT'S AN ALCHEMICAL SYMBOL FOR SATURN.
IN THE SIXTEENTH AND SEVENTEENTH CENTURIES, WHEN THE INQUISITION WAS HUNTING WITCHES...
COVENS IN EUROPE *CO-OPTED* OTHER GROUP'S SYMBOLS TO COMMUNICATE.
SATURN IS *DARK MATTER,* LITERALLY "THE DARK ENDEAVOUR."
COVENS USING DARK MAGIC *MARKED* THEMSELVES TO SEE WHO THEY COULD TRUST.
SO ADA DAVENPORT WAS A *WITCH?* COME ON.
DAVENPORT WAS GIRL WHO GOT MURDERED.
HE GUY HO *DID* IS THE ITCH.
AND YOU KNOW THIS BECAUSE...?
"LET'S NOT TALK ABOUT *ME,* OKAY?"

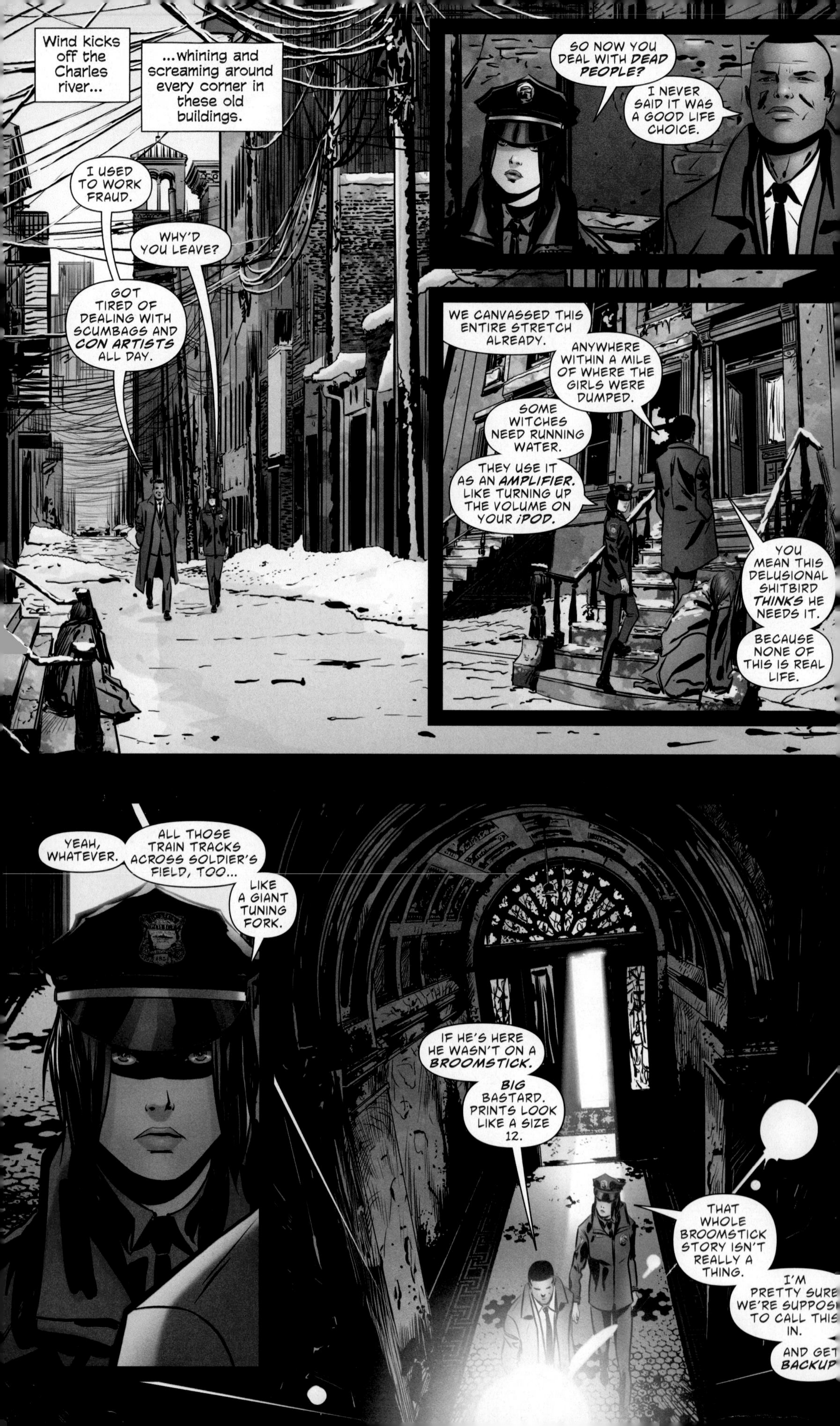
Wind kicks off the Charles river...
...whining and screaming around every corner in these old buildings.
I USED TO WORK FRAUD.
WHY'D YOU LEAVE?
GOT TIRED OF DEALING WITH SCUMBAGS AND CON ARTISTS ALL DAY.
SO NOW YOU DEAL WITH DEAD PEOPLE?
I NEVER SAID IT WAS A GOOD LIFE CHOICE.
WE CANVASSED THIS ENTIRE STRETCH ALREADY.
ANYWHERE WITHIN A MILE OF WHERE THE GIRLS WERE DUMPED.
SOME WITCHES NEED RUNNING WATER.
THEY USE IT AS AN AMPLIFIER. LIKE TURNING UP THE VOLUME ON YOUR iPOD.
YOU MEAN THIS DELUSIONAL SHITBIRD THINKS HE NEEDS IT.
BECAUSE NONE OF THIS IS REAL LIFE.
YEAH, WHATEVER.
ALL THOSE TRAIN TRACKS ACROSS SOLDIER'S FIELD, TOO...
LIKE A GIANT TUNING FORK.
IF HE'S HERE HE WASN'T ON A BROOMSTICK.
BIG BASTARD. PRINTS LOOK LIKE A SIZE 12.
THAT WHOLE BROOMSTICK STORY ISN'T REALLY A THING.
I'M PRETTY SURE WE'RE SUPPOS TO CALL THIS IN.
AND GET BACKUP

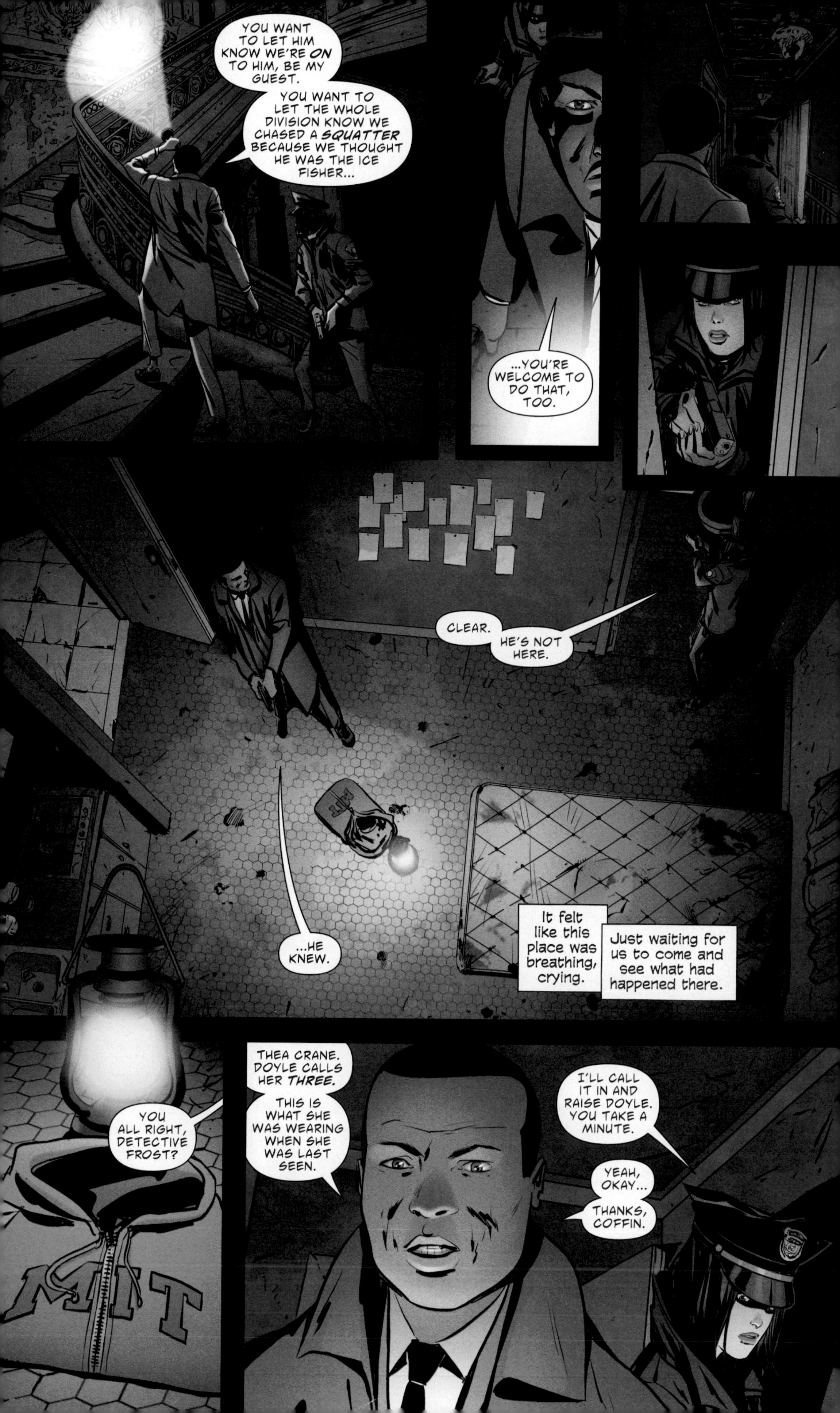

YOU WANT TO LET HIM KNOW WE'RE ON TO HIM, BE MY GUEST.
YOU WANT TO LET THE WHOLE DIVISION KNOW WE CHASED A SQUATTER BECAUSE WE THOUGHT HE WAS THE ICE FISHER...
...YOU'RE WELCOME TO DO THAT, TOO.
CLEAR.
HE'S NOT HERE.
...HE KNEW.
It felt like this place was breathing, crying.
Just waiting for us to come and see what had happened there.
YOU ALL RIGHT, DETECTIVE FROST?
THEA CRANE. DOYLE CALLS HER THREE.
THIS IS WHAT SHE WAS WEARING WHEN SHE WAS LAST SEEN.
I'LL CALL IT IN AND RAISE DOYLE. YOU TAKE A MINUTE.
YEAH, OKAY...
THANKS, COFFIN.
MIT

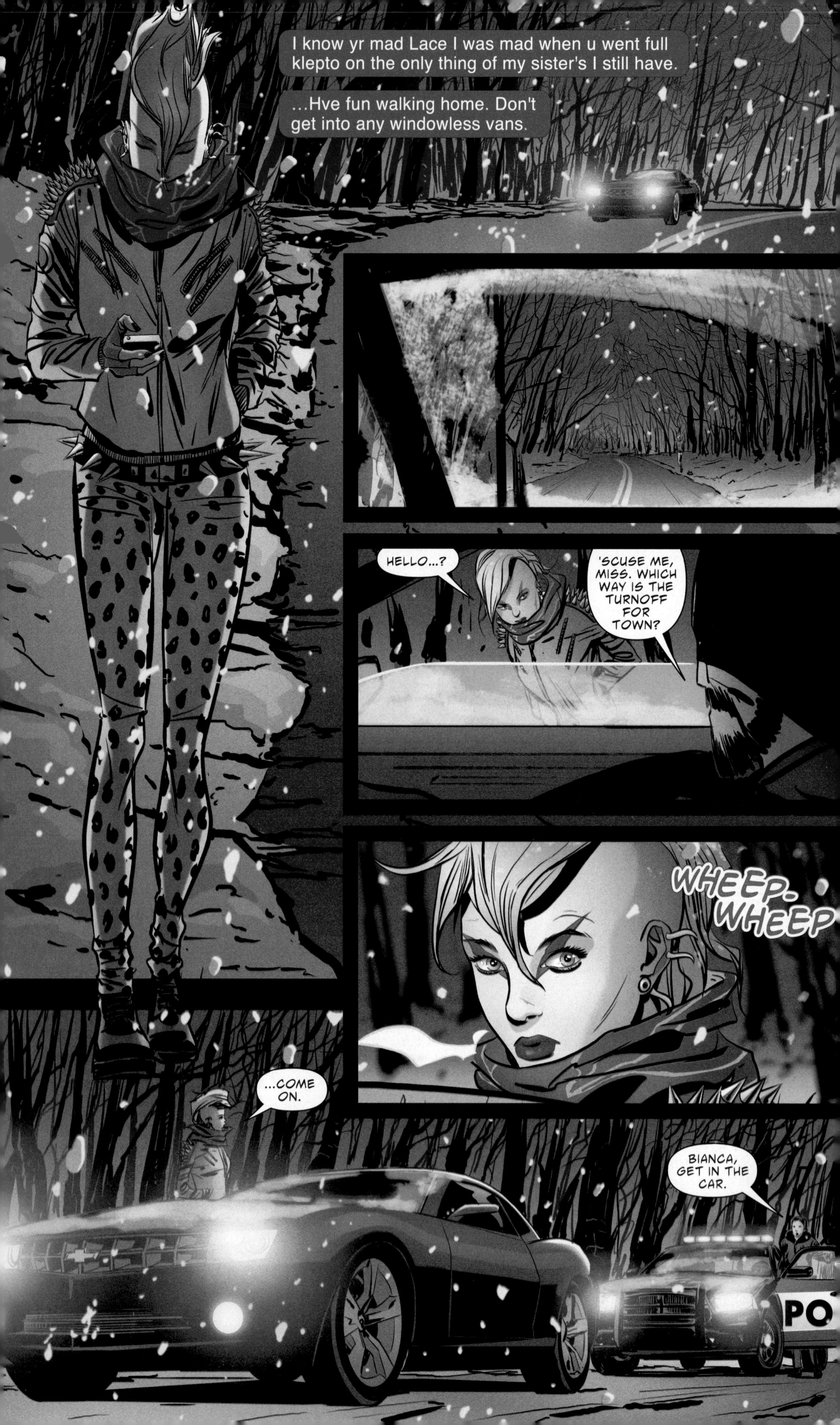
I know yr mad Lace I was mad when u went full klepto on the only thing of my sister's I still have.
...Hve fun walking home. Don't get into any windowless vans.
HELLO...?
'SCUSE ME, MISS. WHICH WAY IS THE TURNOFF FOR TOWN?
WHEEP-WHEEP
...COME ON.
BIANCA, GET IN THE CAR.
PO

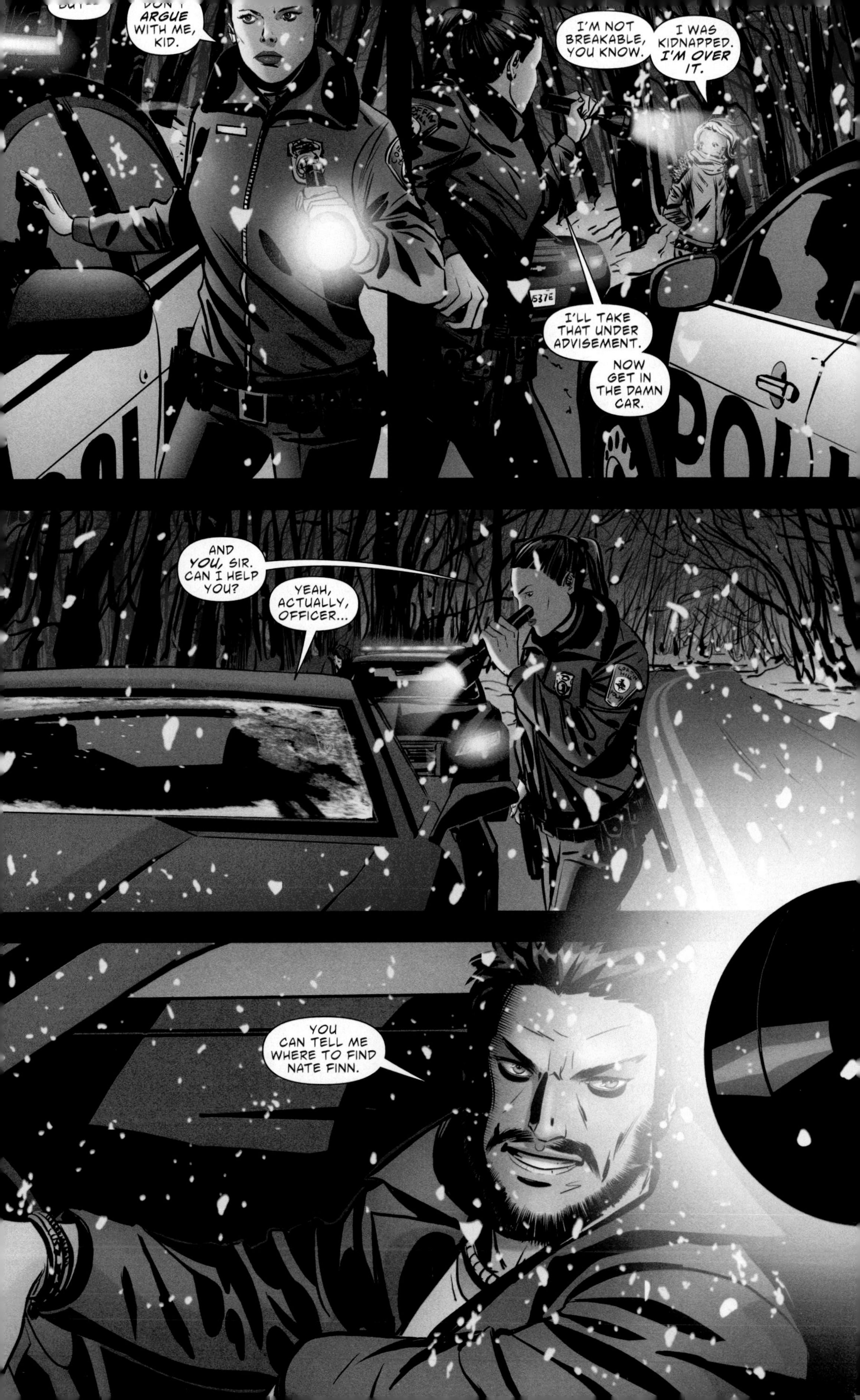
ARGUE WITH ME, KID.
I'M NOT BREAKABLE, YOU KNOW.
I WAS KIDNAPPED. I'M OVER IT.
I'LL TAKE THAT UNDER ADVISEMENT.
NOW GET IN THE DAMN CAR.
AND YOU, SIR. CAN I HELP YOU?
YEAH, ACTUALLY, OFFICER...
YOU CAN TELL ME WHERE TO FIND NATE FINN.

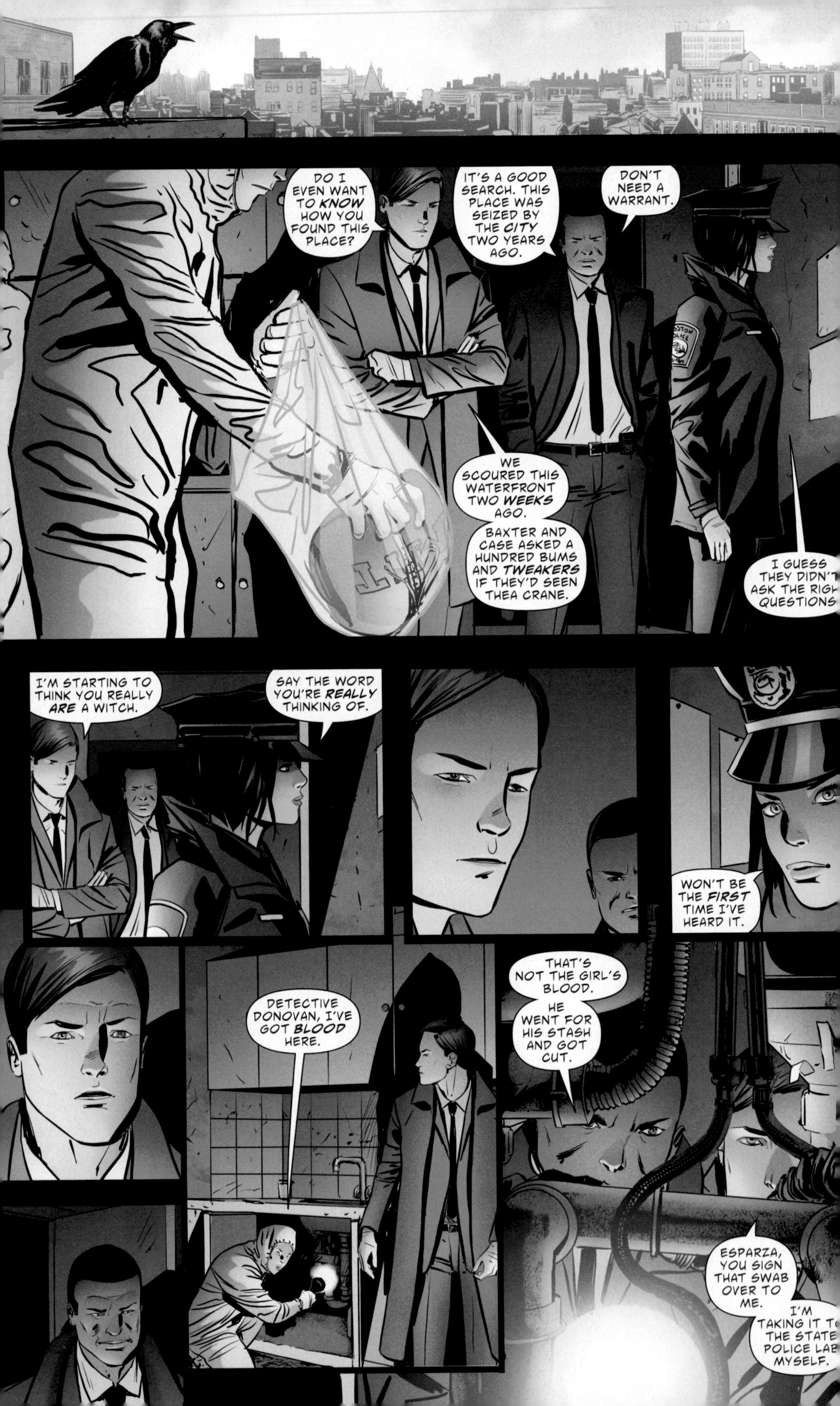
DO I EVEN WANT TO KNOW HOW YOU FOUND THIS PLACE?
IT'S A GOOD SEARCH. THIS PLACE WAS SEIZED BY THE CITY TWO YEARS AGO.
DON'T NEED A WARRANT.
WE SCOURED THIS WATERFRONT TWO WEEKS AGO.
BAXTER AND CASE ASKED A HUNDRED BUMS AND TWEAKERS IF THEY'D SEEN THEA CRANE.
I GUESS THEY DIDN'T ASK THE RIGHT QUESTIONS.
I'M STARTING TO THINK YOU REALLY ARE A WITCH.
SAY THE WORD YOU'RE REALLY THINKING OF.
WON'T BE THE FIRST TIME I'VE HEARD IT.
DETECTIVE DONOVAN, I'VE GOT BLOOD HERE.
THAT'S NOT THE GIRL'S BLOOD.
HE WENT FOR HIS STASH AND GOT CUT.
ESPARZA, YOU SIGN THAT SWAB OVER TO ME.
I'M TAKING IT TO THE STATE POLICE LAB MYSELF.

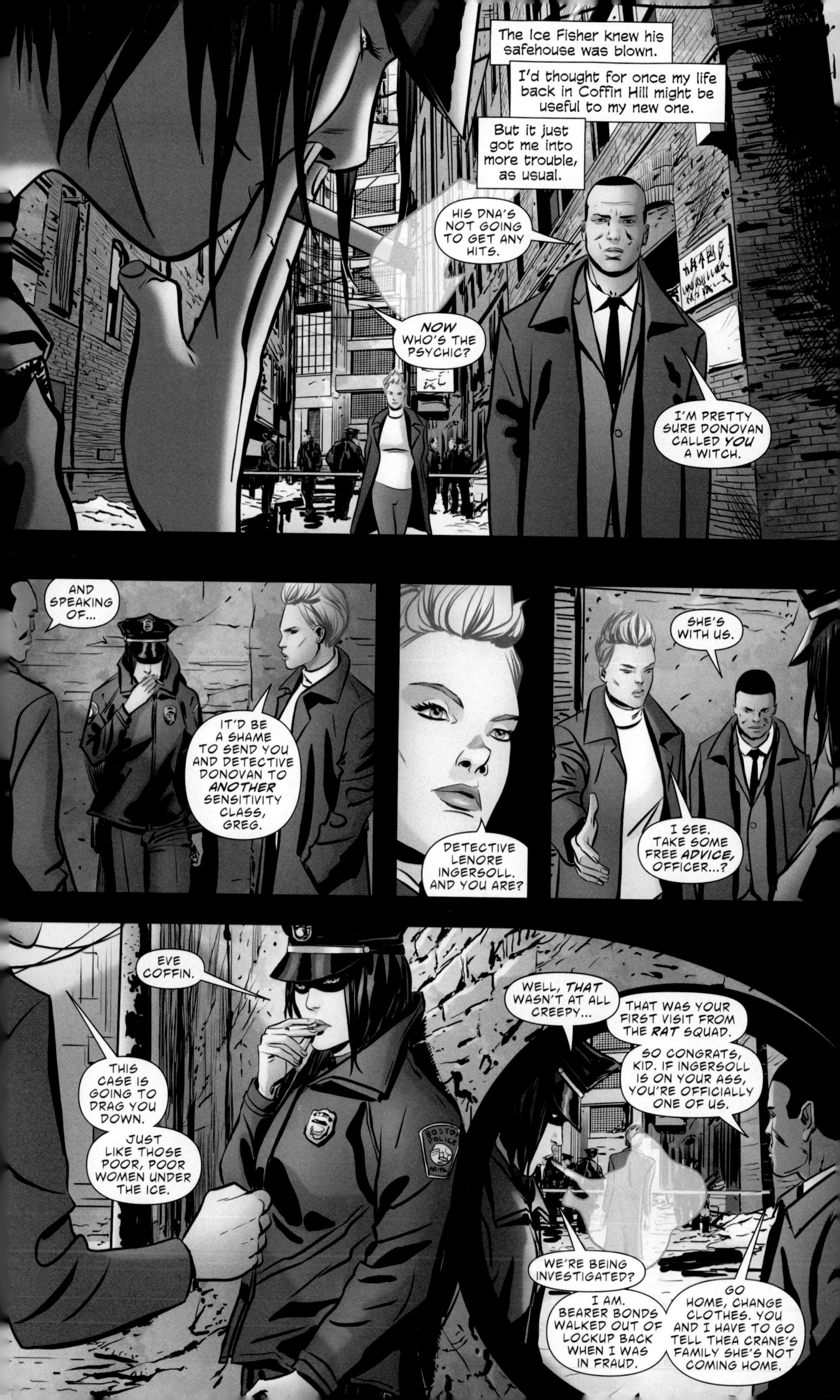

The Ice Fisher knew his safehouse was blown.
I'd thought for once my life back in Coffin Hill might be useful to my new one.
But it just got me into more trouble, as usual.
HIS DNA'S NOT GOING TO GET ANY HITS.
NOW WHO'S THE PSYCHIC?
I'M PRETTY SURE DONOVAN CALLED YOU A WITCH.
AND SPEAKING OF...
IT'D BE A SHAME TO SEND YOU AND DETECTIVE DONOVAN TO ANOTHER SENSITIVITY CLASS, GREG.
DETECTIVE LENORE INGERSOLL. AND YOU ARE?
SHE'S WITH US.
I SEE. TAKE SOME FREE ADVICE, OFFICER...?
EVE COFFIN.
THIS CASE IS GOING TO DRAG YOU DOWN.
JUST LIKE THOSE POOR, POOR WOMEN UNDER THE ICE.
BOSTON POLICE
WELL, THAT WASN'T AT ALL CREEPY...
THAT WAS YOUR FIRST VISIT FROM THE RAT SQUAD.
SO CONGRATS, KID. IF INGERSOLL IS ON YOUR ASS, YOU'RE OFFICIALLY ONE OF US.
WE'RE BEING INVESTIGATED?
I AM. BEARER BONDS WALKED OUT OF LOCKUP BACK WHEN I WAS IN FRAUD.
GO HOME, CHANGE CLOTHES. YOU AND I HAVE TO GO TELL THEA CRANE'S FAMILY SHE'S NOT COMING HOME.

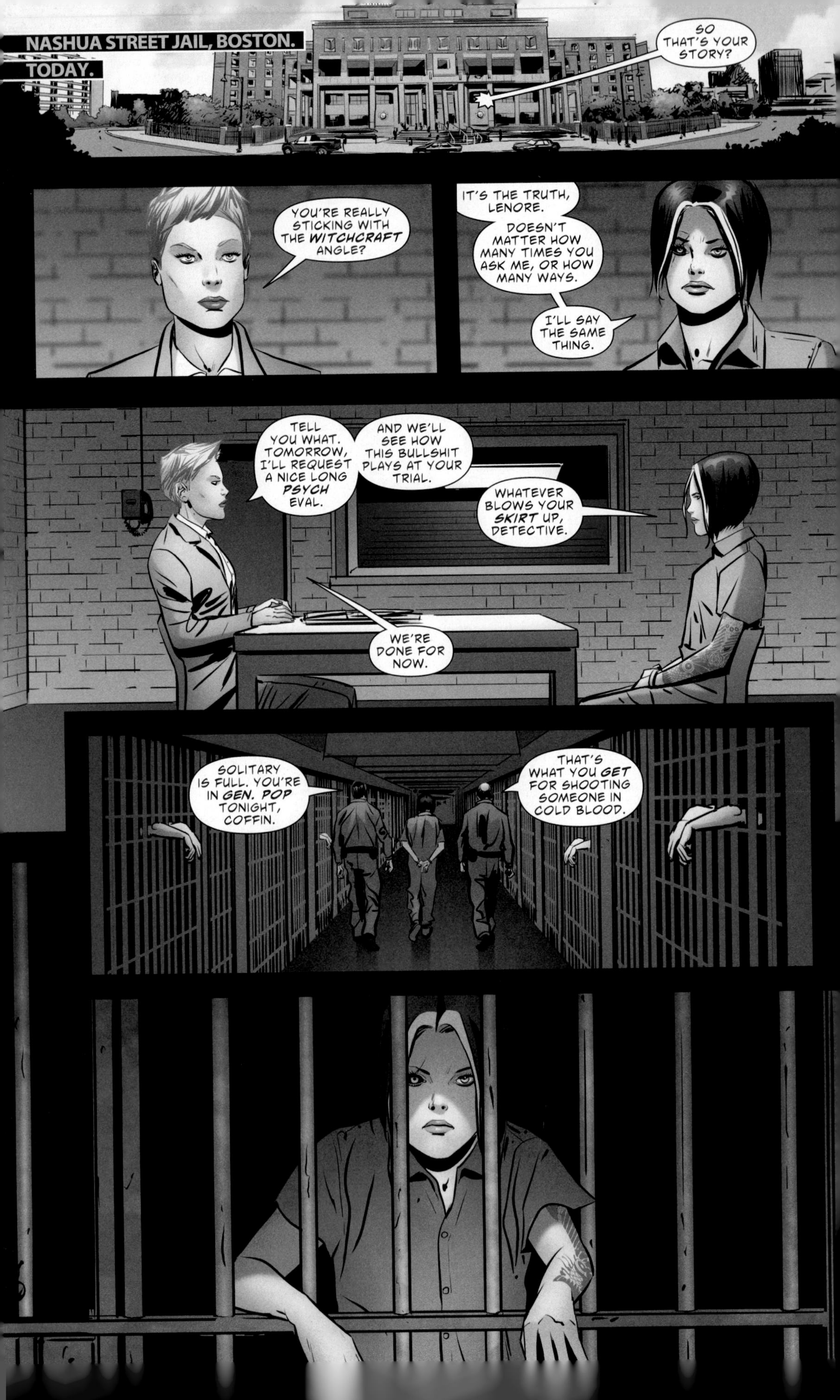
NASHUA STREET JAIL, BOSTON.
TODAY.
SO THAT'S YOUR STORY?
YOU'RE REALLY STICKING WITH THE WITCHCRAFT ANGLE?
IT'S THE TRUTH, LENORE.
DOESN'T MATTER HOW MANY TIMES YOU ASK ME, OR HOW MANY WAYS.
I'LL SAY THE SAME THING.
TELL YOU WHAT. TOMORROW, I'LL REQUEST A NICE LONG PSYCH EVAL.
AND WE'LL SEE HOW THIS BULLSHIT PLAYS AT YOUR TRIAL.
WHATEVER BLOWS YOUR SKIRT UP, DETECTIVE.
WE'RE DONE FOR NOW.
SOLITARY IS FULL. YOU'RE IN GEN. POP TONIGHT, COFFIN.
THAT'S WHAT YOU GET FOR SHOOTING SOMEONE IN COLD BLOOD.

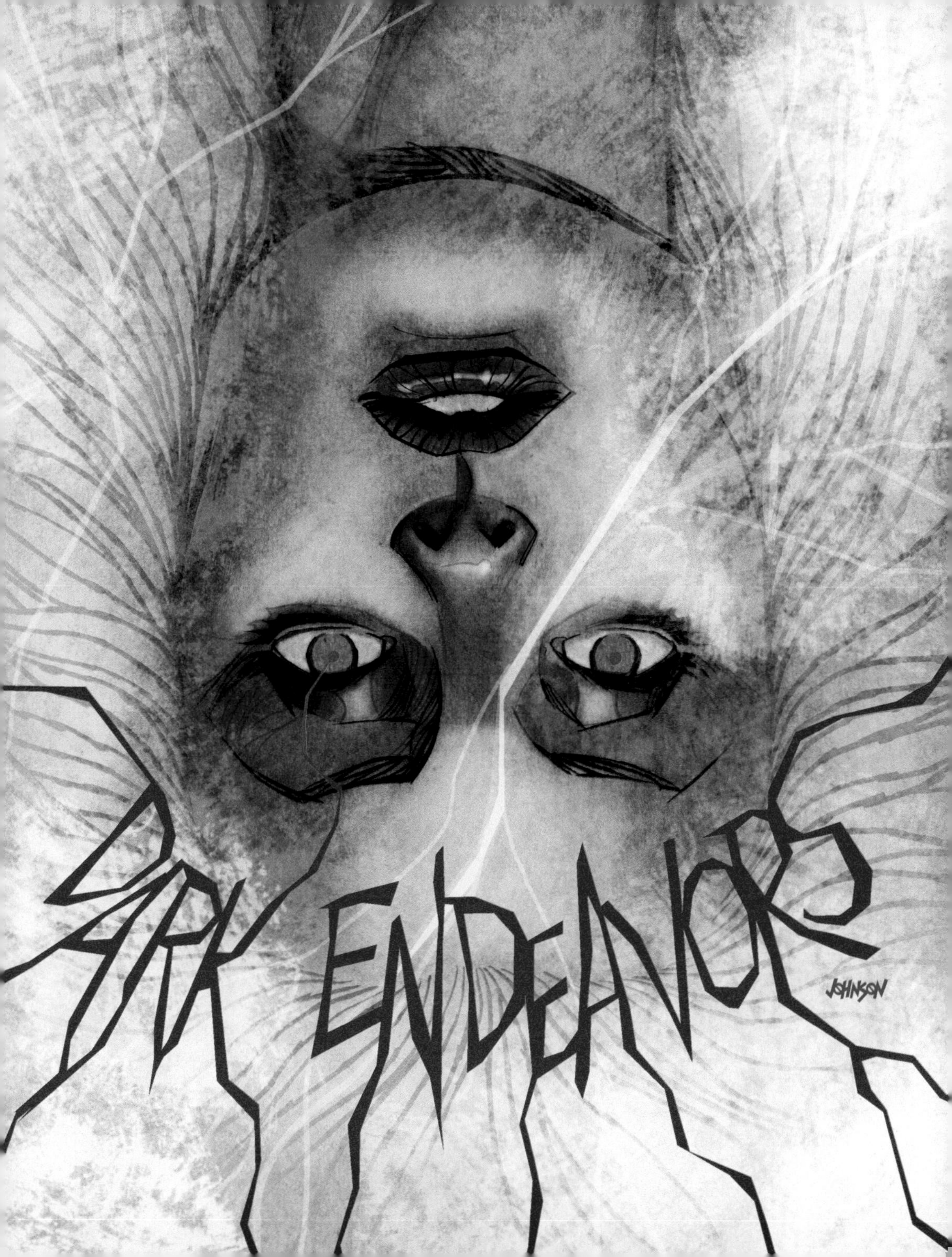
DARK ENDEAVORS
JOHNSON

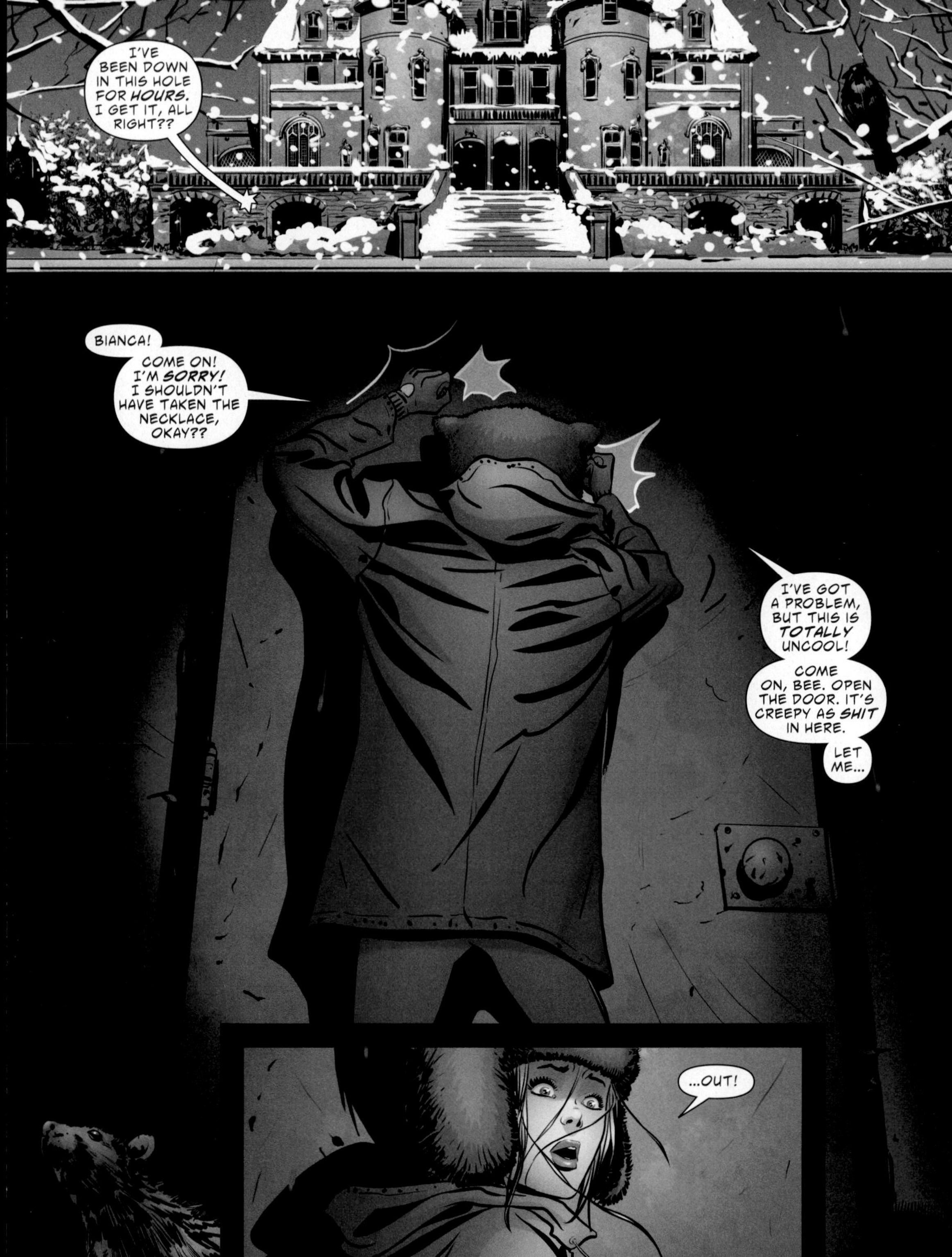
I'VE BEEN DOWN IN THIS HOLE FOR HOURS. I GET IT, ALL RIGHT??
BIANCA!
COME ON! I'M SORRY! I SHOULDN'T HAVE TAKEN THE NECKLACE, OKAY??
I'VE GOT A PROBLEM, BUT THIS IS TOTALLY UNCOOL!
COME ON, BEE. OPEN THE DOOR. IT'S CREEPY AS SHIT IN HERE.
LET ME...
...OUT!

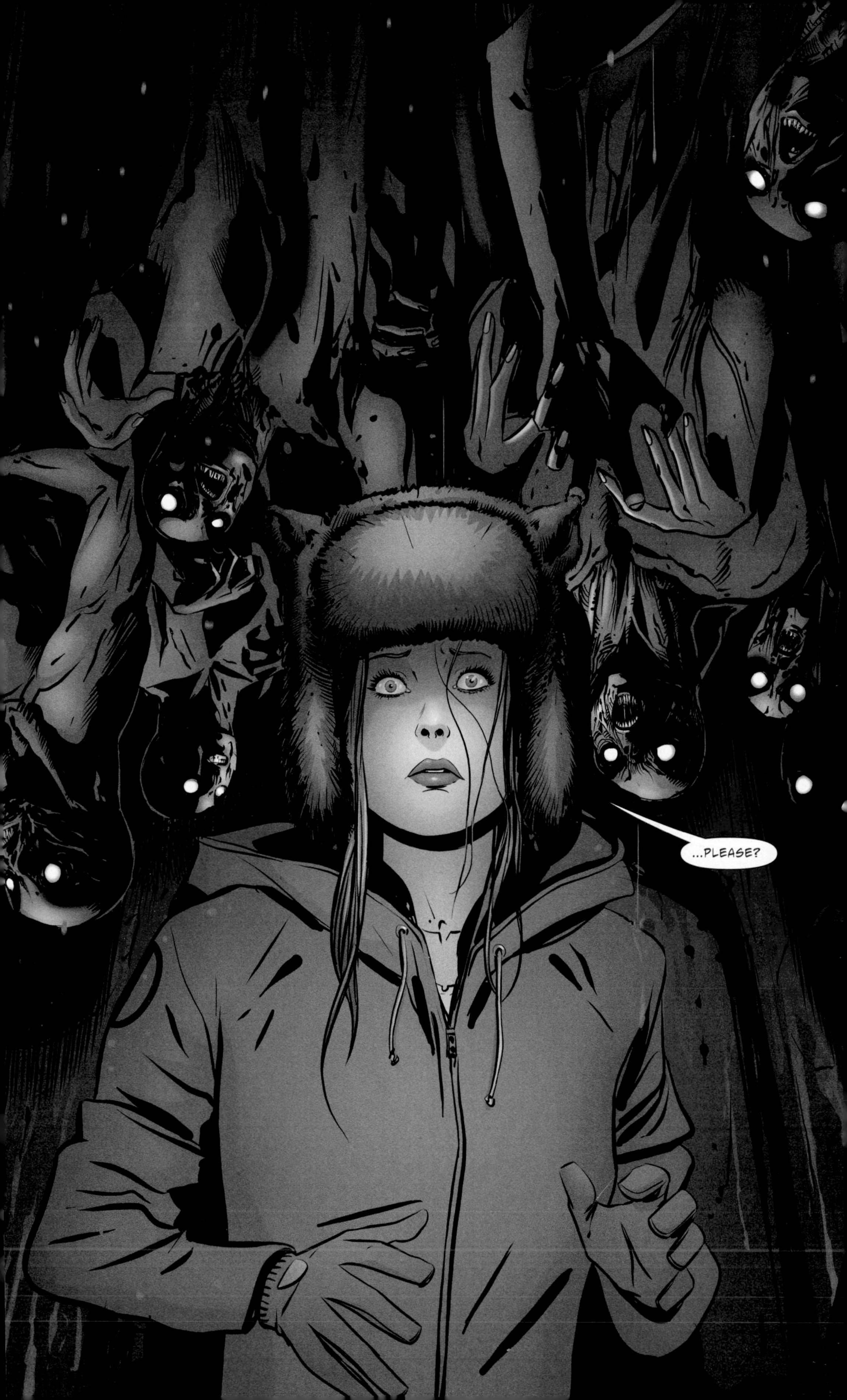
...PLEASE?

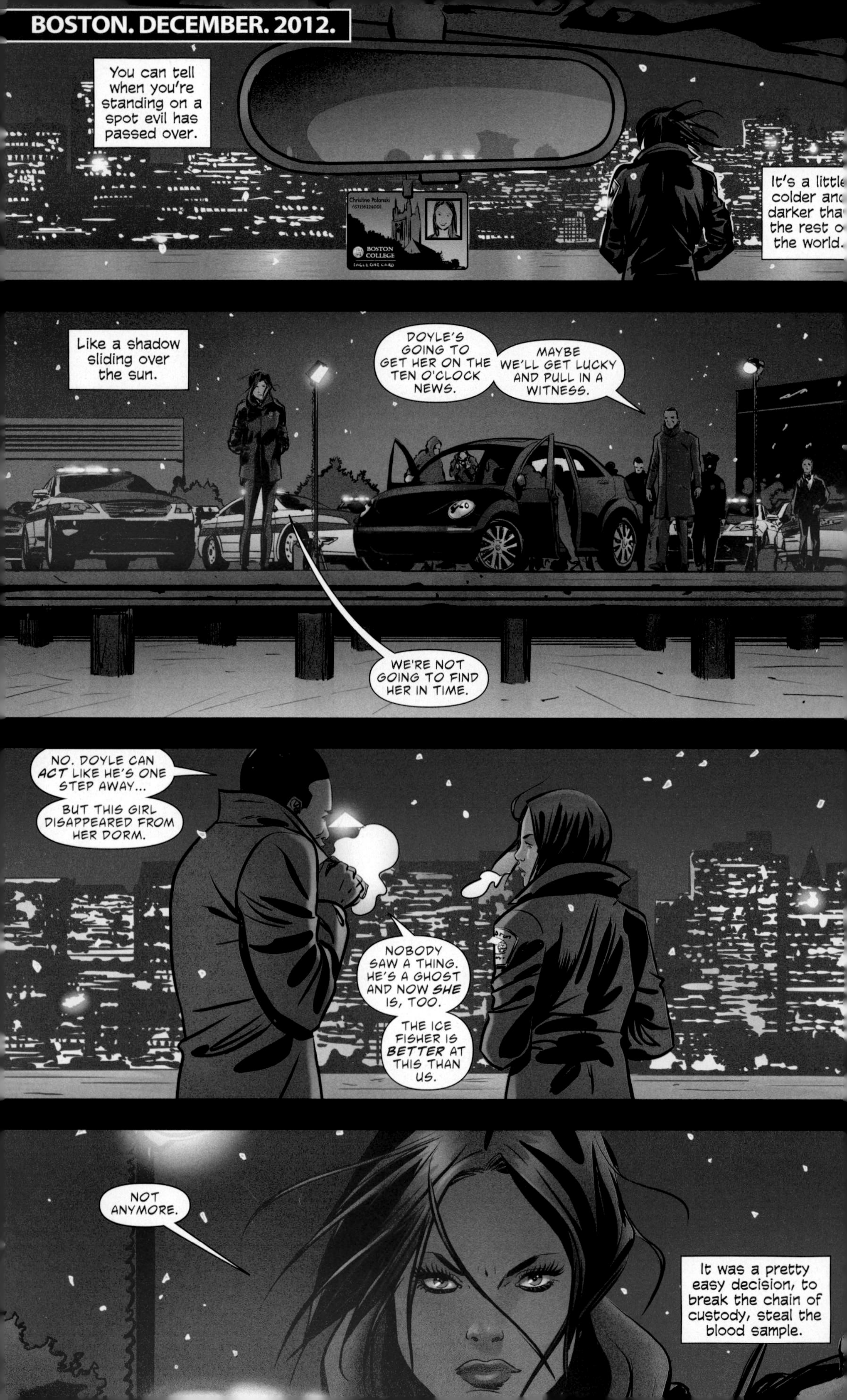
BOSTON. DECEMBER. 2012.
You can tell when you're standing on a spot evil has passed over.
BOSTON COLLEGE
It's a littl colder an darker tha the rest o the world.
Like a shadow sliding over the sun.
DOYLE'S GOING TO GET HER ON THE TEN O'CLOCK NEWS.
MAYBE WE'LL GET LUCKY AND PULL IN A WITNESS.
WE'RE NOT GOING TO FIND HER IN TIME.
NO. DOYLE CAN ACT LIKE HE'S ONE STEP AWAY...
BUT THIS GIRL DISAPPEARED FROM HER DORM.
NOBODY SAW A THING. HE'S A GHOST AND NOW SHE IS, TOO.
THE ICE FISHER IS BETTER AT THIS THAN US.
NOT ANYMORE.
It was a pretty easy decision, to break the chain of custody, steal the blood sample.

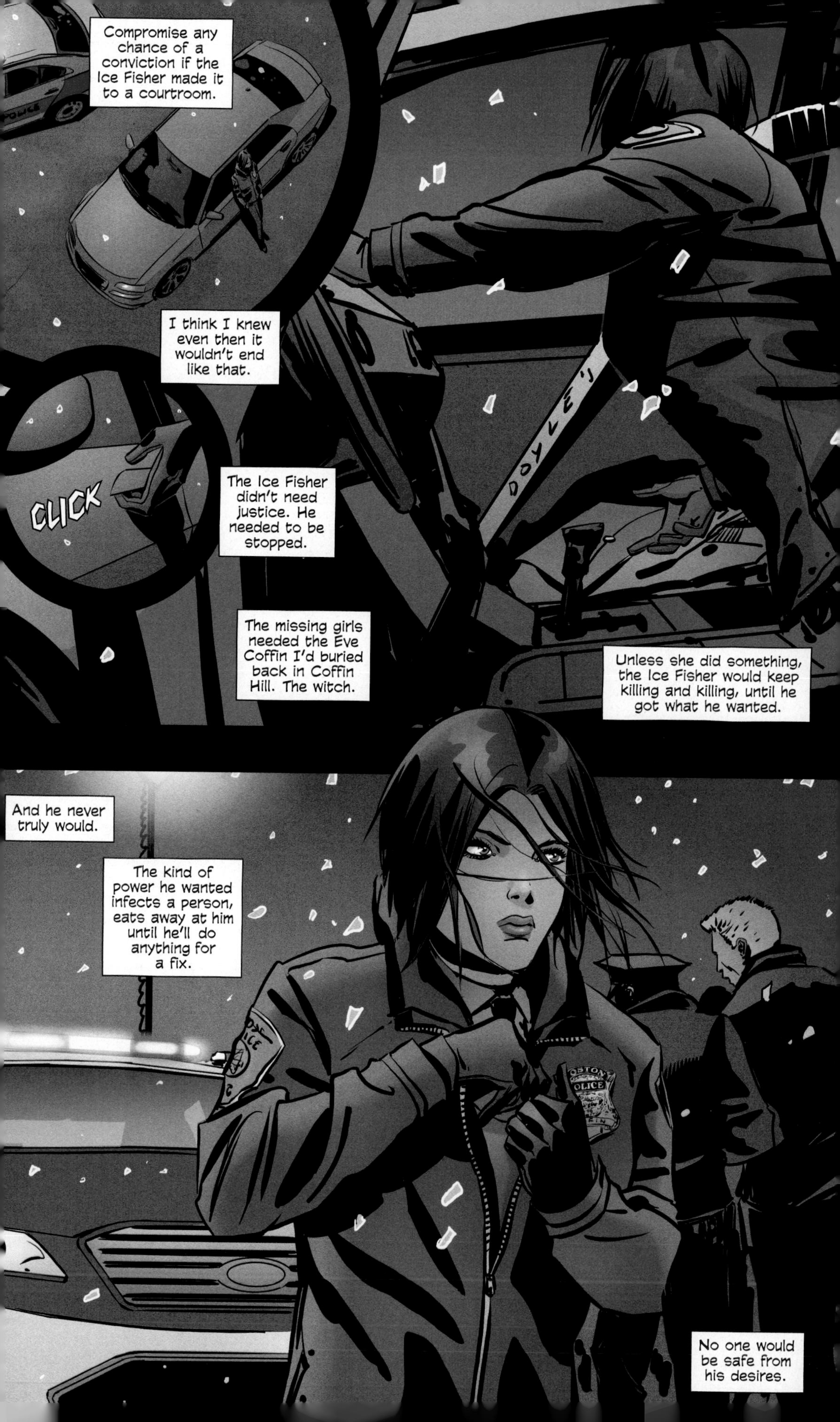
Compromise any chance of a conviction if the Ice Fisher made it to a courtroom.
I think I knew even then it wouldn't end like that.
CLICK
The Ice Fisher didn't need justice. He needed to be stopped.
The missing girls needed the Eve Coffin I'd buried back in Coffin Hill. The witch.
Unless she did something, the Ice Fisher would keep killing and killing, until he got what he wanted.
And he never truly would.
The kind of power he wanted infects a person, eats away at him until he'll do anything for a fix.
No one would be safe from his desires.

DISTRICT 1 STATION HOUSE. 40 SUDBURY ST.

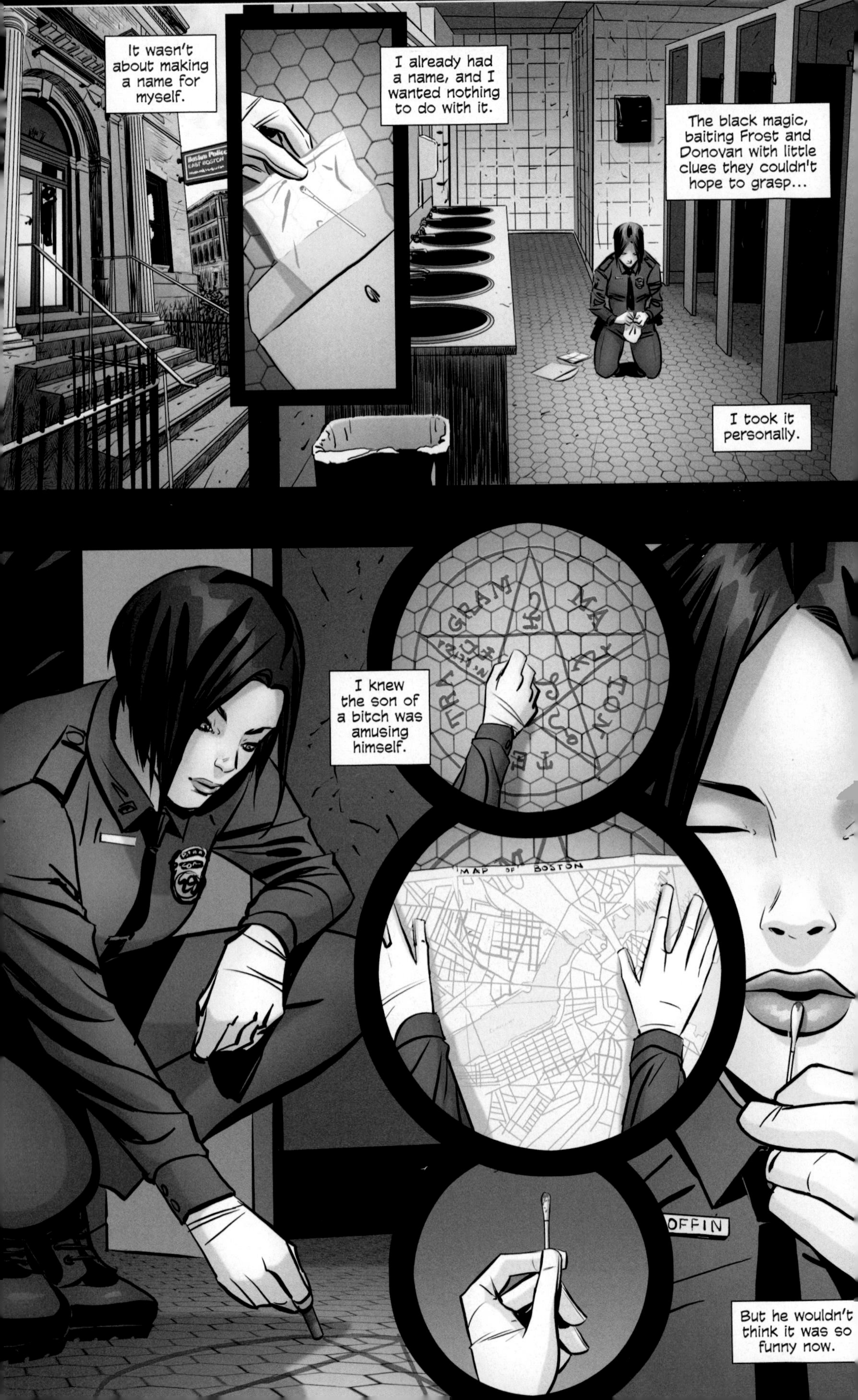

Boston Police
EAST BOSTON
It wasn't about making a name for myself.
I already had a name, and I wanted nothing to do with it.
The black magic, baiting Frost and Donovan with little clues they couldn't hope to grasp...
I took it personally.
I knew the son of a bitch was amusing himself.
MAP OF BOSTON
But he wouldn't think it was so funny now.

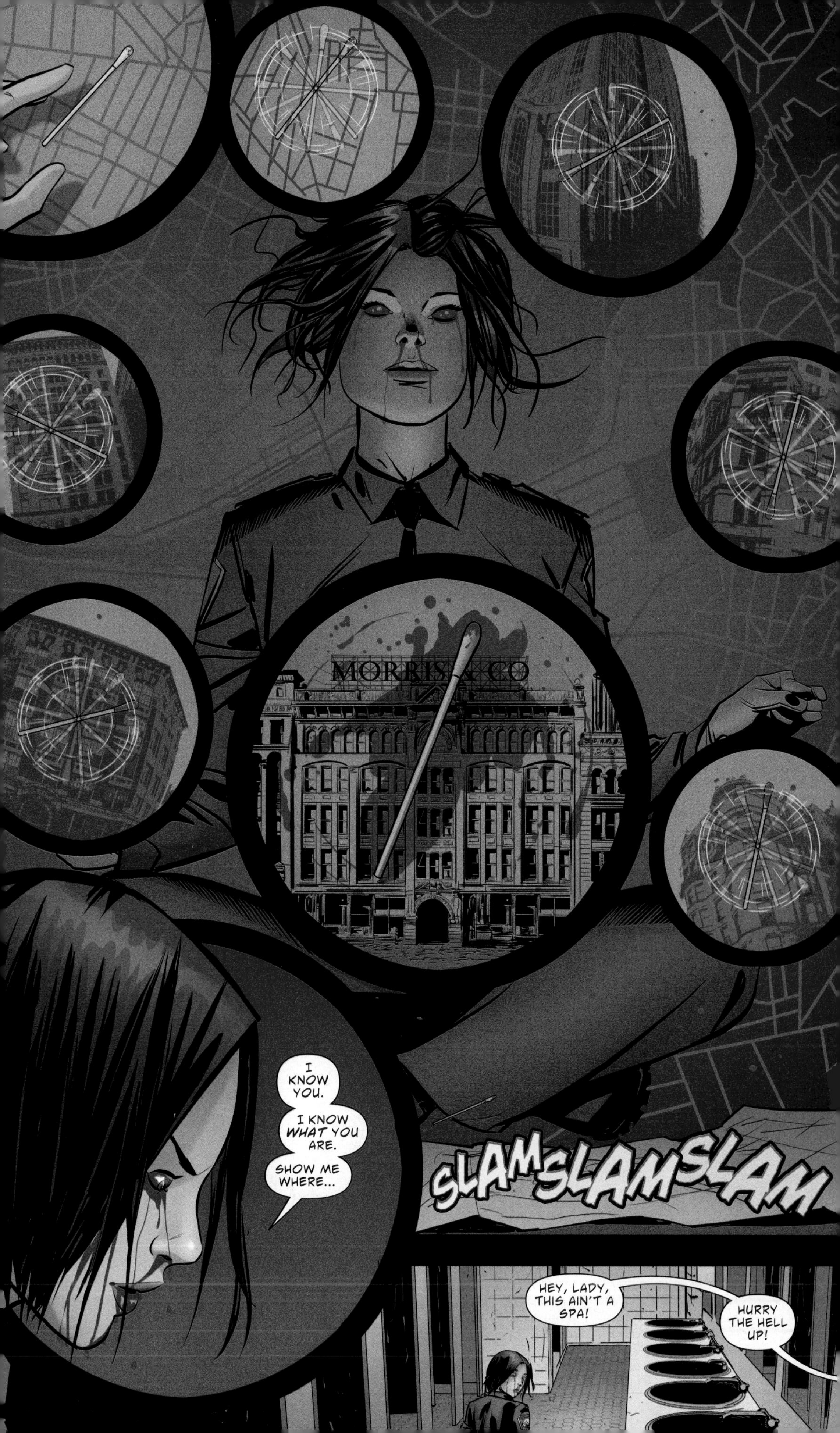
MORRIS & CO
I KNOW YOU.
I KNOW WHAT YOU ARE.
SHOW ME WHERE...
SLAMSLAMSLAM
HEY, LADY, THIS AIN'T A SPA!
HURRY THE HELL UP!

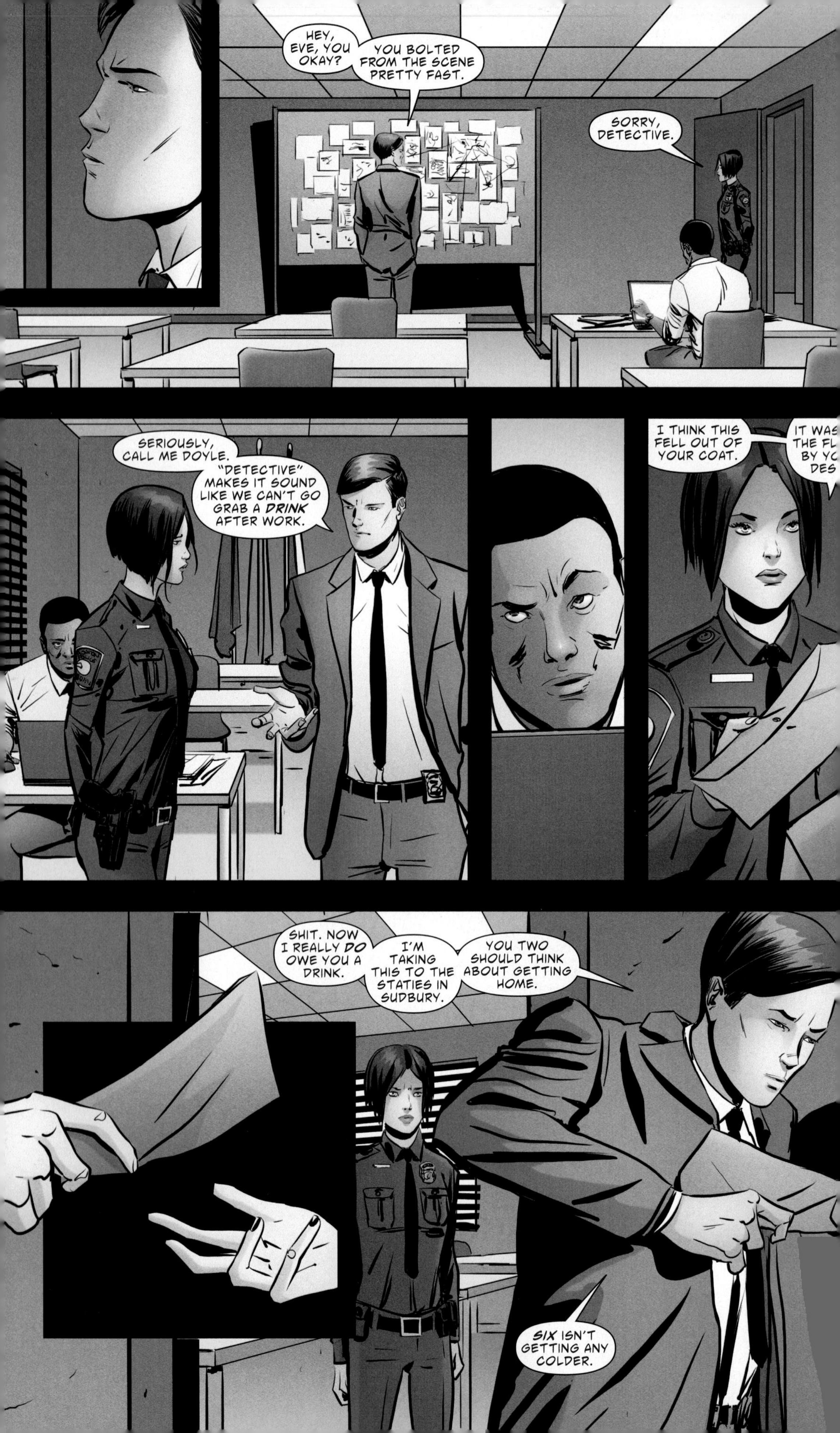
HEY, EVE, YOU OKAY?
YOU BOLTED FROM THE SCENE PRETTY FAST.
SORRY, DETECTIVE.
SERIOUSLY, CALL ME DOYLE.
"DETECTIVE" MAKES IT SOUND LIKE WE CAN'T GO GRAB A DRINK AFTER WORK.
I THINK THIS FELL OUT OF YOUR COAT.
IT WAS THE FL BY YO DES
SHIT. NOW I REALLY DO OWE YOU A DRINK.
I'M TAKING THIS TO THE STATIES IN SUDBURY.
YOU TWO SHOULD THINK ABOUT GETTING HOME.
SIX ISN'T GETTING ANY COLDER.

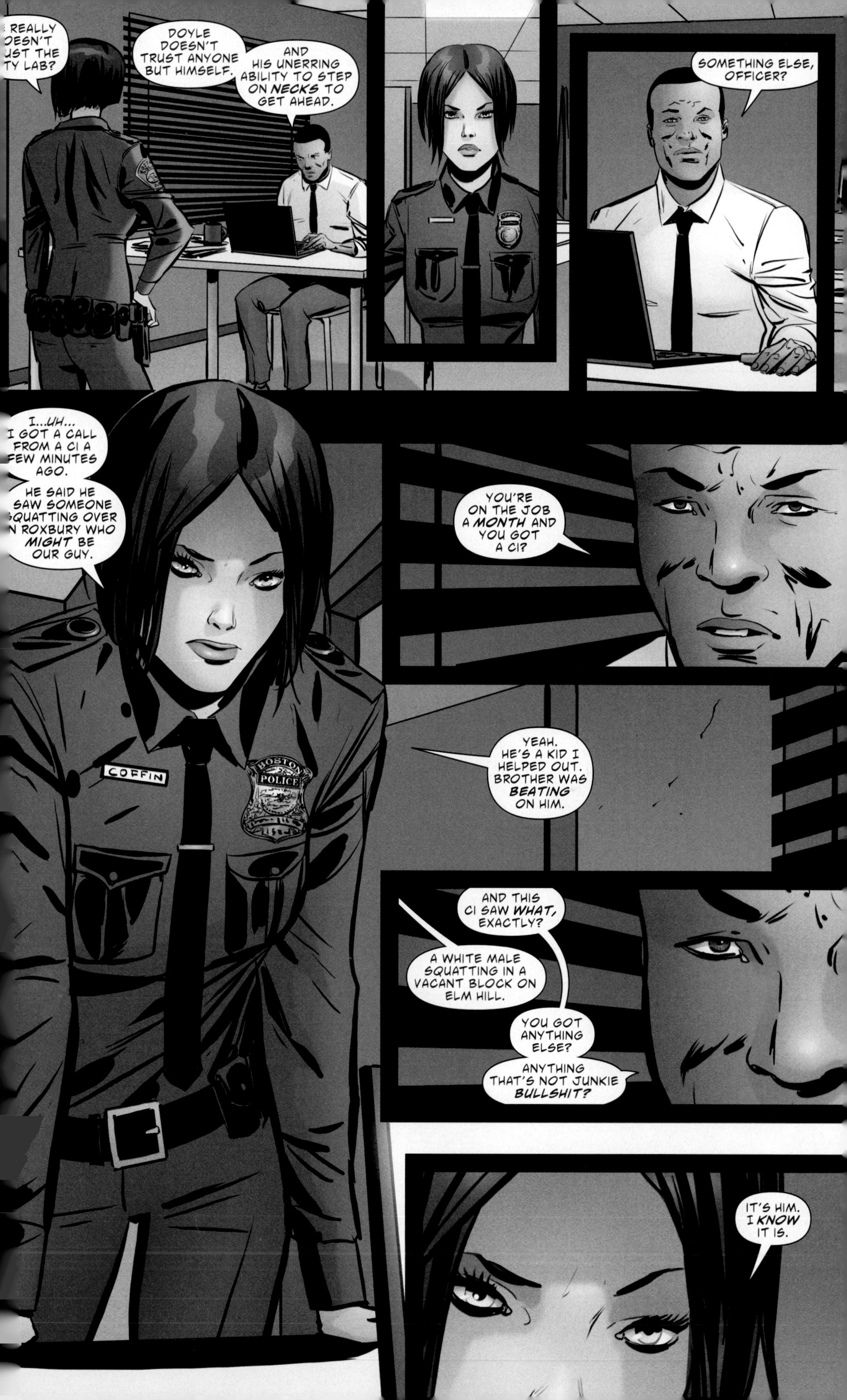
E REALLY OESN'T UST THE TY LAB?
DOYLE DOESN'T TRUST ANYONE BUT HIMSELF.
AND HIS UNERRING ABILITY TO STEP ON NECKS TO GET AHEAD.
SOMETHING ELSE, OFFICER?
I...UH... I GOT A CALL FROM A CI A FEW MINUTES AGO.
HE SAID HE SAW SOMEONE SQUATTING OVER N ROXBURY WHO MIGHT BE OUR GUY.
YOU'RE ON THE JOB A MONTH AND YOU GOT A CI?
YEAH. HE'S A KID I HELPED OUT. BROTHER WAS BEATING ON HIM.
AND THIS CI SAW WHAT, EXACTLY?
A WHITE MALE SQUATTING IN A VACANT BLOCK ON ELM HILL.
YOU GOT ANYTHING ELSE?
ANYTHING THAT'S NOT JUNKIE BULLSHIT?
IT'S HIM. I KNOW IT IS.
COFFIN
BOSTON POLICE

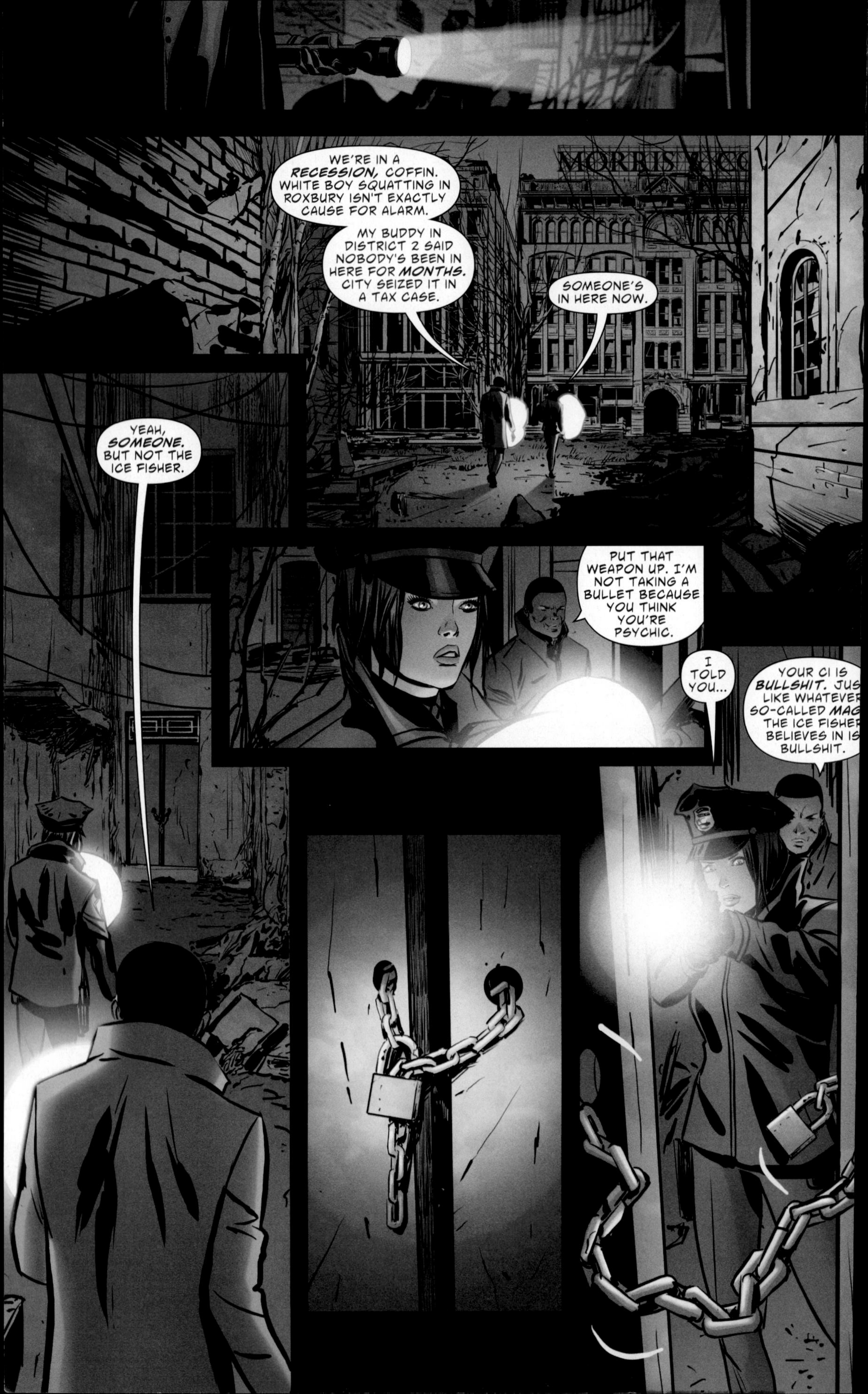
MORRIS & CO
WE'RE IN A RECESSION, COFFIN. WHITE BOY SQUATTING IN ROXBURY ISN'T EXACTLY CAUSE FOR ALARM.
MY BUDDY IN DISTRICT 2 SAID NOBODY'S BEEN IN HERE FOR MONTHS. CITY SEIZED IT IN A TAX CASE.
SOMEONE'S IN HERE NOW.
YEAH, SOMEONE. BUT NOT THE ICE FISHER.
PUT THAT WEAPON UP. I'M NOT TAKING A BULLET BECAUSE YOU THINK YOU'RE PSYCHIC.
I TOLD YOU...
YOUR CI IS BULLSHIT. JUS LIKE WHATEVER SO-CALLED MAG THE ICE FISHER BELIEVES IN IS BULLSHIT.

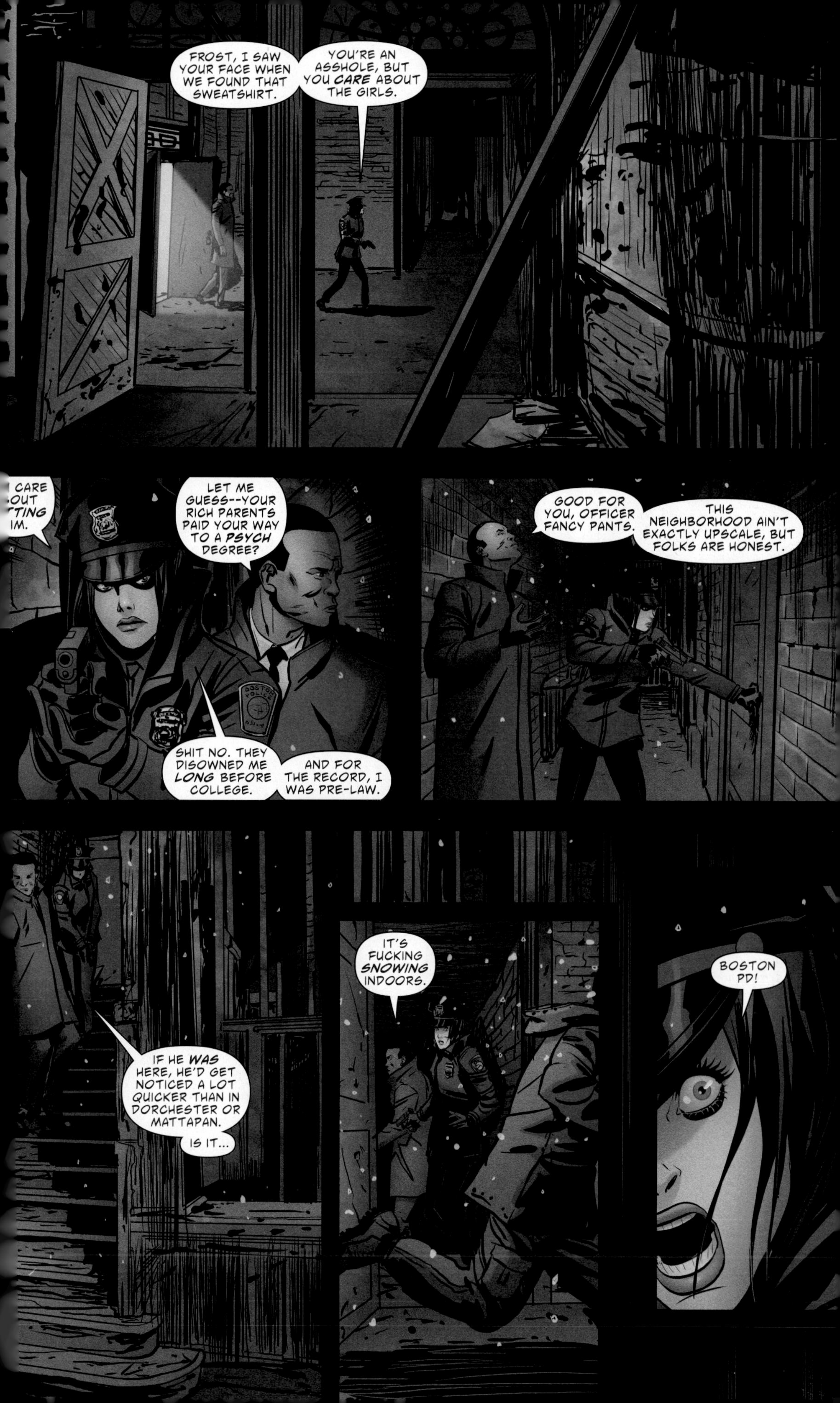
FROST, I SAW YOUR FACE WHEN WE FOUND THAT SWEATSHIRT.
YOU'RE AN ASSHOLE, BUT YOU CARE ABOUT THE GIRLS.
CARE
LET ME GUESS--YOUR RICH PARENTS PAID YOUR WAY TO A PSYCH DEGREE?
SHIT NO. THEY DISOWNED ME LONG BEFORE COLLEGE.
AND FOR THE RECORD, I WAS PRE-LAW.
GOOD FOR YOU, OFFICER FANCY PANTS.
THIS NEIGHBORHOOD AIN'T EXACTLY UPSCALE, BUT FOLKS ARE HONEST.
IF HE WAS HERE, HE'D GET NOTICED A LOT QUICKER THAN IN DORCHESTER OR MATTAPAN.
IS IT...
IT'S FUCKING SNOWING INDOORS.
BOSTON PD!

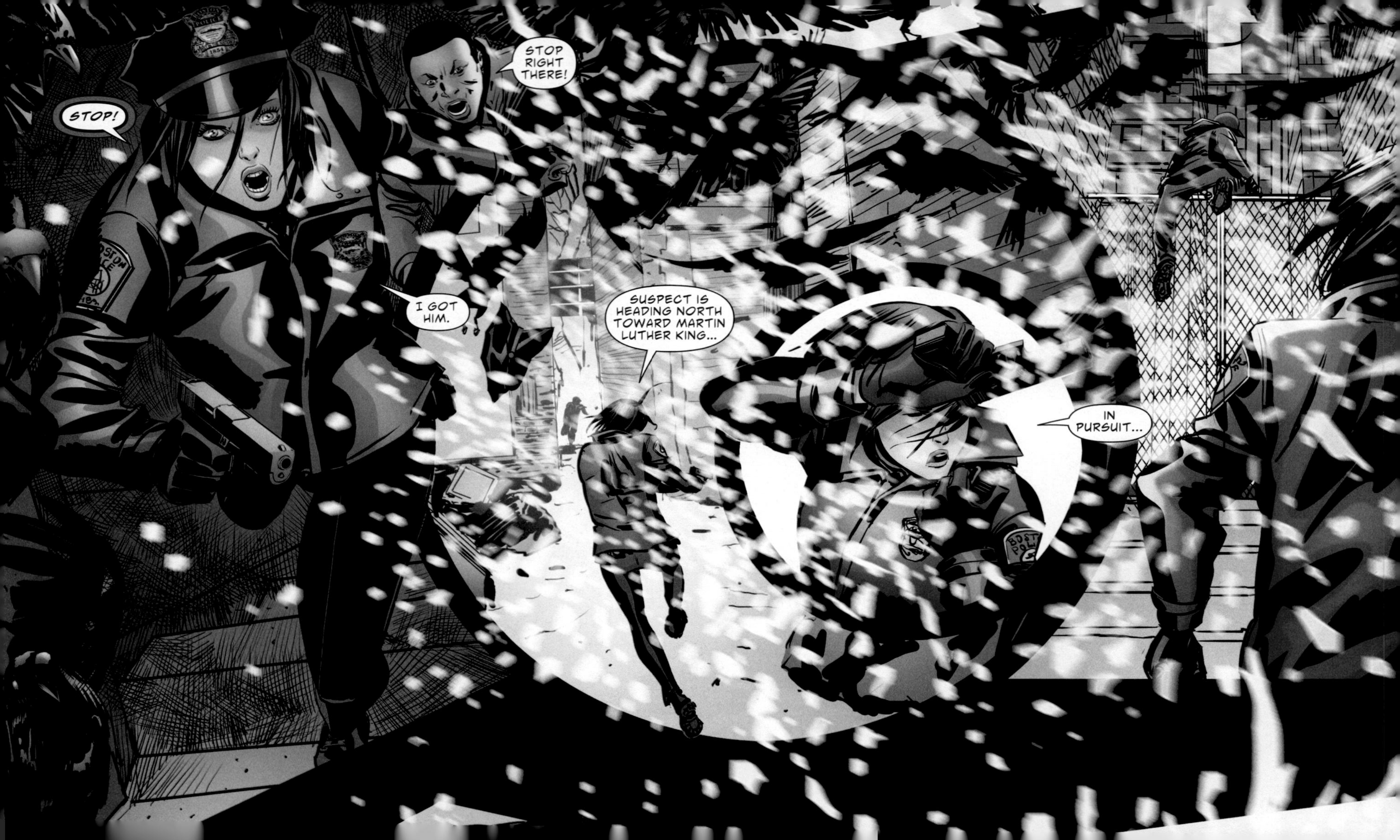
STOP!
STOP RIGHT THERE!
I GOT HIM.
SUSPECT IS HEADING NORTH TOWARD MARTIN LUTHER KING...
IN PURSUIT...

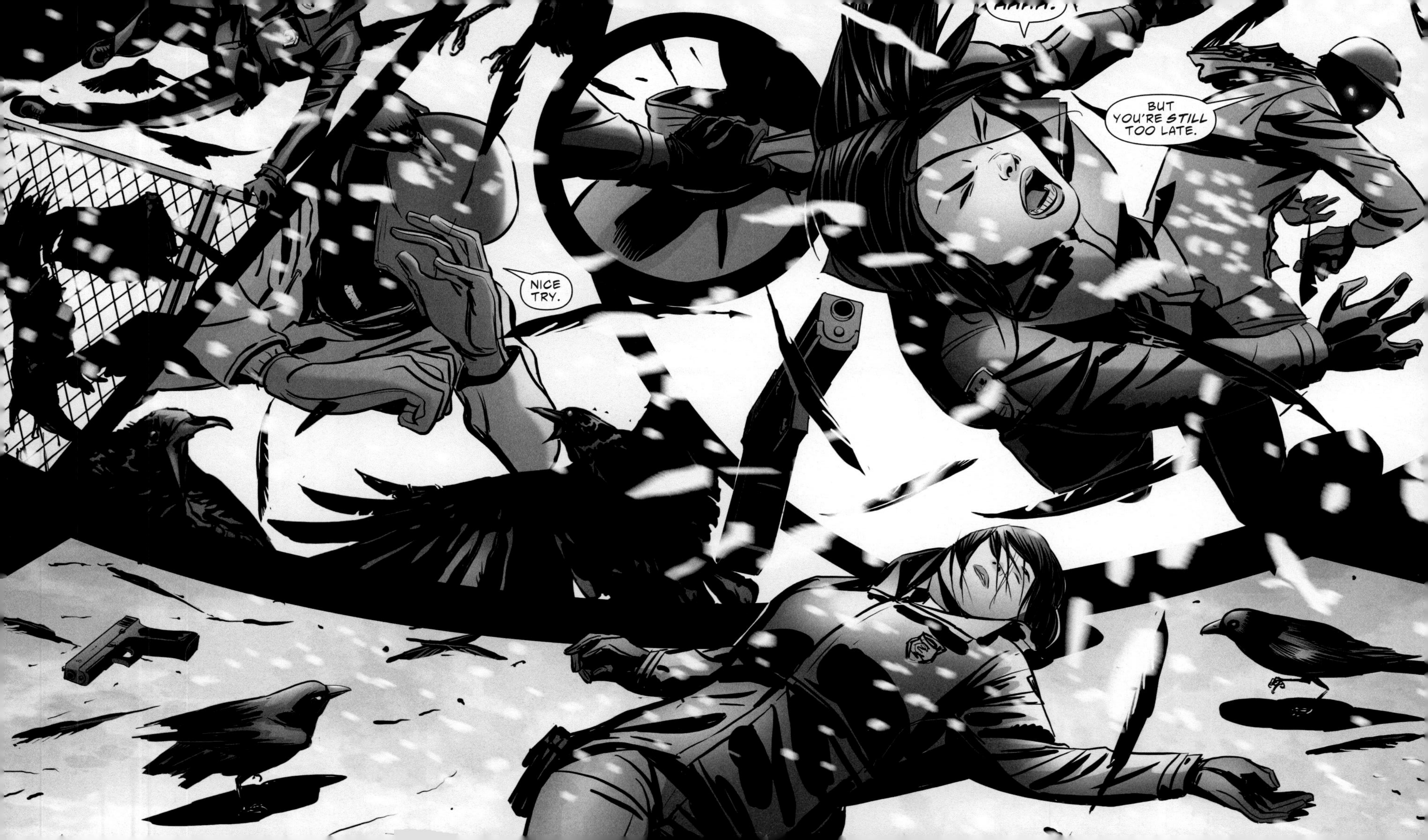
NICE TRY.
BUT YOU'RE STILL TOO LATE.

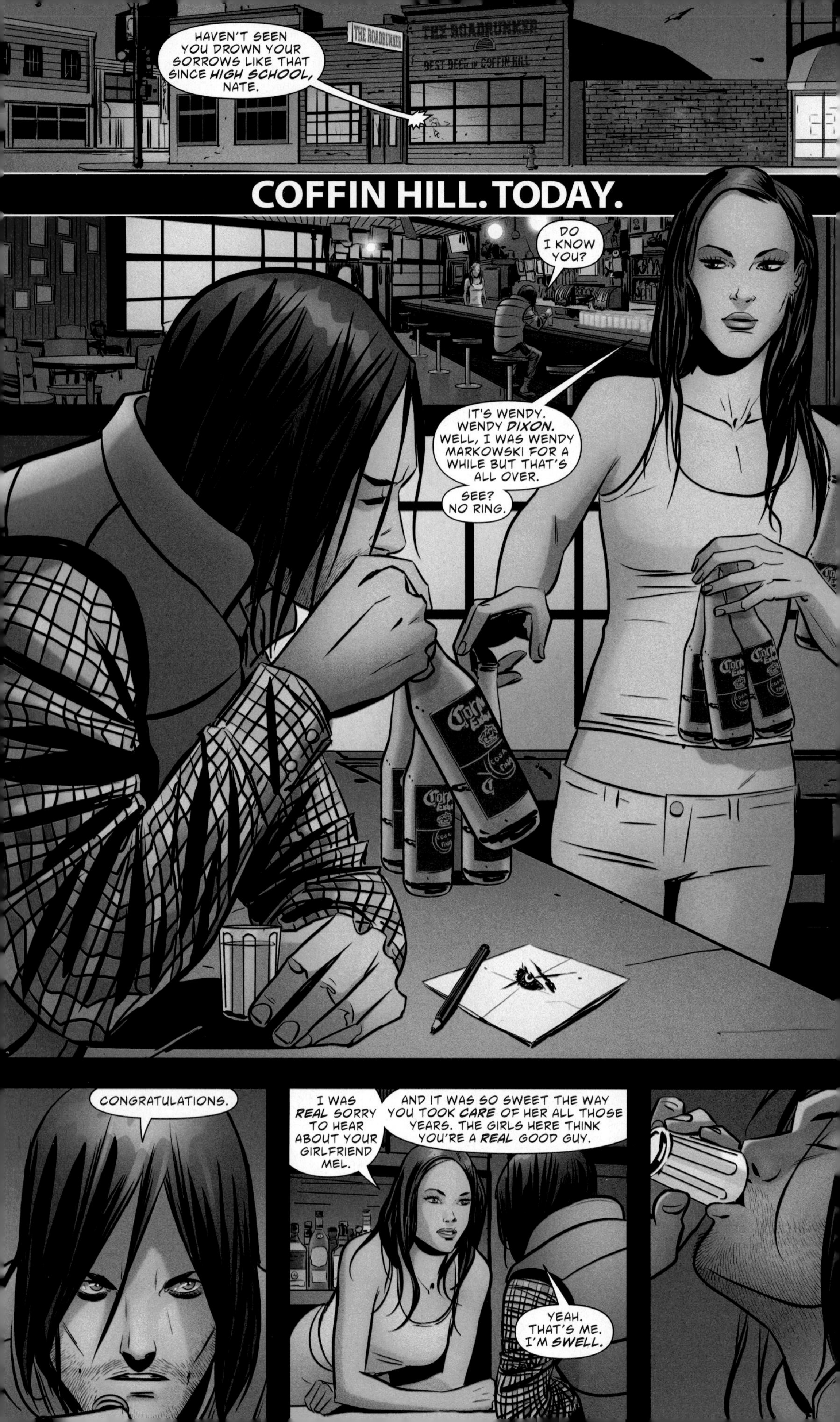
THE ROADRUNNER
THE ROADRUNNER
BEST DEG IN COFFIN HILL
HAVEN'T SEEN YOU DROWN YOUR SORROWS LIKE THAT SINCE HIGH SCHOOL, NATE.
COFFIN HILL. TODAY.
DO I KNOW YOU?
IT'S WENDY. WENDY DIXON. WELL, I WAS WENDY MARKOWSKI FOR A WHILE BUT THAT'S ALL OVER.
SEE? NO RING.
CONGRATULATIONS.
I WAS REAL SORRY TO HEAR ABOUT YOUR GIRLFRIEND MEL.
AND IT WAS SO SWEET THE WAY YOU TOOK CARE OF HER ALL THOSE YEARS. THE GIRLS HERE THINK YOU'RE A REAL GOOD GUY.
YEAH. THAT'S ME. I'M SWELL.

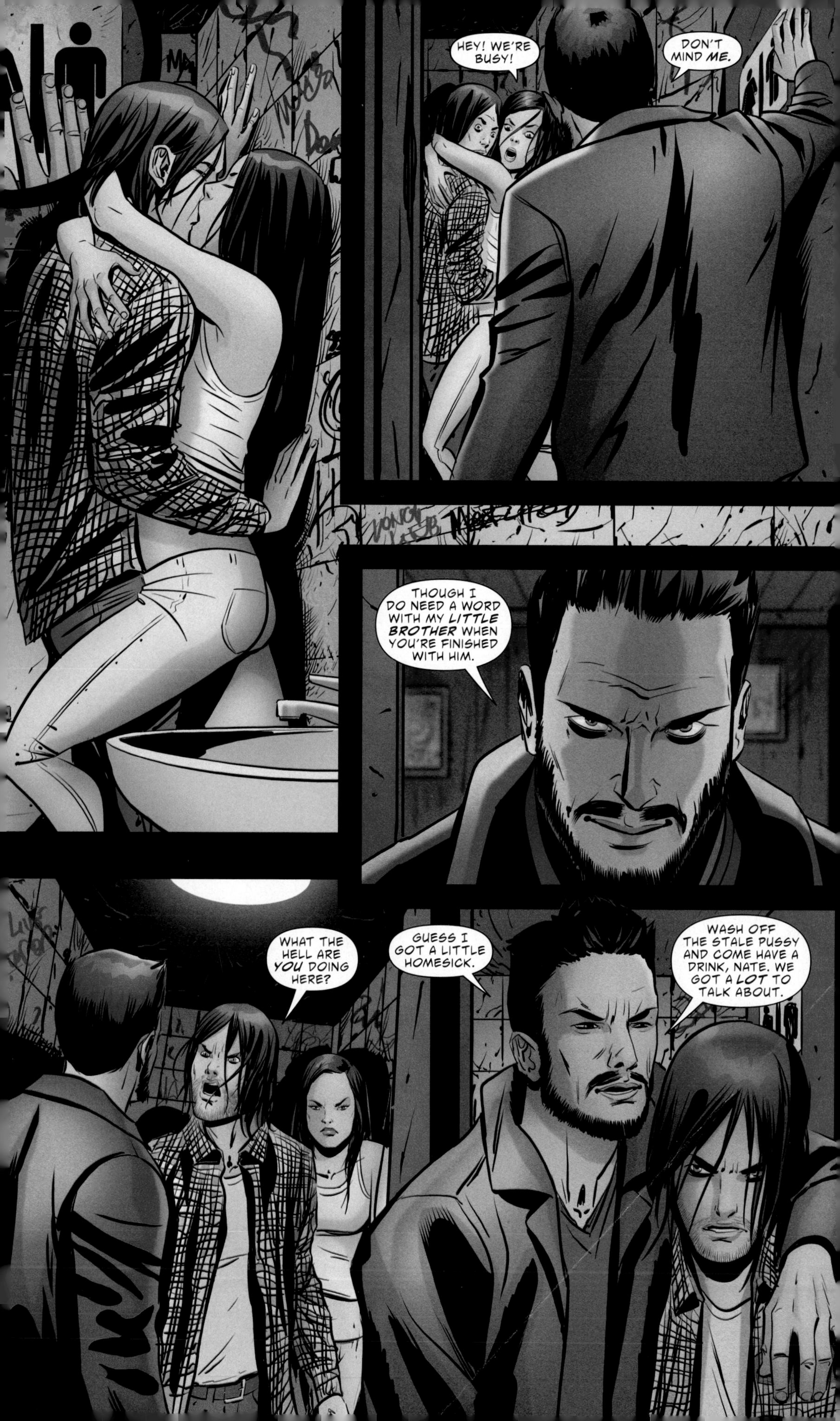
HEY! WE'RE BUSY!
DON'T MIND ME.
THOUGH I DO NEED A WORD WITH MY LITTLE BROTHER WHEN YOU'RE FINISHED WITH HIM.
WHAT THE HELL ARE YOU DOING HERE?
GUESS I GOT A LITTLE HOMESICK.
WASH OFF THE STALE PUSSY AND COME HAVE A DRINK, NATE. WE GOT A LOT TO TALK ABOUT.

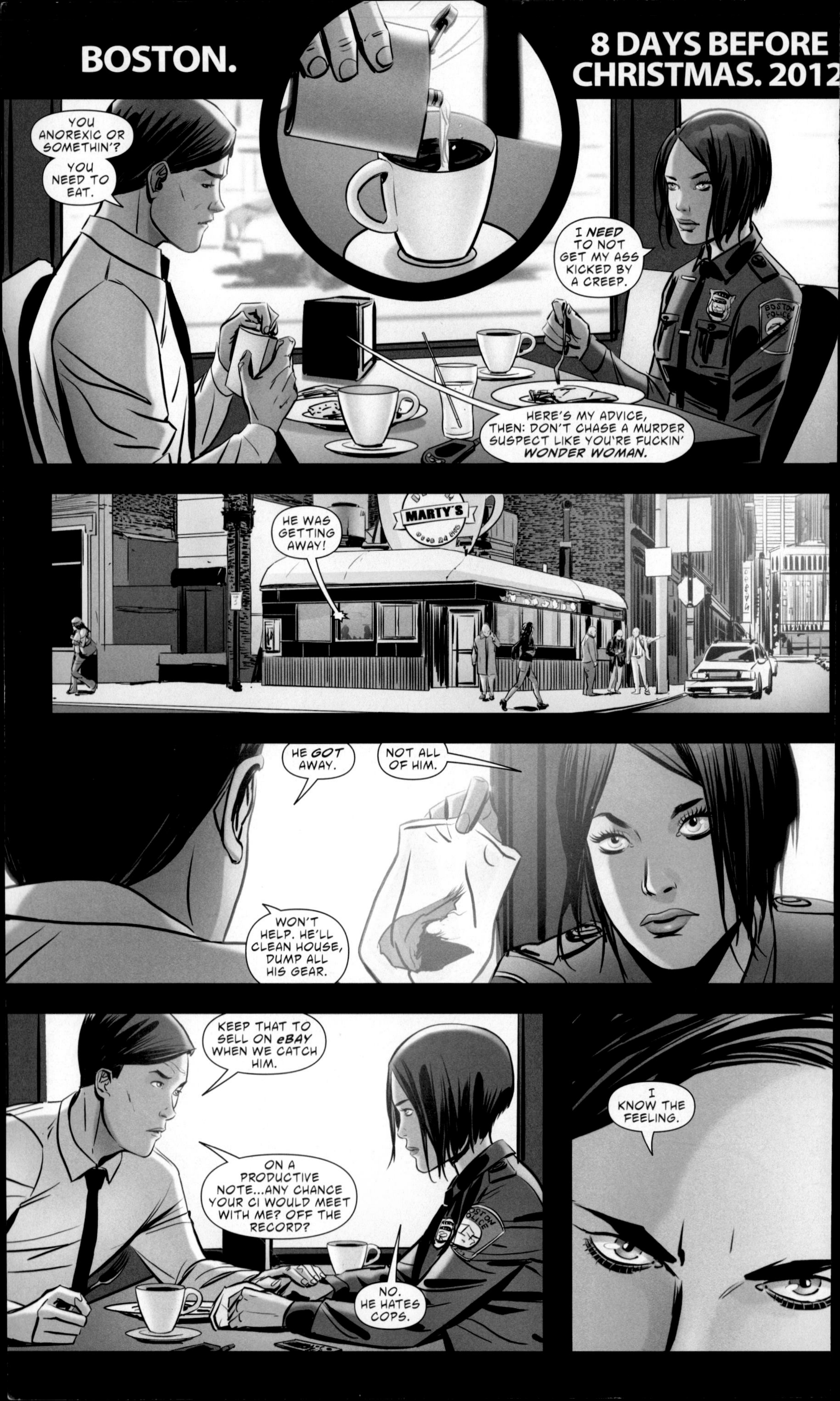
BOSTON.
8 DAYS BEFORE CHRISTMAS. 2012
YOU ANOREXIC OR SOMETHIN'?
YOU NEED TO EAT.
I NEED TO NOT GET MY ASS KICKED BY A CREEP.
HERE'S MY ADVICE, THEN: DON'T CHASE A MURDER SUSPECT LIKE YOU'RE FUCKIN' WONDER WOMAN.
MARTY'S
HE WAS GETTING AWAY!
HE GOT AWAY.
NOT ALL OF HIM.
WON'T HELP. HE'LL CLEAN HOUSE, DUMP ALL HIS GEAR.
KEEP THAT TO SELL ON eBAY WHEN WE CATCH HIM.
ON A PRODUCTIVE NOTE...ANY CHANCE YOUR CI WOULD MEET WITH ME? OFF THE RECORD?
NO. HE HATES COPS.
I KNOW THE FEELING.

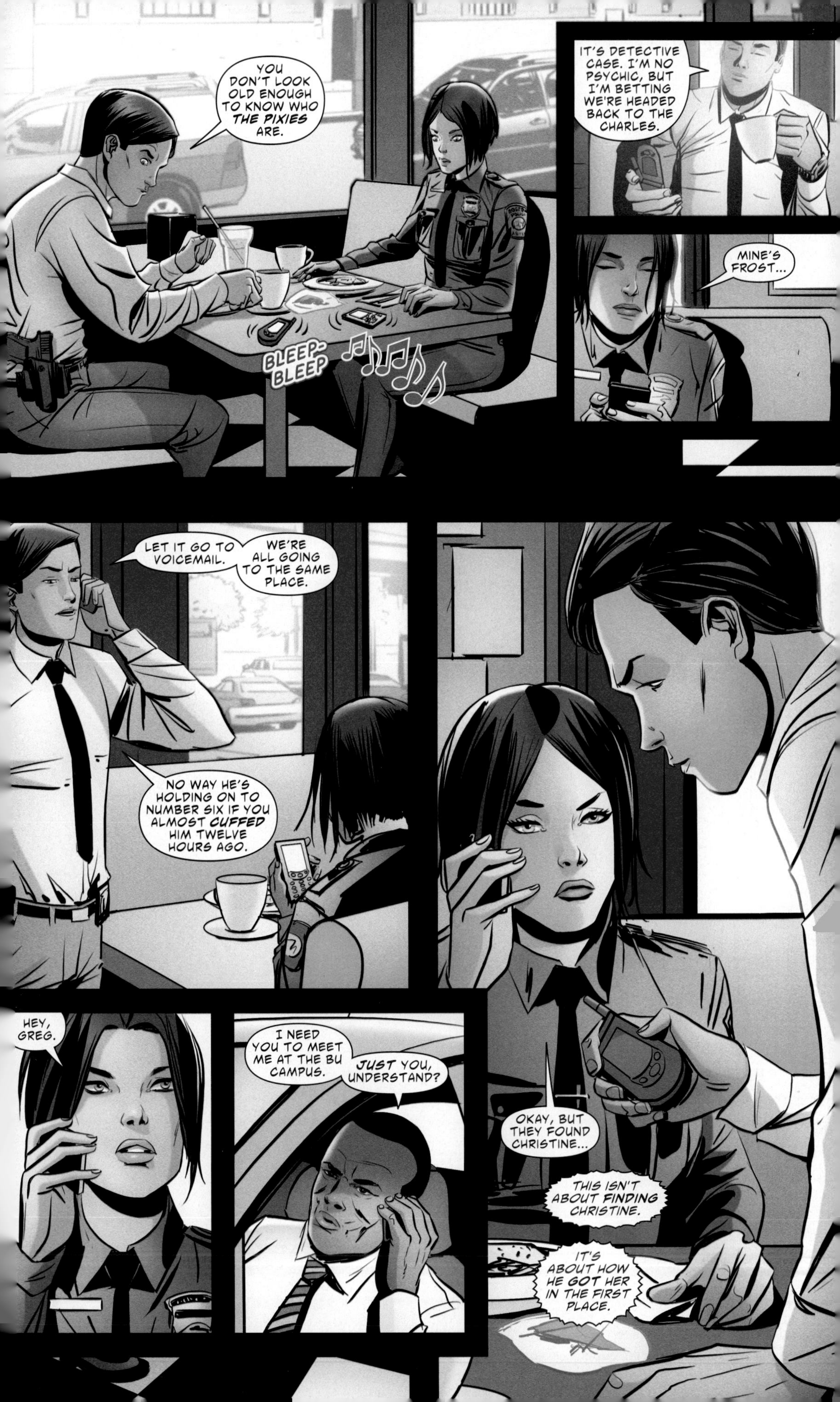
YOU DON'T LOOK OLD ENOUGH TO KNOW WHO THE PIXIES ARE.
BLEEP-BLEEP
IT'S DETECTIVE CASE. I'M NO PSYCHIC, BUT I'M BETTING WE'RE HEADED BACK TO THE CHARLES.
MINE'S FROST...
LET IT GO TO VOICEMAIL.
WE'RE ALL GOING TO THE SAME PLACE.
NO WAY HE'S HOLDING ON TO NUMBER SIX IF YOU ALMOST CUFFED HIM TWELVE HOURS AGO.
HEY, GREG.
I NEED YOU TO MEET ME AT THE BU CAMPUS.
JUST YOU, UNDERSTAND?
OKAY, BUT THEY FOUND CHRISTINE...
THIS ISN'T ABOUT FINDING CHRISTINE.
IT'S ABOUT HOW HE GOT HER IN THE FIRST PLACE.

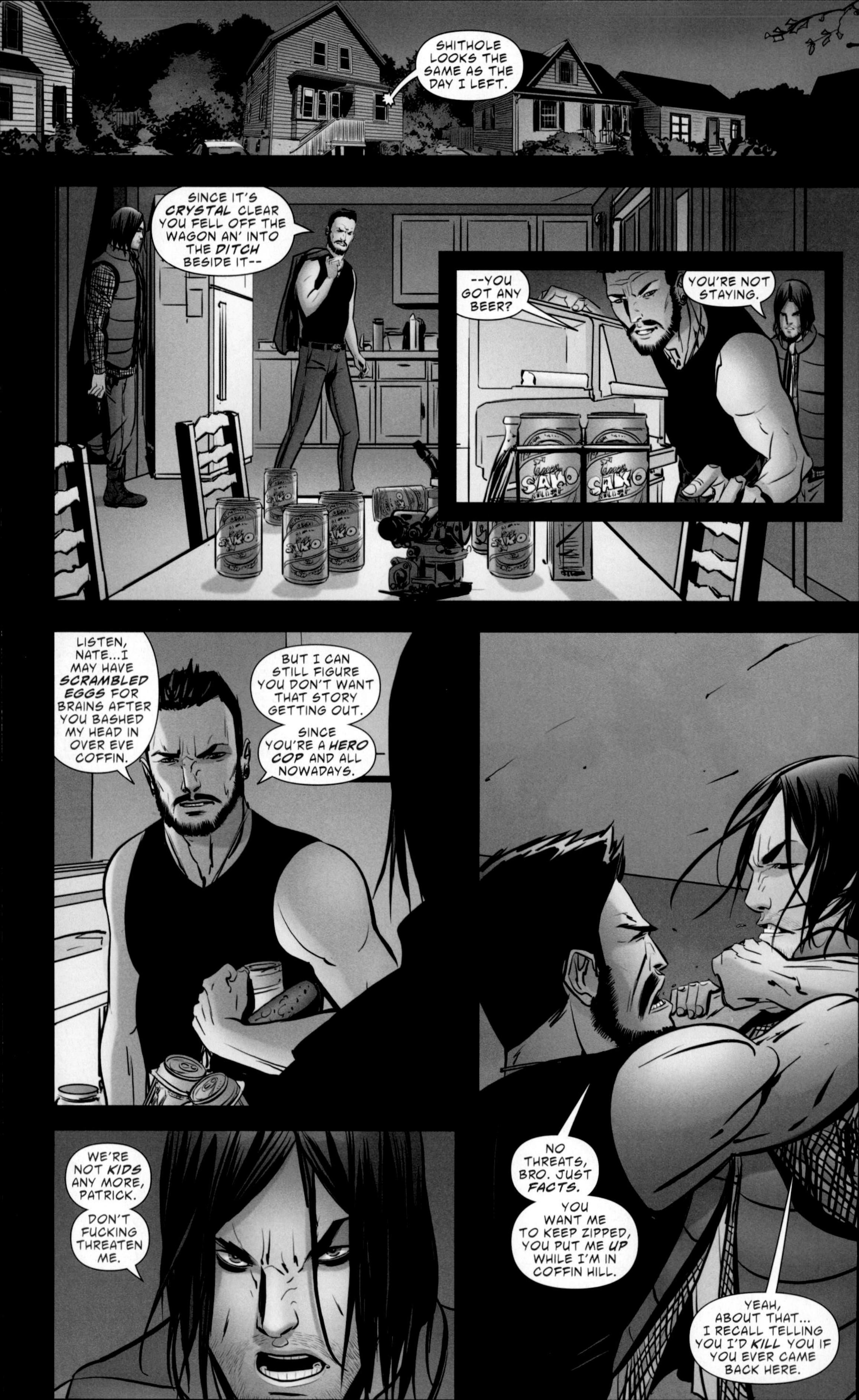
SHITHOLE LOOKS THE SAME AS THE DAY I LEFT.
SINCE IT'S CRYSTAL CLEAR YOU FELL OFF THE WAGON AN' INTO THE DITCH BESIDE IT--
--YOU GOT ANY BEER?
YOU'RE NOT STAYING.
LISTEN, NATE...I MAY HAVE SCRAMBLED EGGS FOR BRAINS AFTER YOU BASHED MY HEAD IN OVER EVE COFFIN.
BUT I CAN STILL FIGURE YOU DON'T WANT THAT STORY GETTING OUT.
SINCE YOU'RE A HERO COP AND ALL NOWADAYS.
WE'RE NOT KIDS ANY MORE, PATRICK.
DON'T FUCKING THREATEN ME.
NO THREATS, BRO. JUST FACTS.
YOU WANT ME TO KEEP ZIPPED, YOU PUT ME UP WHILE I'M IN COFFIN HILL.
YEAH, ABOUT THAT... I RECALL TELLING YOU I'D KILL YOU IF YOU EVER CAME BACK HERE.

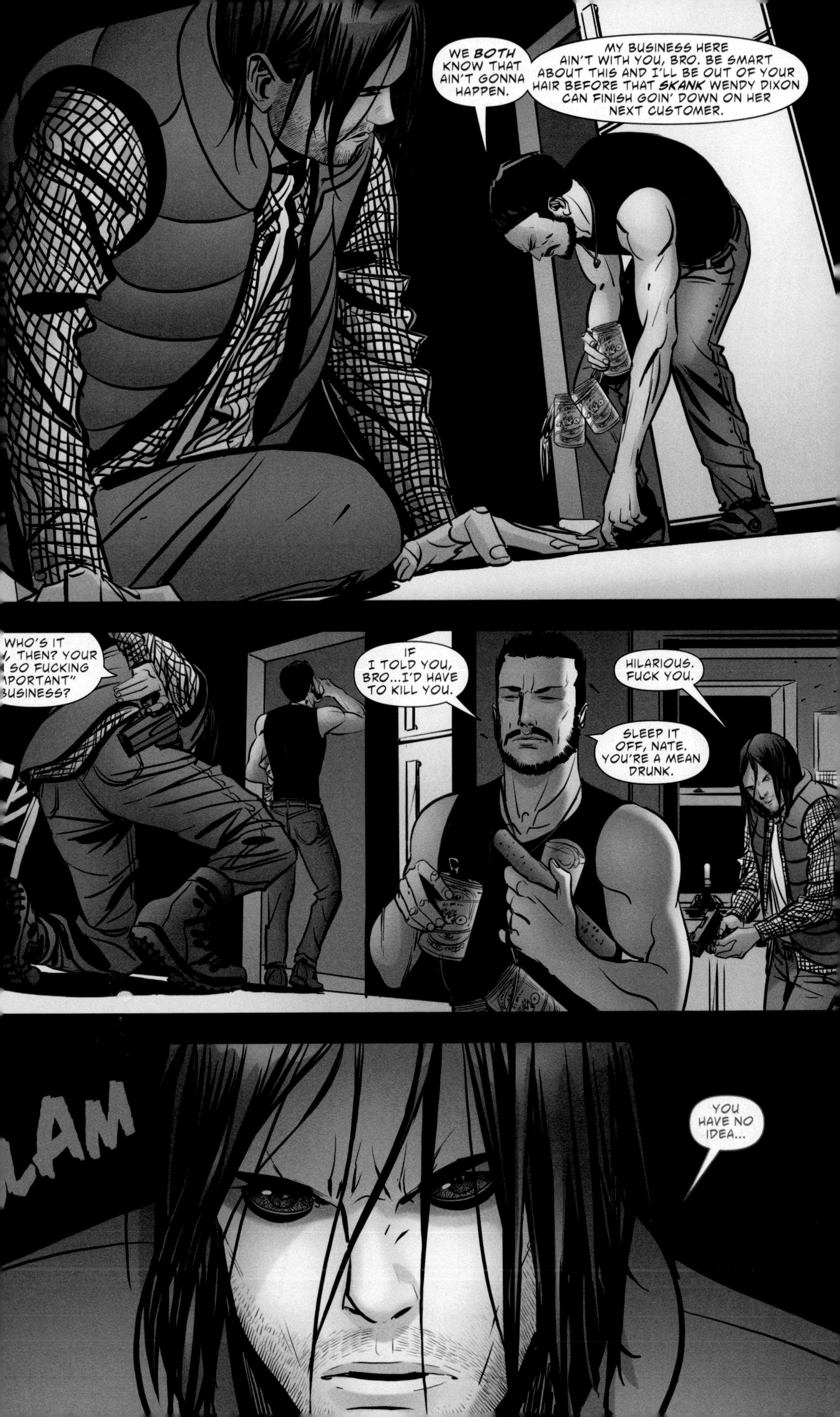
MY BUSINESS HERE AIN'T WITH YOU, BRO. BE SMART ABOUT THIS AND I'LL BE OUT OF YOUR HAIR BEFORE THAT SKANK WENDY DIXON CAN FINISH GOIN' DOWN ON HER NEXT CUSTOMER.
WE BOTH KNOW THAT AIN'T GONNA HAPPEN.
IF I TOLD YOU, BRO...I'D HAVE TO KILL YOU.
HILARIOUS. FUCK YOU.
SLEEP IT OFF, NATE. YOU'RE A MEAN DRUNK.
YOU HAVE NO IDEA...

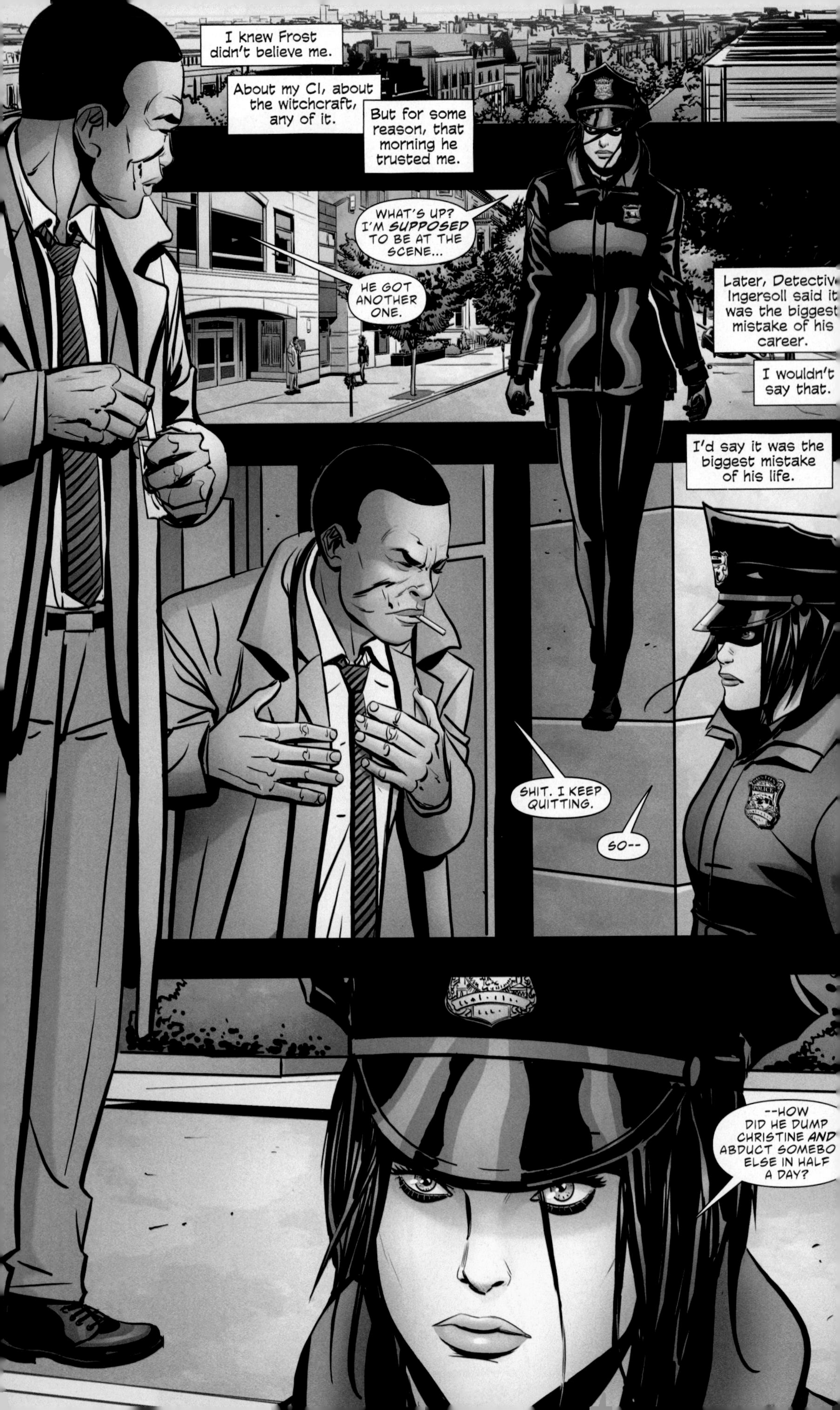

I knew Frost didn't believe me.
About my CI, about the witchcraft, any of it.
But for some reason, that morning he trusted me.
WHAT'S UP? I'M SUPPOSED TO BE AT THE SCENE...
HE GOT ANOTHER ONE.
Later, Detectiv Ingersoll said it was the biggest mistake of his career.
I wouldn't say that.
I'd say it was the biggest mistake of his life.
SHIT. I KEEP QUITTING.
SO--
--HOW DID HE DUMP CHRISTINE AND ABDUCT SOMEBO ELSE IN HALF A DAY?

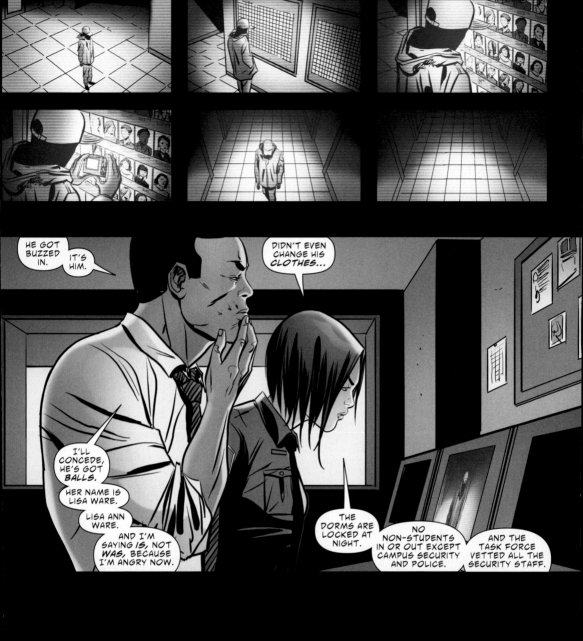

HE GOT BUZZED IN.

IT'S HIM.

DIDN'T EVEN CHANGE HIS *CLOTHES...*

I'LL CONCEDE, HE'S GOT *BALLS.*

HER NAME IS LISA WARE.

LISA ANN WARE.

AND I'M SAYING *IS,* NOT *WAS,* BECAUSE I'M ANGRY NOW.

THE DORMS ARE LOCKED AT NIGHT.

NO NON-STUDENTS IN OR OUT EXCEPT CAMPUS SECURITY AND POLICE.

AND THE TASK FORCE VETTED ALL THE SECURITY STAFF.

"I'M ANGRY HE'S GOTTEN SEVEN."

"YOU WANNA KNOW WHAT *ELSE* I'M ANGRY ABOUT?"

"*YOU* SAY IT, EVE. I WANNA KNOW I'M NOT CRAZY."

"I MUST BE CRAZY, TOO."

"BECAUSE I'M THINKING THE ICE FISHER IS A *COP.*"

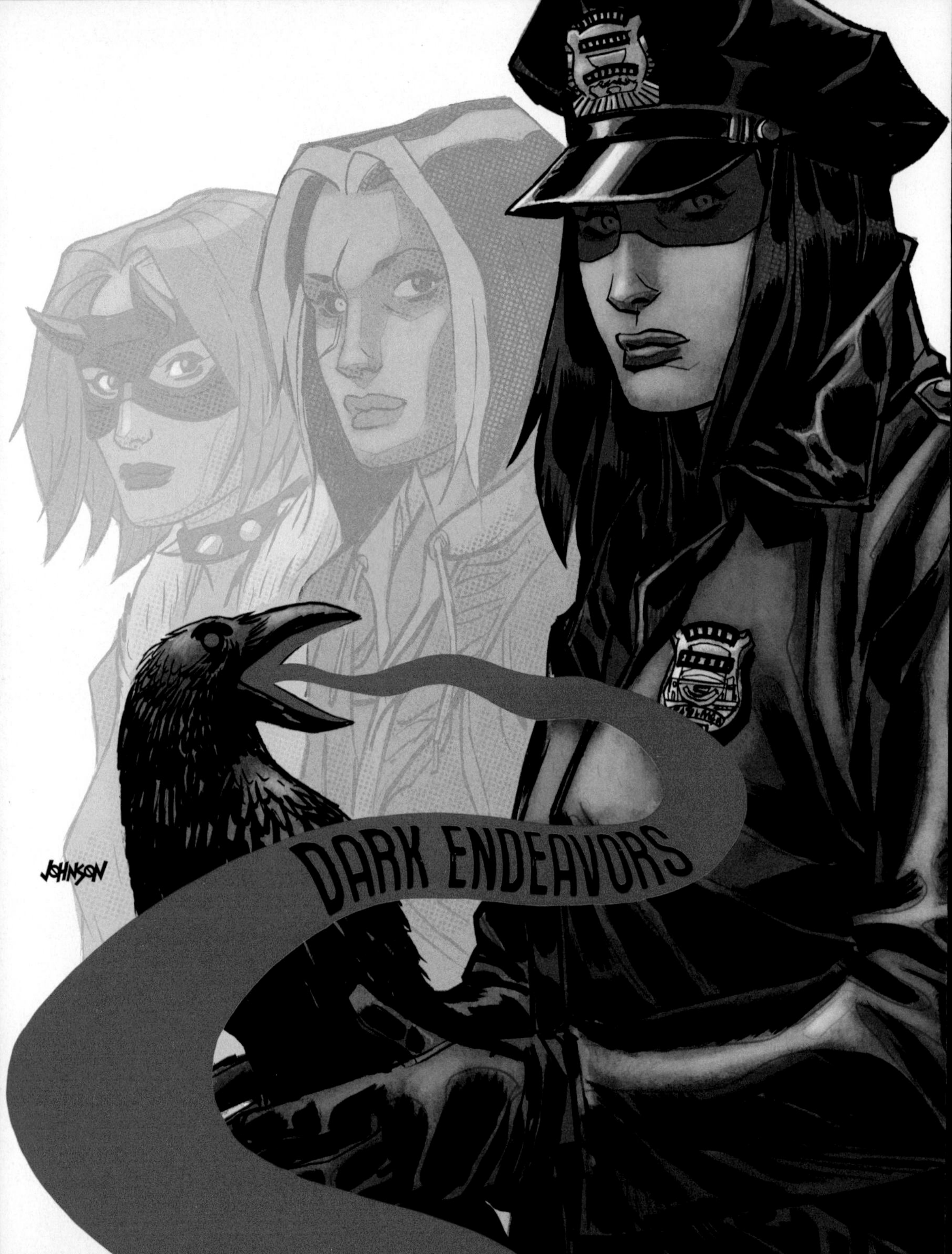
DARK ENDEAVORS
JOHNSON

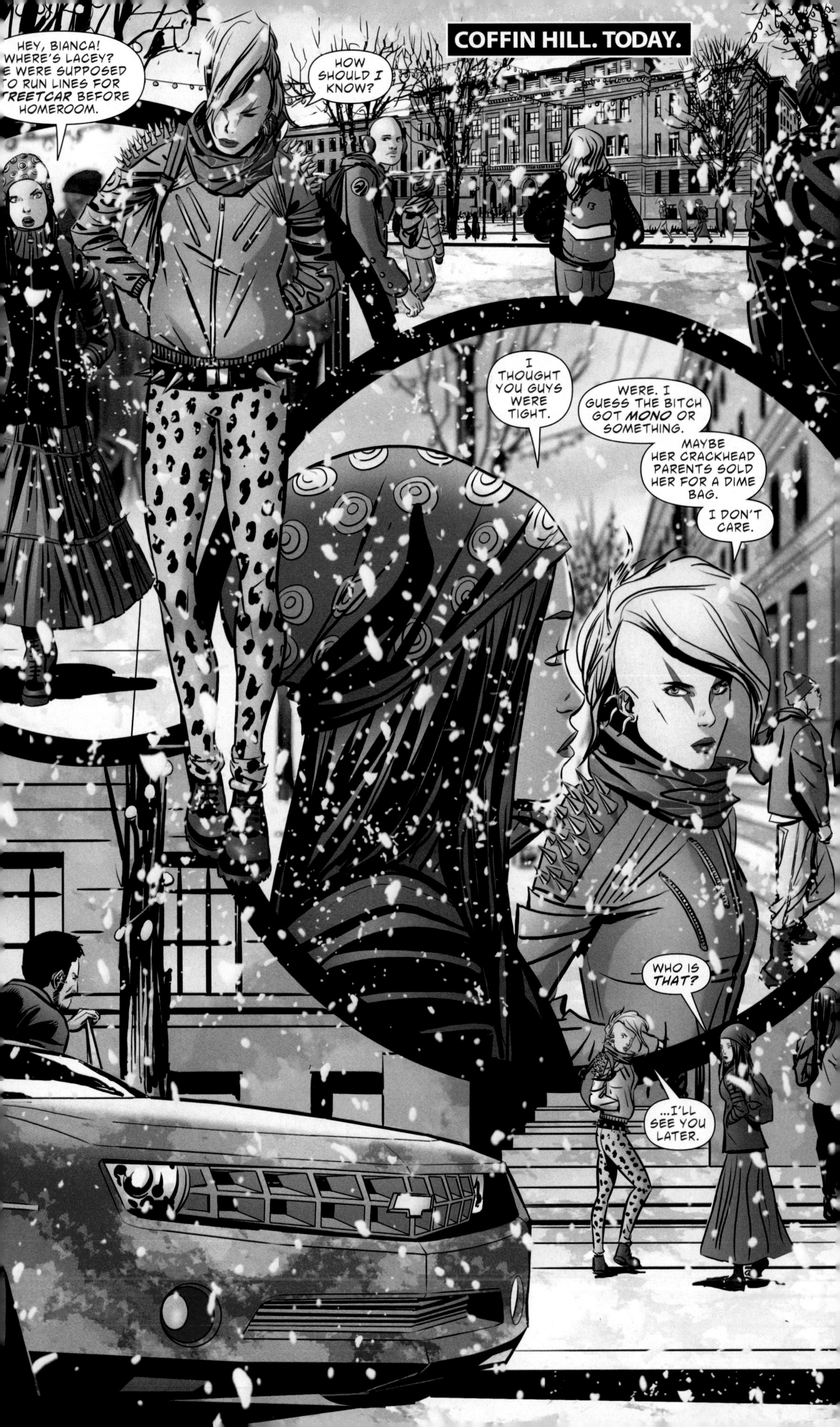
COFFIN HILL. TODAY.
HEY, BIANCA! WHERE'S LACEY? E WERE SUPPOSED TO RUN LINES FOR TREETCAR BEFORE HOMEROOM.
HOW SHOULD I KNOW?
I THOUGHT YOU GUYS WERE TIGHT.
WERE. I GUESS THE BITCH GOT MONO OR SOMETHING.
MAYBE HER CRACKHEAD PARENTS SOLD HER FOR A DIME BAG.
I DON'T CARE.
WHO IS THAT?
...I'LL SEE YOU LATER.

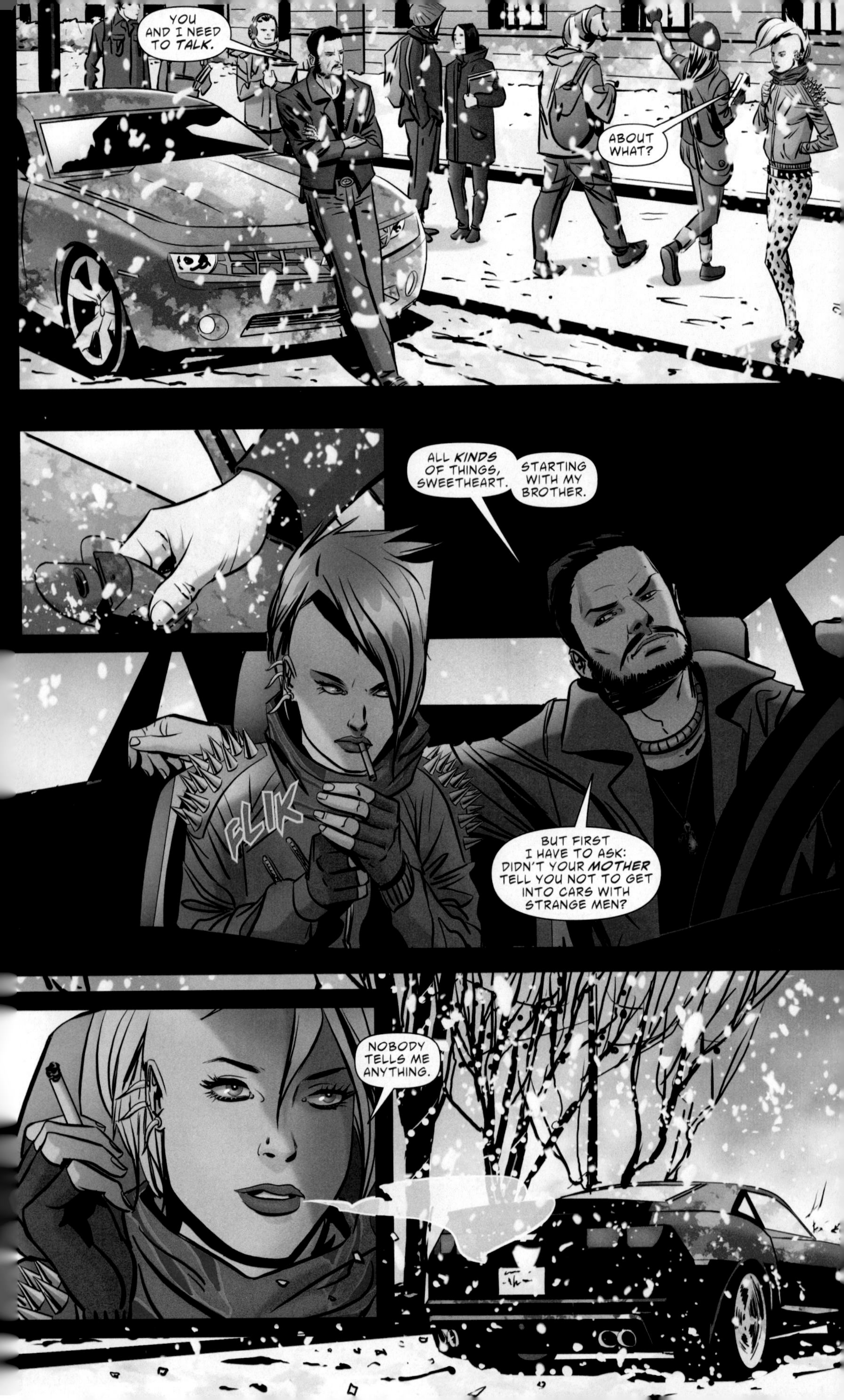
YOU AND I NEED TO TALK.
ABOUT WHAT?
ALL KINDS OF THINGS, SWEETHEART.
STARTING WITH MY BROTHER.
FLIK
BUT FIRST I HAVE TO ASK: DIDN'T YOUR MOTHER TELL YOU NOT TO GET INTO CARS WITH STRANGE MEN?
NOBODY TELLS ME ANYTHING.

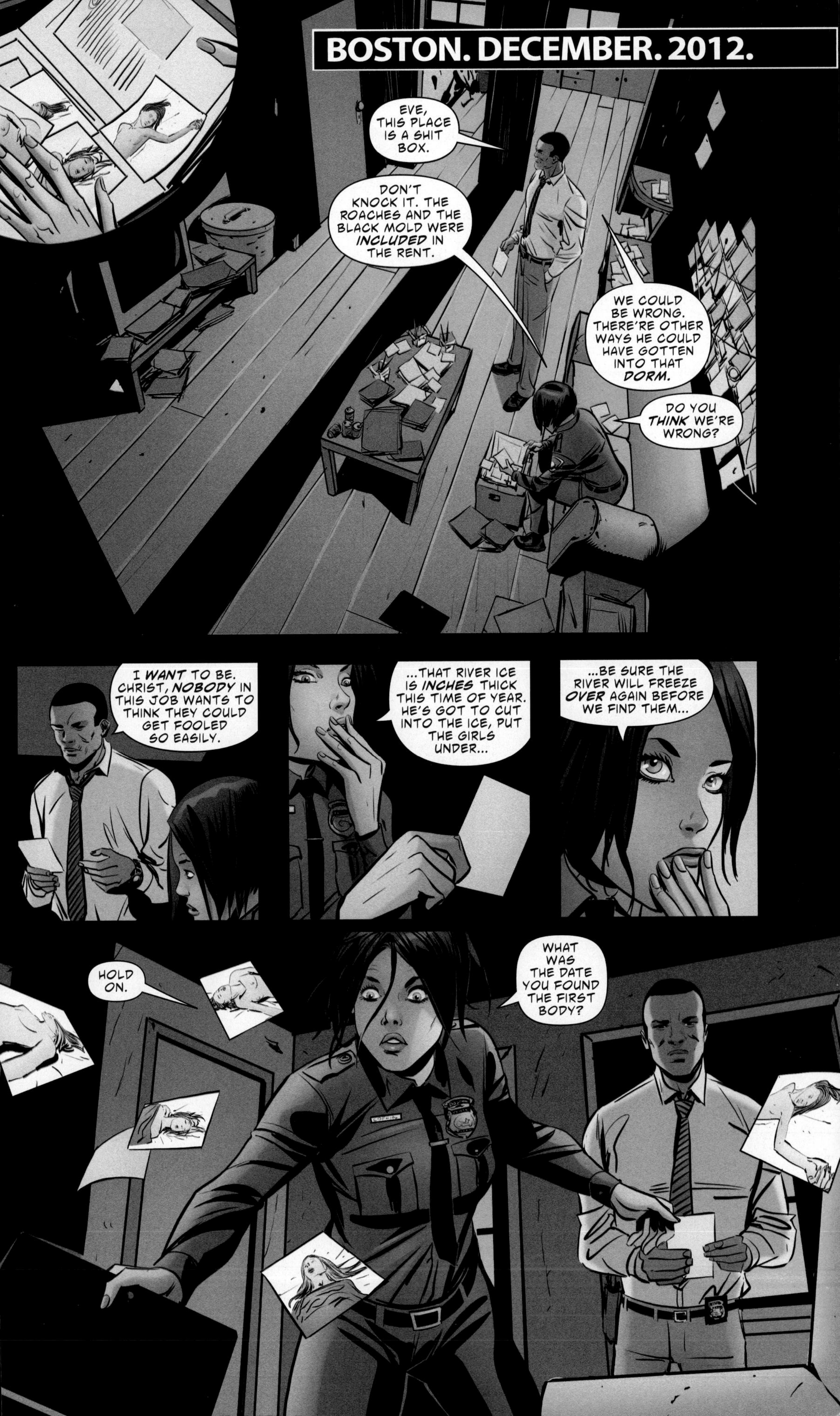
BOSTON. DECEMBER. 2012.
EVE, THIS PLACE IS A SHIT BOX.
DON'T KNOCK IT. THE ROACHES AND THE BLACK MOLD WERE INCLUDED IN THE RENT.
WE COULD BE WRONG. THERE'RE OTHER WAYS HE COULD HAVE GOTTEN INTO THAT DORM.
DO YOU THINK WE'RE WRONG?
I WANT TO BE. CHRIST, NOBODY IN THIS JOB WANTS TO THINK THEY COULD GET FOOLED SO EASILY.
...THAT RIVER ICE IS INCHES THICK THIS TIME OF YEAR. HE'S GOT TO CUT INTO THE ICE, PUT THE GIRLS UNDER...
...BE SURE THE RIVER WILL FREEZE OVER AGAIN BEFORE WE FIND THEM...
HOLD ON.
WHAT WAS THE DATE YOU FOUND THE FIRST BODY?

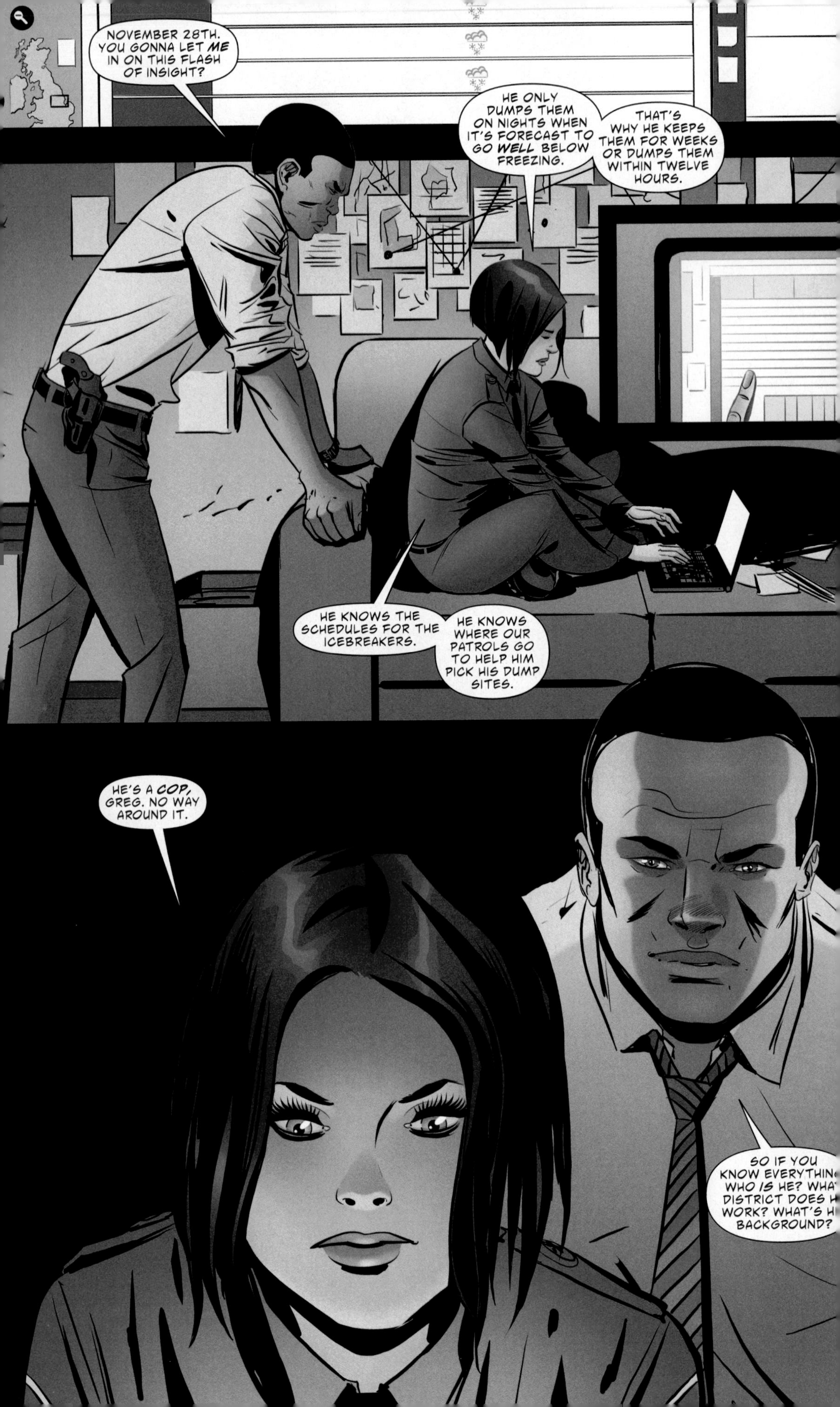
NOVEMBER 28TH. YOU GONNA LET *ME* IN ON THIS FLASH OF INSIGHT?
HE ONLY DUMPS THEM ON NIGHTS WHEN IT'S FORECAST TO GO *WELL* BELOW FREEZING.
THAT'S WHY HE KEEPS THEM FOR WEEKS OR DUMPS THEM WITHIN TWELVE HOURS.
HE KNOWS THE SCHEDULES FOR THE ICEBREAKERS.
HE KNOWS WHERE OUR PATROLS GO TO HELP HIM PICK HIS DUMP SITES.
HE'S A *COP*, GREG. NO WAY AROUND IT.

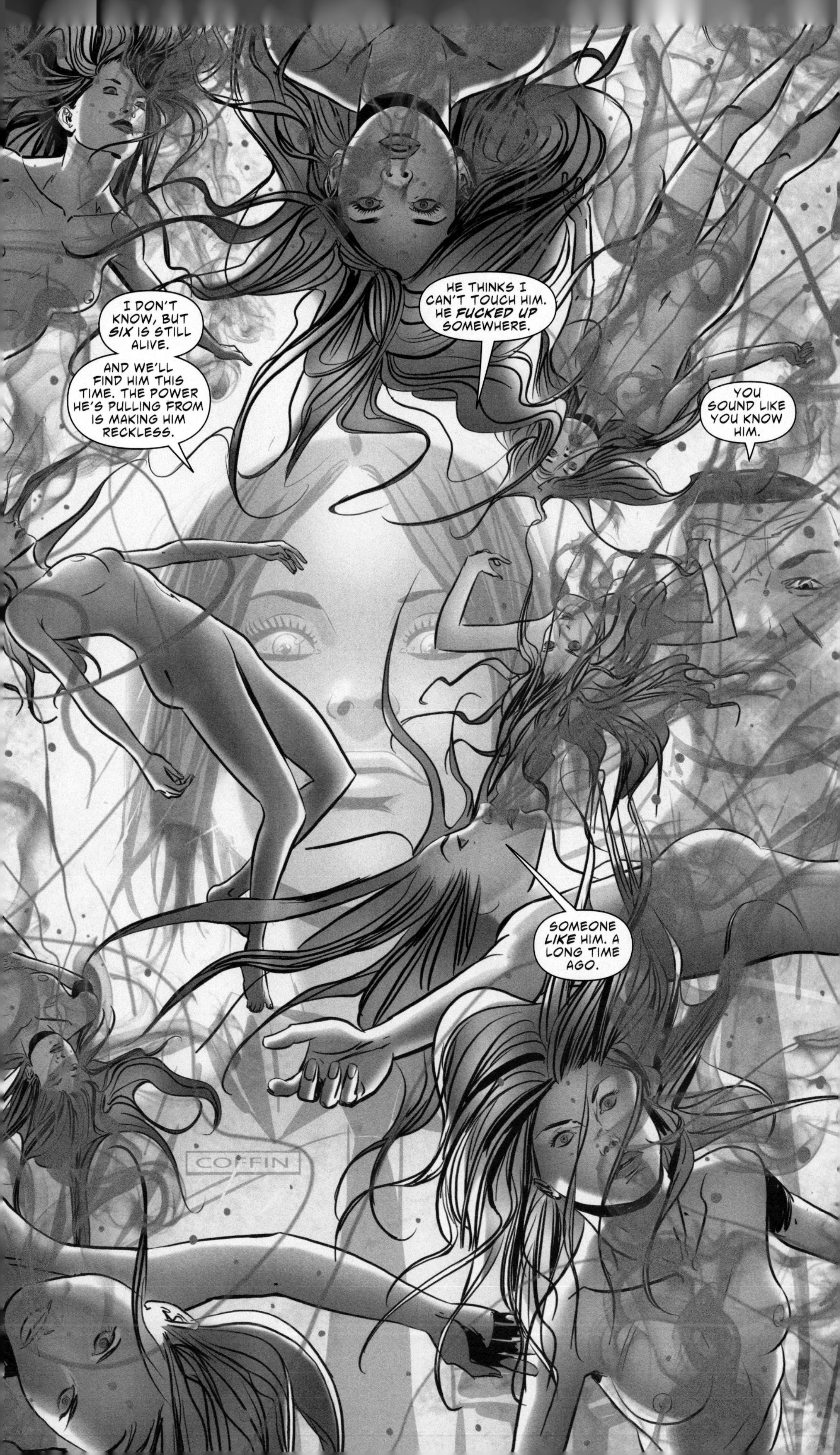
I DON'T KNOW, BUT SIX IS STILL ALIVE.
AND WE'LL FIND HIM THIS TIME. THE POWER HE'S PULLING FROM IS MAKING HIM RECKLESS.
HE THINKS I CAN'T TOUCH HIM. HE FUCKED UP SOMEWHERE.
YOU SOUND LIKE YOU KNOW HIM.
SOMEONE LIKE HIM. A LONG TIME AGO.
COFFIN

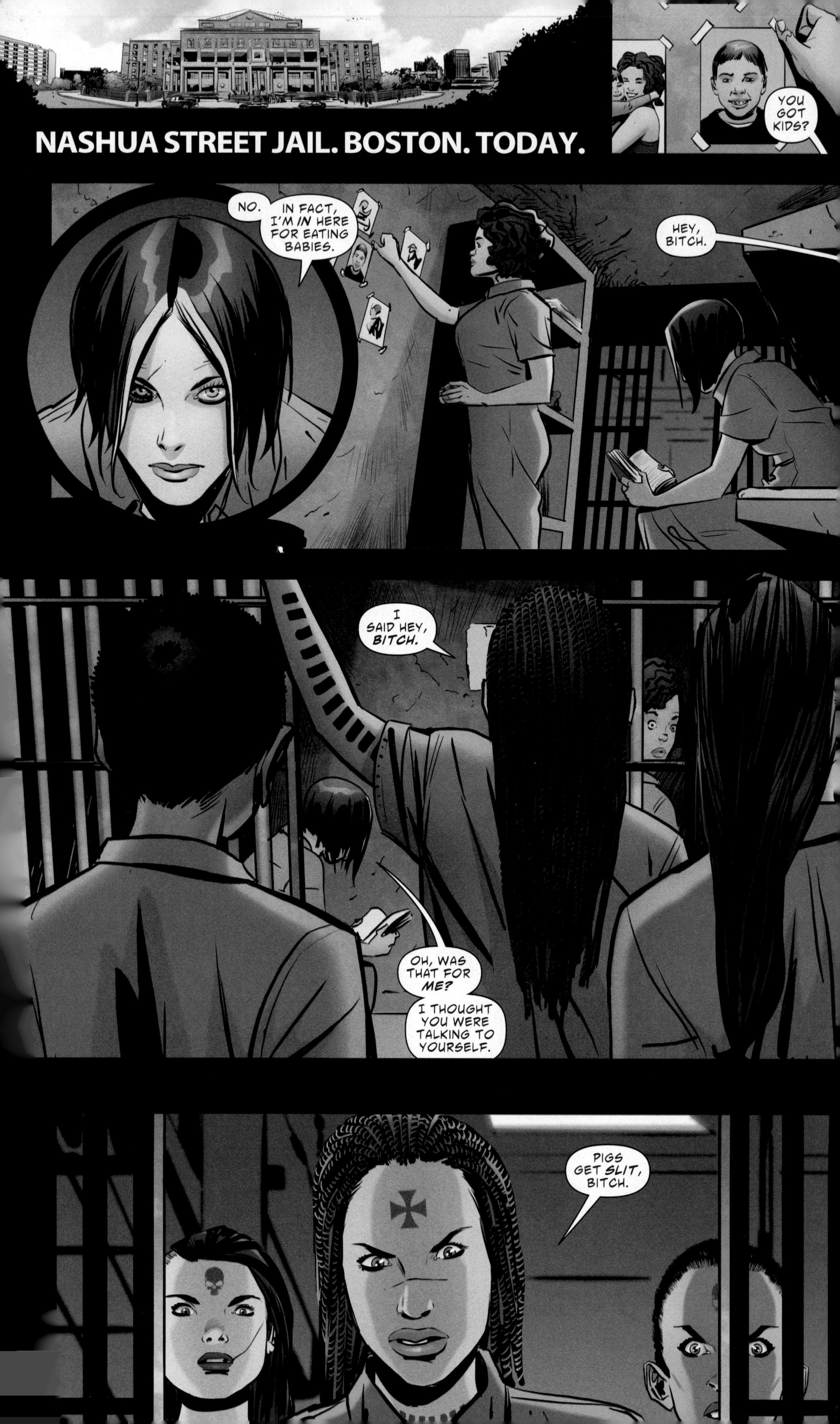
NASHUA STREET JAIL. BOSTON. TODAY.
YOU GOT KIDS?
NO.
IN FACT, I'M IN HERE FOR EATING BABIES.
HEY, BITCH.
I SAID HEY, BITCH.
OH, WAS THAT FOR ME?
I THOUGHT YOU WERE TALKING TO YOURSELF.
PIGS GET SLIT, BITCH.

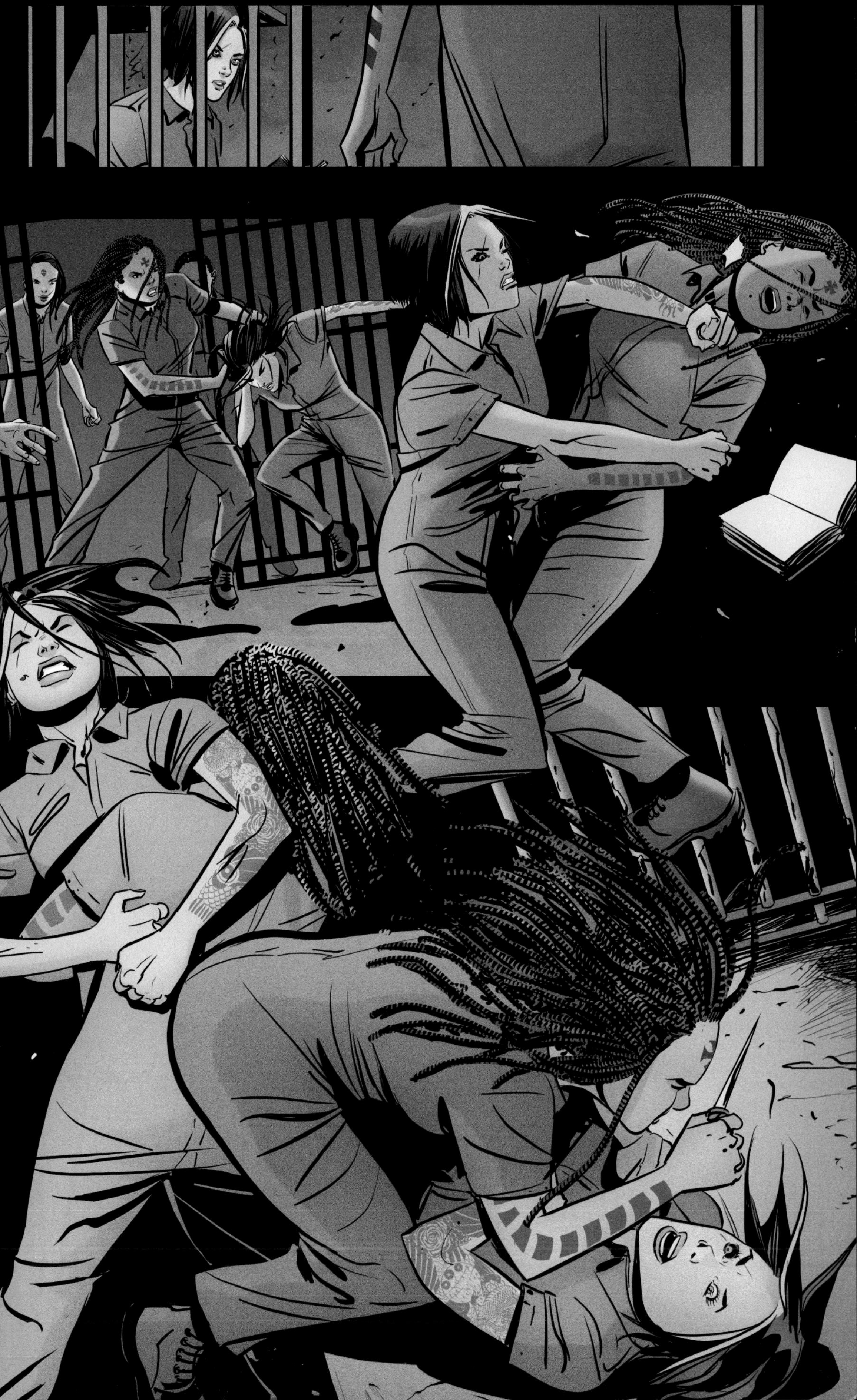

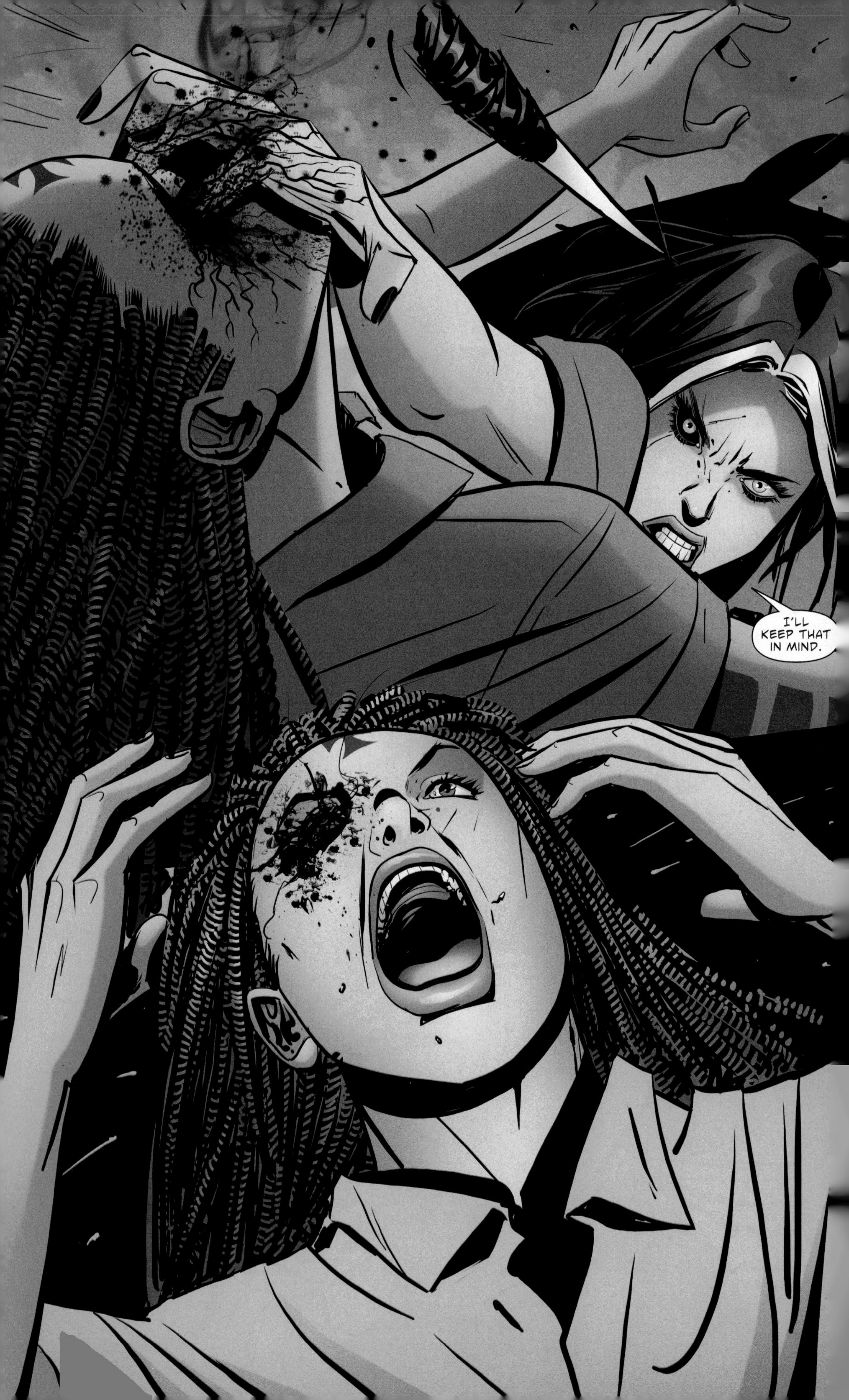
I'LL KEEP THAT IN MIND.

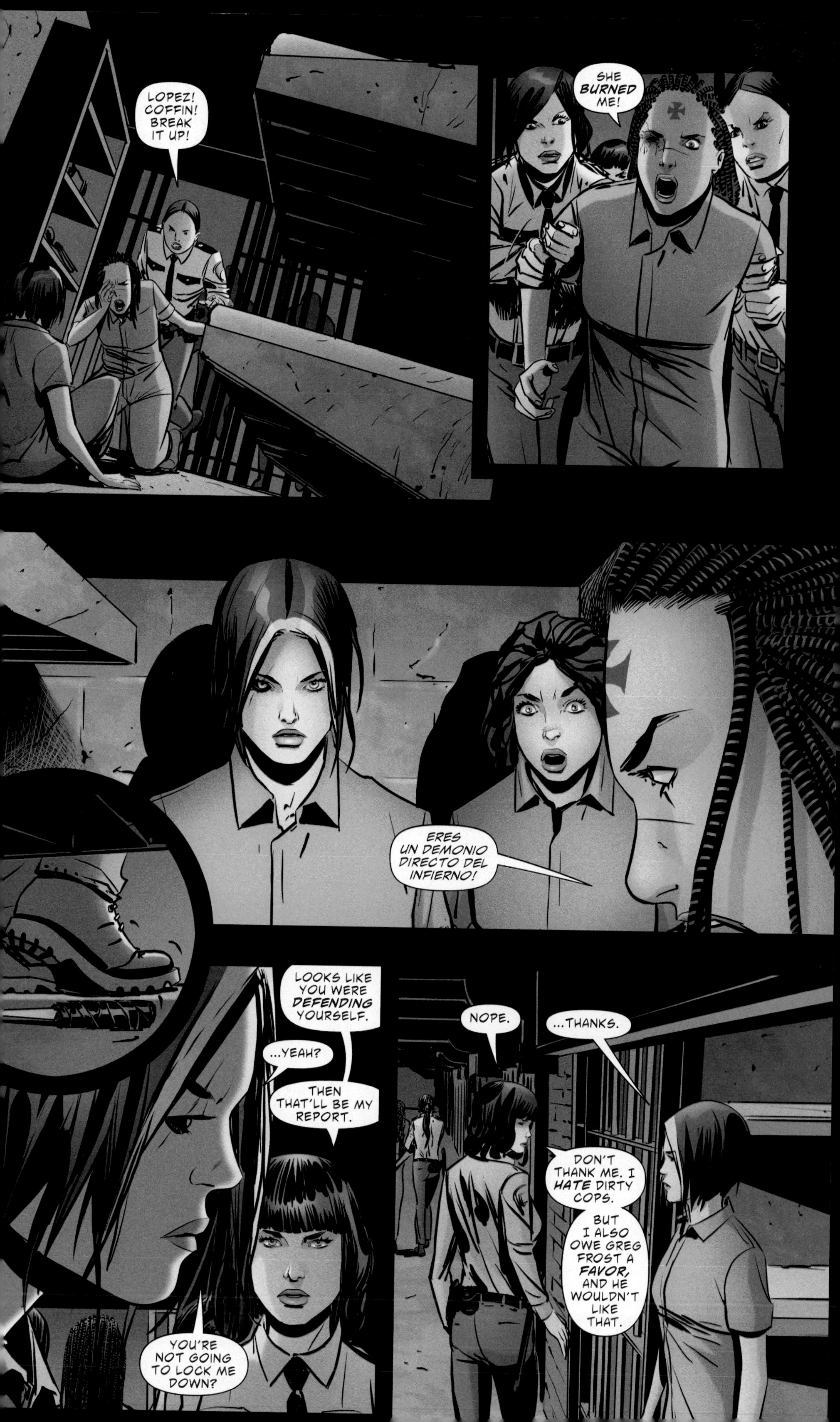
LOPEZ! COFFIN! BREAK IT UP!
SHE BURNED ME!
ERES UN DEMONIO DIRECTO DEL INFIERNO!
LOOKS LIKE YOU WERE DEFENDING YOURSELF.
...YEAH?
THEN THAT'LL BE MY REPORT.
YOU'RE NOT GOING TO LOCK ME DOWN?
NOPE.
...THANKS.
DON'T THANK ME. I HATE DIRTY COPS.
BUT I ALSO OWE GREG FROST A FAVOR, AND HE WOULDN'T LIKE THAT.

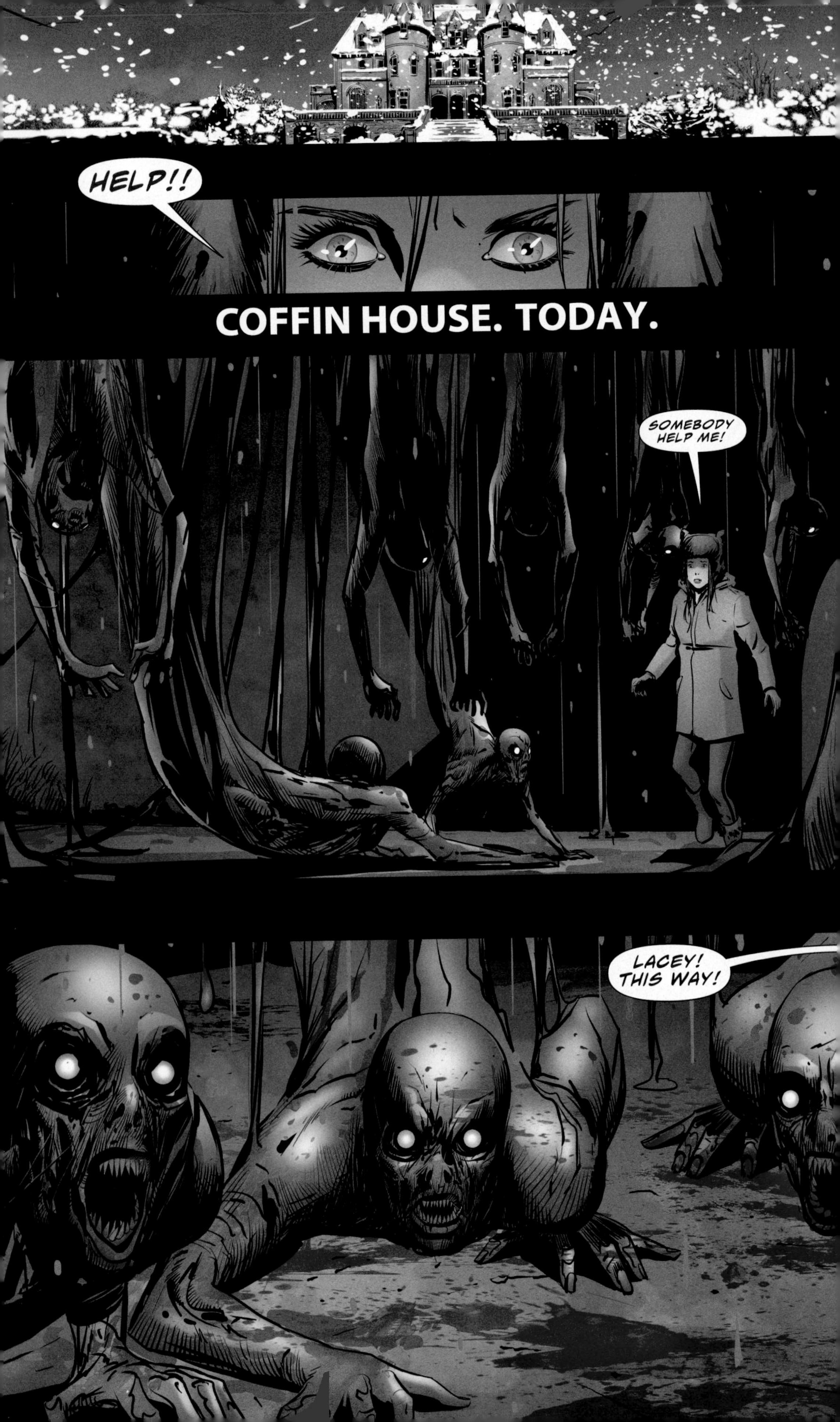
HELP!!
COFFIN HOUSE. TODAY.
SOMEBODY HELP ME!
LACEY! THIS WAY!

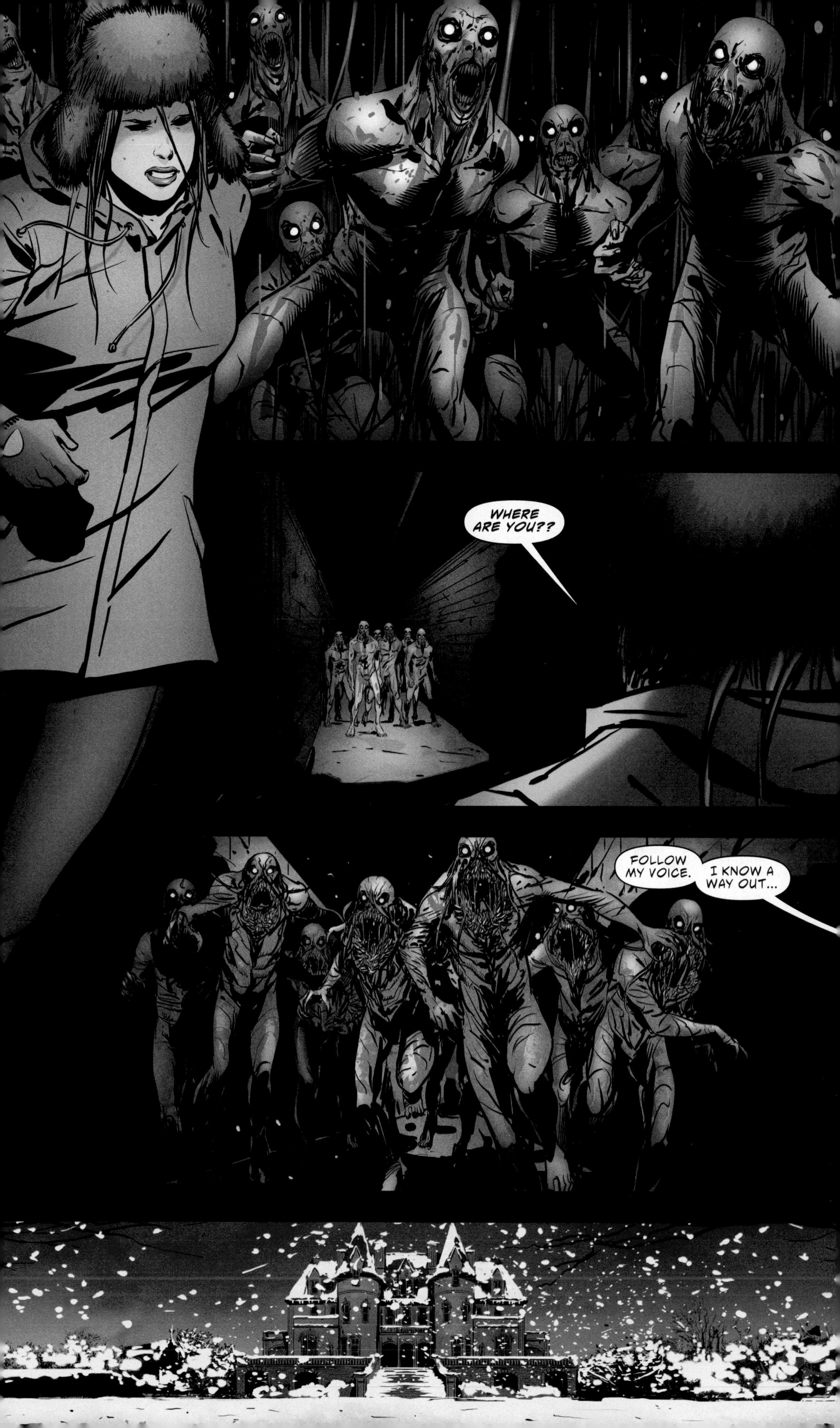
WHERE ARE YOU??
FOLLOW MY VOICE.
I KNOW A WAY OUT...

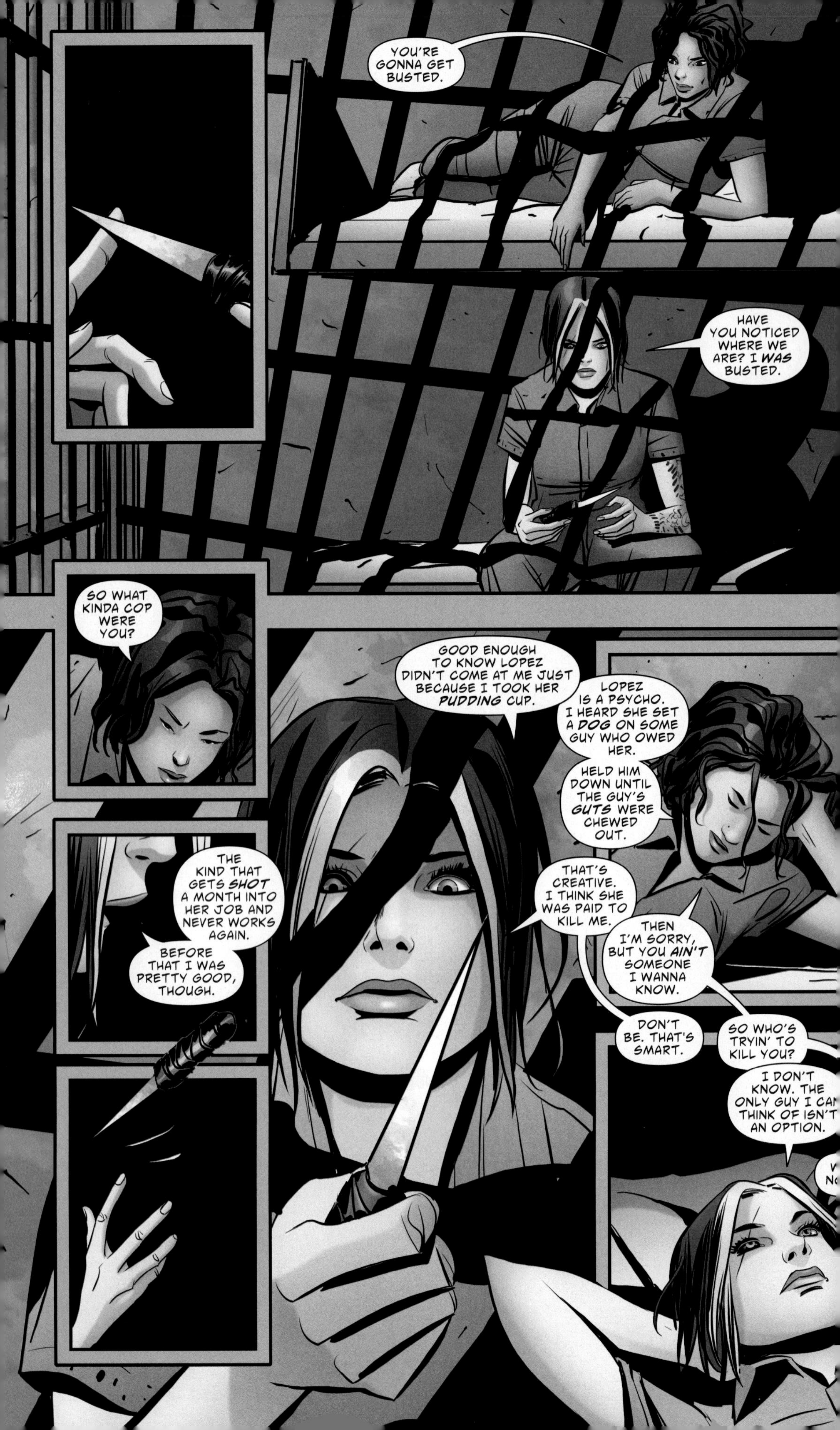
YOU'RE GONNA GET BUSTED.
HAVE YOU NOTICED WHERE WE ARE? I *WAS* BUSTED.
SO WHAT KINDA COP WERE YOU?
GOOD ENOUGH TO KNOW LOPEZ DIDN'T COME AT ME JUST BECAUSE I TOOK HER *PUDDING* CUP.
LOPEZ IS A PSYCHO. I HEARD SHE SET A *DOG* ON SOME GUY WHO OWED HER.
HELD HIM DOWN UNTIL THE GUY'S *GUTS* WERE CHEWED OUT.
THE KIND THAT GETS *SHOT* A MONTH INTO HER JOB AND NEVER WORKS AGAIN.
BEFORE THAT I WAS PRETTY GOOD, THOUGH.
THAT'S CREATIVE. I THINK SHE WAS PAID TO KILL ME.
THEN I'M SORRY, BUT YOU *AIN'T* SOMEONE I WANNA KNOW.
DON'T BE. THAT'S SMART.
SO WHO'S TRYIN' TO KILL YOU?
I DON'T KNOW. THE ONLY GUY I CA THINK OF ISN'T AN OPTION.

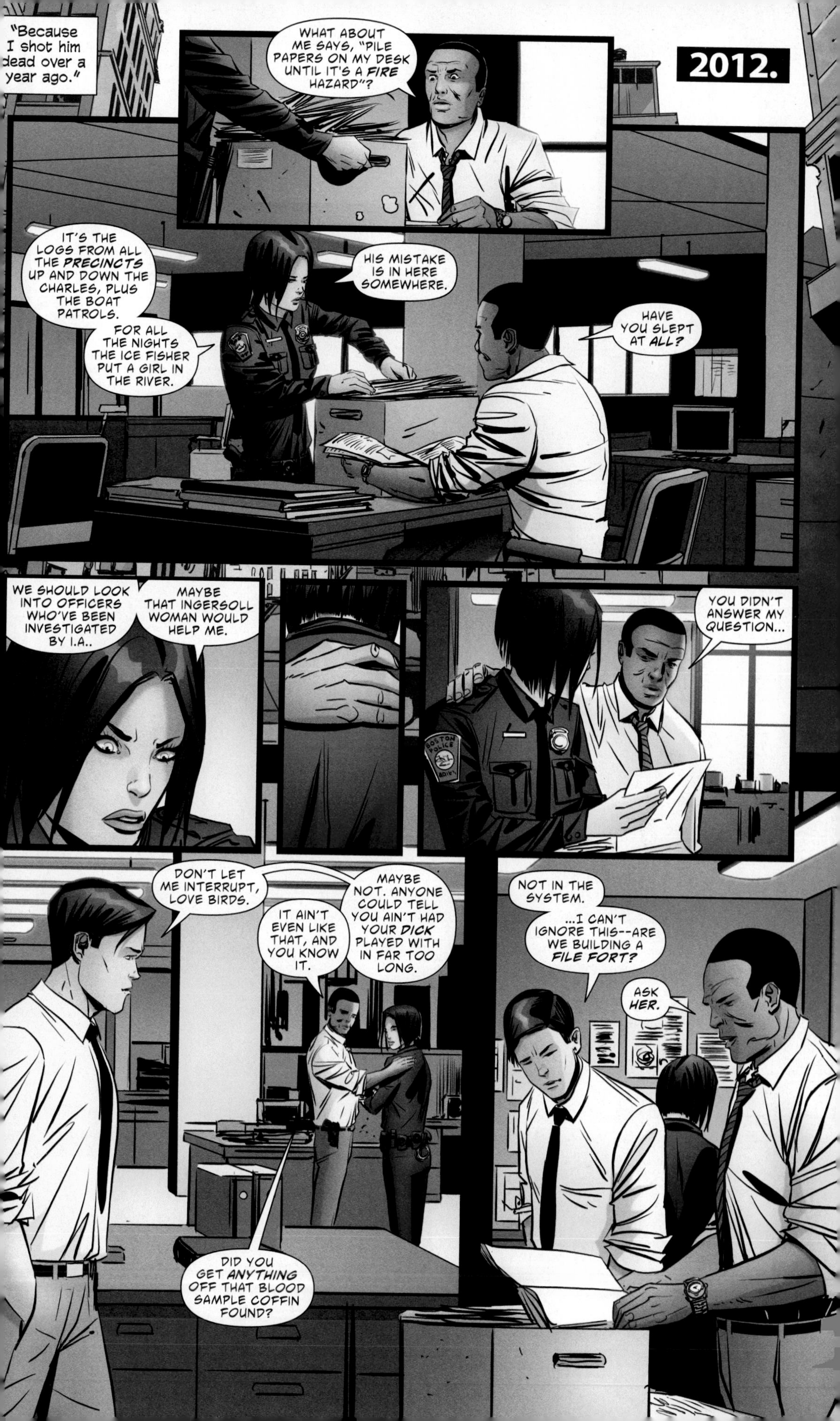
"Because I shot him dead over a year ago."
2012.
WHAT ABOUT ME SAYS, "PILE PAPERS ON MY DESK UNTIL IT'S A FIRE HAZARD"?
IT'S THE LOGS FROM ALL THE PRECINCTS UP AND DOWN THE CHARLES, PLUS THE BOAT PATROLS.
FOR ALL THE NIGHTS THE ICE FISHER PUT A GIRL IN THE RIVER.
HIS MISTAKE IS IN HERE SOMEWHERE.
HAVE YOU SLEPT AT ALL?
WE SHOULD LOOK INTO OFFICERS WHO'VE BEEN INVESTIGATED BY I.A..
MAYBE THAT INGERSOLL WOMAN WOULD HELP ME.
YOU DIDN'T ANSWER MY QUESTION...
DON'T LET ME INTERRUPT, LOVE BIRDS.
IT AIN'T EVEN LIKE THAT, AND YOU KNOW IT.
MAYBE NOT. ANYONE COULD TELL YOU AIN'T HAD YOUR DICK PLAYED WITH IN FAR TOO LONG.
DID YOU GET ANYTHING OFF THAT BLOOD SAMPLE COFFIN FOUND?
NOT IN THE SYSTEM.
...I CAN'T IGNORE THIS--ARE WE BUILDING A FILE FORT?
ASK HER.

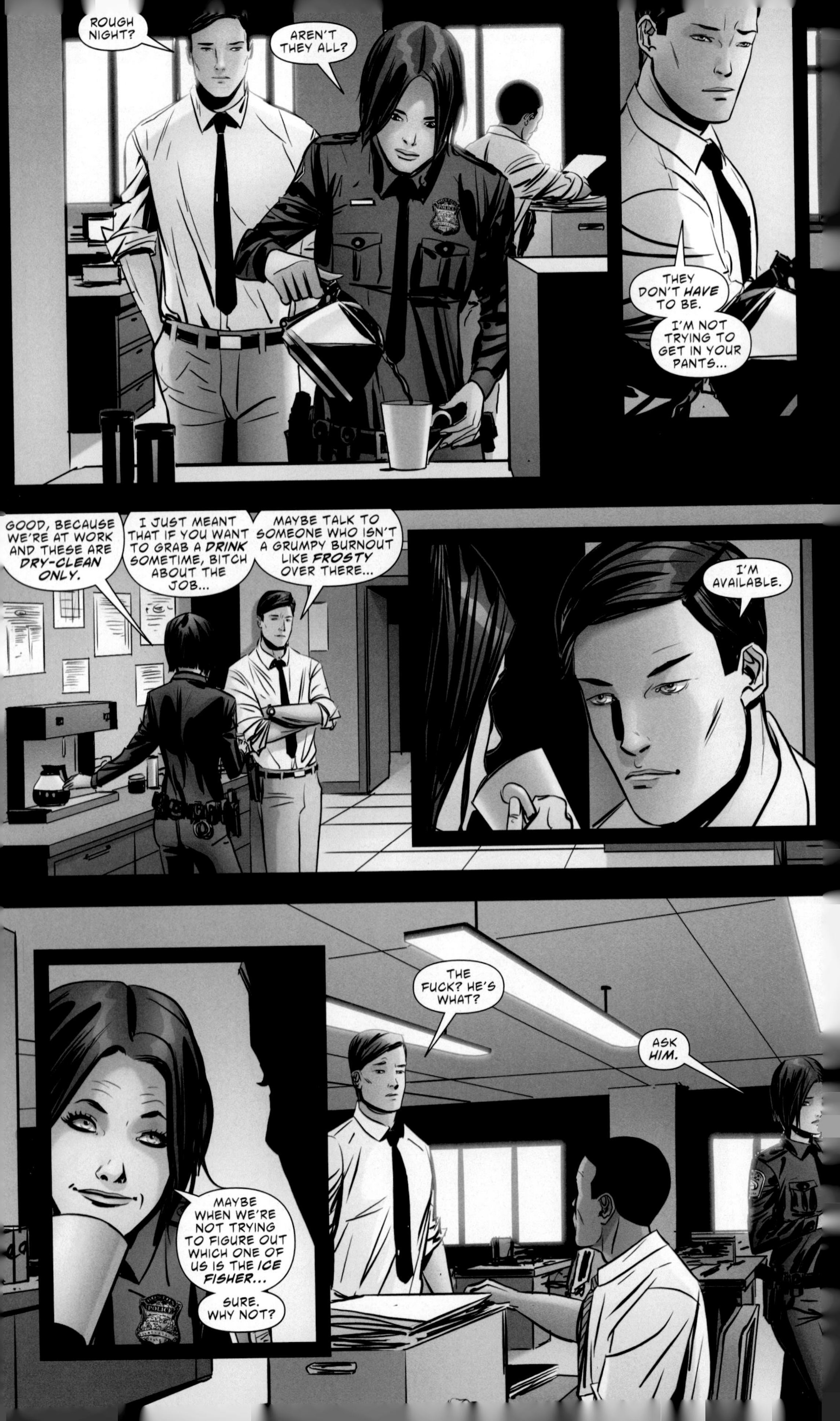
ROUGH NIGHT?
AREN'T THEY ALL?
THEY DON'T HAVE TO BE.
I'M NOT TRYING TO GET IN YOUR PANTS...
GOOD, BECAUSE WE'RE AT WORK AND THESE ARE DRY-CLEAN ONLY.
I JUST MEANT THAT IF YOU WANT TO GRAB A DRINK SOMETIME, BITCH ABOUT THE JOB...
MAYBE TALK TO SOMEONE WHO ISN'T A GRUMPY BURNOUT LIKE FROSTY OVER THERE...
I'M AVAILABLE.
MAYBE WHEN WE'RE NOT TRYING TO FIGURE OUT WHICH ONE OF US IS THE ICE FISHER...
SURE. WHY NOT?
THE FUCK? HE'S WHAT?
ASK HIM.

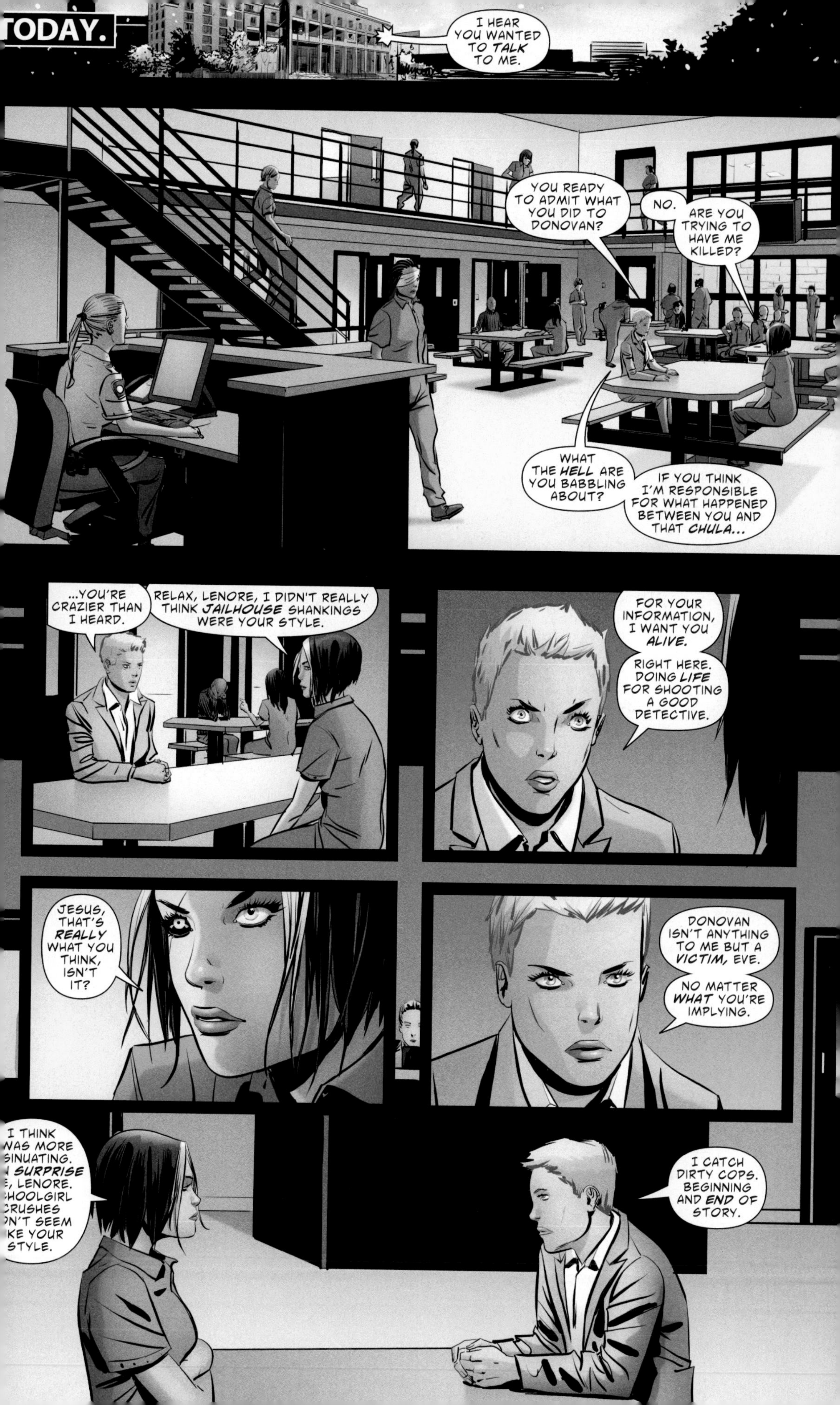
TODAY.
I HEAR YOU WANTED TO TALK TO ME.
YOU READY TO ADMIT WHAT YOU DID TO DONOVAN?
NO.
ARE YOU TRYING TO HAVE ME KILLED?
WHAT THE HELL ARE YOU BABBLING ABOUT?
IF YOU THINK I'M RESPONSIBLE FOR WHAT HAPPENED BETWEEN YOU AND THAT CHULA...
...YOU'RE CRAZIER THAN I HEARD.
RELAX, LENORE, I DIDN'T REALLY THINK JAILHOUSE SHANKINGS WERE YOUR STYLE.
FOR YOUR INFORMATION, I WANT YOU ALIVE.
RIGHT HERE. DOING LIFE FOR SHOOTING A GOOD DETECTIVE.
JESUS, THAT'S REALLY WHAT YOU THINK, ISN'T IT?
DONOVAN ISN'T ANYTHING TO ME BUT A VICTIM, EVE.
NO MATTER WHAT YOU'RE IMPLYING.
I CATCH DIRTY COPS. BEGINNING AND END OF STORY.

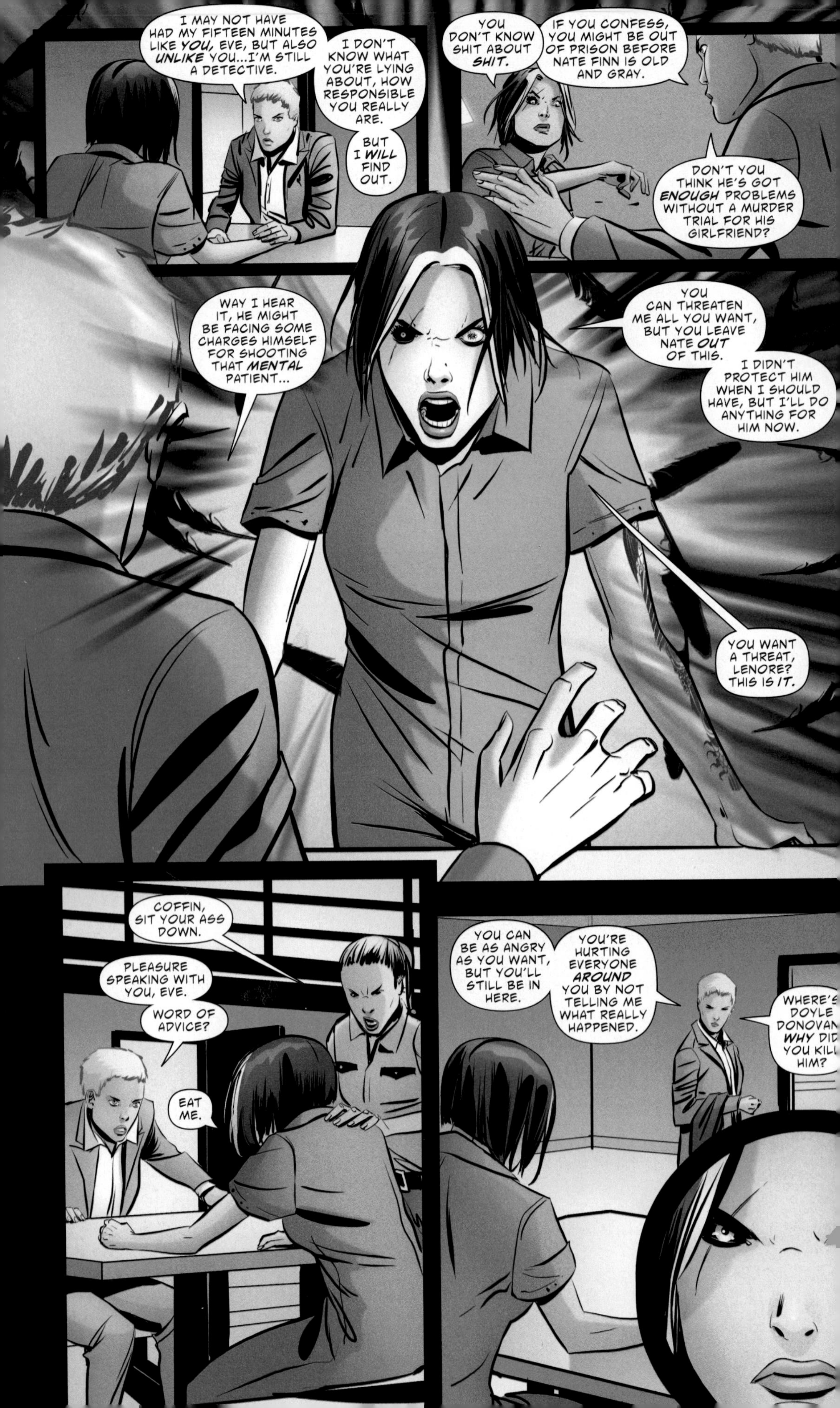
I MAY NOT HAVE HAD MY FIFTEEN MINUTES LIKE YOU, EVE, BUT ALSO UNLIKE YOU...I'M STILL A DETECTIVE.
I DON'T KNOW WHAT YOU'RE LYING ABOUT, HOW RESPONSIBLE YOU REALLY ARE.
BUT I WILL FIND OUT.
YOU DON'T KNOW SHIT ABOUT SHIT.
IF YOU CONFESS, YOU MIGHT BE OUT OF PRISON BEFORE NATE FINN IS OLD AND GRAY.
DON'T YOU THINK HE'S GOT ENOUGH PROBLEMS WITHOUT A MURDER TRIAL FOR HIS GIRLFRIEND?
WAY I HEAR IT, HE MIGHT BE FACING SOME CHARGES HIMSELF FOR SHOOTING THAT MENTAL PATIENT...
YOU CAN THREATEN ME ALL YOU WANT, BUT YOU LEAVE NATE OUT OF THIS.
I DIDN'T PROTECT HIM WHEN I SHOULD HAVE, BUT I'LL DO ANYTHING FOR HIM NOW.
YOU WANT A THREAT, LENORE? THIS IS IT.
COFFIN, SIT YOUR ASS DOWN.
PLEASURE SPEAKING WITH YOU, EVE.
WORD OF ADVICE?
EAT ME.
YOU CAN BE AS ANGRY AS YOU WANT, BUT YOU'LL STILL BE IN HERE.
YOU'RE HURTING EVERYONE AROUND YOU BY NOT TELLING ME WHAT REALLY HAPPENED.
WHERE'S DOYLE DONOVAN WHY DID YOU KILL HIM?

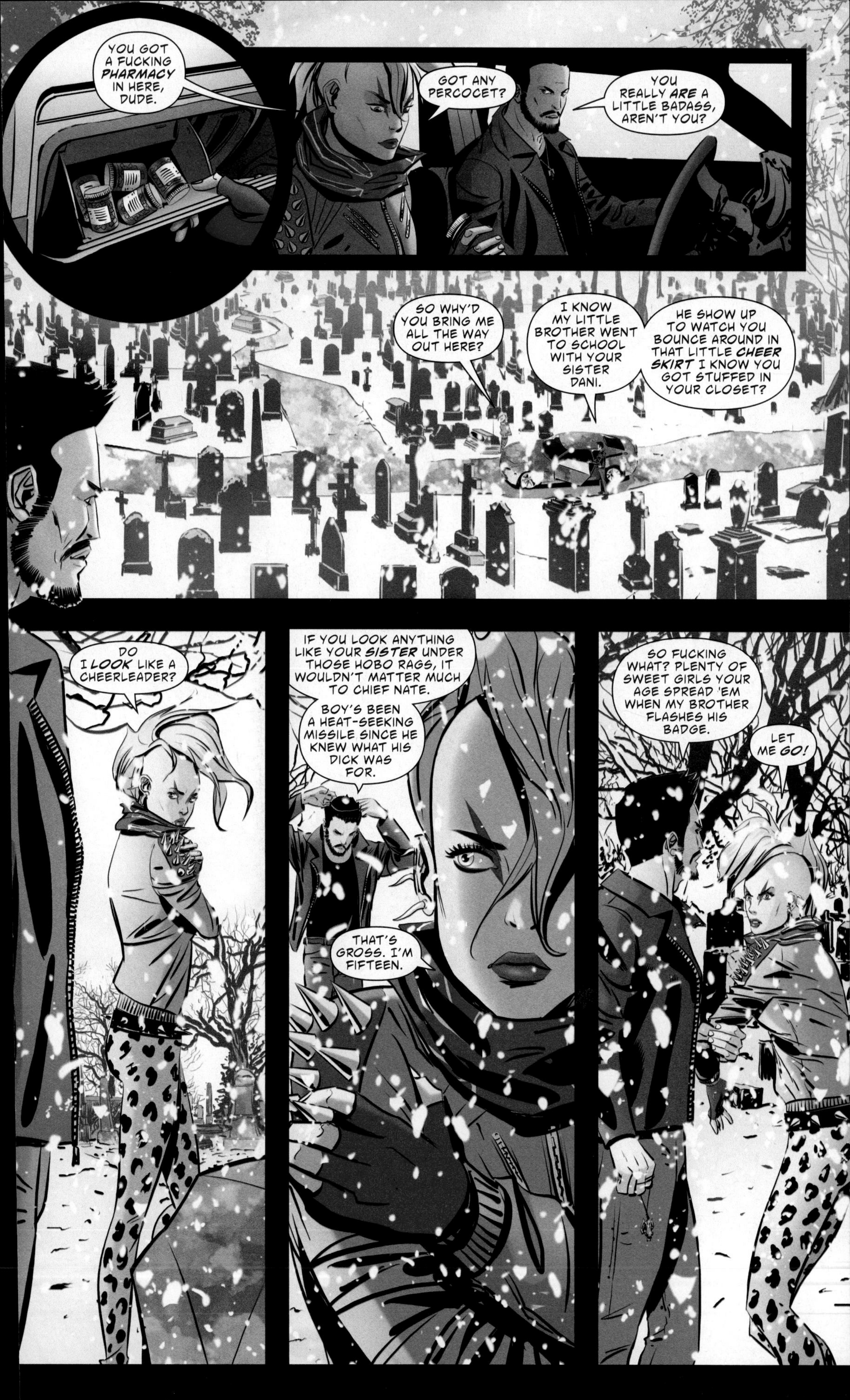
YOU GOT A FUCKING PHARMACY IN HERE, DUDE.
GOT ANY PERCOCET?
YOU REALLY ARE A LITTLE BADASS, AREN'T YOU?
SO WHY'D YOU BRING ME ALL THE WAY OUT HERE?
I KNOW MY LITTLE BROTHER WENT TO SCHOOL WITH YOUR SISTER DANI.
HE SHOW UP TO WATCH YOU BOUNCE AROUND IN THAT LITTLE CHEER SKIRT I KNOW YOU GOT STUFFED IN YOUR CLOSET?
DO I LOOK LIKE A CHEERLEADER?
IF YOU LOOK ANYTHING LIKE YOUR SISTER UNDER THOSE HOBO RAGS, IT WOULDN'T MATTER MUCH TO CHIEF NATE.
BOY'S BEEN A HEAT-SEEKING MISSILE SINCE HE KNEW WHAT HIS DICK WAS FOR.
THAT'S GROSS. I'M FIFTEEN.
SO FUCKING WHAT? PLENTY OF SWEET GIRLS YOUR AGE SPREAD 'EM WHEN MY BROTHER FLASHES HIS BADGE.
LET ME GO!

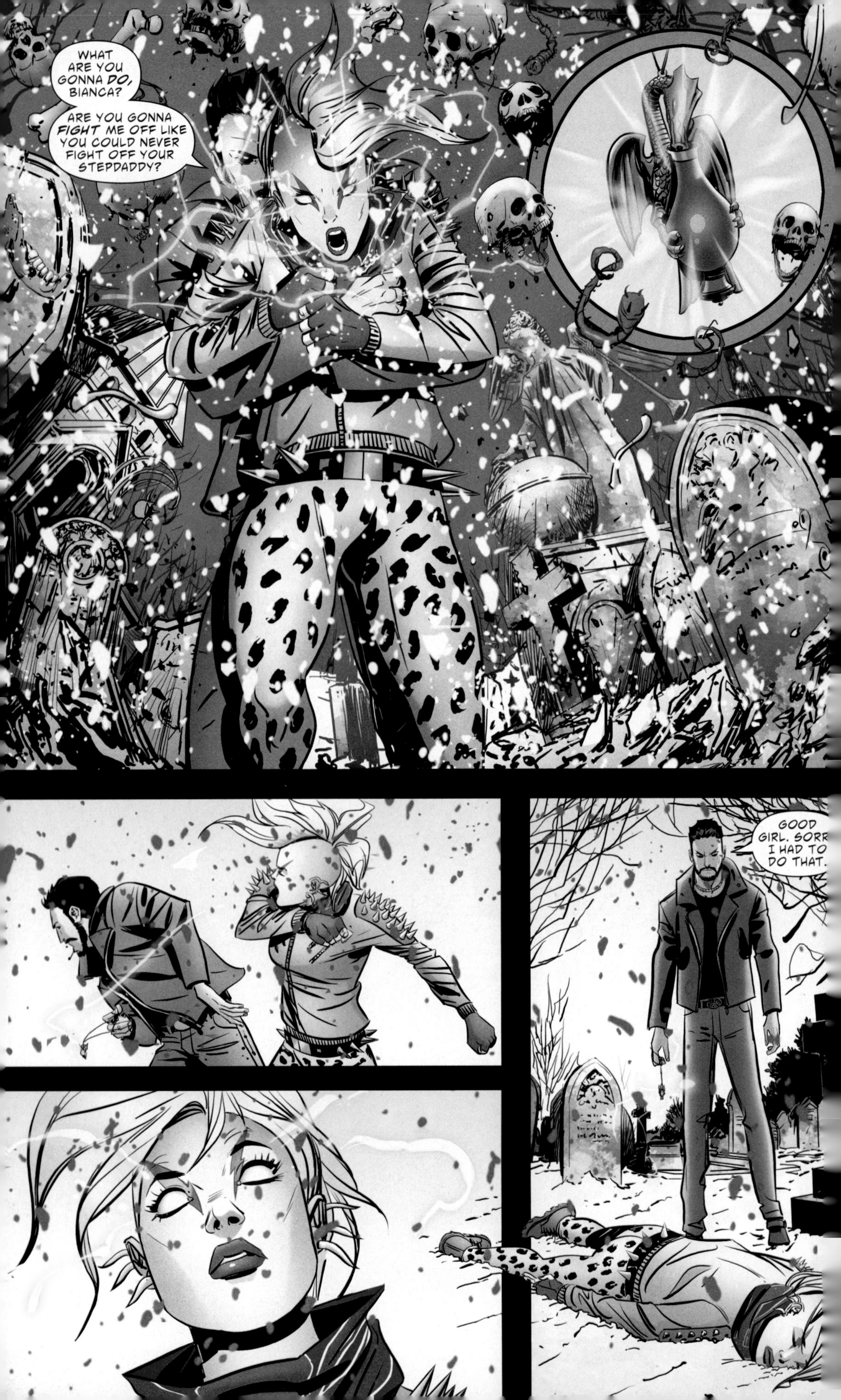
WHAT ARE YOU GONNA *DO,* BIANCA?
ARE YOU GONNA *FIGHT* ME OFF LIKE YOU COULD NEVER FIGHT OFF YOUR STEPDADDY?
GOOD GIRL. SORR I HAD TO DO THAT.

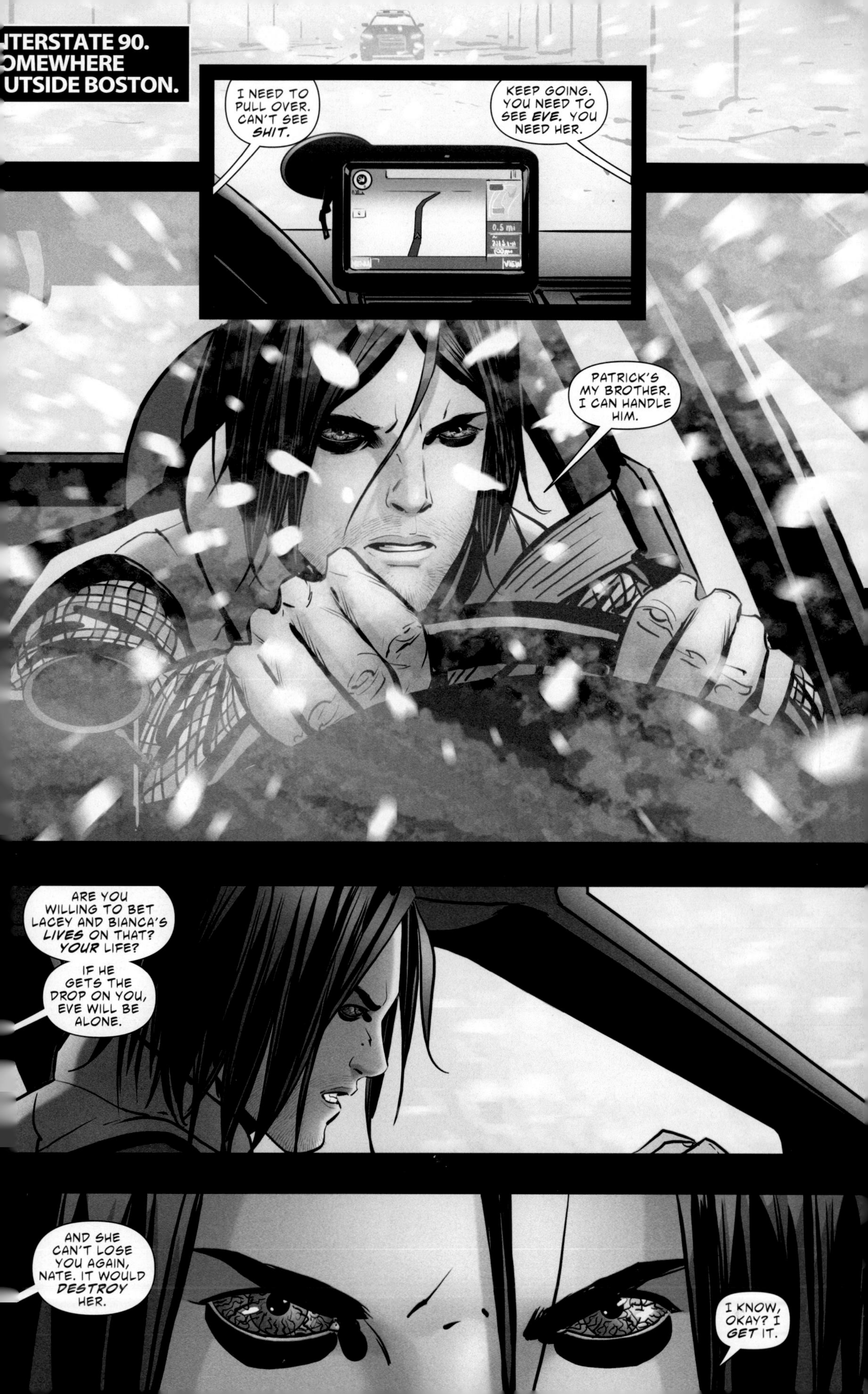
ITERSTATE 90. OMEWHERE UTSIDE BOSTON.
I NEED TO PULL OVER. CAN'T SEE SHIT.
KEEP GOING. YOU NEED TO SEE EVE. YOU NEED HER.
PATRICK'S MY BROTHER. I CAN HANDLE HIM.
ARE YOU WILLING TO BET LACEY AND BIANCA'S LIVES ON THAT? YOUR LIFE?
IF HE GETS THE DROP ON YOU, EVE WILL BE ALONE.
AND SHE CAN'T LOSE YOU AGAIN, NATE. IT WOULD DESTROY HER.
I KNOW, OKAY? I GET IT.

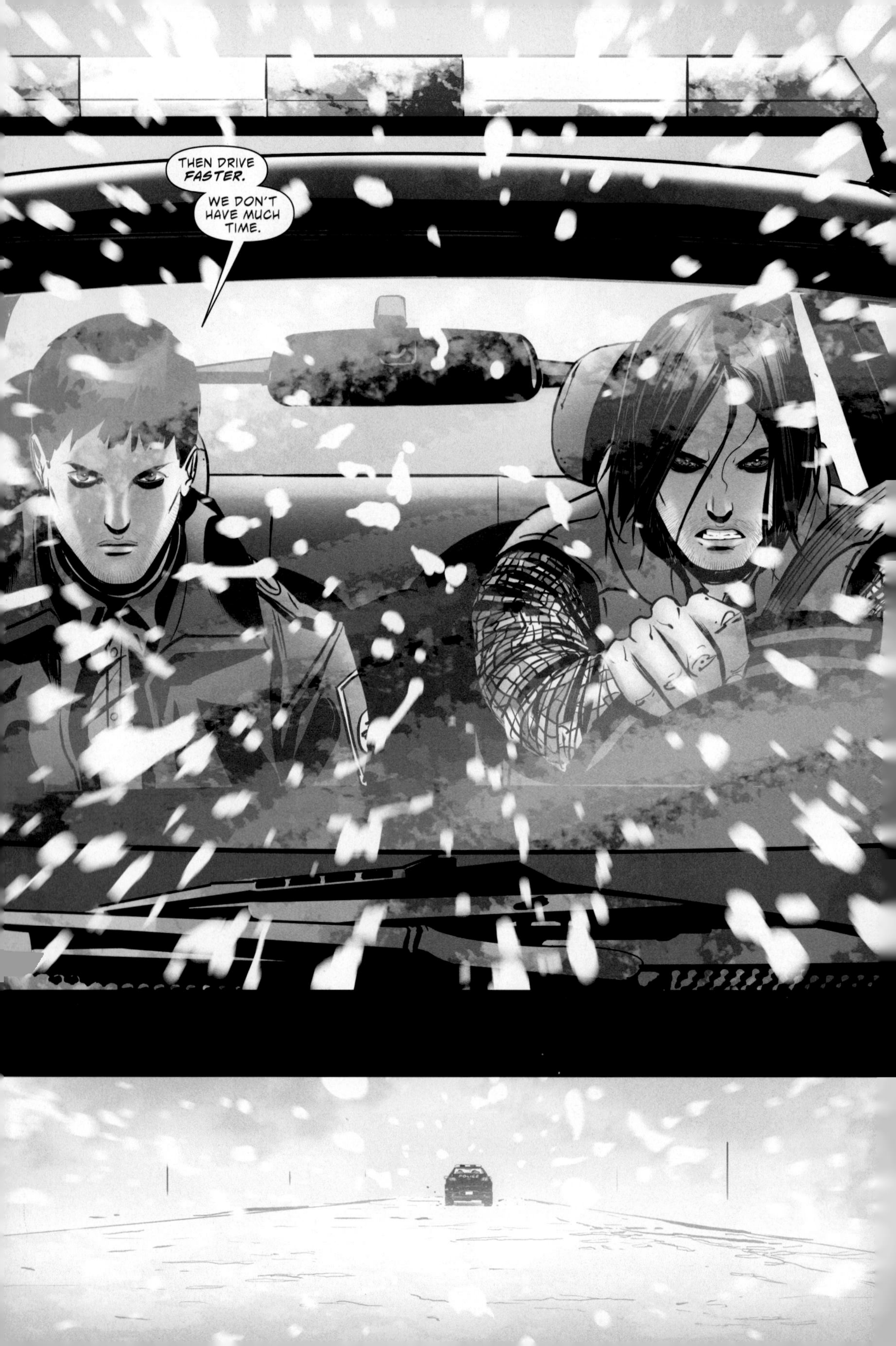
THEN DRIVE *FASTER.*
WE DON'T HAVE MUCH TIME.

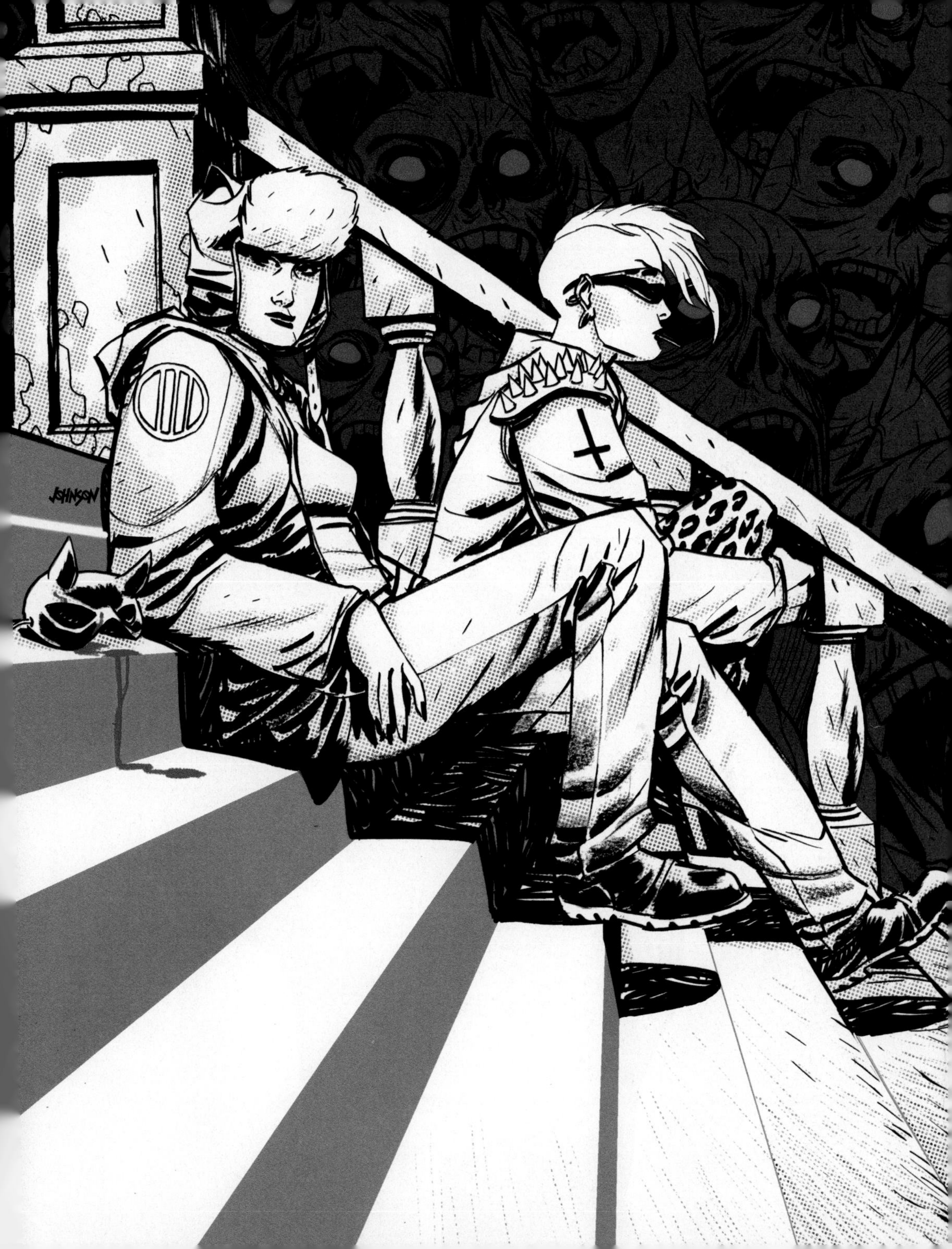

JOHNSON

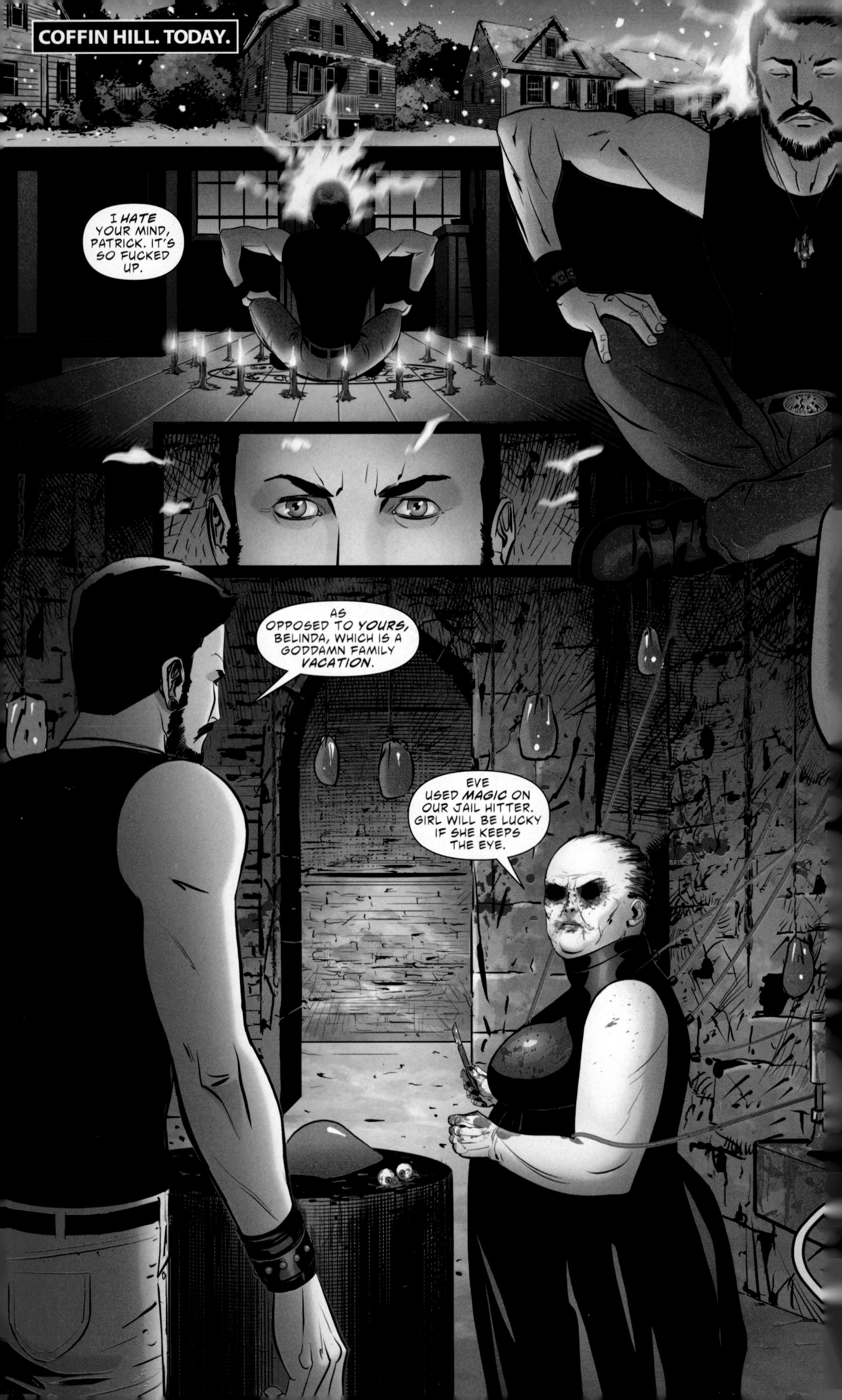

COFFIN HILL. TODAY.
I HATE YOUR MIND, PATRICK. IT'S SO FUCKED UP.
AS OPPOSED TO YOURS, BELINDA, WHICH IS A GODDAMN FAMILY VACATION.
EVE USED MAGIC ON OUR JAIL HITTER. GIRL WILL BE LUCKY IF SHE KEEPS THE EYE.

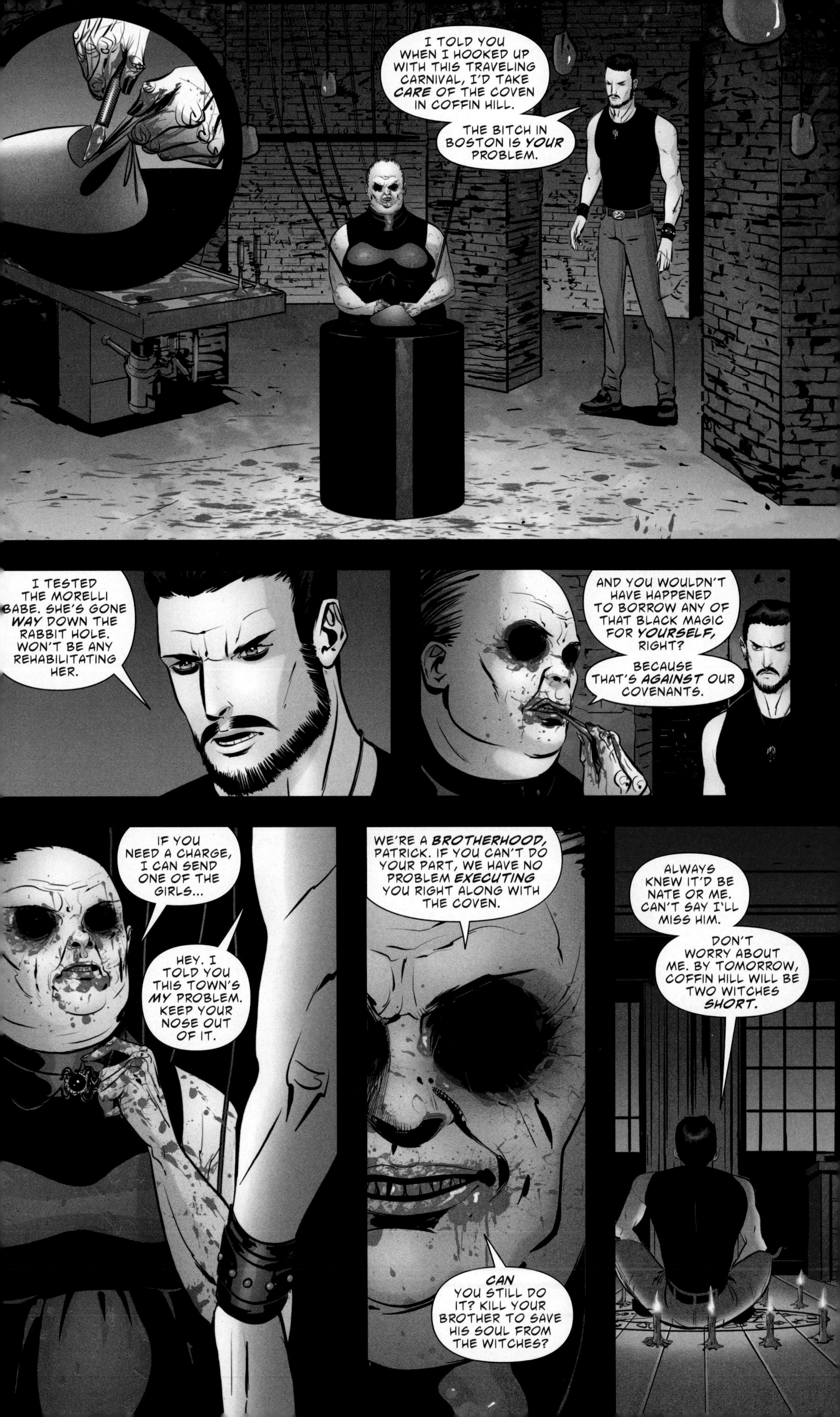
I TOLD YOU WHEN I HOOKED UP WITH THIS TRAVELING CARNIVAL, I'D TAKE *CARE* OF THE COVEN IN COFFIN HILL.
THE BITCH IN BOSTON IS *YOUR* PROBLEM.
I TESTED THE MORELLI BABE. SHE'S GONE *WAY* DOWN THE RABBIT HOLE. WON'T BE ANY REHABILITATING HER.
AND YOU WOULDN'T HAVE HAPPENED TO BORROW ANY OF THAT BLACK MAGIC FOR *YOURSELF,* RIGHT?
BECAUSE THAT'S *AGAINST* OUR COVENANTS.
IF YOU NEED A CHARGE, I CAN SEND ONE OF THE GIRLS...
HEY. I TOLD YOU THIS TOWN'S *MY* PROBLEM. KEEP YOUR NOSE OUT OF IT.
WE'RE A *BROTHERHOOD,* PATRICK. IF YOU CAN'T DO YOUR PART, WE HAVE NO PROBLEM *EXECUTING* YOU RIGHT ALONG WITH THE COVEN.
CAN YOU STILL DO IT? KILL YOUR BROTHER TO SAVE HIS SOUL FROM THE WITCHES?
ALWAYS KNEW IT'D BE NATE OR ME. CAN'T SAY I'LL MISS HIM.
DON'T WORRY ABOUT ME. BY TOMORROW, COFFIN HILL WILL BE TWO WITCHES *SHORT.*

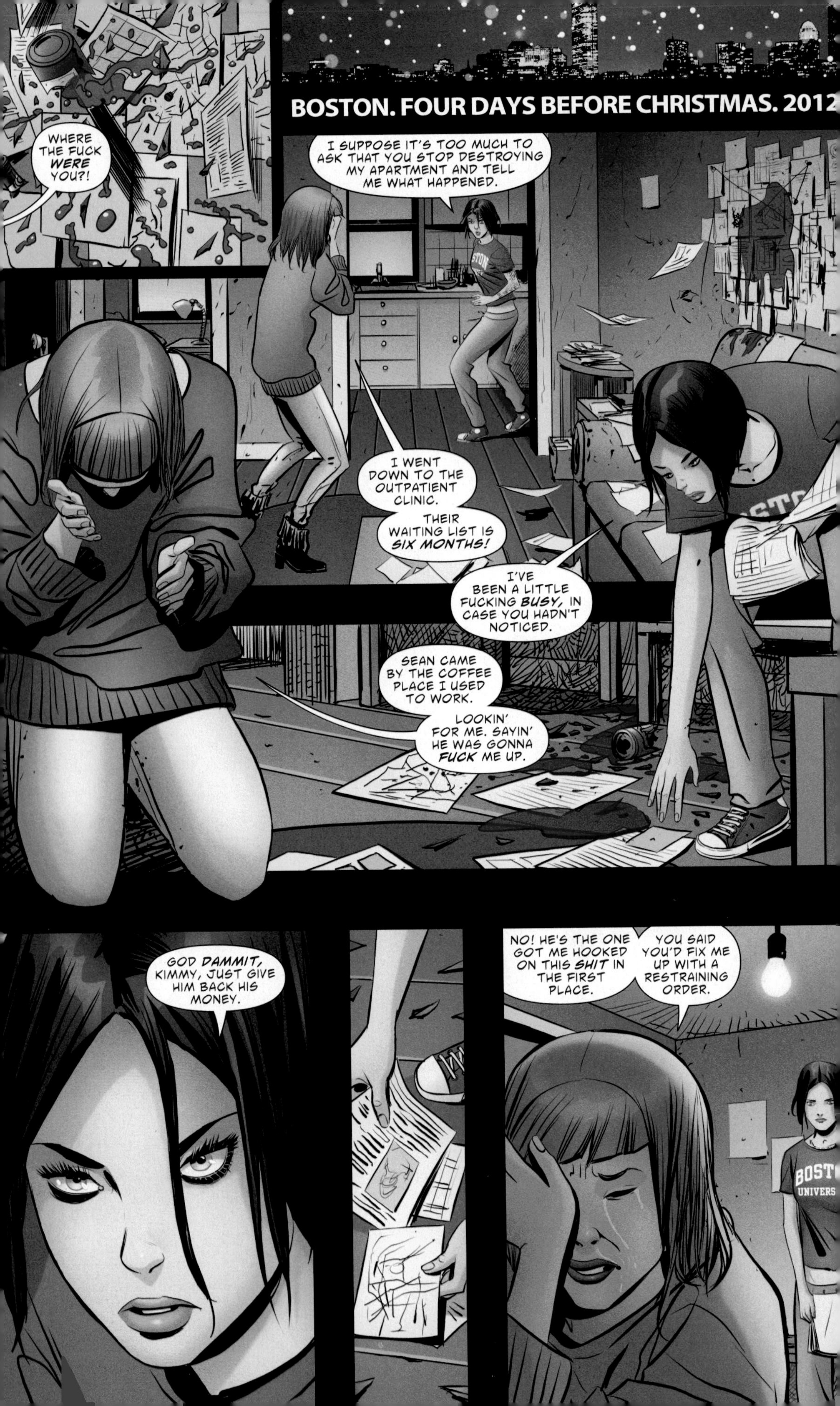
BOSTON. FOUR DAYS BEFORE CHRISTMAS. 2012
WHERE THE FUCK WERE YOU?!
I SUPPOSE IT'S TOO MUCH TO ASK THAT YOU STOP DESTROYING MY APARTMENT AND TELL ME WHAT HAPPENED.
I WENT DOWN TO THE OUTPATIENT CLINIC.
THEIR WAITING LIST IS SIX MONTHS!
I'VE BEEN A LITTLE FUCKING BUSY, IN CASE YOU HADN'T NOTICED.
SEAN CAME BY THE COFFEE PLACE I USED TO WORK.
LOOKIN' FOR ME. SAYIN' HE WAS GONNA FUCK ME UP.
GOD DAMMIT, KIMMY, JUST GIVE HIM BACK HIS MONEY.
NO! HE'S THE ONE GOT ME HOOKED ON THIS SHIT IN THE FIRST PLACE.
YOU SAID YOU'D FIX ME UP WITH A RESTRAINING ORDER.

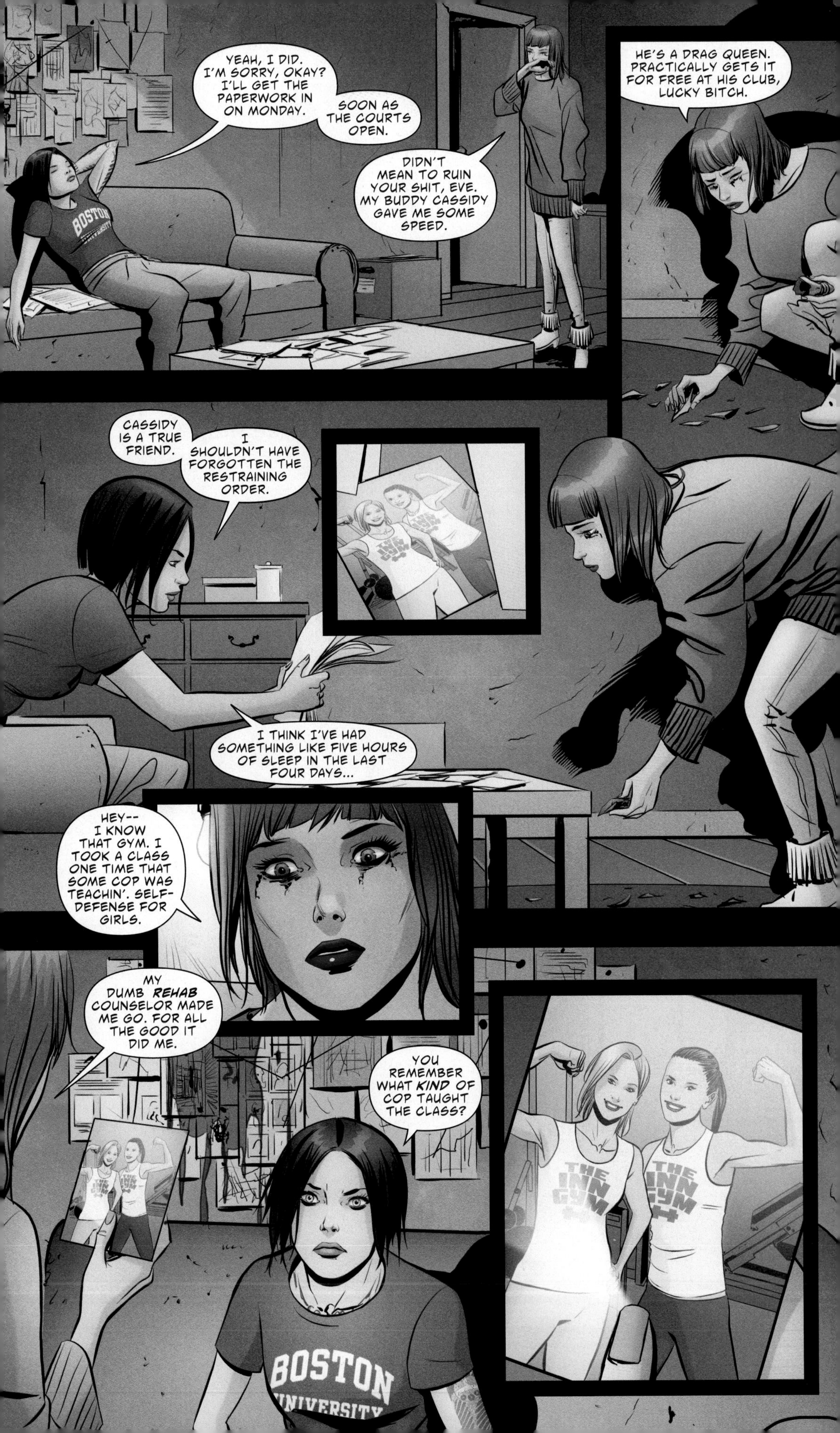
YEAH, I DID. I'M SORRY, OKAY? I'LL GET THE PAPERWORK IN ON MONDAY.
SOON AS THE COURTS OPEN.
DIDN'T MEAN TO RUIN YOUR SHIT, EVE. MY BUDDY CASSIDY GAVE ME SOME SPEED.
HE'S A DRAG QUEEN. PRACTICALLY GETS IT FOR FREE AT HIS CLUB, LUCKY BITCH.
CASSIDY IS A TRUE FRIEND.
I SHOULDN'T HAVE FORGOTTEN THE RESTRAINING ORDER.
I THINK I'VE HAD SOMETHING LIKE FIVE HOURS OF SLEEP IN THE LAST FOUR DAYS...
HEY-- I KNOW THAT GYM. I TOOK A CLASS ONE TIME THAT SOME COP WAS TEACHIN'. SELF-DEFENSE FOR GIRLS.
MY DUMB *REHAB* COUNSELOR MADE ME GO. FOR ALL THE GOOD IT DID ME.
YOU REMEMBER WHAT *KIND* OF COP TAUGHT THE CLASS?
THE INN GYM
BOSTON UNIVERSITY

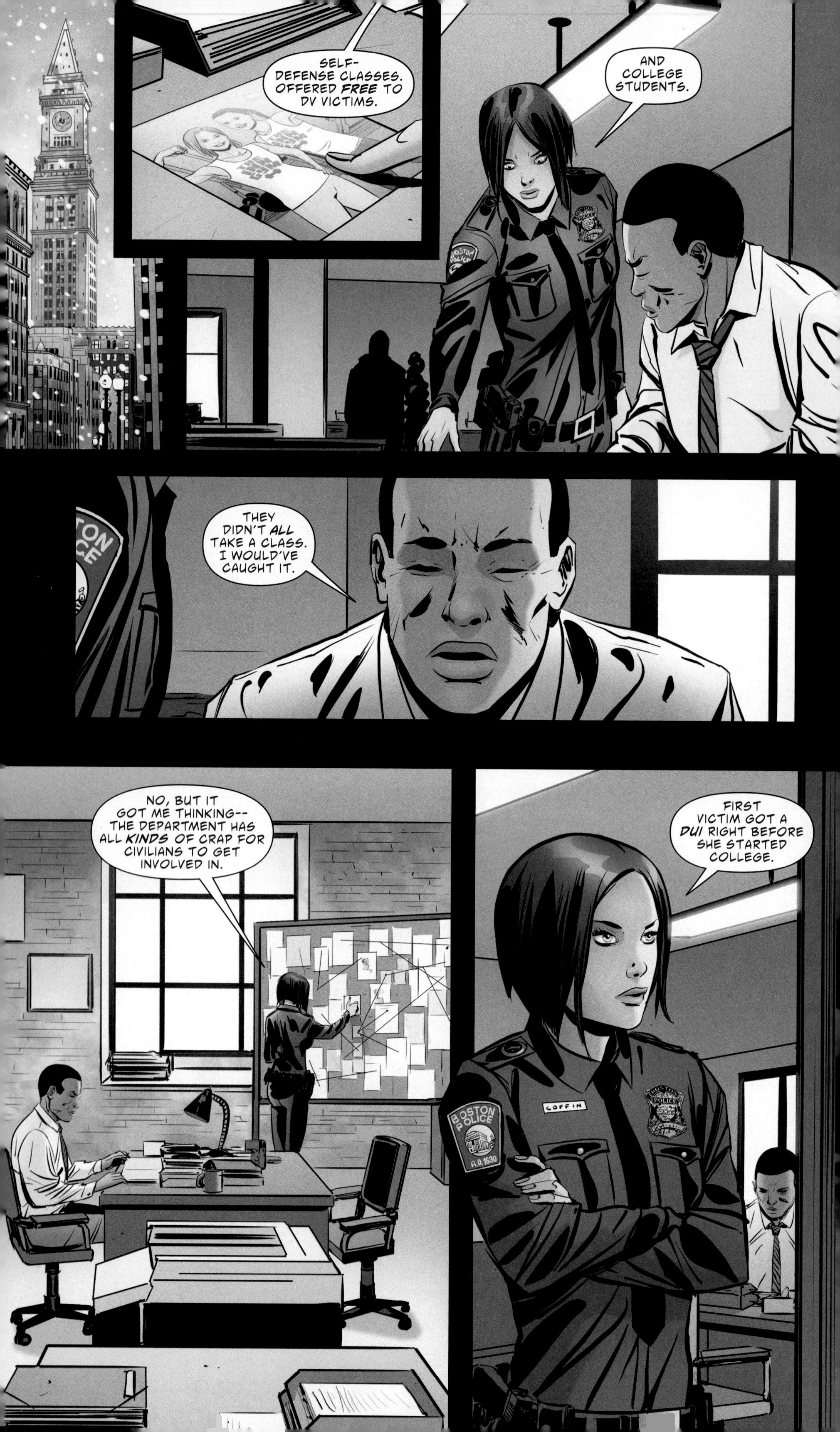
SELF-DEFENSE CLASSES. OFFERED FREE TO DV VICTIMS.
AND COLLEGE STUDENTS.
THEY DIDN'T ALL TAKE A CLASS. I WOULD'VE CAUGHT IT.
NO, BUT IT GOT ME THINKING-- THE DEPARTMENT HAS ALL KINDS OF CRAP FOR CIVILIANS TO GET INVOLVED IN.
FIRST VICTIM GOT A DUI RIGHT BEFORE SHE STARTED COLLEGE.

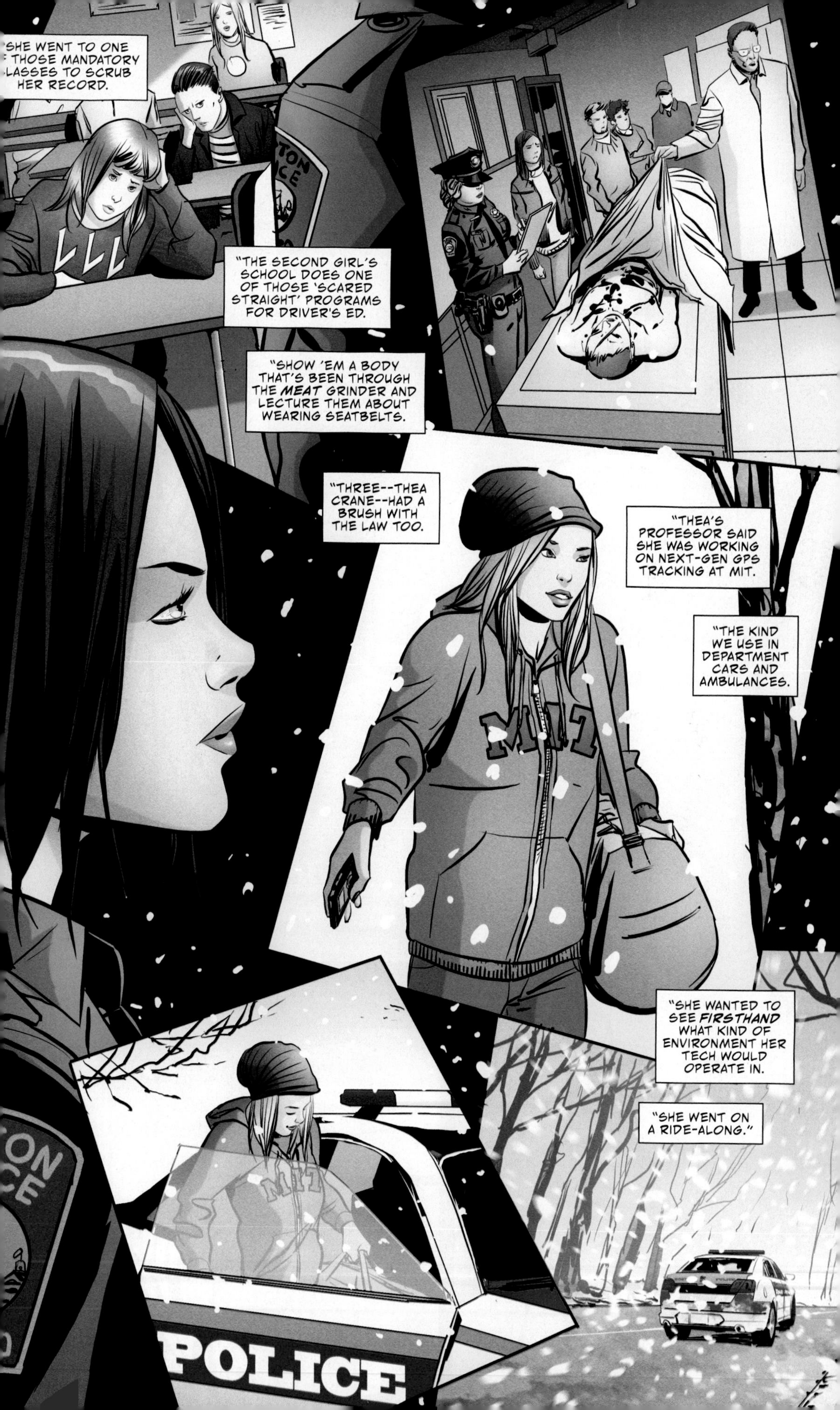

SHE WENT TO ONE
F THOSE MANDATORY
LASSES TO SCRUB
HER RECORD.
"THE SECOND GIRL'S SCHOOL DOES ONE OF THOSE 'SCARED STRAIGHT' PROGRAMS FOR DRIVER'S ED.
"SHOW 'EM A BODY THAT'S BEEN THROUGH THE *MEAT* GRINDER AND LECTURE THEM ABOUT WEARING SEATBELTS.
"THREE--THEA CRANE--HAD A BRUSH WITH THE LAW TOO.
"THEA'S PROFESSOR SAID SHE WAS WORKING ON NEXT-GEN GPS TRACKING AT MIT.
"THE KIND WE USE IN DEPARTMENT CARS AND AMBULANCES.
"SHE WANTED TO SEE *FIRSTHAND* WHAT KIND OF ENVIRONMENT HER TECH WOULD OPERATE IN.
"SHE WENT ON A RIDE-ALONG."
MIT
POLICE

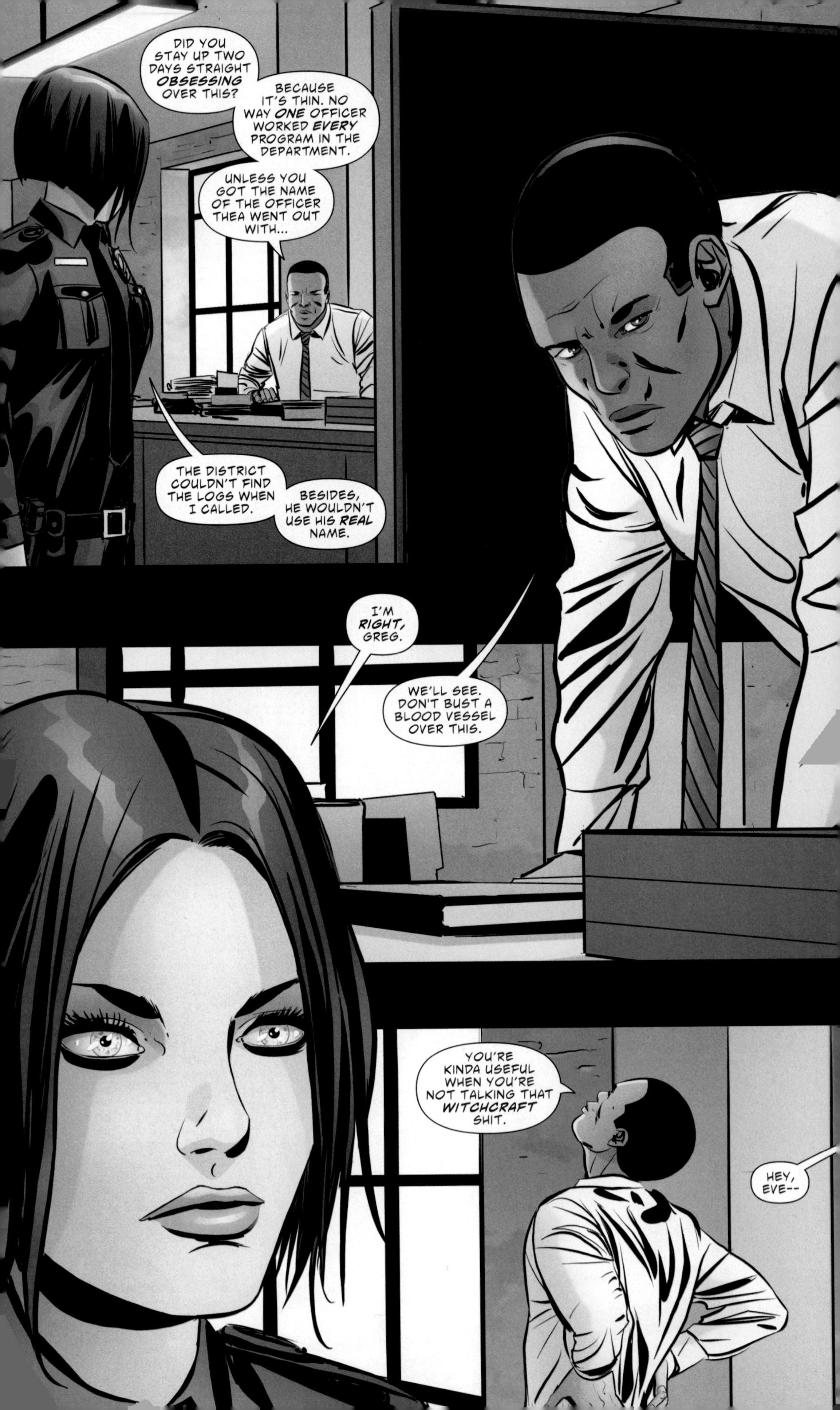

DID YOU STAY UP TWO DAYS STRAIGHT OBSESSING OVER THIS?
BECAUSE IT'S THIN. NO WAY ONE OFFICER WORKED EVERY PROGRAM IN THE DEPARTMENT.
UNLESS YOU GOT THE NAME OF THE OFFICER THEA WENT OUT WITH...
THE DISTRICT COULDN'T FIND THE LOGS WHEN I CALLED.
BESIDES, HE WOULDN'T USE HIS REAL NAME.
I'M RIGHT, GREG.
WE'LL SEE. DON'T BUST A BLOOD VESSEL OVER THIS.
YOU'RE KINDA USEFUL WHEN YOU'RE NOT TALKING THAT WITCHCRAFT SHIT.
HEY, EVE--

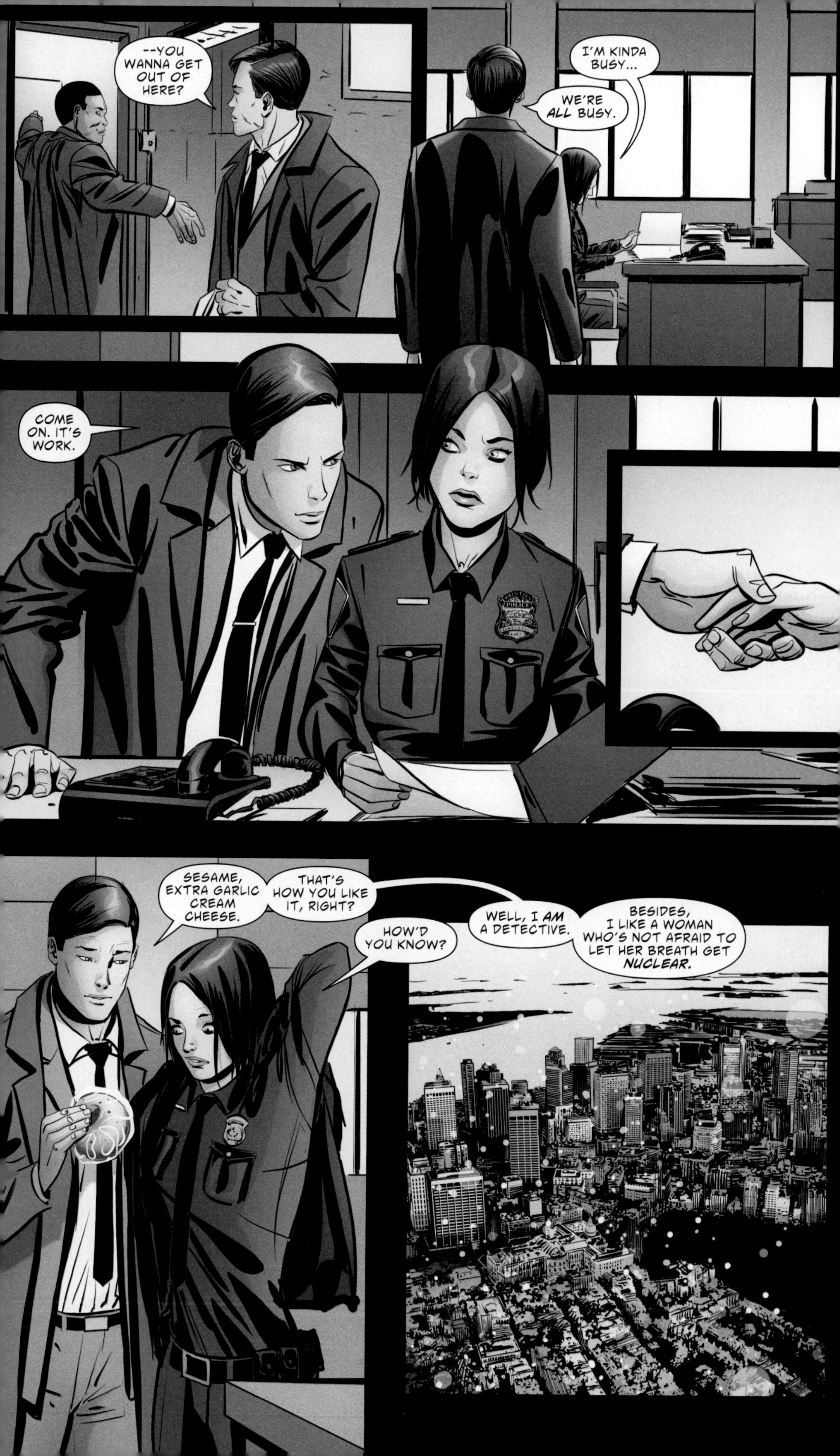

--YOU WANNA GET OUT OF HERE?
I'M KINDA BUSY...
WE'RE ALL BUSY.
COME ON. IT'S WORK.
SESAME, EXTRA GARLIC CREAM CHEESE.
THAT'S HOW YOU LIKE IT, RIGHT?
HOW'D YOU KNOW?
WELL, I AM A DETECTIVE.
BESIDES, I LIKE A WOMAN WHO'S NOT AFRAID TO LET HER BREATH GET NUCLEAR.

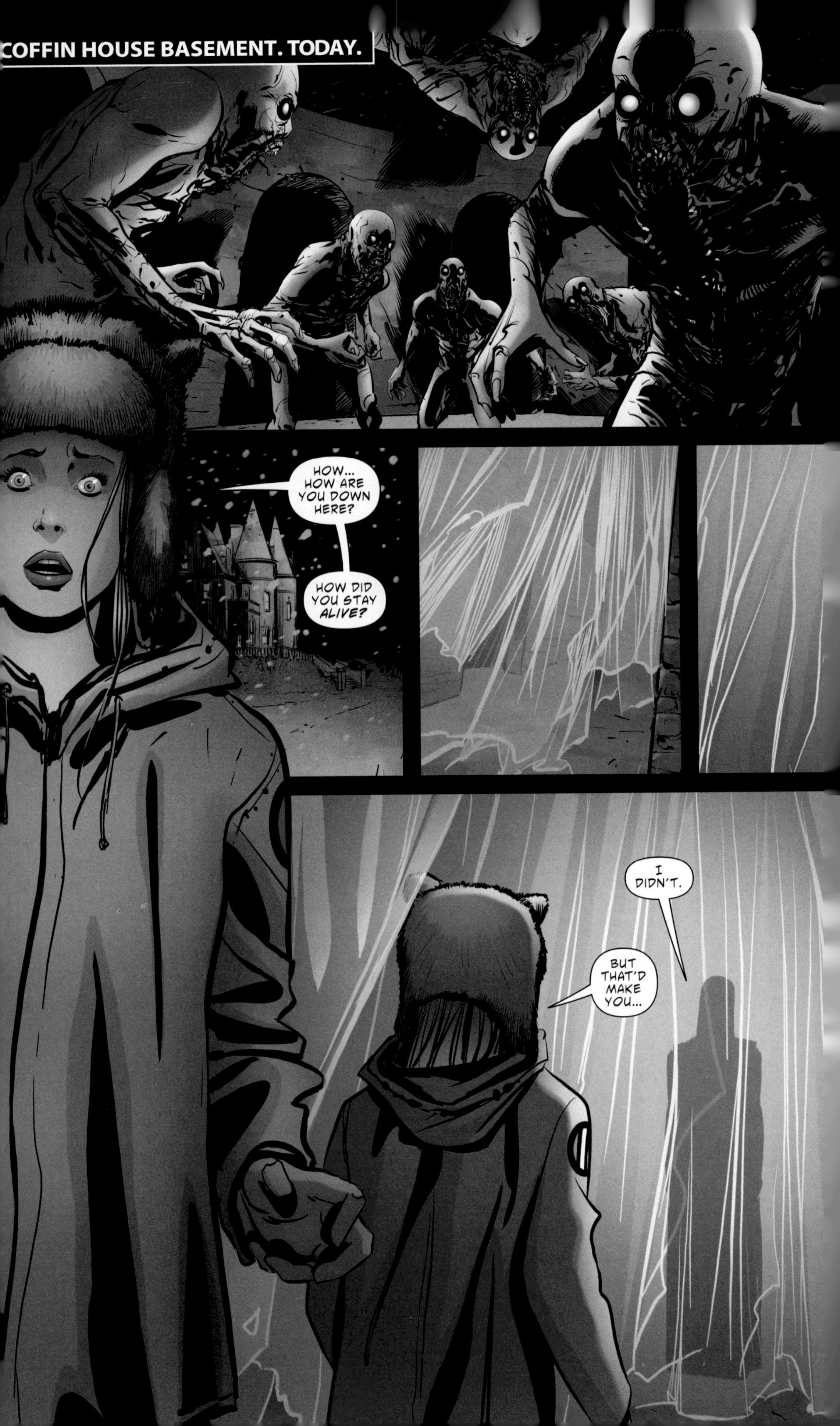
COFFIN HOUSE BASEMENT. TODAY.
HOW... HOW ARE YOU DOWN HERE?
HOW DID YOU STAY ALIVE?
I DIDN'T.
BUT THAT'D MAKE YOU...

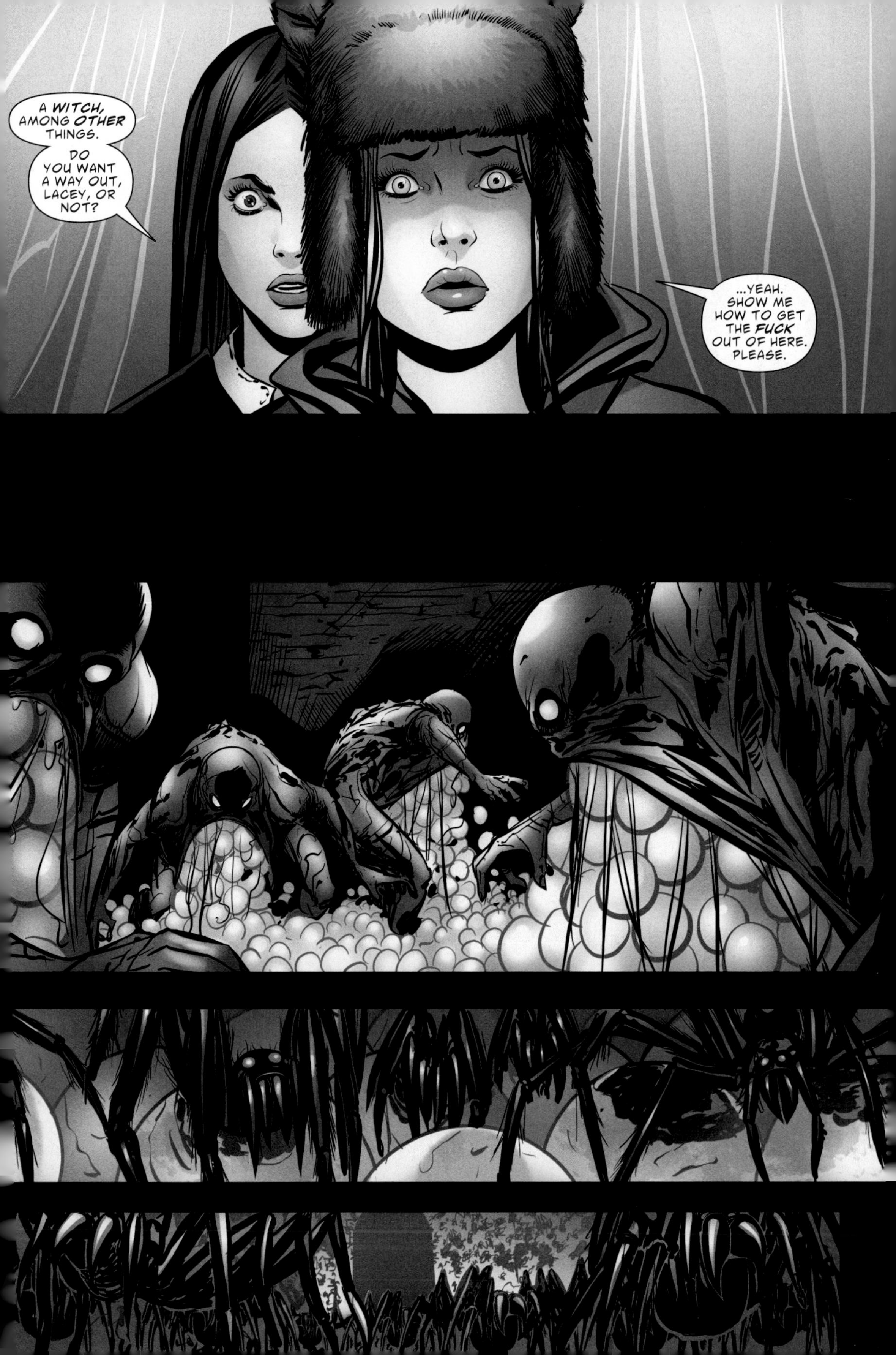
A WITCH, AMONG OTHER THINGS.
DO YOU WANT A WAY OUT, LACEY, OR NOT?
...YEAH. SHOW ME HOW TO GET THE FUCK OUT OF HERE. PLEASE.

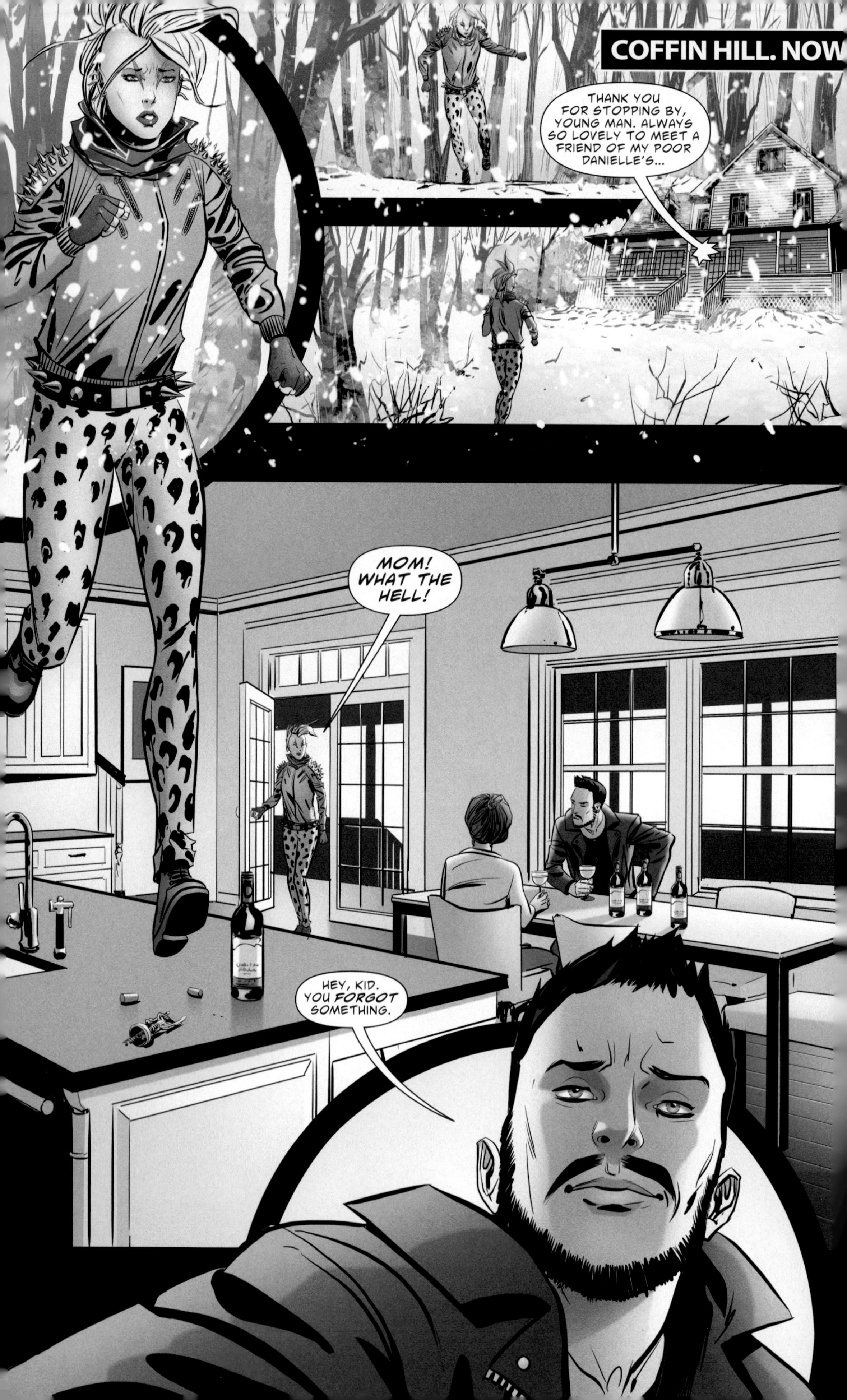
COFFIN HILL. NOW
THANK YOU FOR STOPPING BY, YOUNG MAN. ALWAYS SO LOVELY TO MEET A FRIEND OF MY POOR DANIELLE'S...
MOM! WHAT THE HELL!
HEY, KID. YOU FORGOT SOMETHING.

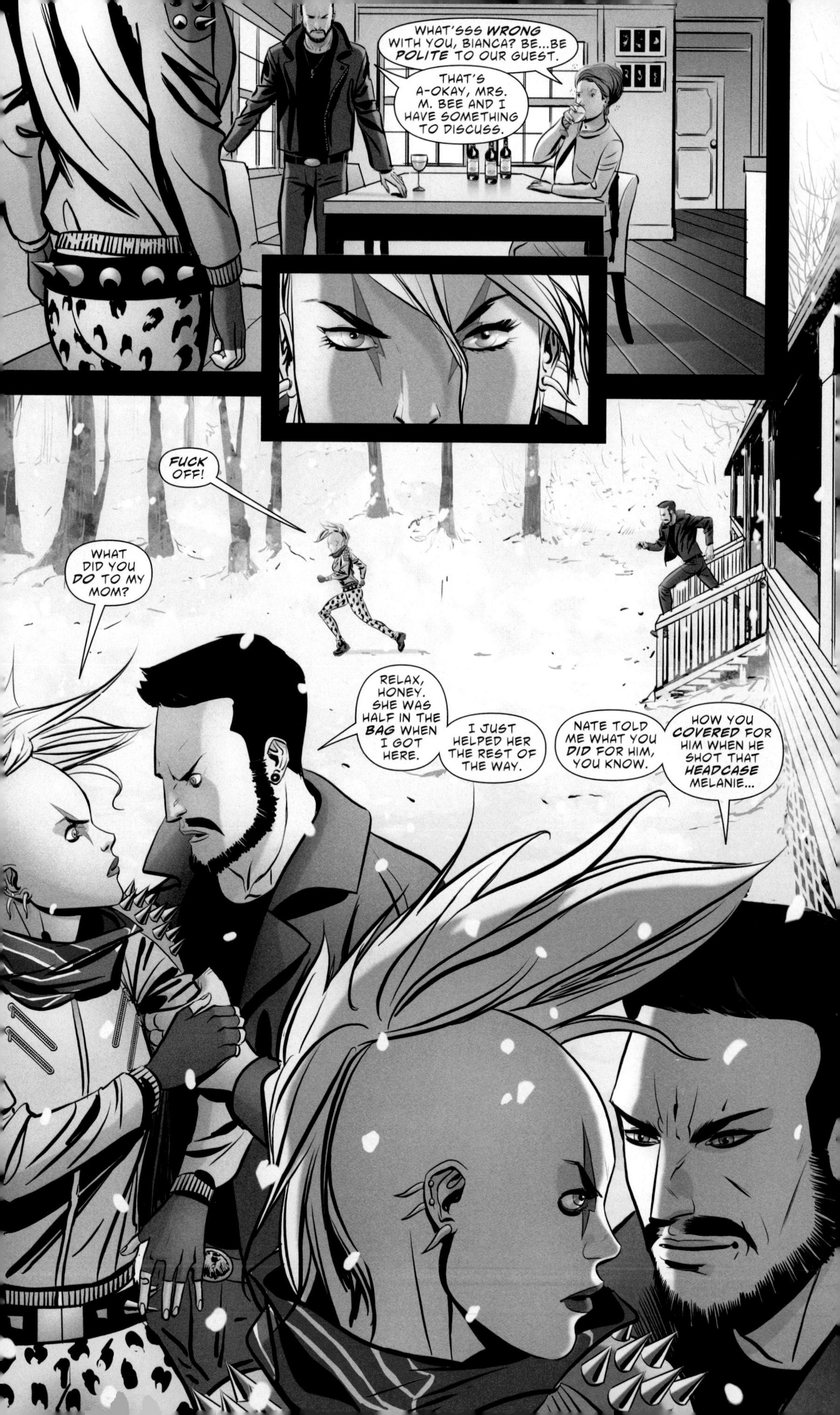
WHAT'SSS **WRONG** WITH YOU, BIANCA? BE...BE **POLITE** TO OUR GUEST.
THAT'S A-OKAY, MRS. M. BEE AND I HAVE SOMETHING TO DISCUSS.
FUCK OFF!
WHAT DID YOU ***DO*** TO MY MOM?
RELAX, HONEY. SHE WAS HALF IN THE ***BAG*** WHEN I GOT HERE.
I JUST HELPED HER THE REST OF THE WAY.
NATE TOLD ME WHAT YOU ***DID*** FOR HIM, YOU KNOW.
HOW YOU ***COVERED*** FOR HIM WHEN HE SHOT THAT ***HEADCASE*** MELANIE...

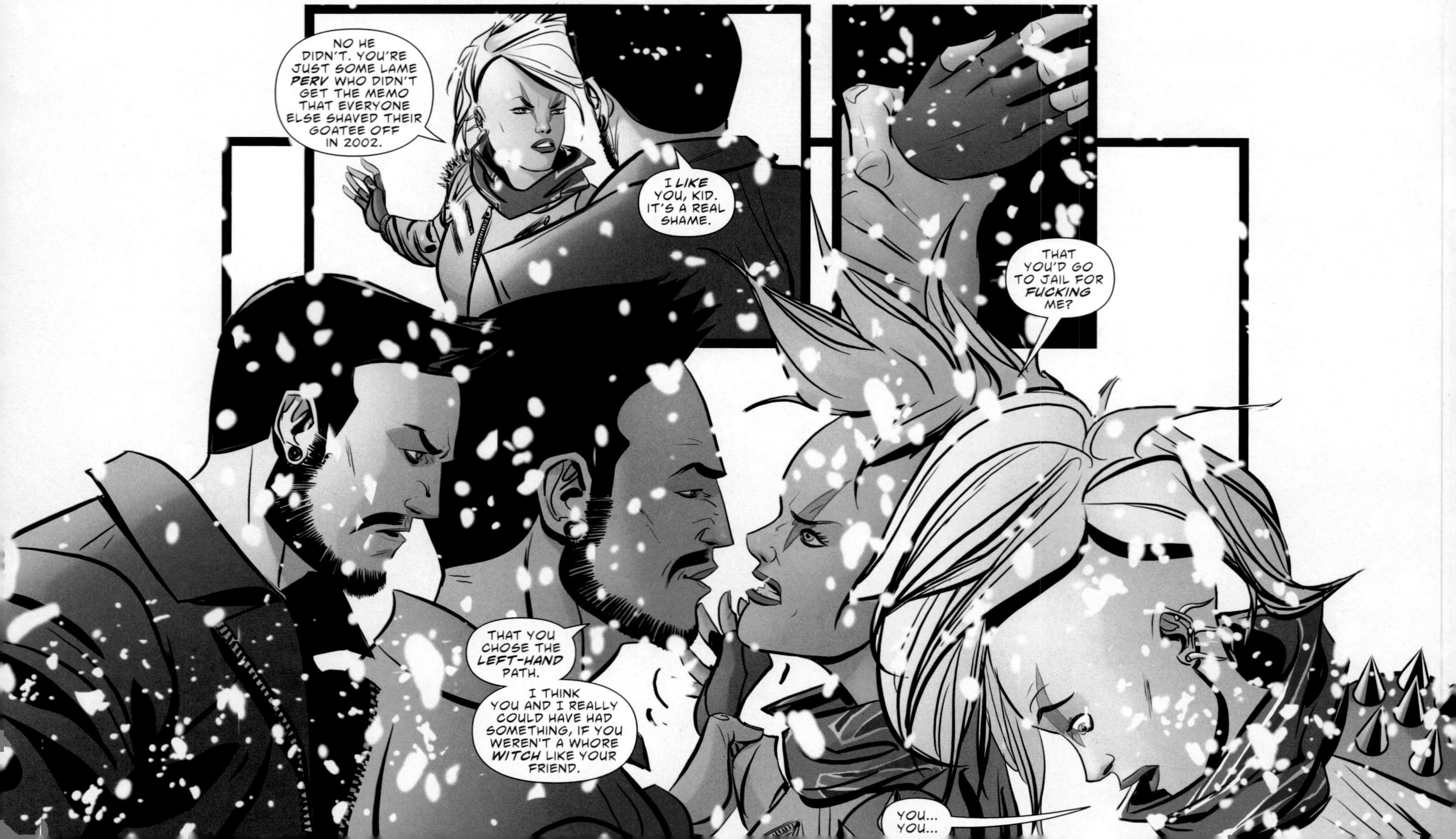
NO HE DIDN'T. YOU'RE JUST SOME LAME *PERV* WHO DIDN'T GET THE MEMO THAT EVERYONE ELSE SHAVED THEIR GOATEE OFF IN 2002.
I *LIKE* YOU, KID. IT'S A REAL SHAME.
THAT YOU'D GO TO JAIL FOR *FUCKING* ME?
YOU... YOU...
THAT YOU CHOSE THE *LEFT-HAND* PATH.
I THINK YOU AND I REALLY COULD HAVE HAD SOMETHING, IF YOU WEREN'T A WHORE *WITCH* LIKE YOUR FRIEND.

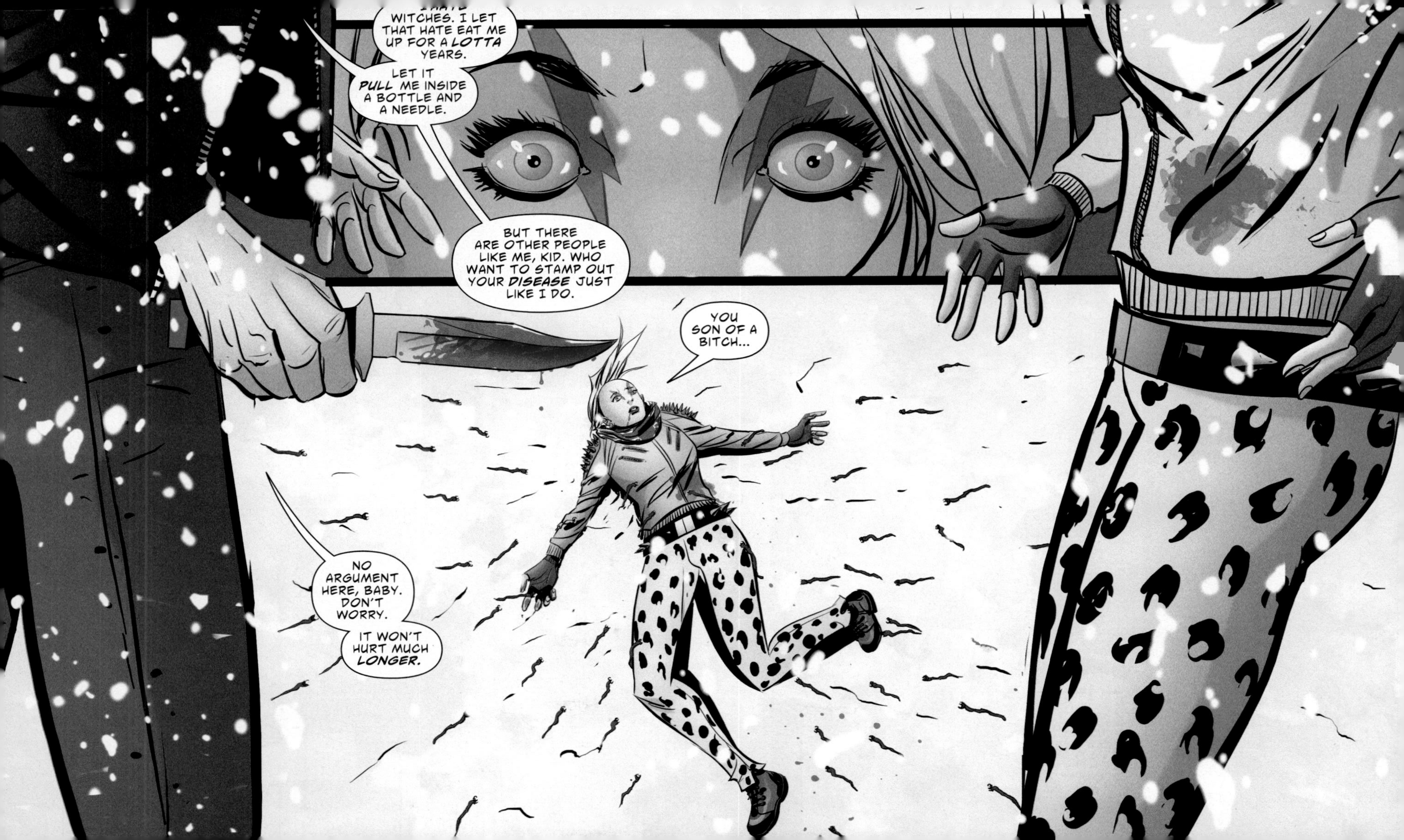
WITCHES. I LET THAT HATE EAT ME UP FOR A LOTTA YEARS.
LET IT PULL ME INSIDE A BOTTLE AND A NEEDLE.
BUT THERE ARE OTHER PEOPLE LIKE ME, KID. WHO WANT TO STAMP OUT YOUR DISEASE JUST LIKE I DO.
YOU SON OF A BITCH...
NO ARGUMENT HERE, BABY. DON'T WORRY.
IT WON'T HURT MUCH LONGER.

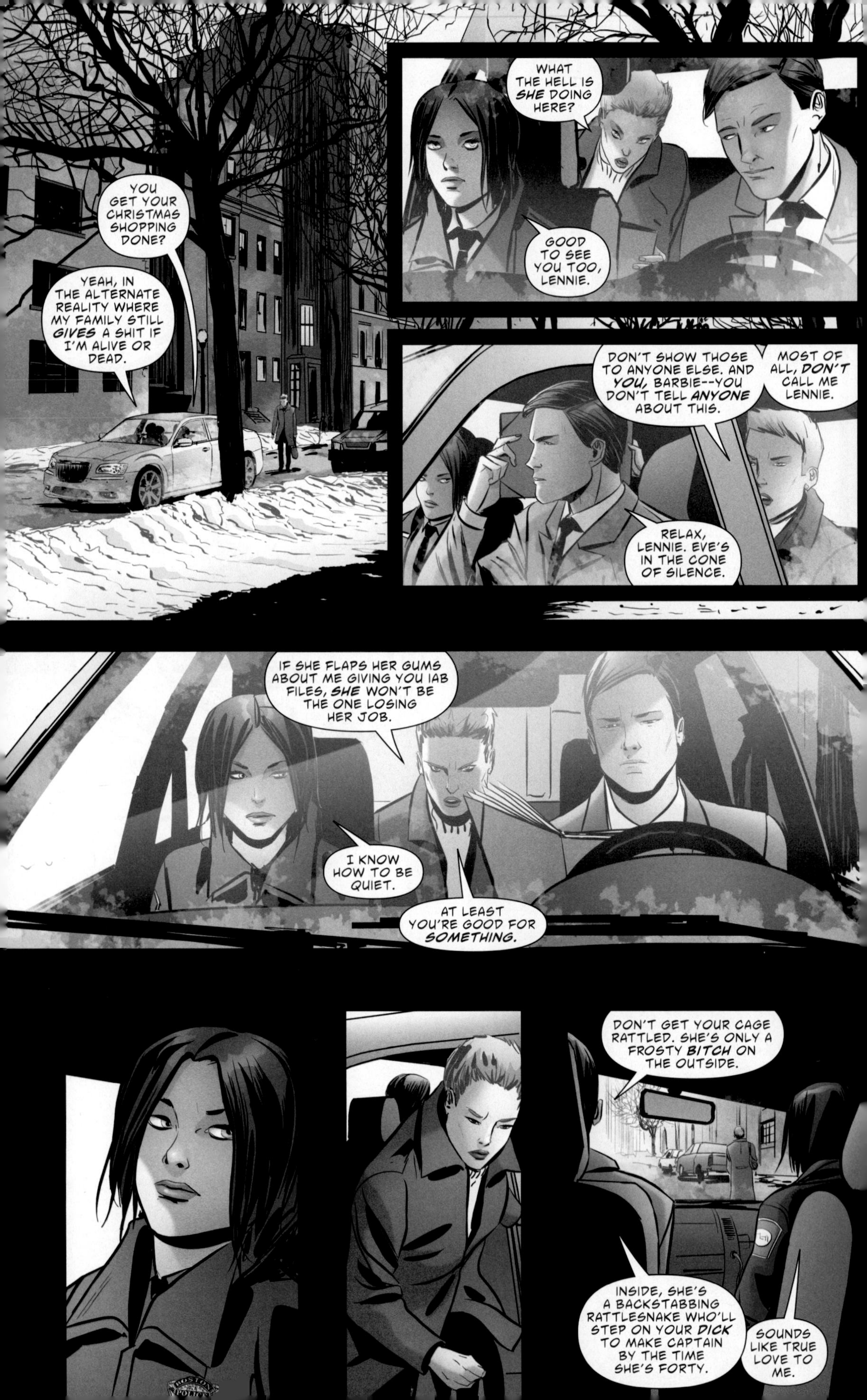
YOU GET YOUR CHRISTMAS SHOPPING DONE?
YEAH, IN THE ALTERNATE REALITY WHERE MY FAMILY STILL GIVES A SHIT IF I'M ALIVE OR DEAD.
WHAT THE HELL IS SHE DOING HERE?
GOOD TO SEE YOU TOO, LENNIE.
DON'T SHOW THOSE TO ANYONE ELSE. AND YOU, BARBIE--YOU DON'T TELL ANYONE ABOUT THIS.
MOST OF ALL, DON'T CALL ME LENNIE.
RELAX, LENNIE. EVE'S IN THE CONE OF SILENCE.
IF SHE FLAPS HER GUMS ABOUT ME GIVING YOU IAB FILES, SHE WON'T BE THE ONE LOSING HER JOB.
I KNOW HOW TO BE QUIET.
AT LEAST YOU'RE GOOD FOR SOMETHING.
DON'T GET YOUR CAGE RATTLED. SHE'S ONLY A FROSTY BITCH ON THE OUTSIDE.
INSIDE, SHE'S A BACKSTABBING RATTLESNAKE WHO'LL STEP ON YOUR DICK TO MAKE CAPTAIN BY THE TIME SHE'S FORTY.
SOUNDS LIKE TRUE LOVE TO ME.

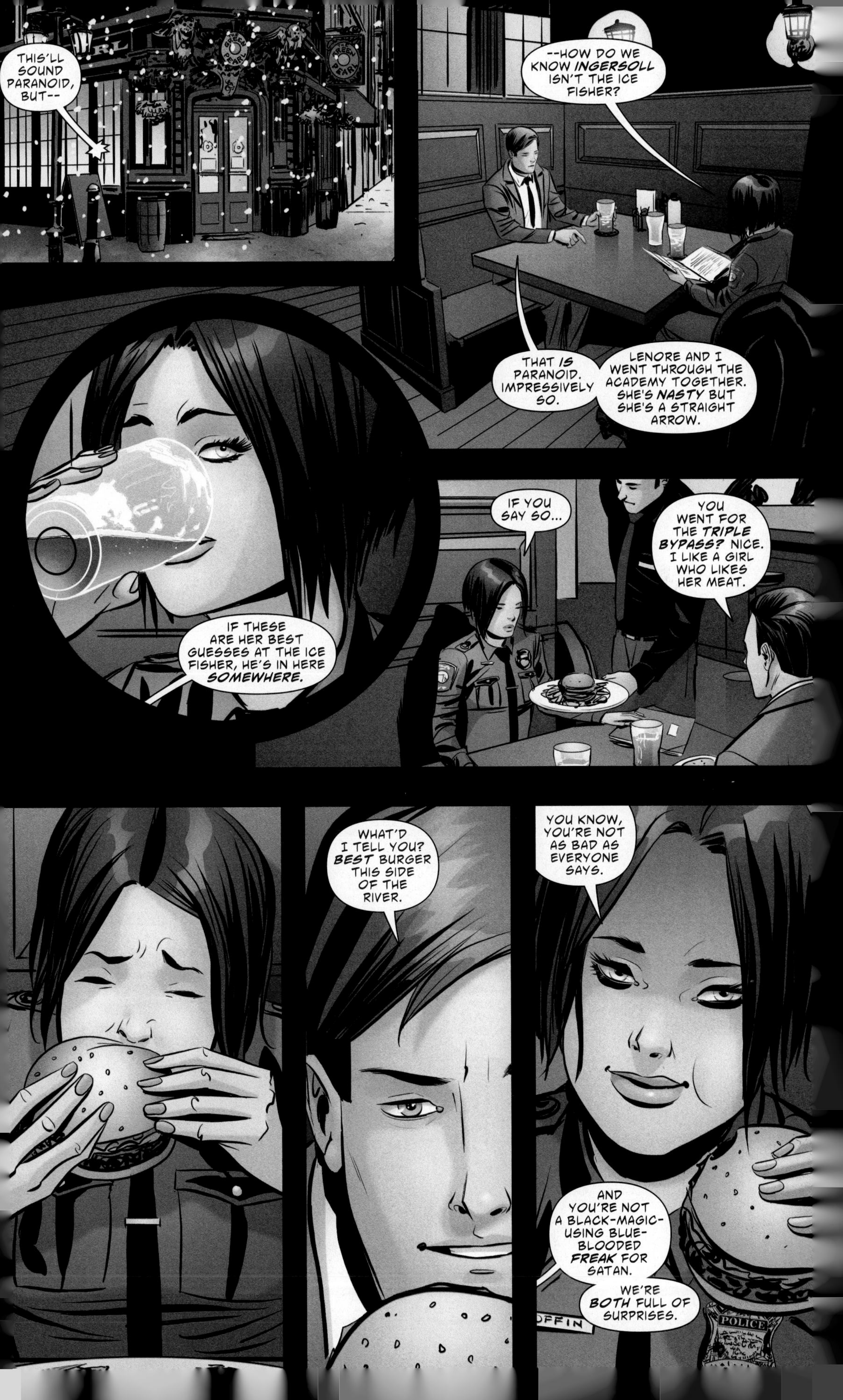

THIS'LL SOUND PARANOID, BUT--
--HOW DO WE KNOW INGERSOLL ISN'T THE ICE FISHER?
THAT IS PARANOID. IMPRESSIVELY SO.
LENORE AND I WENT THROUGH THE ACADEMY TOGETHER. SHE'S NASTY BUT SHE'S A STRAIGHT ARROW.
IF THESE ARE HER BEST GUESSES AT THE ICE FISHER, HE'S IN HERE SOMEWHERE.
IF YOU SAY SO...
YOU WENT FOR THE TRIPLE BYPASS? NICE. I LIKE A GIRL WHO LIKES HER MEAT.
WHAT'D I TELL YOU? BEST BURGER THIS SIDE OF THE RIVER.
YOU KNOW, YOU'RE NOT AS BAD AS EVERYONE SAYS.
AND YOU'RE NOT A BLACK-MAGIC-USING BLUE-BLOODED FREAK FOR SATAN.
WE'RE BOTH FULL OF SURPRISES.

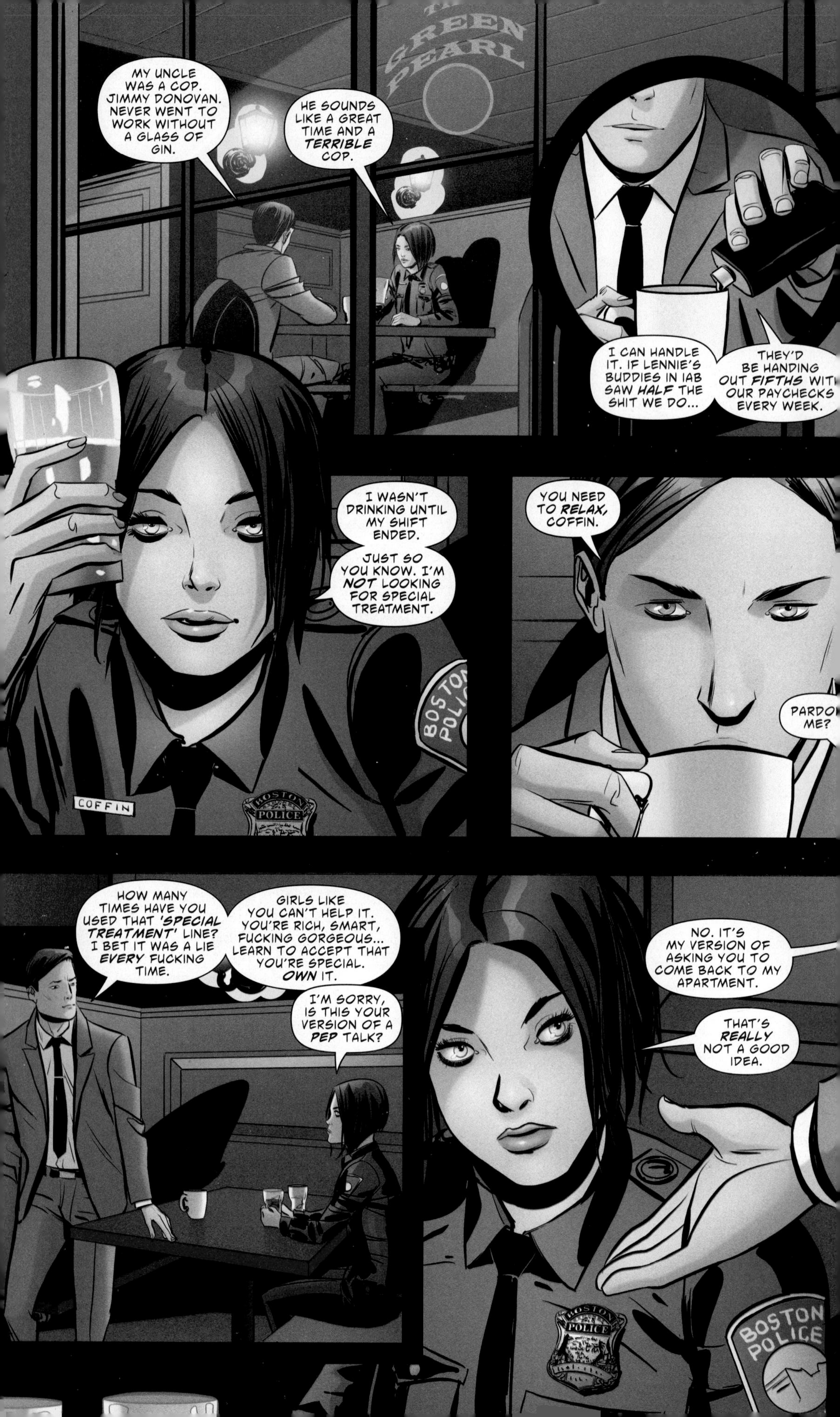
THE GREEN PEARL
MY UNCLE WAS A COP. JIMMY DONOVAN. NEVER WENT TO WORK WITHOUT A GLASS OF GIN.
HE SOUNDS LIKE A GREAT TIME AND A *TERRIBLE* COP.
I CAN HANDLE IT. IF LENNIE'S BUDDIES IN IAB SAW *HALF* THE SHIT WE DO...
THEY'D BE HANDING OUT *FIFTHS* WIT OUR PAYCHECKS EVERY WEEK.
I WASN'T DRINKING UNTIL MY SHIFT ENDED.
JUST SO YOU KNOW. I'M *NOT* LOOKING FOR SPECIAL TREATMENT.
BOSTON POLICE
COFFIN
YOU NEED TO *RELAX,* COFFIN.
PARDO ME?
HOW MANY TIMES HAVE YOU USED THAT *'SPECIAL TREATMENT'* LINE? I BET IT WAS A LIE *EVERY* FUCKING TIME.
GIRLS LIKE YOU CAN'T HELP IT. YOU'RE RICH, SMART, FUCKING GORGEOUS... LEARN TO ACCEPT THAT YOU'RE SPECIAL. *OWN* IT.
I'M SORRY, IS THIS YOUR VERSION OF A *PEP* TALK?
NO. IT'S MY VERSION OF ASKING YOU TO COME BACK TO MY APARTMENT.
THAT'S *REALLY* NOT A GOOD IDEA.
BOSTON POLICE

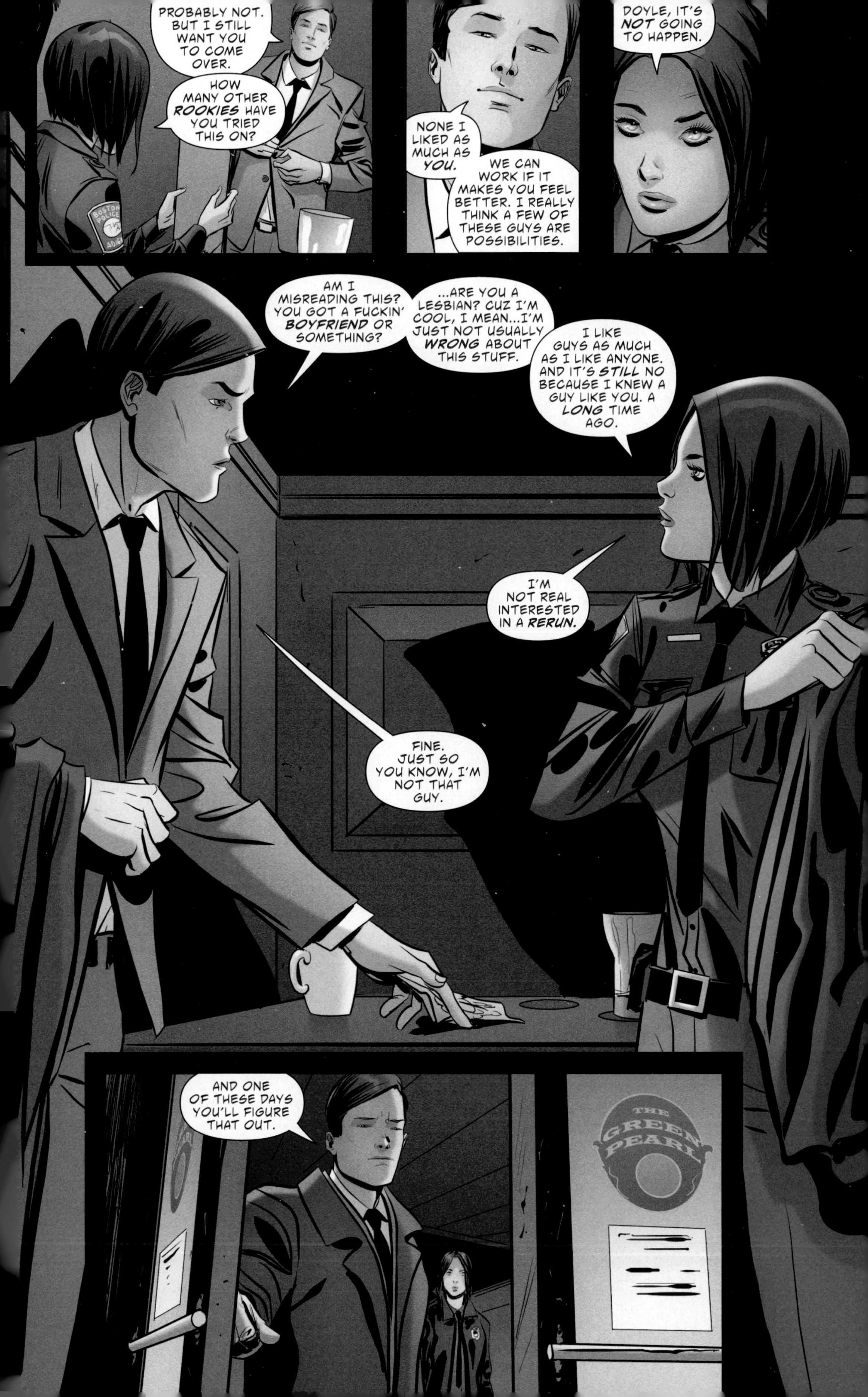
PROBABLY NOT. BUT I STILL WANT YOU TO COME OVER.
HOW MANY OTHER ROOKIES HAVE YOU TRIED THIS ON?
NONE I LIKED AS MUCH AS YOU.
WE CAN WORK IF IT MAKES YOU FEEL BETTER. I REALLY THINK A FEW OF THESE GUYS ARE POSSIBILITIES.
DOYLE, IT'S NOT GOING TO HAPPEN.
AM I MISREADING THIS? YOU GOT A FUCKIN' BOYFRIEND OR SOMETHING?
...ARE YOU A LESBIAN? CUZ I'M COOL, I MEAN...I'M JUST NOT USUALLY WRONG ABOUT THIS STUFF.
I LIKE GUYS AS MUCH AS I LIKE ANYONE. AND IT'S STILL NO BECAUSE I KNEW A GUY LIKE YOU. A LONG TIME AGO.
I'M NOT REAL INTERESTED IN A RERUN.
FINE. JUST SO YOU KNOW, I'M NOT THAT GUY.
AND ONE OF THESE DAYS YOU'LL FIGURE THAT OUT.
THE GREEN PEARL

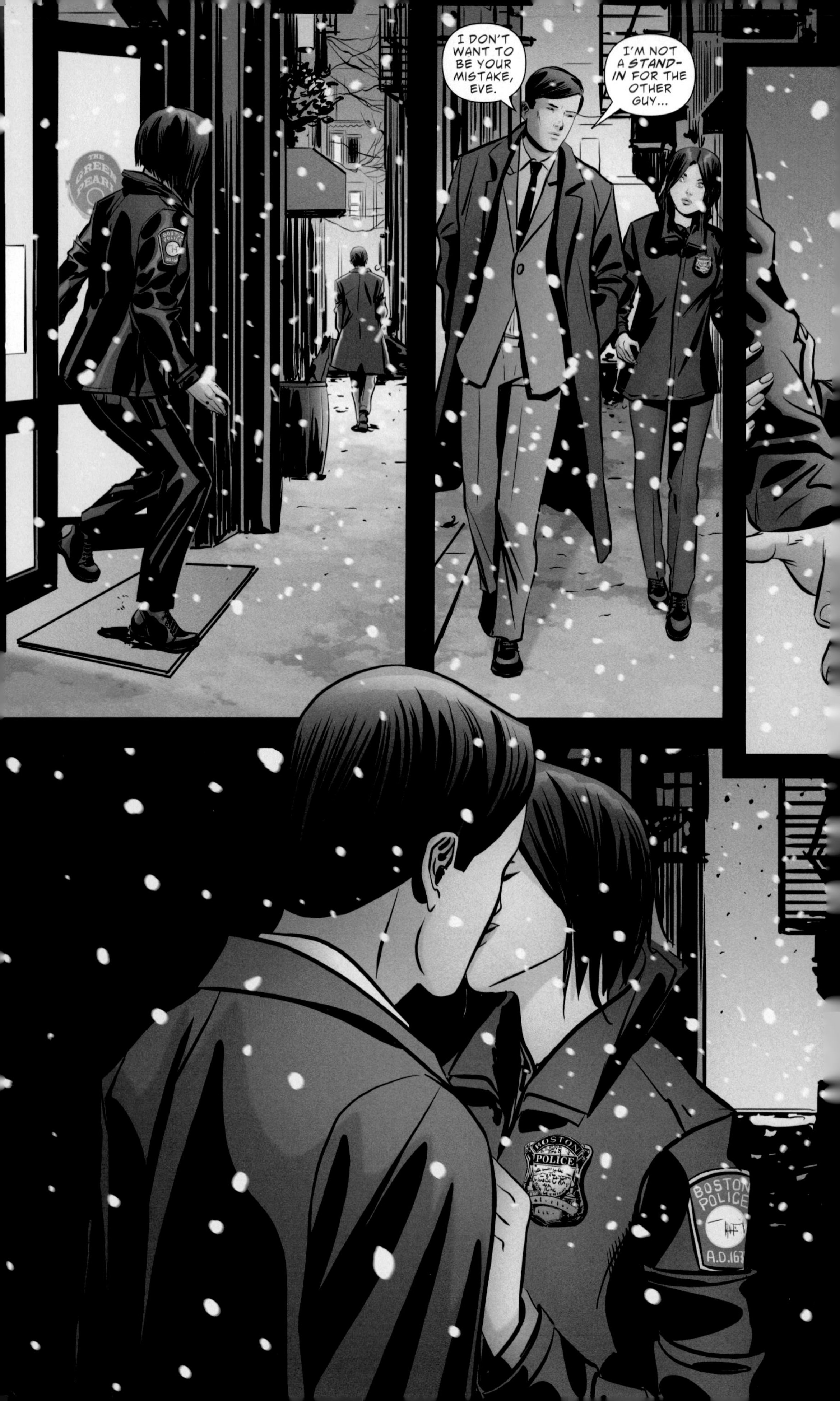
I DON'T WANT TO BE YOUR MISTAKE, EVE.
I'M NOT A *STAND-IN* FOR THE OTHER GUY...
BOSTON POLICE
BOSTON POLICE A.D.1630

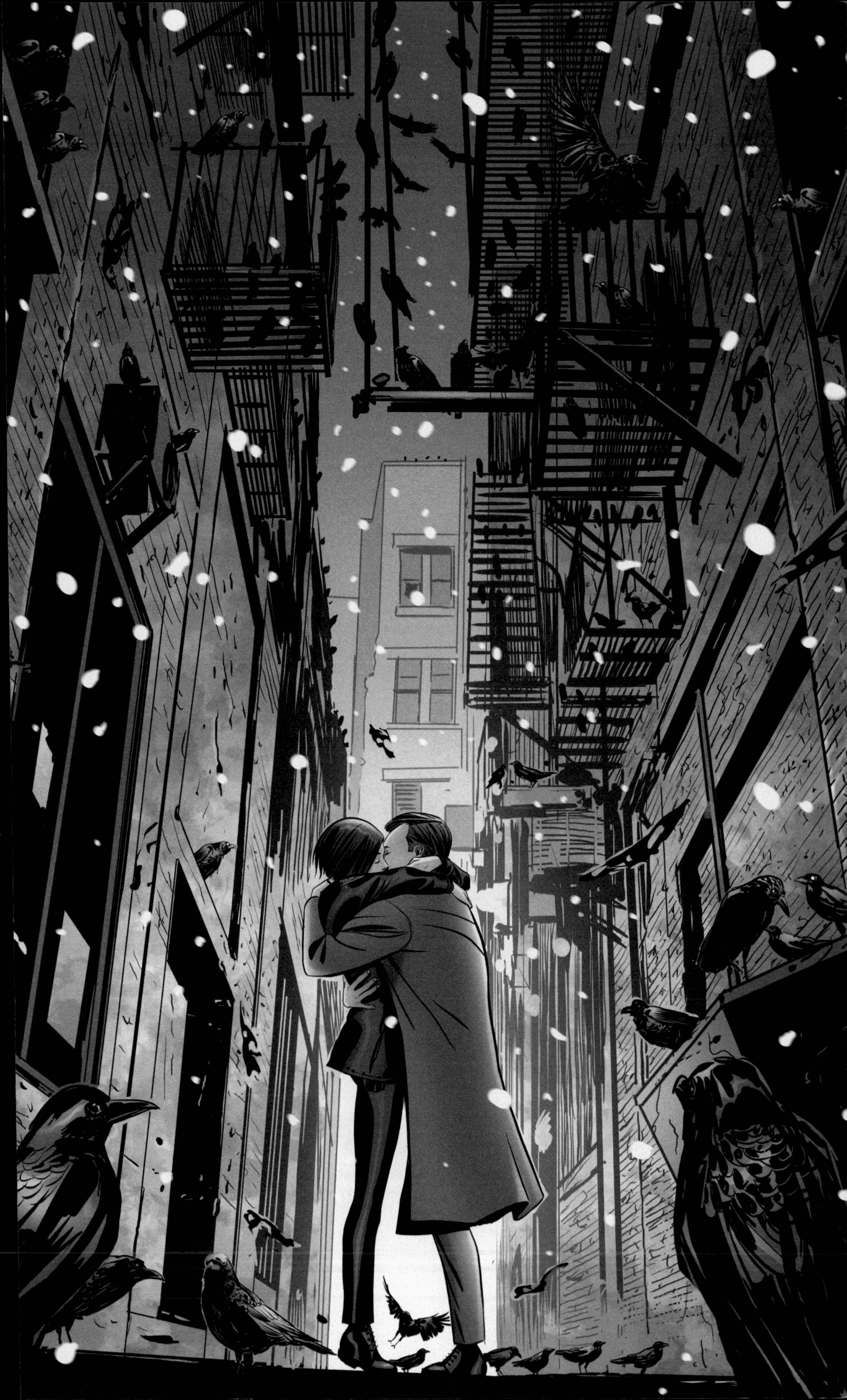

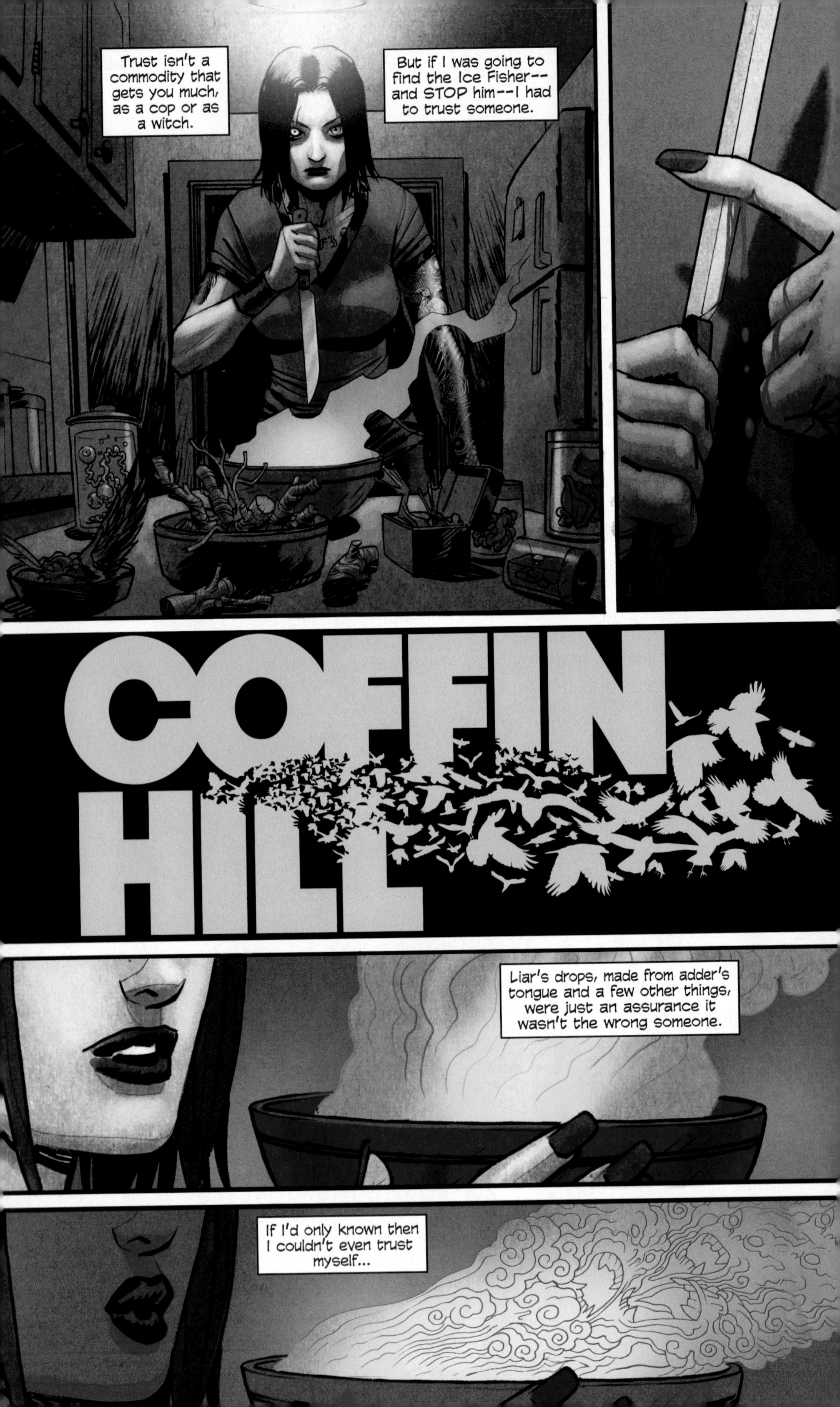
Trust isn't a commodity that gets you much, as a cop or as a witch.
But if I was going to find the Ice Fisher-- and STOP him--I had to trust someone.
COFFIN HILL
Liar's drops, made from adder's tongue and a few other things, were just an assurance it wasn't the wrong someone.
If I'd only known then I couldn't even trust myself...

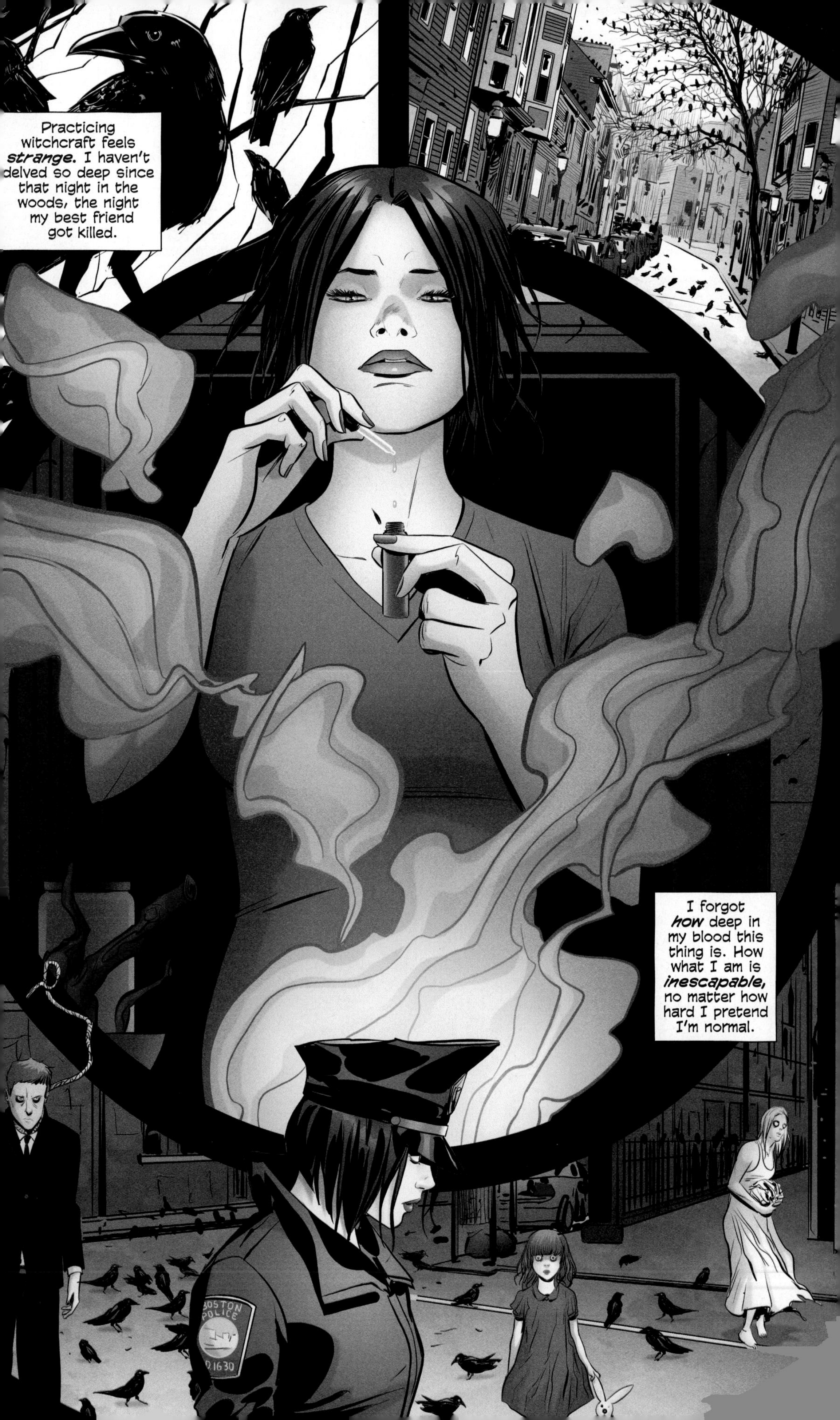
Practicing witchcraft feels **strange.** I haven't delved so deep since that night in the woods, the night my best friend got killed.
I forgot **how** deep in my blood this thing is. How what I am is **inescapable,** no matter how hard I pretend I'm normal.

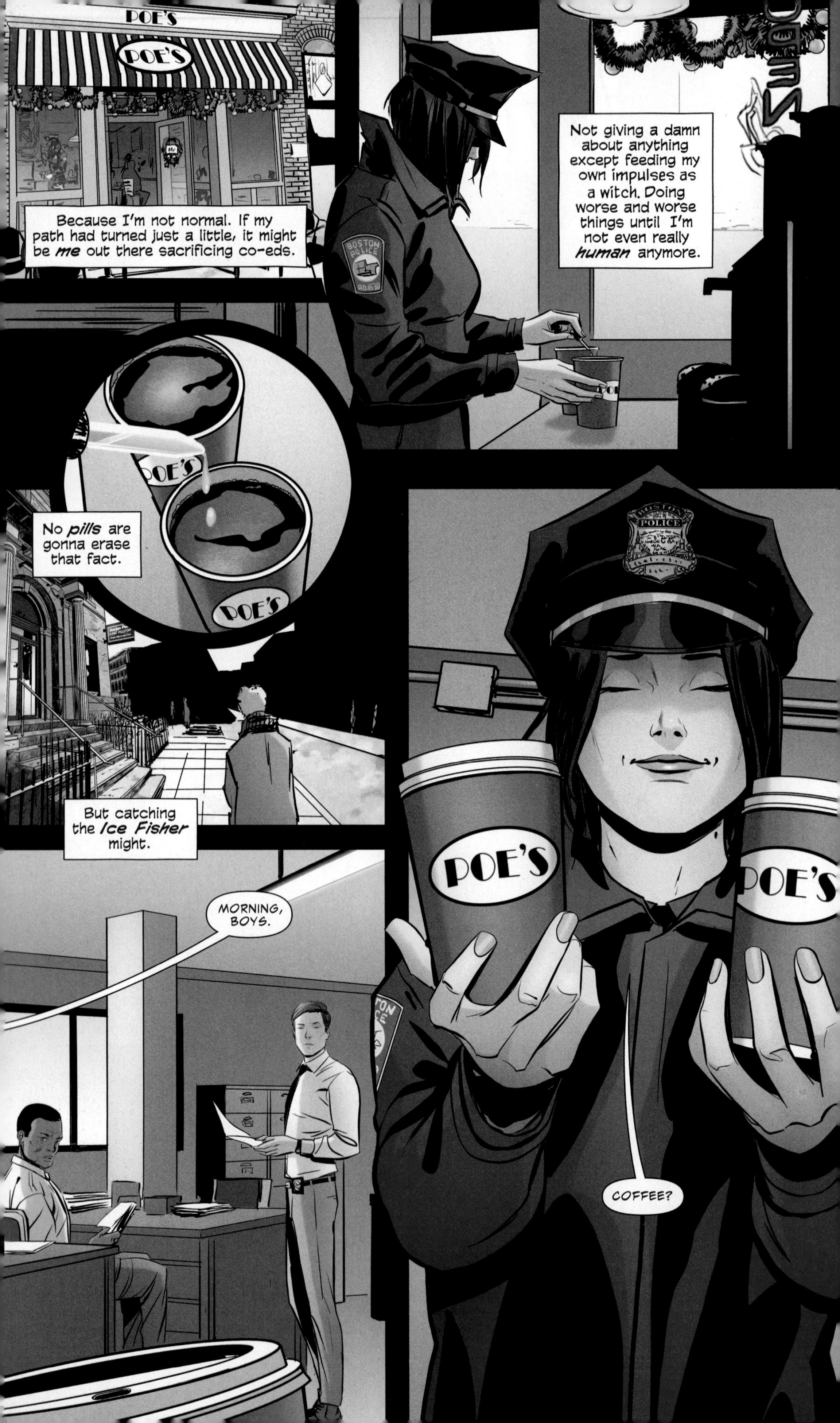
POE'S
POE'S
Because I'm not normal. If my path had turned just a little, it might be *me* out there sacrificing co-eds.
BOSTON POLICE
Not giving a damn about anything except feeding my own impulses as a witch. Doing worse and worse things until I'm not even really *human* anymore.
POE'S
POE'S
No *pills* are gonna erase that fact.
But catching the *Ice Fisher* might.
BOSTON POLICE
POE'S
POE'S
MORNING, BOYS.
COFFEE?

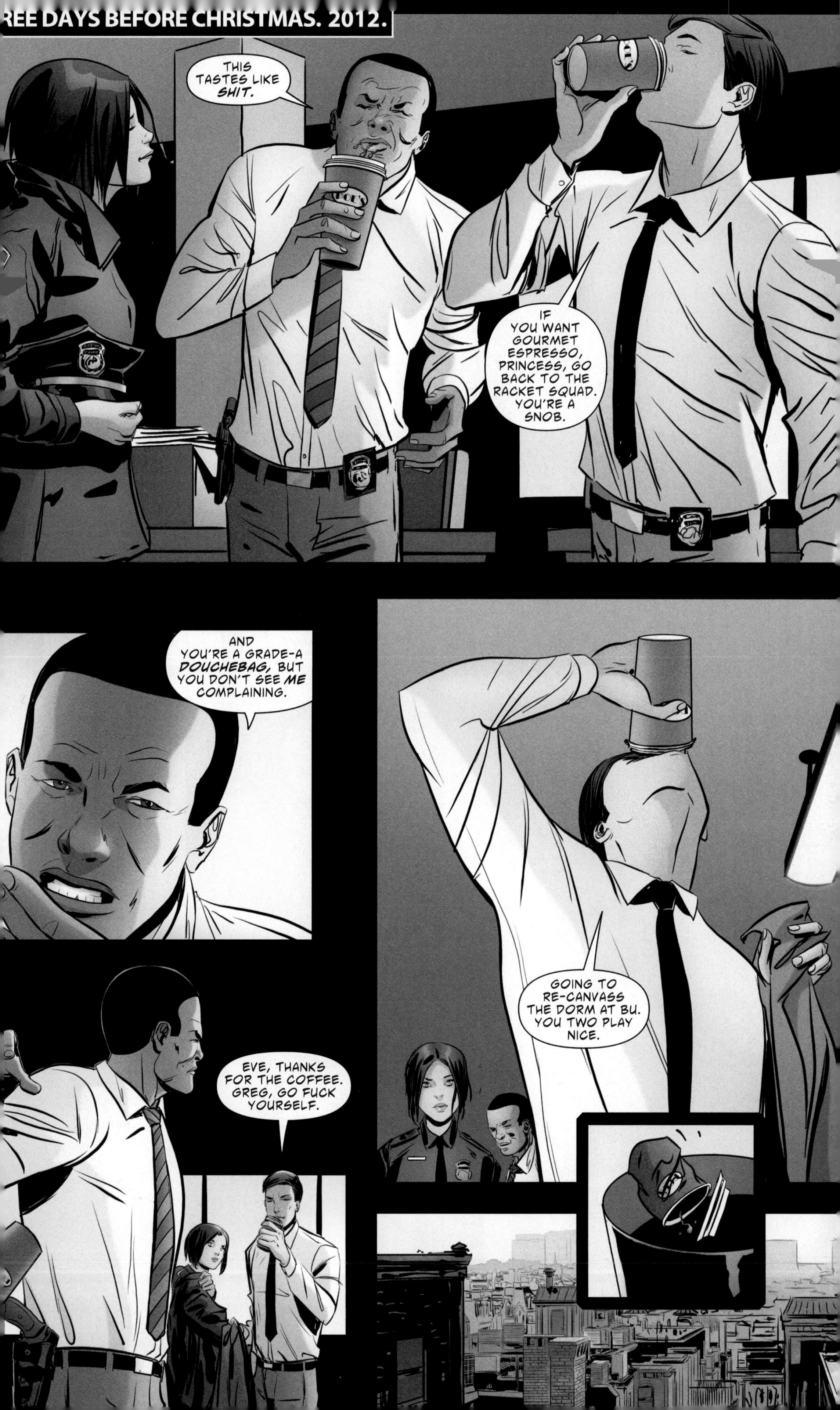
REE DAYS BEFORE CHRISTMAS. 2012.
THIS TASTES LIKE SHIT.
IF YOU WANT GOURMET ESPRESSO, PRINCESS, GO BACK TO THE RACKET SQUAD. YOU'RE A SNOB.
AND YOU'RE A GRADE-A DOUCHEBAG, BUT YOU DON'T SEE ME COMPLAINING.
GOING TO RE-CANVASS THE DORM AT BU. YOU TWO PLAY NICE.
EVE, THANKS FOR THE COFFEE. GREG, GO FUCK YOURSELF.

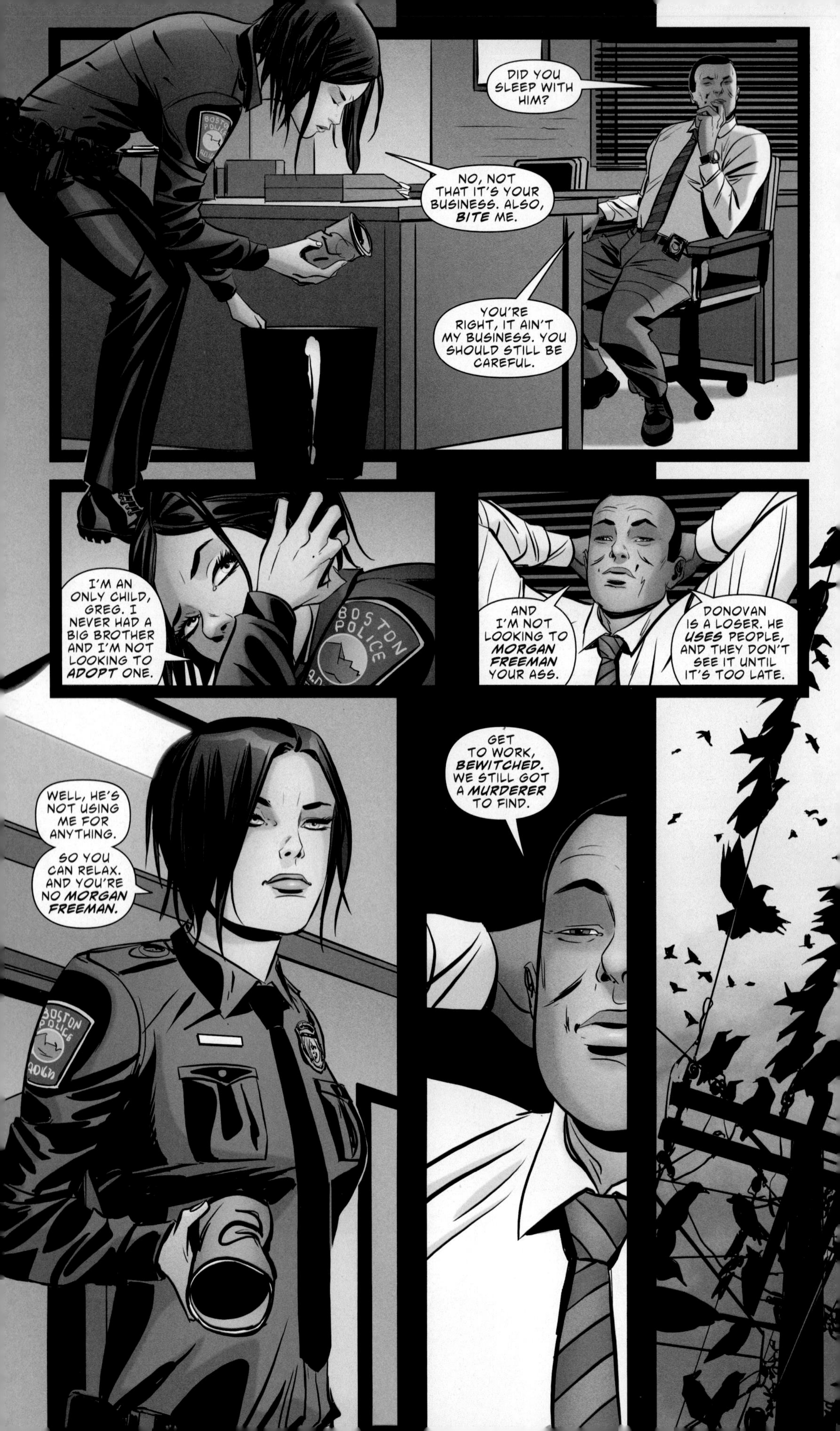
DID YOU SLEEP WITH HIM?
NO, NOT THAT IT'S YOUR BUSINESS. ALSO, *BITE* ME.
YOU'RE RIGHT, IT AIN'T MY BUSINESS. YOU SHOULD STILL BE CAREFUL.
I'M AN ONLY CHILD, GREG. I NEVER HAD A BIG BROTHER AND I'M NOT LOOKING TO *ADOPT* ONE.
DONOVAN IS A LOSER. HE *USES* PEOPLE, AND THEY DON'T SEE IT UNTIL IT'S TOO LATE.
AND I'M NOT LOOKING TO *MORGAN FREEMAN* YOUR ASS.
WELL, HE'S NOT USING ME FOR ANYTHING.
SO YOU CAN RELAX. AND YOU'RE NO *MORGAN FREEMAN.*
GET TO WORK, *BEWITCHED.* WE STILL GOT A *MURDERER* TO FIND.
BOSTON POLICE

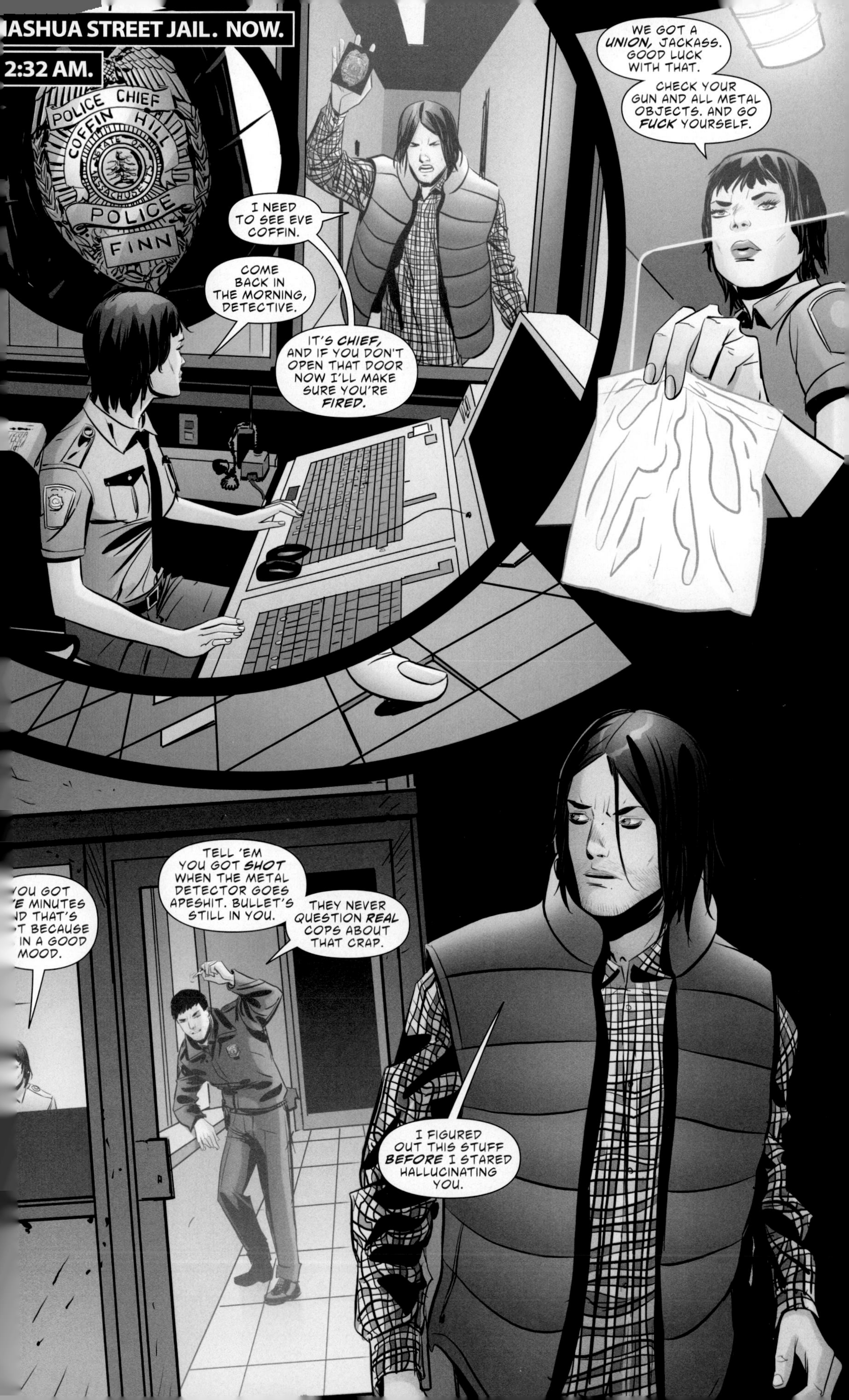

ASHUA STREET JAIL. NOW.
2:32 AM.
POLICE CHIEF
COFFIN HILL
STATE OF MASSACHUSETTS
POLICE
FINN
I NEED TO SEE EVE COFFIN.
COME BACK IN THE MORNING, DETECTIVE.
IT'S CHIEF, AND IF YOU DON'T OPEN THAT DOOR NOW I'LL MAKE SURE YOU'RE FIRED.
WE GOT A UNION, JACKASS. GOOD LUCK WITH THAT.
CHECK YOUR GUN AND ALL METAL OBJECTS. AND GO FUCK YOURSELF.
OU GOT
E MINUTES
D THAT'S
T BECAUSE
IN A GOOD
MOOD.
TELL 'EM YOU GOT SHOT WHEN THE METAL DETECTOR GOES APESHIT. BULLET'S STILL IN YOU.
THEY NEVER QUESTION REAL COPS ABOUT THAT CRAP.
I FIGURED OUT THIS STUFF BEFORE I STARED HALLUCINATING YOU.

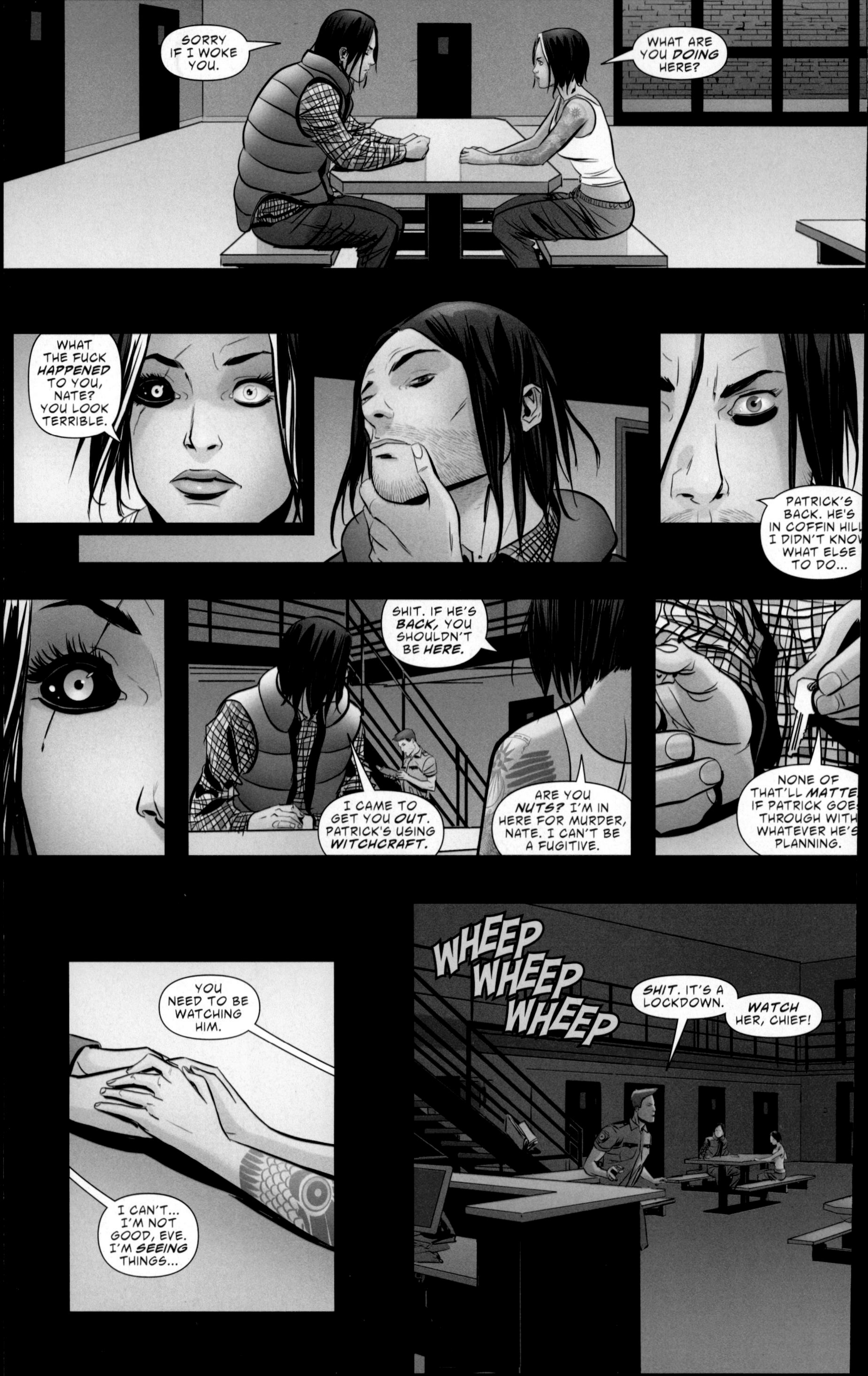
SORRY IF I WOKE YOU.
WHAT ARE YOU DOING HERE?
WHAT THE FUCK HAPPENED TO YOU, NATE? YOU LOOK TERRIBLE.
PATRICK'S BACK. HE'S IN COFFIN HILL I DIDN'T KNOW WHAT ELSE TO DO...
SHIT. IF HE'S BACK, YOU SHOULDN'T BE HERE.
I CAME TO GET YOU OUT. PATRICK'S USING WITCHCRAFT.
ARE YOU NUTS? I'M IN HERE FOR MURDER, NATE. I CAN'T BE A FUGITIVE.
NONE OF THAT'LL MATTE IF PATRICK GOES THROUGH WITH WHATEVER HE'S PLANNING.
YOU NEED TO BE WATCHING HIM.
I CAN'T... I'M NOT GOOD, EVE. I'M SEEING THINGS...
WHEEP
WHEEP
WHEEP
SHIT. IT'S A LOCKDOWN.
WATCH HER, CHIEF!

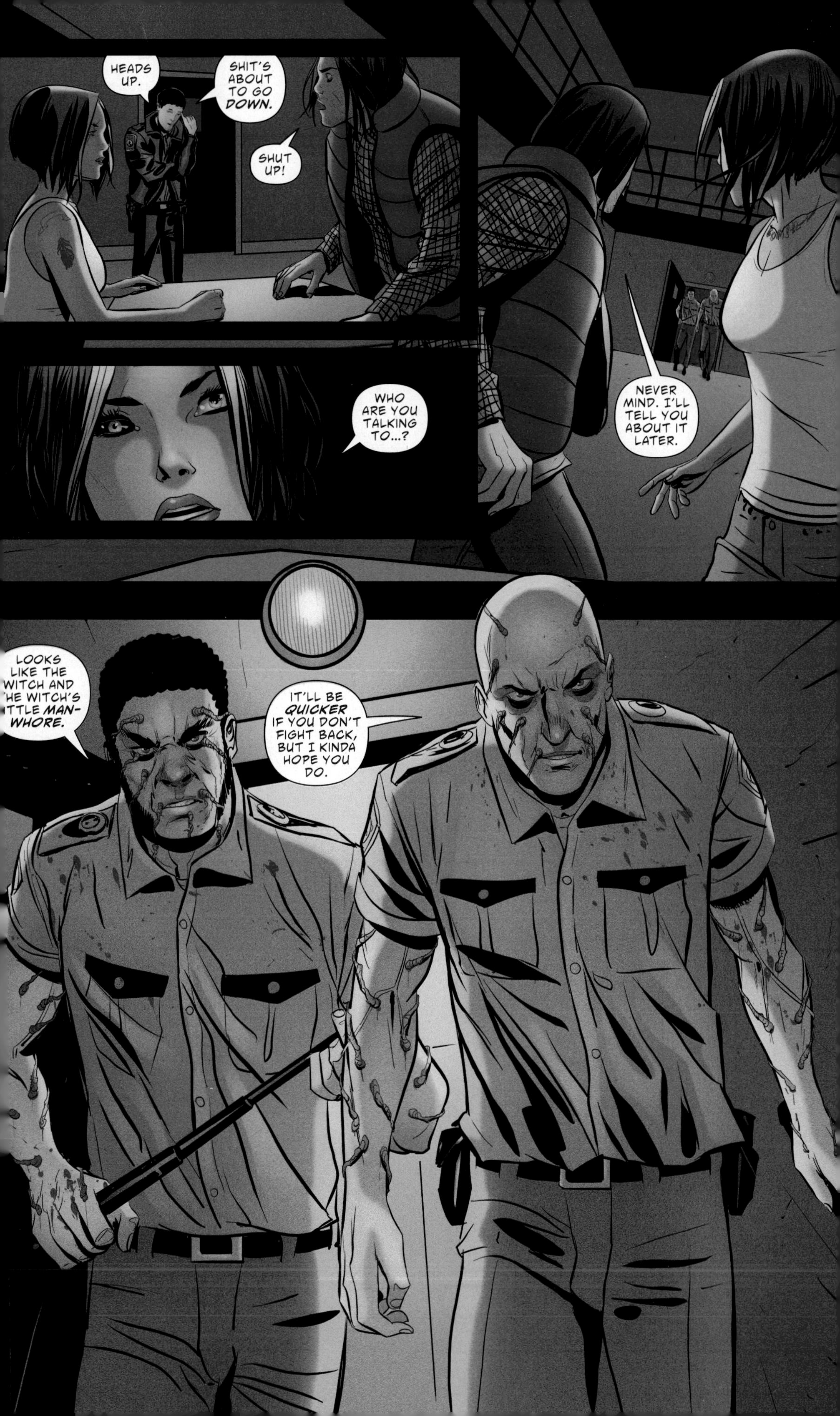
HEADS UP.
SHIT'S ABOUT TO GO ***DOWN.***
SHUT UP!
WHO ARE YOU TALKING TO...?
NEVER MIND. I'LL TELL YOU ABOUT IT LATER.
LOOKS LIKE THE WITCH AND HE WITCH'S TTLE ***MAN-WHORE.***
IT'LL BE ***QUICKER*** IF YOU DON'T FIGHT BACK, BUT I KINDA HOPE YOU DO.

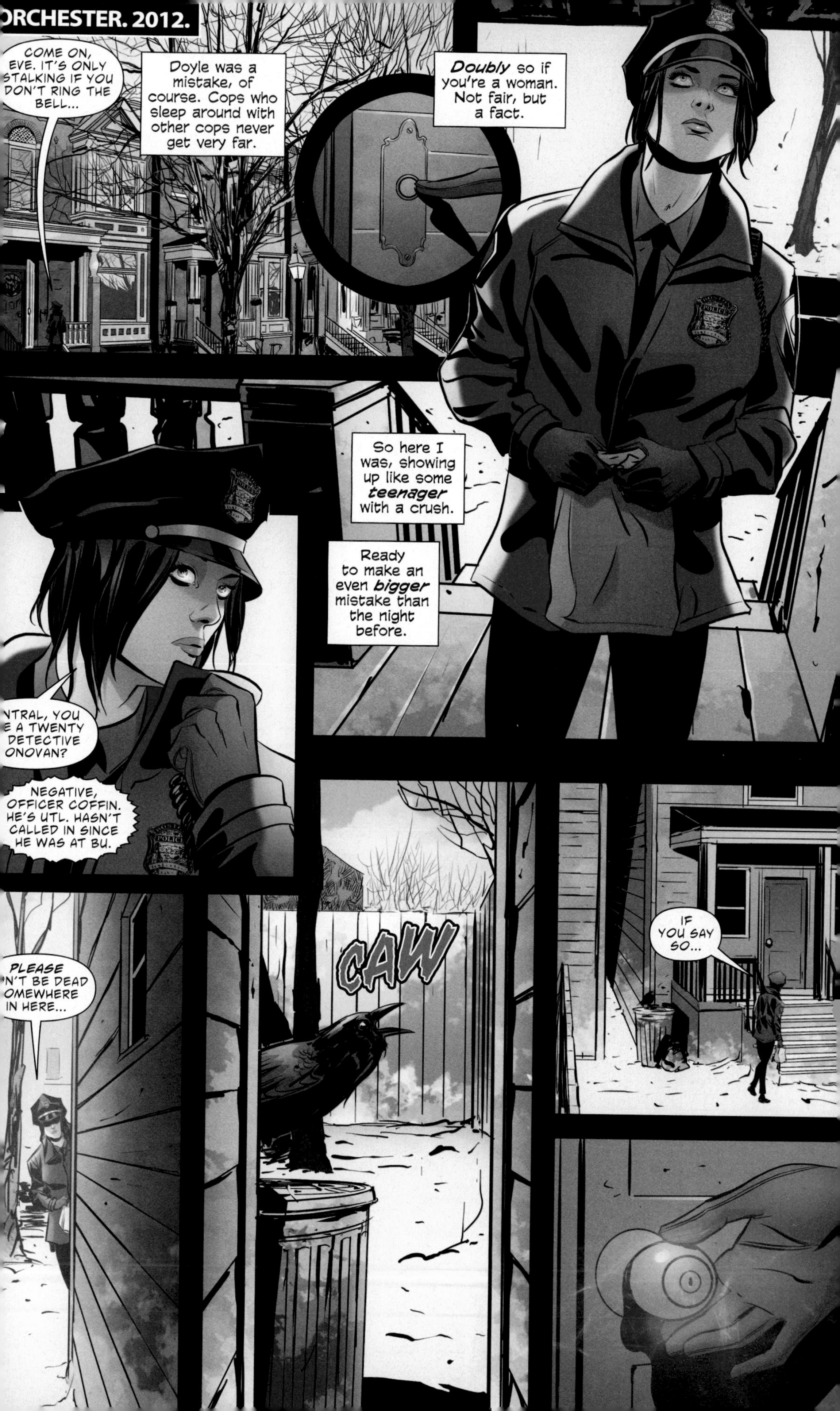

ORCHESTER. 2012.
COME ON, EVE. IT'S ONLY STALKING IF YOU DON'T RING THE BELL...
Doyle was a mistake, of course. Cops who sleep around with other cops never get very far.
Doubly so if you're a woman. Not fair, but a fact.
So here I was, showing up like some teenager with a crush.
Ready to make an even bigger mistake than the night before.
NTRAL, YOU E A TWENTY DETECTIVE ONOVAN?
NEGATIVE, OFFICER COFFIN. HE'S UTL. HASN'T CALLED IN SINCE HE WAS AT BU.
IF YOU SAY SO...
PLEASE N'T BE DEAD OMEWHERE IN HERE...
CAW

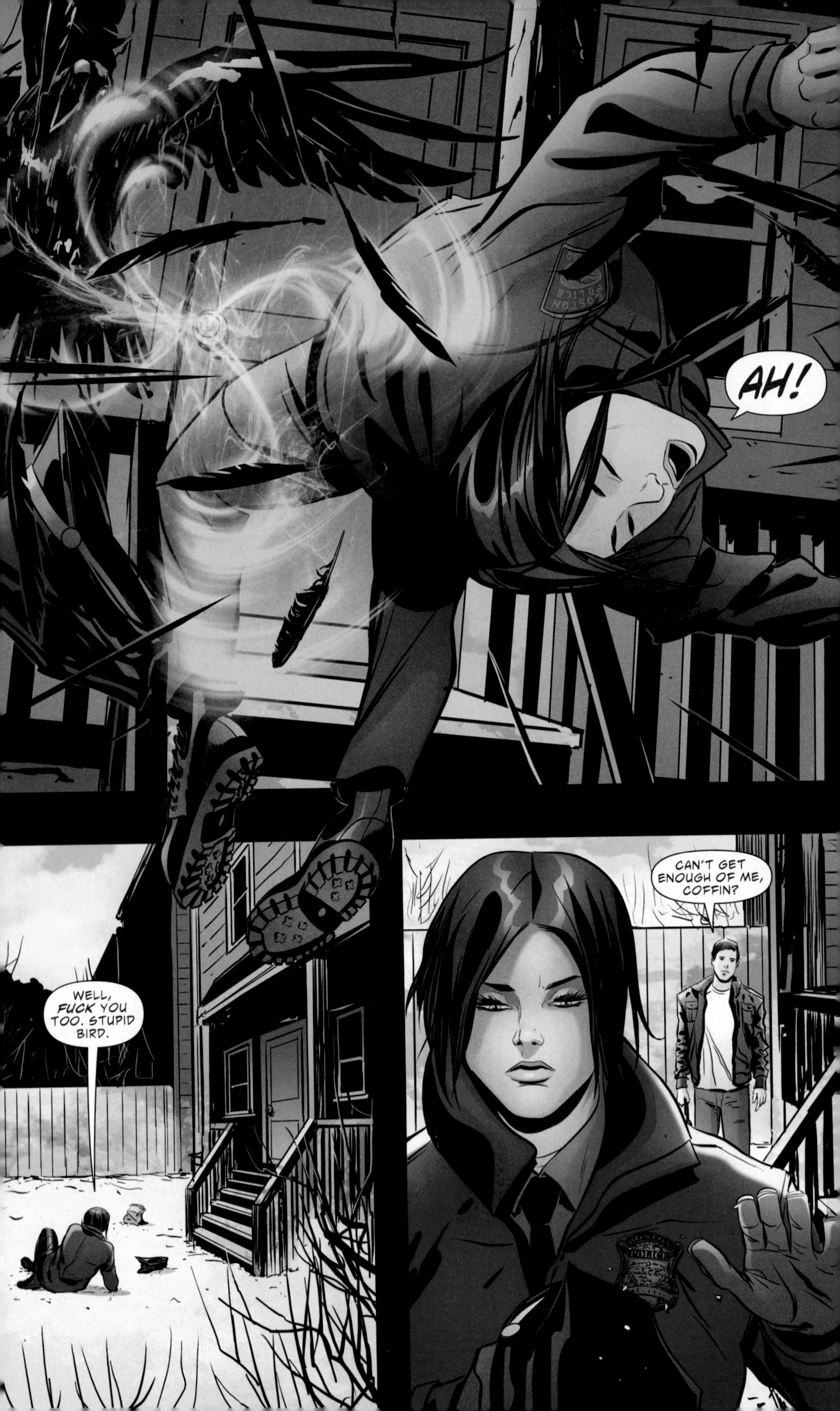
AH!
WELL, FUCK YOU TOO. STUPID BIRD.
CAN'T GET ENOUGH OF ME, COFFIN?

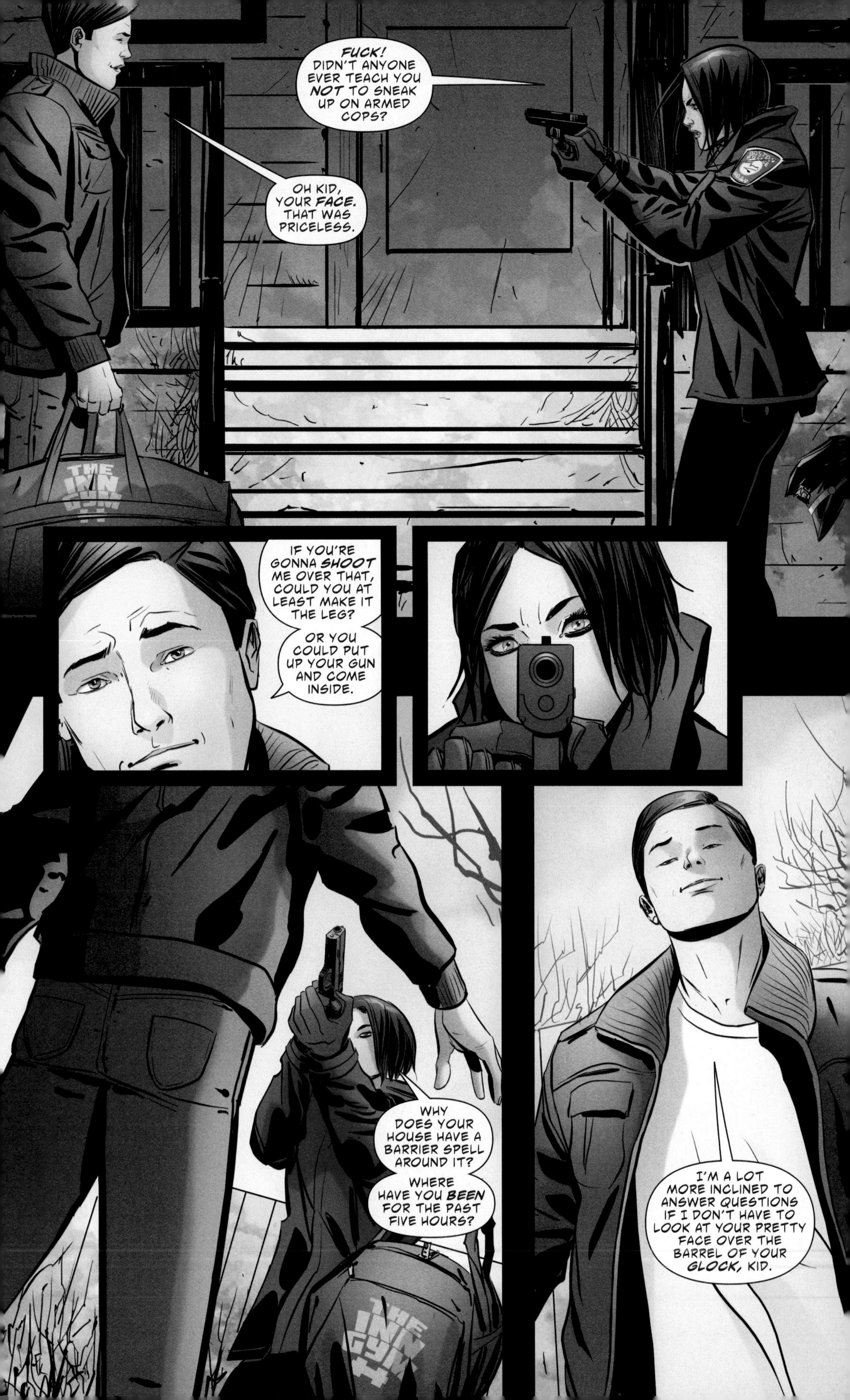
FUCK! DIDN'T ANYONE EVER TEACH YOU NOT TO SNEAK UP ON ARMED COPS?
OH KID, YOUR FACE. THAT WAS PRICELESS.
IF YOU'RE GONNA SHOOT ME OVER THAT, COULD YOU AT LEAST MAKE IT THE LEG?
OR YOU COULD PUT UP YOUR GUN AND COME INSIDE.
WHY DOES YOUR HOUSE HAVE A BARRIER SPELL AROUND IT?
WHERE HAVE YOU BEEN FOR THE PAST FIVE HOURS?
I'M A LOT MORE INCLINED TO ANSWER QUESTIONS IF I DON'T HAVE TO LOOK AT YOUR PRETTY FACE OVER THE BARREL OF YOUR GLOCK, KID.

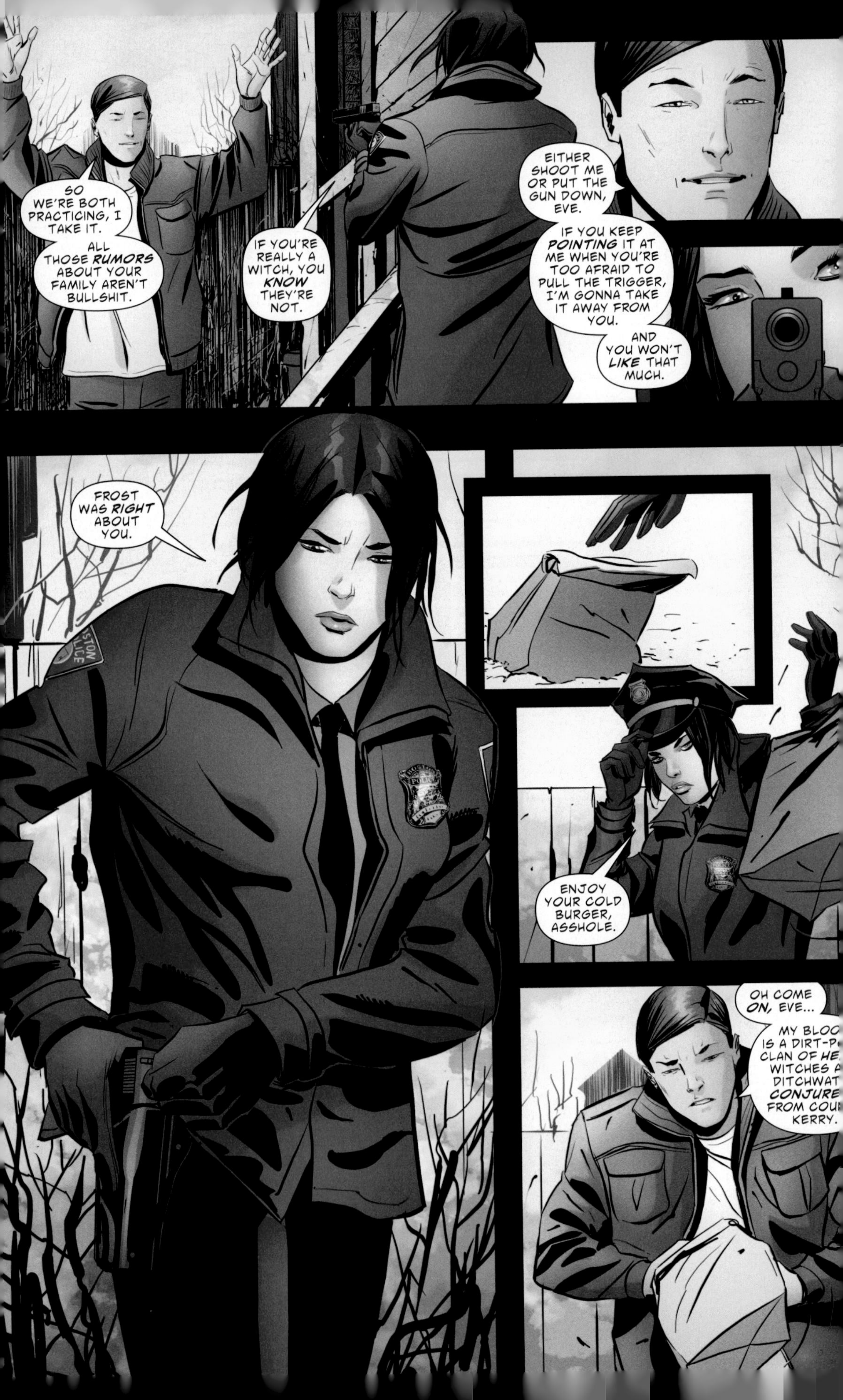
SO WE'RE BOTH PRACTICING, I TAKE IT.
ALL THOSE RUMORS ABOUT YOUR FAMILY AREN'T BULLSHIT.
IF YOU'RE REALLY A WITCH, YOU KNOW THEY'RE NOT.
EITHER SHOOT ME OR PUT THE GUN DOWN, EVE.
IF YOU KEEP POINTING IT AT ME WHEN YOU'RE TOO AFRAID TO PULL THE TRIGGER, I'M GONNA TAKE IT AWAY FROM YOU.
AND YOU WON'T LIKE THAT MUCH.
FROST WAS RIGHT ABOUT YOU.
ENJOY YOUR COLD BURGER, ASSHOLE.
OH COME ON, EVE...
MY BLOO IS A DIRT-P CLAN OF HE WITCHES A DITCHWAT CONJURE FROM COU KERRY.

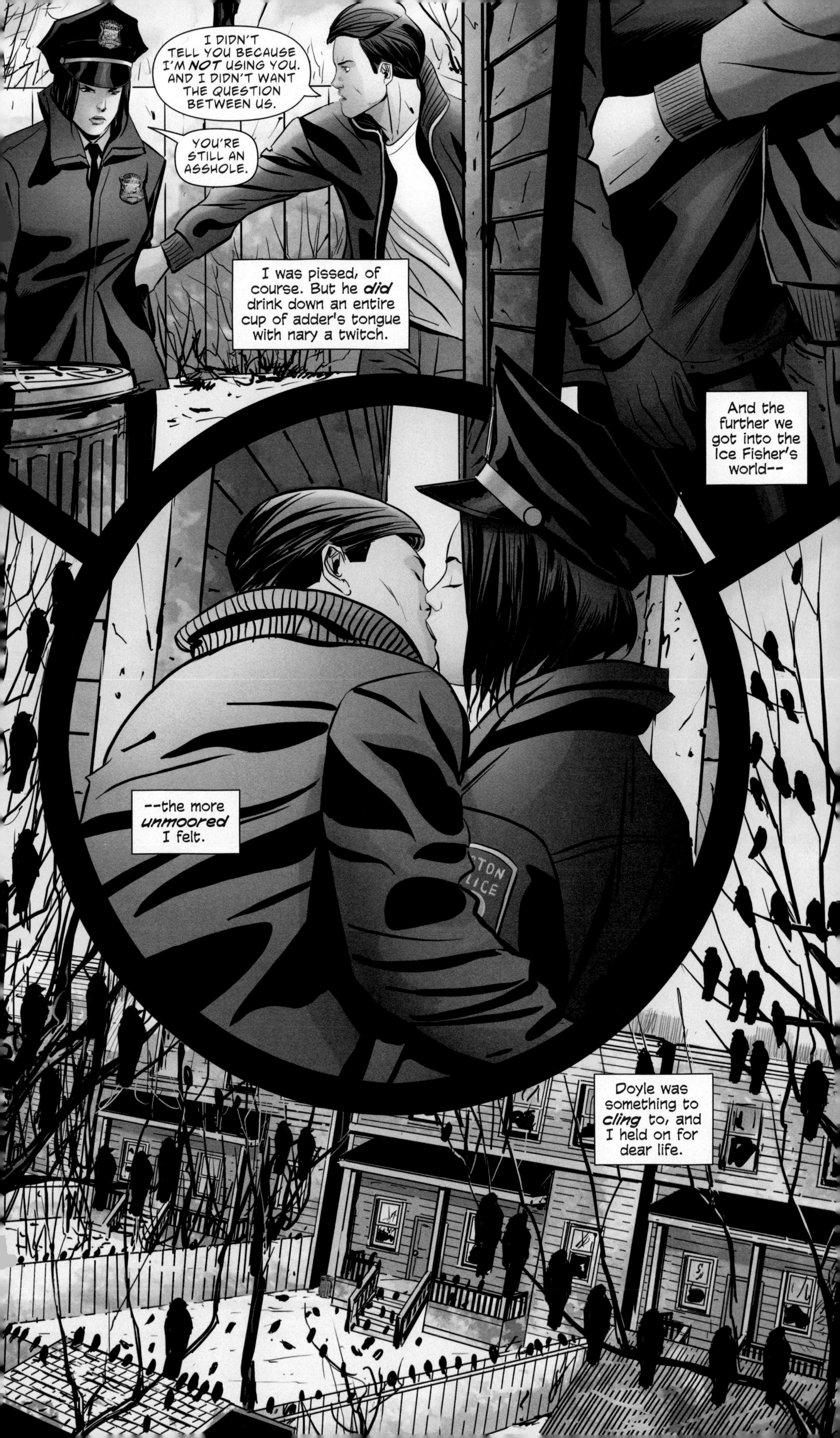

I DIDN'T TELL YOU BECAUSE I'M **NOT** USING YOU. AND I DIDN'T WANT THE QUESTION BETWEEN US.
YOU'RE STILL AN ASSHOLE.
I was pissed, of course. But he ***did*** drink down an entire cup of adder's tongue with nary a twitch.
And the further we got into the Ice Fisher's world--
--the more ***unmoored*** I felt.
Doyle was something to ***cling*** to, and I held on for dear life.

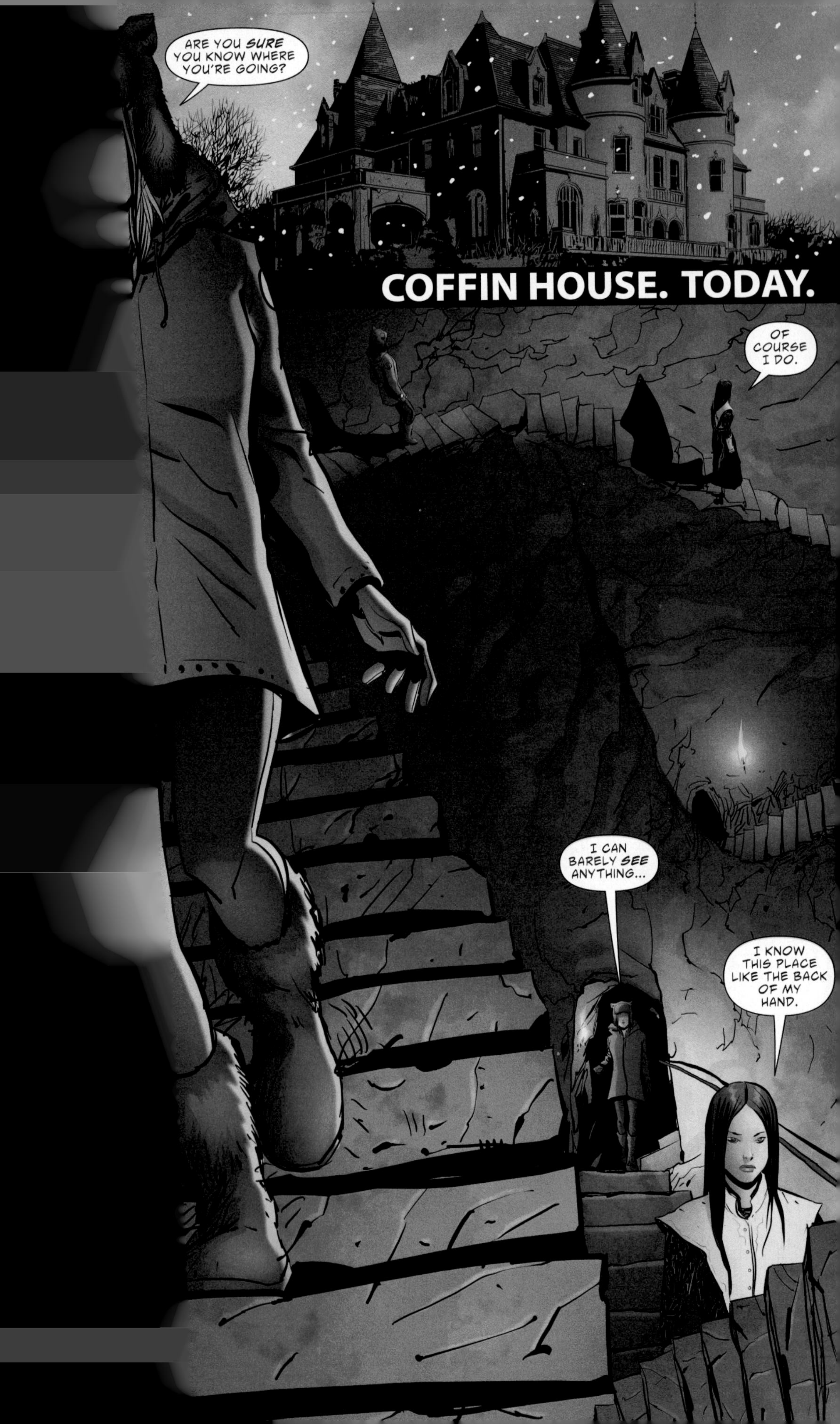
ARE YOU SURE YOU KNOW WHERE YOU'RE GOING?
COFFIN HOUSE. TODAY.
OF COURSE I DO.
I CAN BARELY SEE ANYTHING...
I KNOW THIS PLACE LIKE THE BACK OF MY HAND.

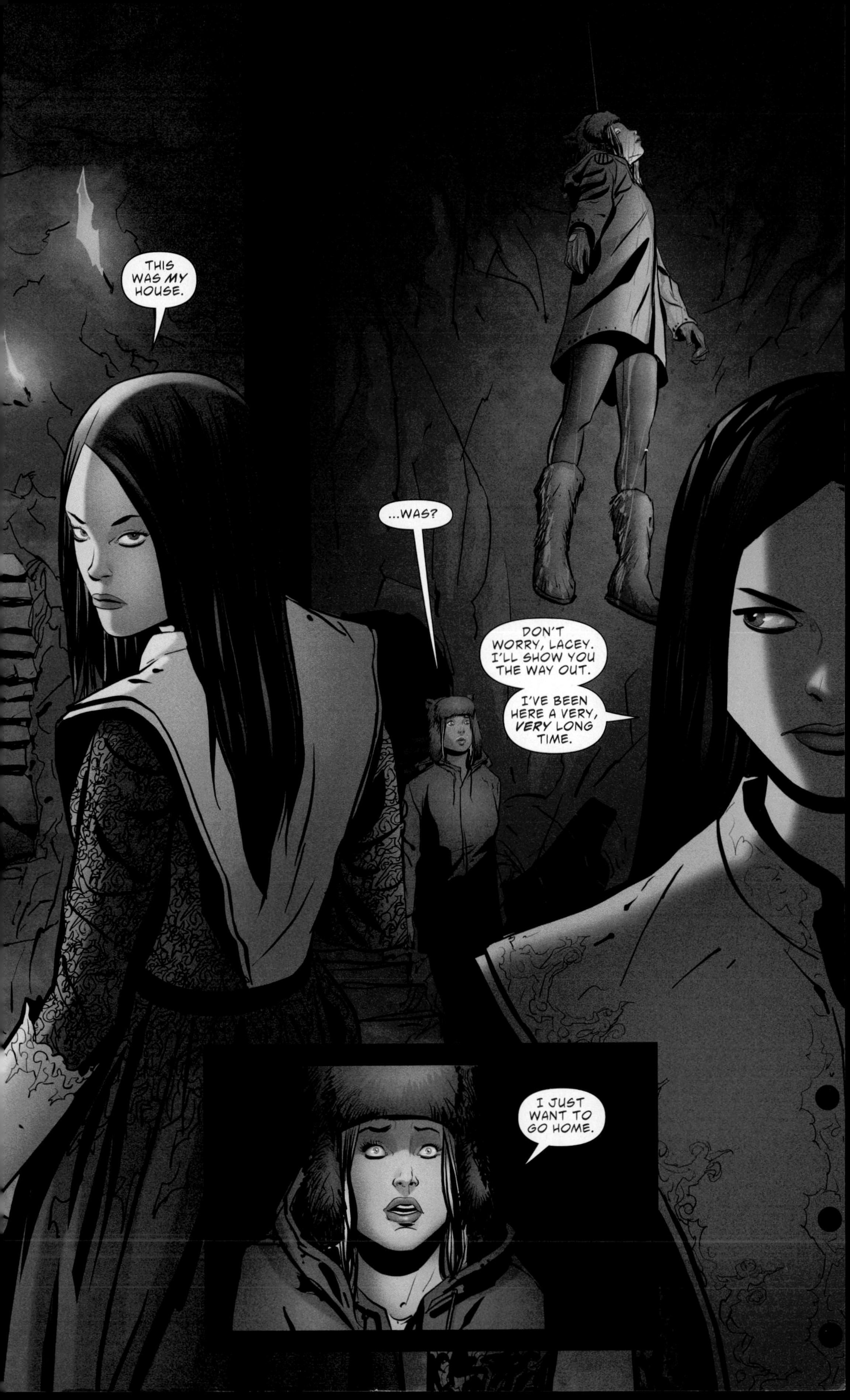
THIS WAS MY HOUSE.
...WAS?
DON'T WORRY, LACEY. I'LL SHOW YOU THE WAY OUT.
I'VE BEEN HERE A VERY, VERY LONG TIME.
I JUST WANT TO GO HOME.

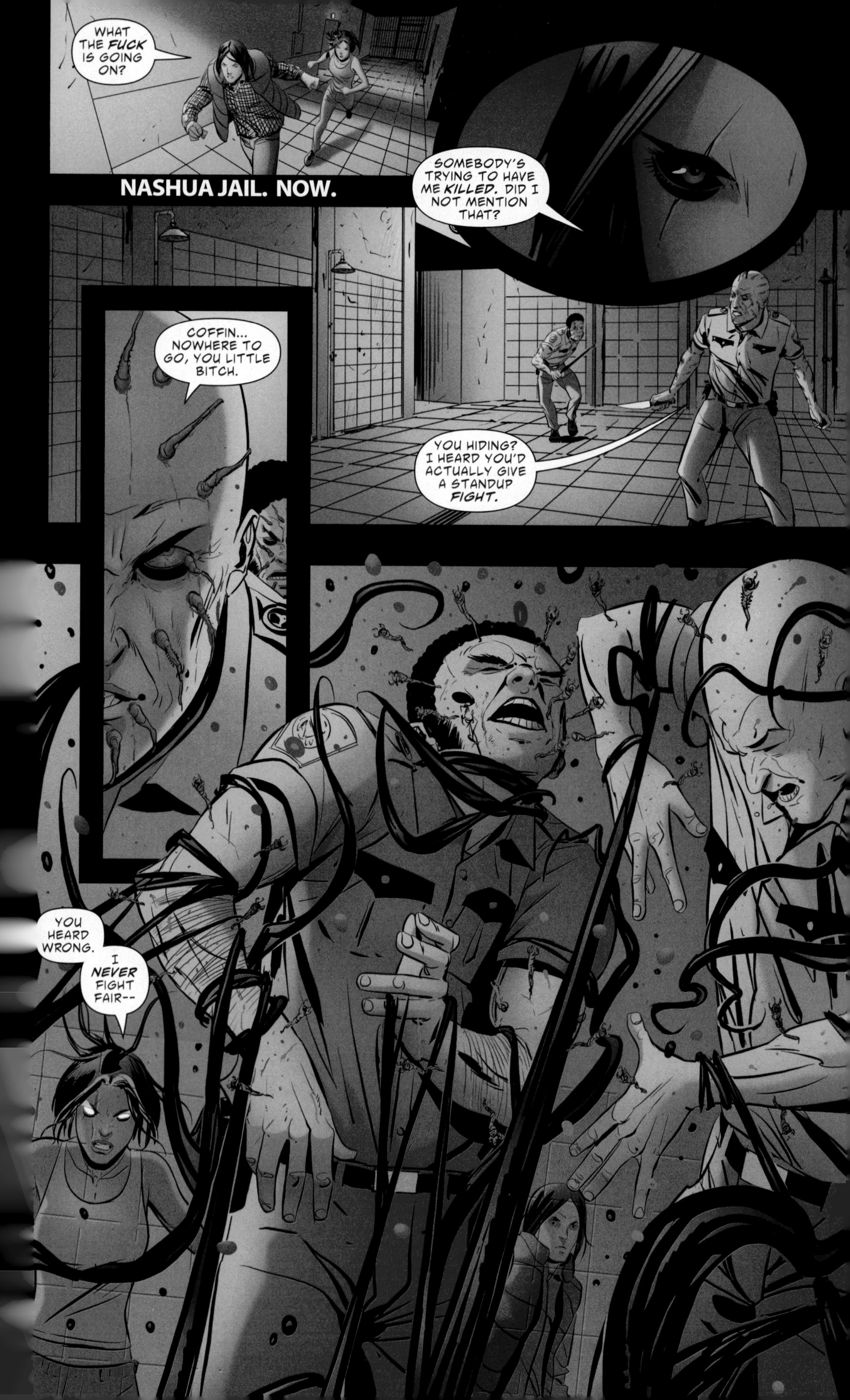

WHAT THE FUCK IS GOING ON?
SOMEBODY'S TRYING TO HAVE ME KILLED. DID I NOT MENTION THAT?
NASHUA JAIL. NOW.
COFFIN... NOWHERE TO GO, YOU LITTLE BITCH.
YOU HIDING? I HEARD YOU'D ACTUALLY GIVE A STANDUP FIGHT.
YOU HEARD WRONG.
I NEVER FIGHT FAIR--

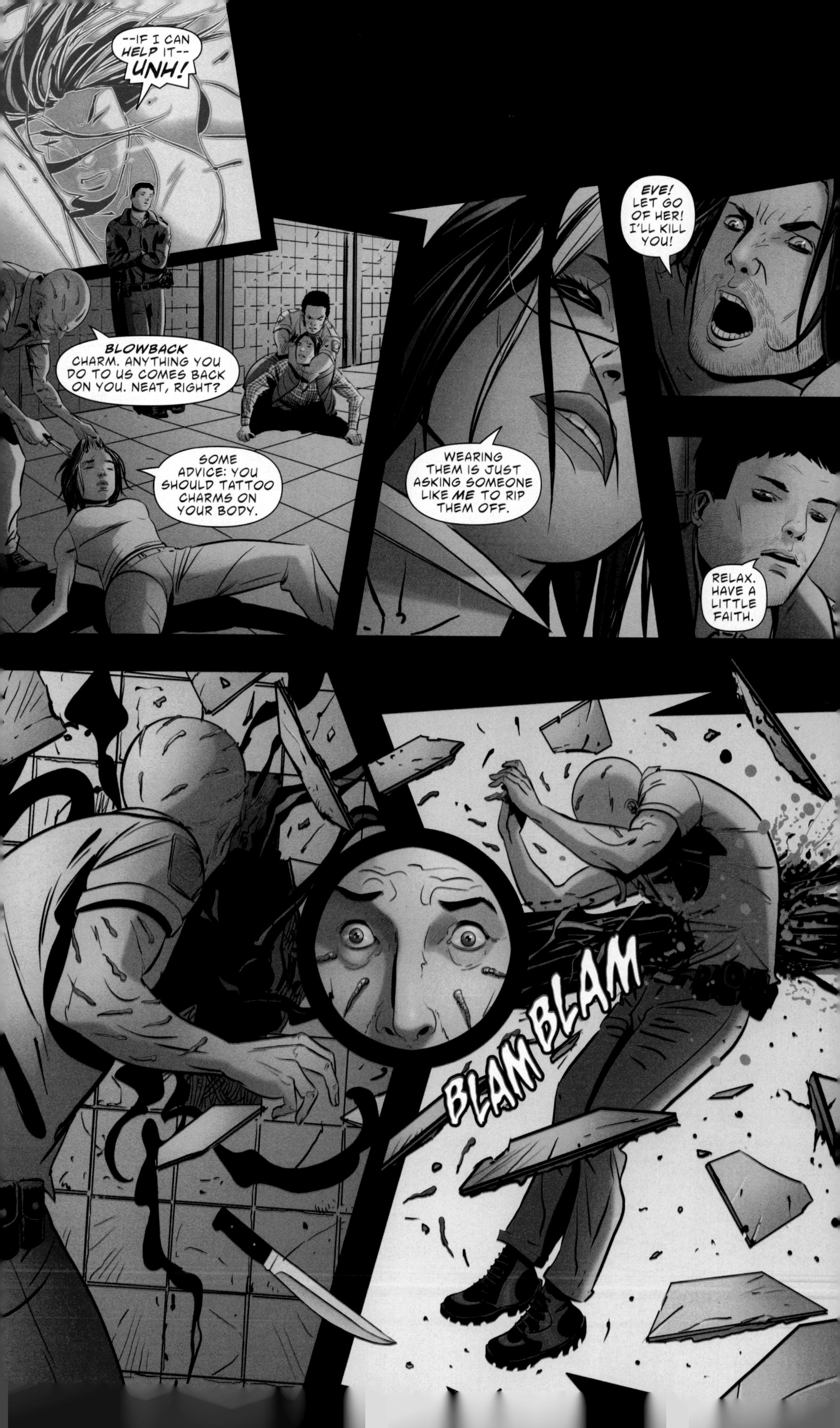

--IF I CAN HELP IT-- UNH!
BLOWBACK CHARM. ANYTHING YOU DO TO US COMES BACK ON YOU. NEAT, RIGHT?
SOME ADVICE: YOU SHOULD TATTOO CHARMS ON YOUR BODY.
WEARING THEM IS JUST ASKING SOMEONE LIKE ME TO RIP THEM OFF.
EVE! LET GO OF HER! I'LL KILL YOU!
RELAX. HAVE A LITTLE FAITH.
BLAM BLAM

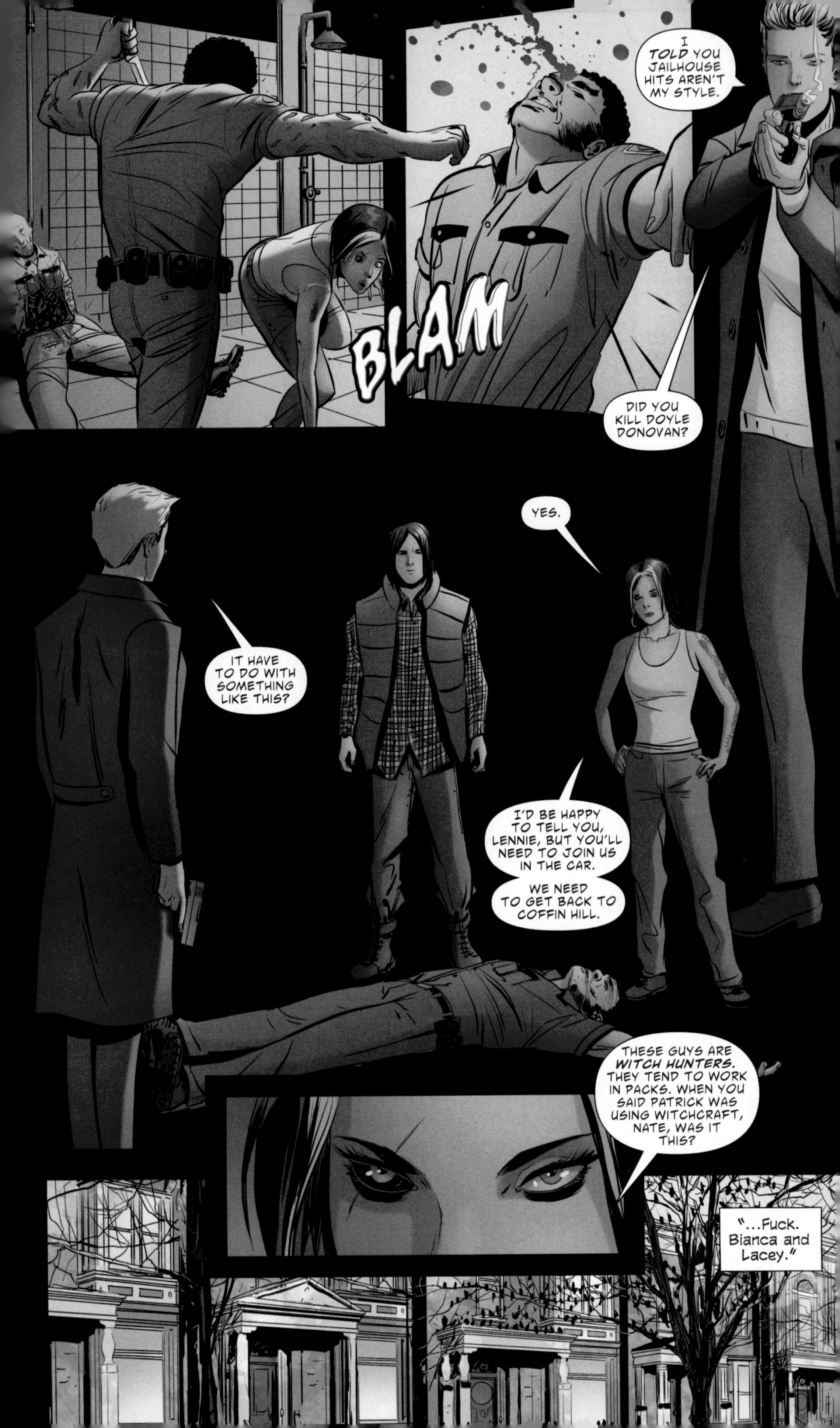
BLAM
I TOLD YOU JAILHOUSE HITS AREN'T MY STYLE.
DID YOU KILL DOYLE DONOVAN?
YES.
IT HAVE TO DO WITH SOMETHING LIKE THIS?
I'D BE HAPPY TO TELL YOU, LENNIE, BUT YOU'LL NEED TO JOIN US IN THE CAR.
WE NEED TO GET BACK TO COFFIN HILL.
THESE GUYS ARE WITCH HUNTERS. THEY TEND TO WORK IN PACKS. WHEN YOU SAID PATRICK WAS USING WITCHCRAFT, NATE, WAS IT THIS?
"...Fuck. Bianca and Lacey."

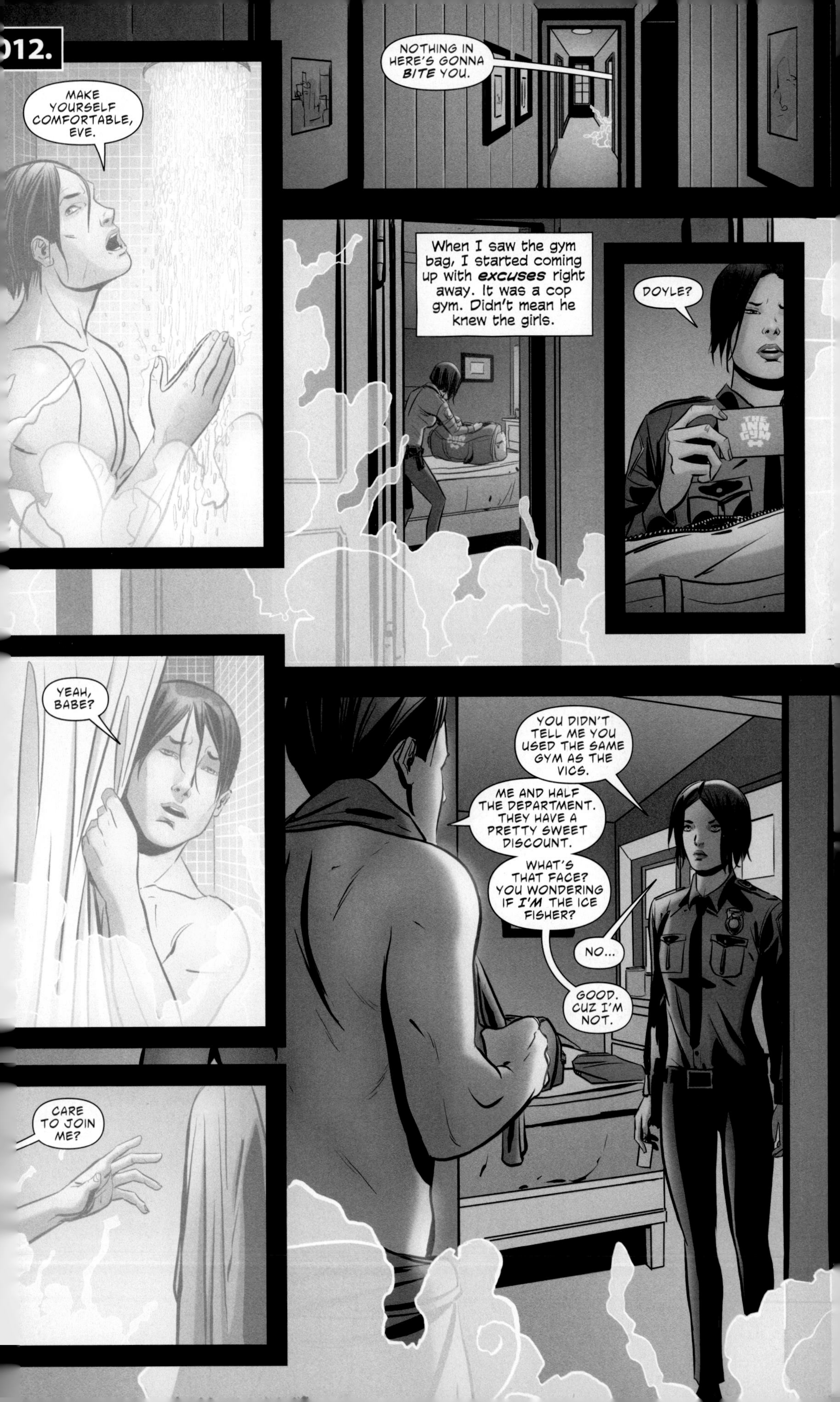
MAKE YOURSELF COMFORTABLE, EVE.
NOTHING IN HERE'S GONNA *BITE* YOU.
When I saw the gym bag, I started coming up with ***excuses*** right away. It was a cop gym. Didn't mean he knew the girls.
DOYLE?
THE INN GYM
YEAH, BABE?
YOU DIDN'T TELL ME YOU USED THE SAME GYM AS THE VICS.
ME AND HALF THE DEPARTMENT. THEY HAVE A PRETTY SWEET DISCOUNT.
WHAT'S THAT FACE? YOU WONDERING IF *I'M* THE ICE FISHER?
NO...
GOOD. CUZ I'M NOT.
CARE TO JOIN ME?

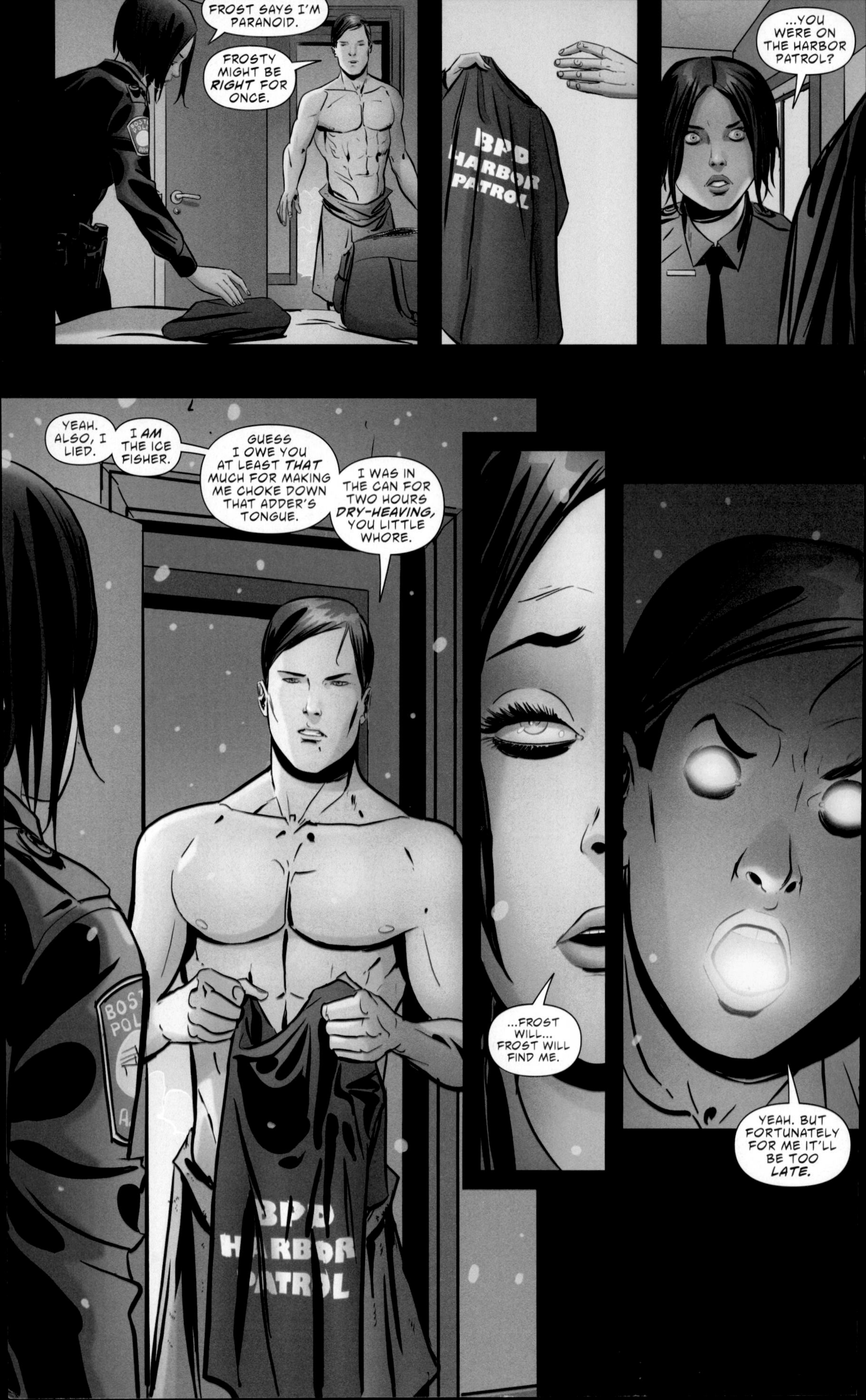
FROST SAYS I'M PARANOID.
FROSTY MIGHT BE RIGHT FOR ONCE.
BPD HARBOR PATROL
...YOU WERE ON THE HARBOR PATROL?
YEAH. ALSO, I LIED.
I AM THE ICE FISHER.
GUESS I OWE YOU AT LEAST THAT MUCH FOR MAKING ME CHOKE DOWN THAT ADDER'S TONGUE.
I WAS IN THE CAN FOR TWO HOURS DRY-HEAVING, YOU LITTLE WHORE.
BPD HARBOR PATROL
...FROST WILL... FROST WILL FIND ME.
YEAH. BUT FORTUNATELY FOR ME IT'LL BE TOO LATE.

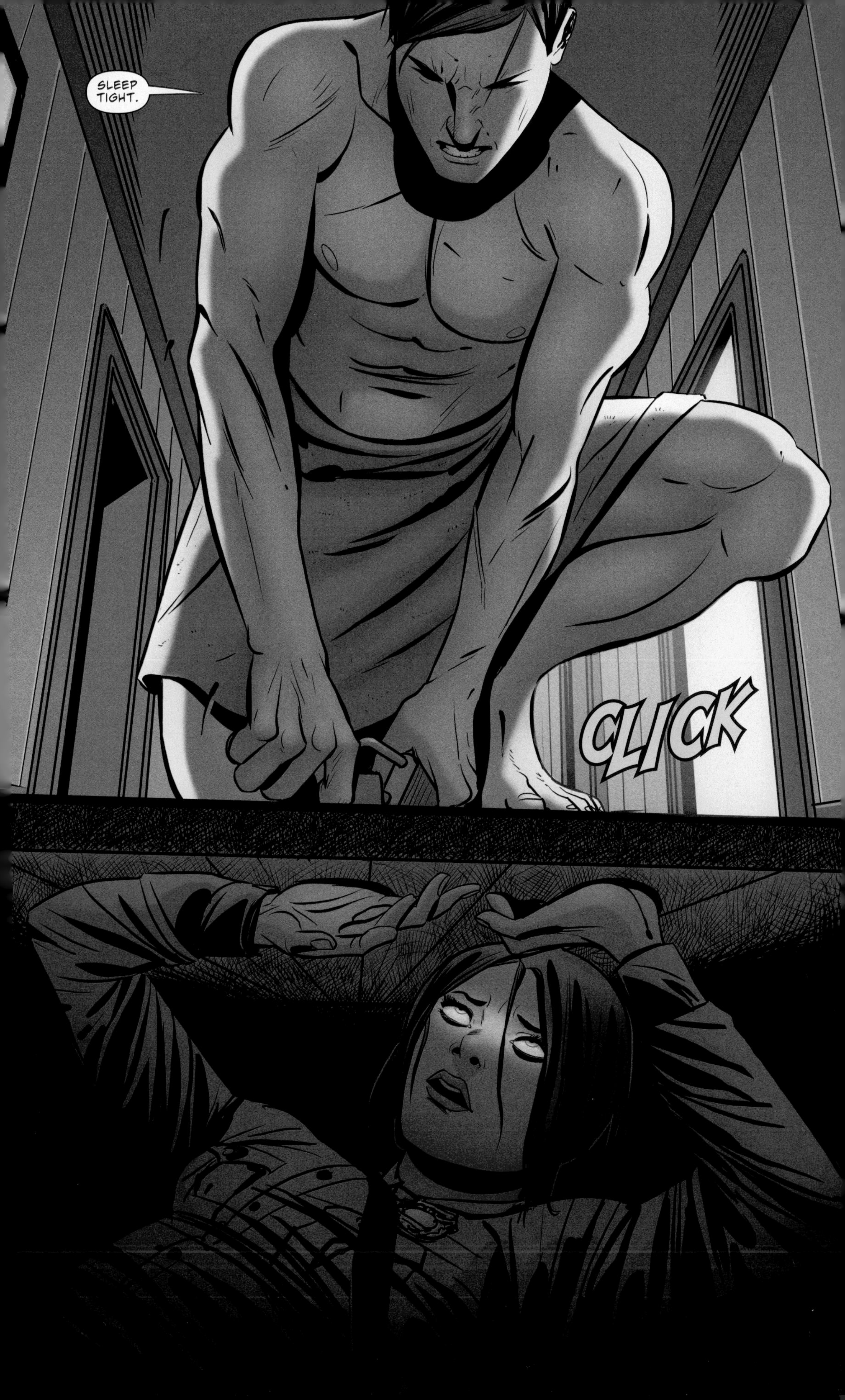
SLEEP TIGHT.
CLICK

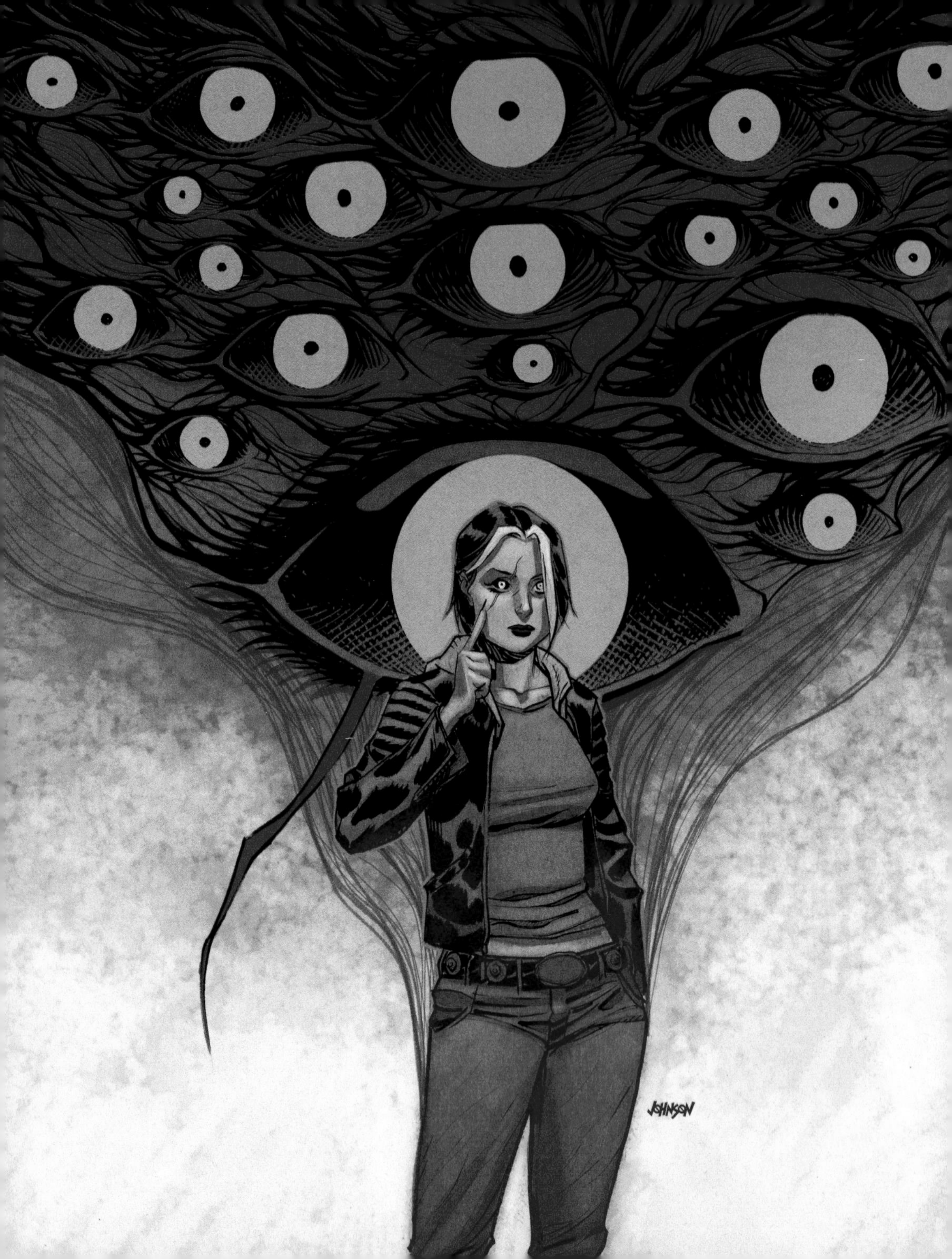
JOHNSON

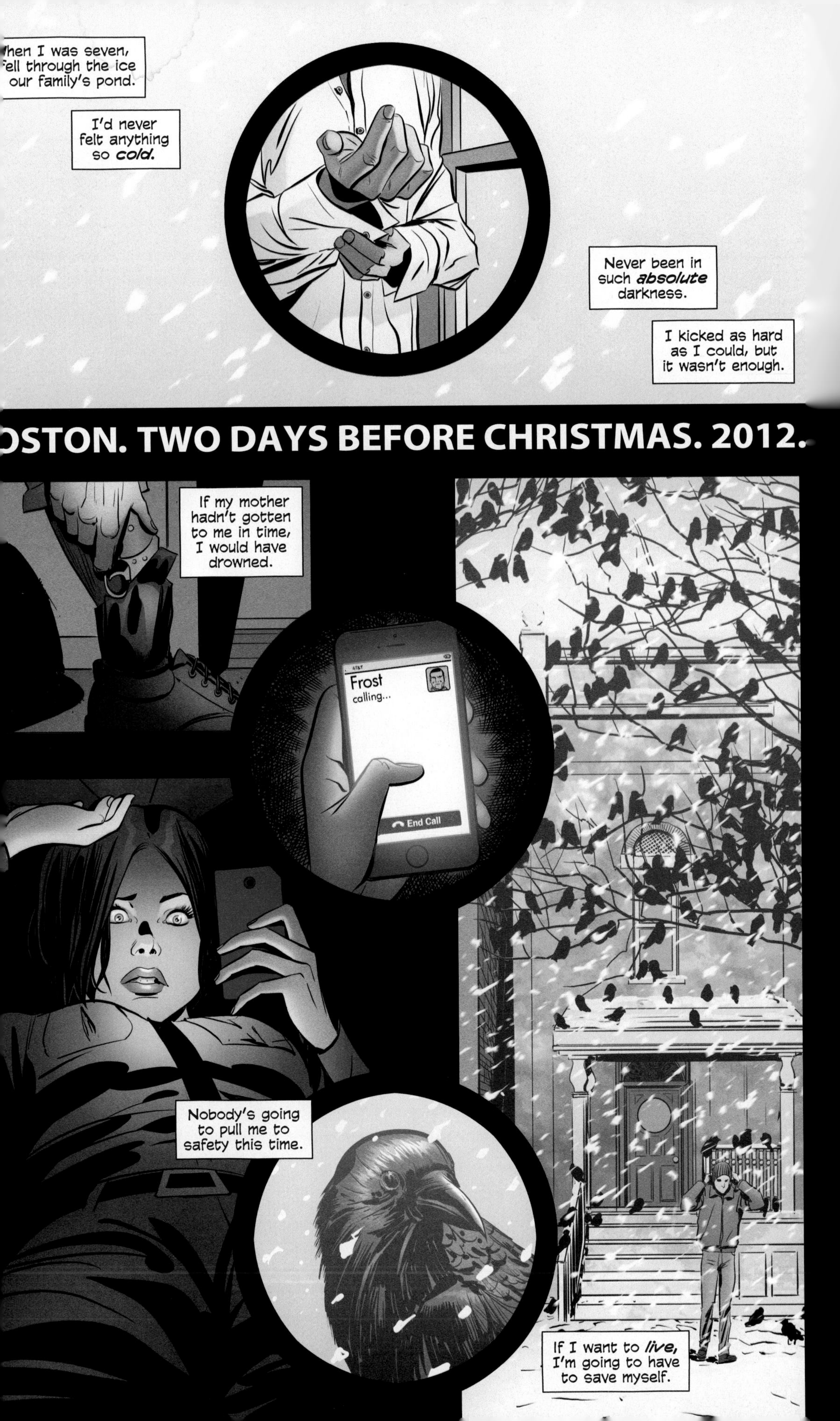

hen I was seven, fell through the ice our family's pond.
I'd never felt anything so *cold.*
Never been in such *absolute* darkness.
I kicked as hard as I could, but it wasn't enough.
OSTON. TWO DAYS BEFORE CHRISTMAS. 2012.
If my mother hadn't gotten to me in time, I would have drowned.
Frost
calling...
End Call
Nobody's going to pull me to safety this time.
If I want to *live,* I'm going to have to save myself.

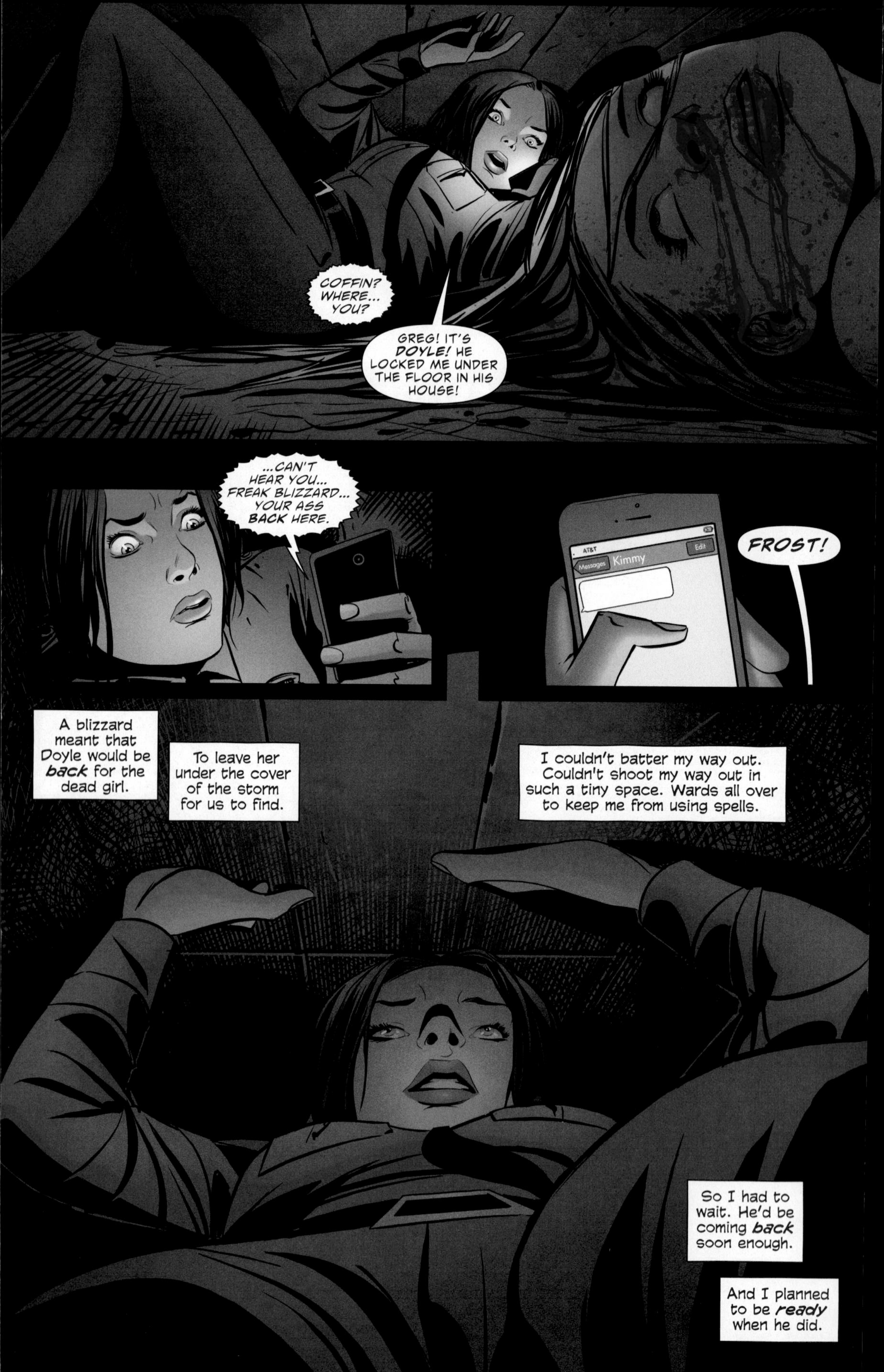
COFFIN? WHERE... YOU?
GREG! IT'S DOYLE! HE LOCKED ME UNDER THE FLOOR IN HIS HOUSE!
...CAN'T HEAR YOU... FREAK BLIZZARD... YOUR ASS BACK HERE.
AT&T
Messages
Kimmy
Edit
FROST!
A blizzard meant that Doyle would be back for the dead girl.
To leave her under the cover of the storm for us to find.
I couldn't batter my way out. Couldn't shoot my way out in such a tiny space. Wards all over to keep me from using spells.
So I had to wait. He'd be coming back soon enough.
And I planned to be ready when he did.

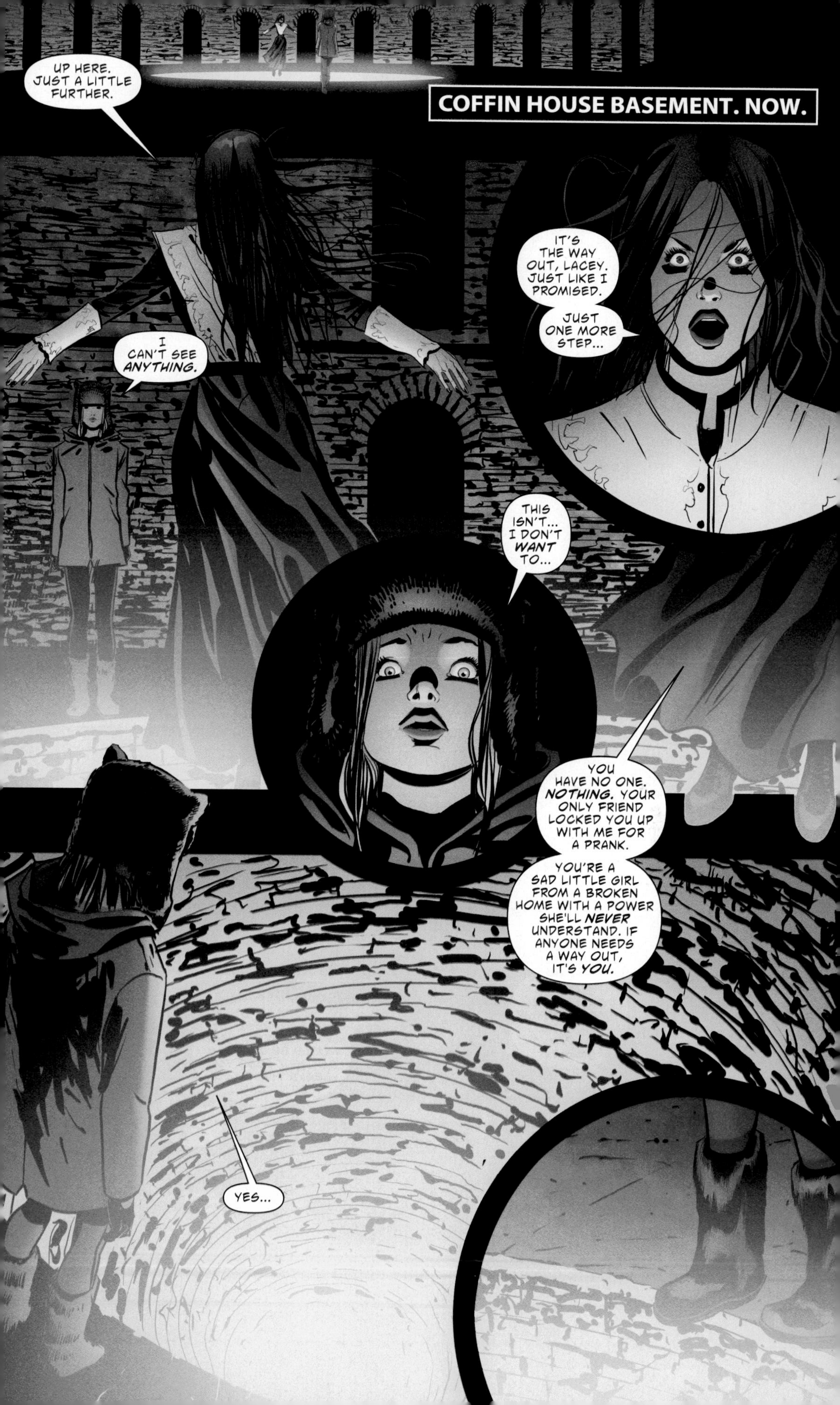
UP HERE. JUST A LITTLE FURTHER.
COFFIN HOUSE BASEMENT. NOW.
I CAN'T SEE *ANYTHING.*
IT'S THE WAY OUT, LACEY. JUST LIKE I PROMISED.
JUST ONE MORE STEP...
THIS ISN'T... I DON'T *WANT* TO...
YOU HAVE NO ONE. *NOTHING.* YOUR ONLY FRIEND LOCKED YOU UP WITH ME FOR A PRANK.
YOU'RE A SAD LITTLE GIRL FROM A BROKEN HOME WITH A POWER SHE'LL *NEVER* UNDERSTAND. IF ANYONE NEEDS A WAY OUT, IT'S *YOU.*
YES...

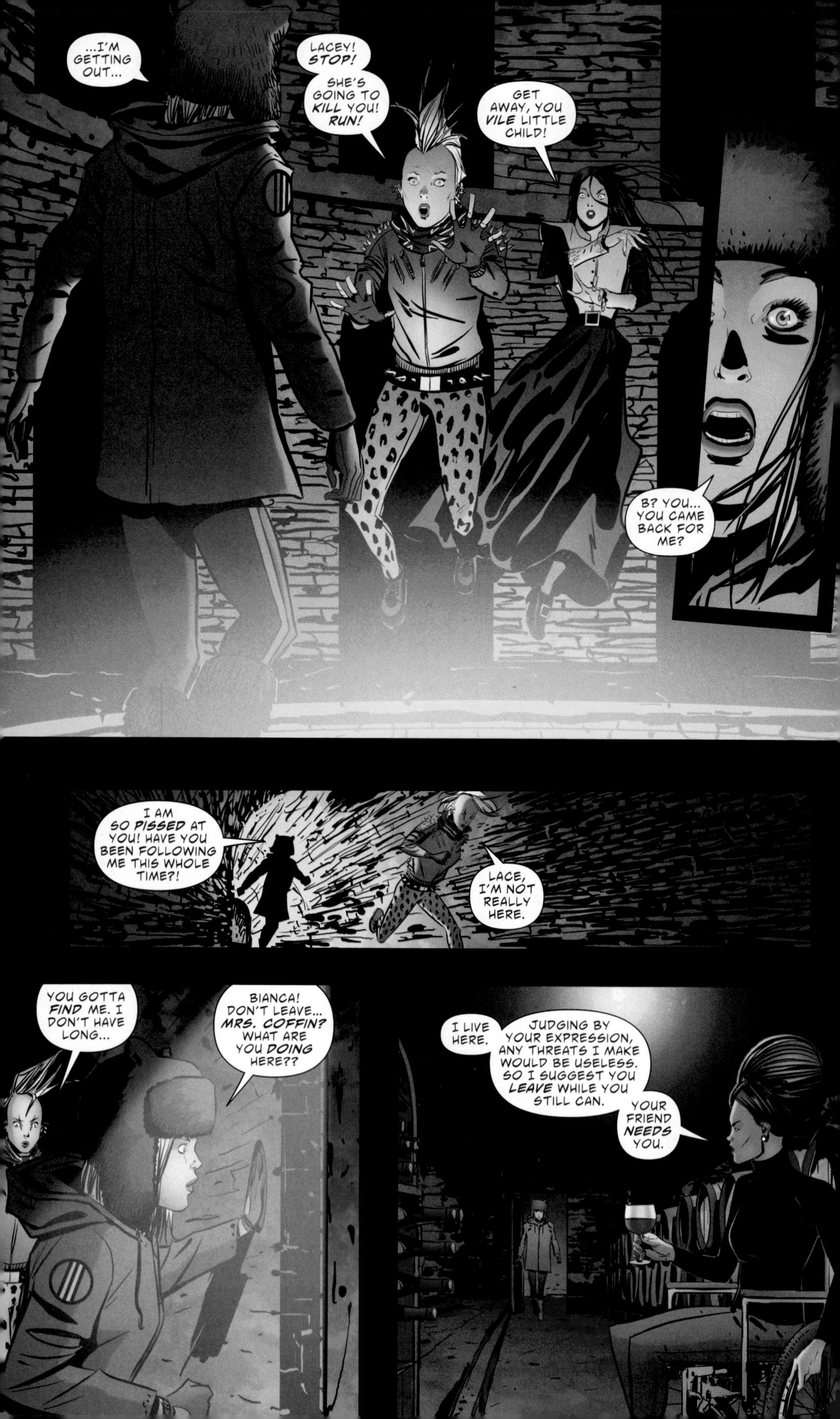
...I'M GETTING OUT...
LACEY! STOP!
SHE'S GOING TO KILL YOU! RUN!
GET AWAY, YOU VILE LITTLE CHILD!
B? YOU... YOU CAME BACK FOR ME?
I AM SO PISSED AT YOU! HAVE YOU BEEN FOLLOWING ME THIS WHOLE TIME?!
LACE, I'M NOT REALLY HERE.
YOU GOTTA FIND ME. I DON'T HAVE LONG...
BIANCA! DON'T LEAVE... MRS. COFFIN? WHAT ARE YOU DOING HERE??
I LIVE HERE.
JUDGING BY YOUR EXPRESSION, ANY THREATS I MAKE WOULD BE USELESS. SO I SUGGEST YOU LEAVE WHILE YOU STILL CAN.
YOUR FRIEND NEEDS YOU.

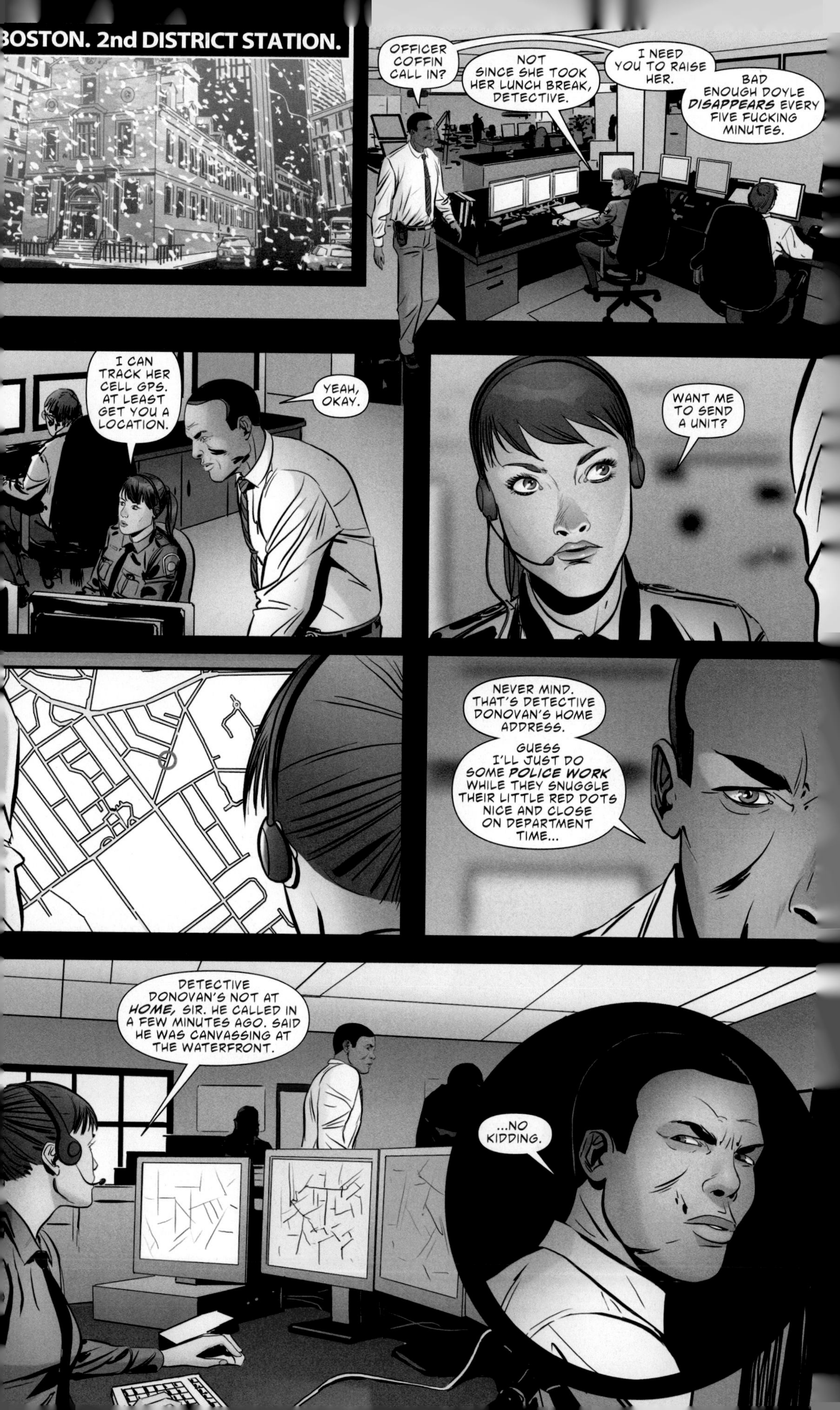
BOSTON. 2nd DISTRICT STATION.
OFFICER COFFIN CALL IN?
NOT SINCE SHE TOOK HER LUNCH BREAK, DETECTIVE.
I NEED YOU TO RAISE HER.
BAD ENOUGH DOYLE DISAPPEARS EVERY FIVE FUCKING MINUTES.
I CAN TRACK HER CELL GPS. AT LEAST GET YOU A LOCATION.
YEAH, OKAY.
WANT ME TO SEND A UNIT?
NEVER MIND. THAT'S DETECTIVE DONOVAN'S HOME ADDRESS.
GUESS I'LL JUST DO SOME POLICE WORK WHILE THEY SNUGGLE THEIR LITTLE RED DOTS NICE AND CLOSE ON DEPARTMENT TIME...
DETECTIVE DONOVAN'S NOT AT HOME, SIR. HE CALLED IN A FEW MINUTES AGO. SAID HE WAS CANVASSING AT THE WATERFRONT.
...NO KIDDING.

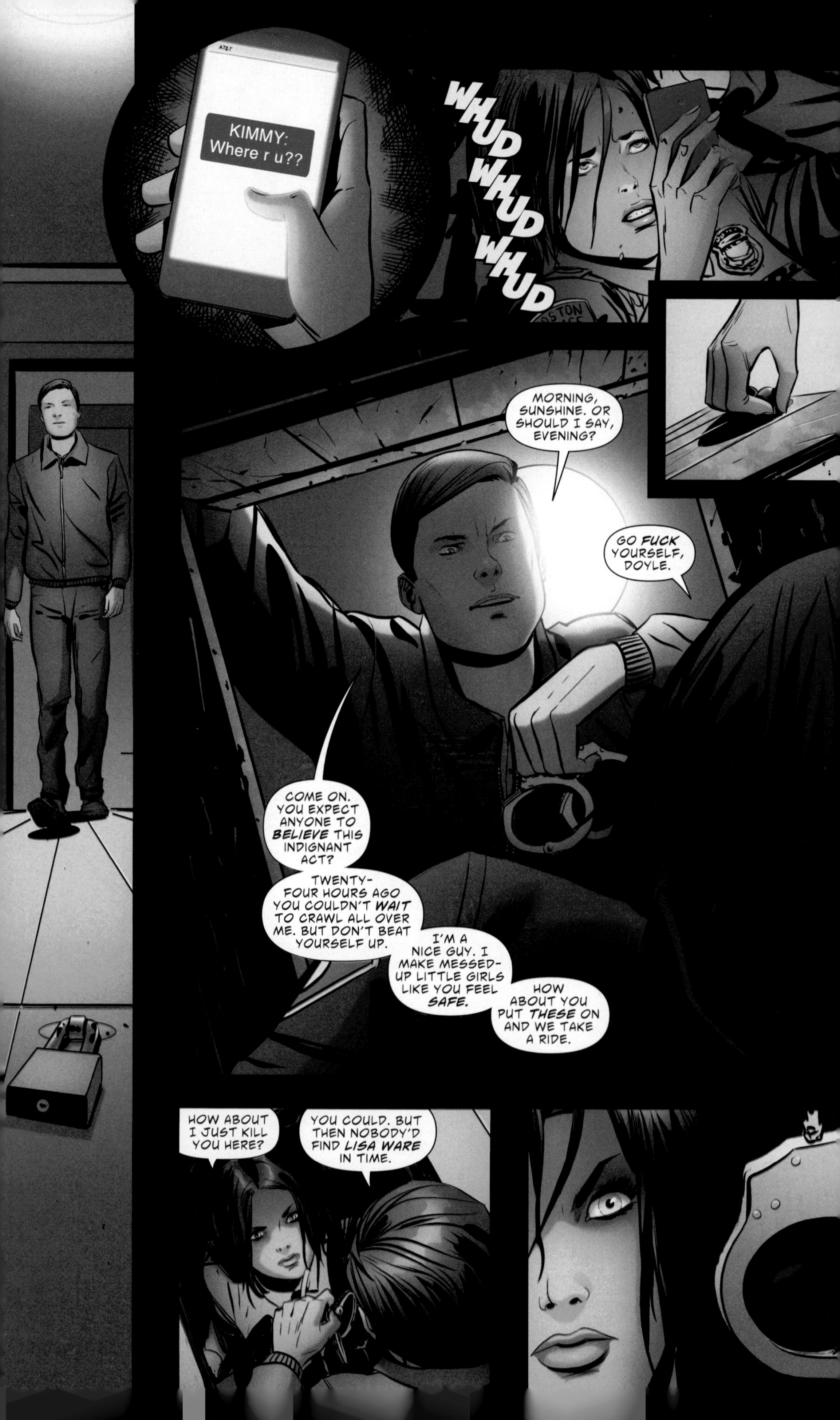
AT&T
KIMMY: Where r u??
WHUD WHUD WHUD
MORNING, SUNSHINE. OR SHOULD I SAY, EVENING?
GO FUCK YOURSELF, DOYLE.
COME ON. YOU EXPECT ANYONE TO BELIEVE THIS INDIGNANT ACT?
TWENTY-FOUR HOURS AGO YOU COULDN'T WAIT TO CRAWL ALL OVER ME. BUT DON'T BEAT YOURSELF UP.
I'M A NICE GUY. I MAKE MESSED-UP LITTLE GIRLS LIKE YOU FEEL SAFE.
HOW ABOUT YOU PUT THESE ON AND WE TAKE A RIDE.
HOW ABOUT I JUST KILL YOU HERE?
YOU COULD. BUT THEN NOBODY'D FIND LISA WARE IN TIME.

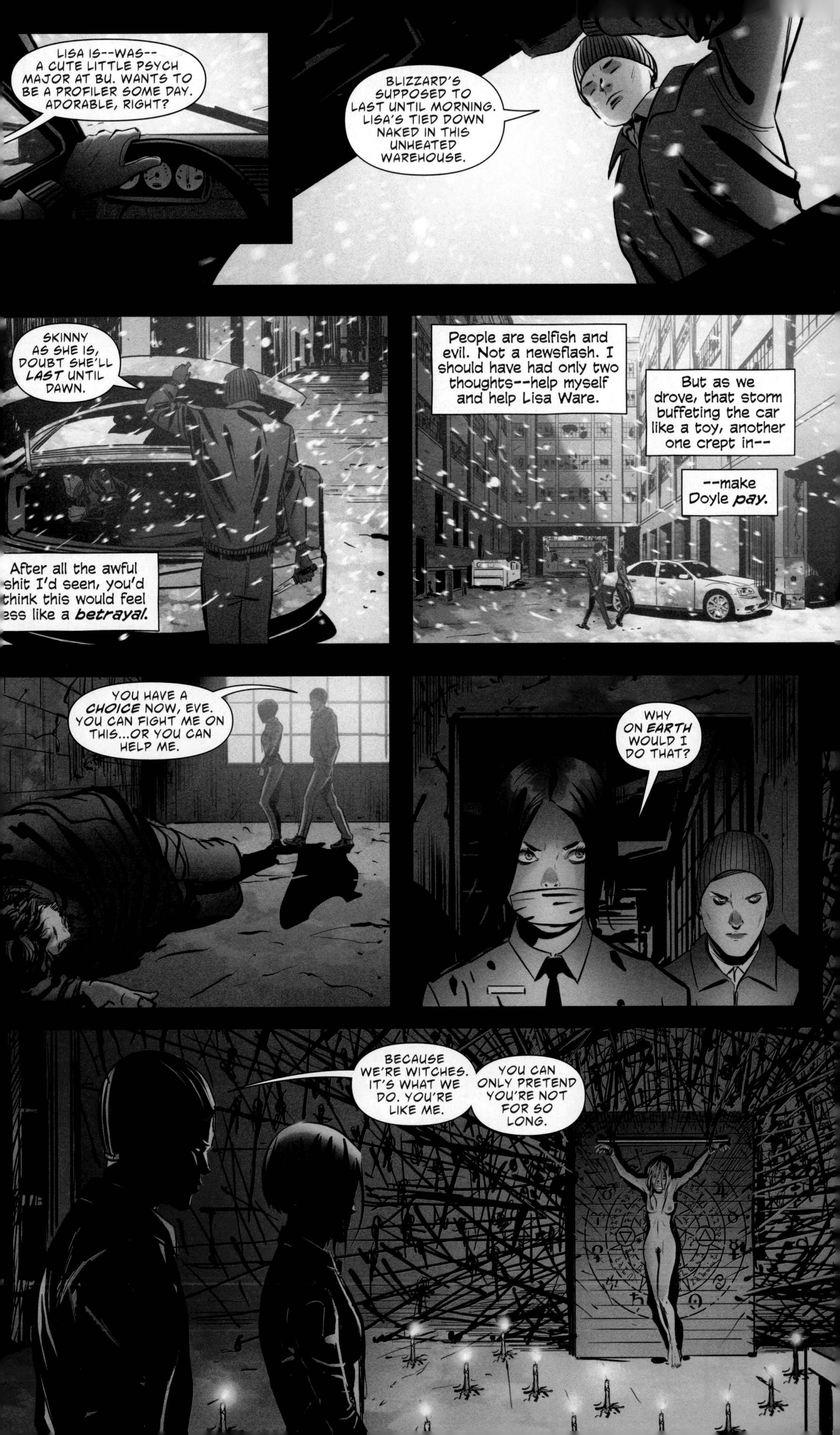
LISA IS--WAS-- A CUTE LITTLE PSYCH MAJOR AT BU. WANTS TO BE A PROFILER SOME DAY. ADORABLE, RIGHT?
BLIZZARD'S SUPPOSED TO LAST UNTIL MORNING. LISA'S TIED DOWN NAKED IN THIS UNHEATED WAREHOUSE.
SKINNY AS SHE IS, DOUBT SHE'LL LAST UNTIL DAWN.
After all the awful shit I'd seen, you'd think this would feel less like a betrayal.
People are selfish and evil. Not a newsflash. I should have had only two thoughts--help myself and help Lisa Ware.
But as we drove, that storm buffeting the car like a toy, another one crept in--
--make Doyle pay.
YOU HAVE A CHOICE NOW, EVE. YOU CAN FIGHT ME ON THIS...OR YOU CAN HELP ME.
WHY ON EARTH WOULD I DO THAT?
BECAUSE WE'RE WITCHES. IT'S WHAT WE DO. YOU'RE LIKE ME.
YOU CAN ONLY PRETEND YOU'RE NOT FOR SO LONG.

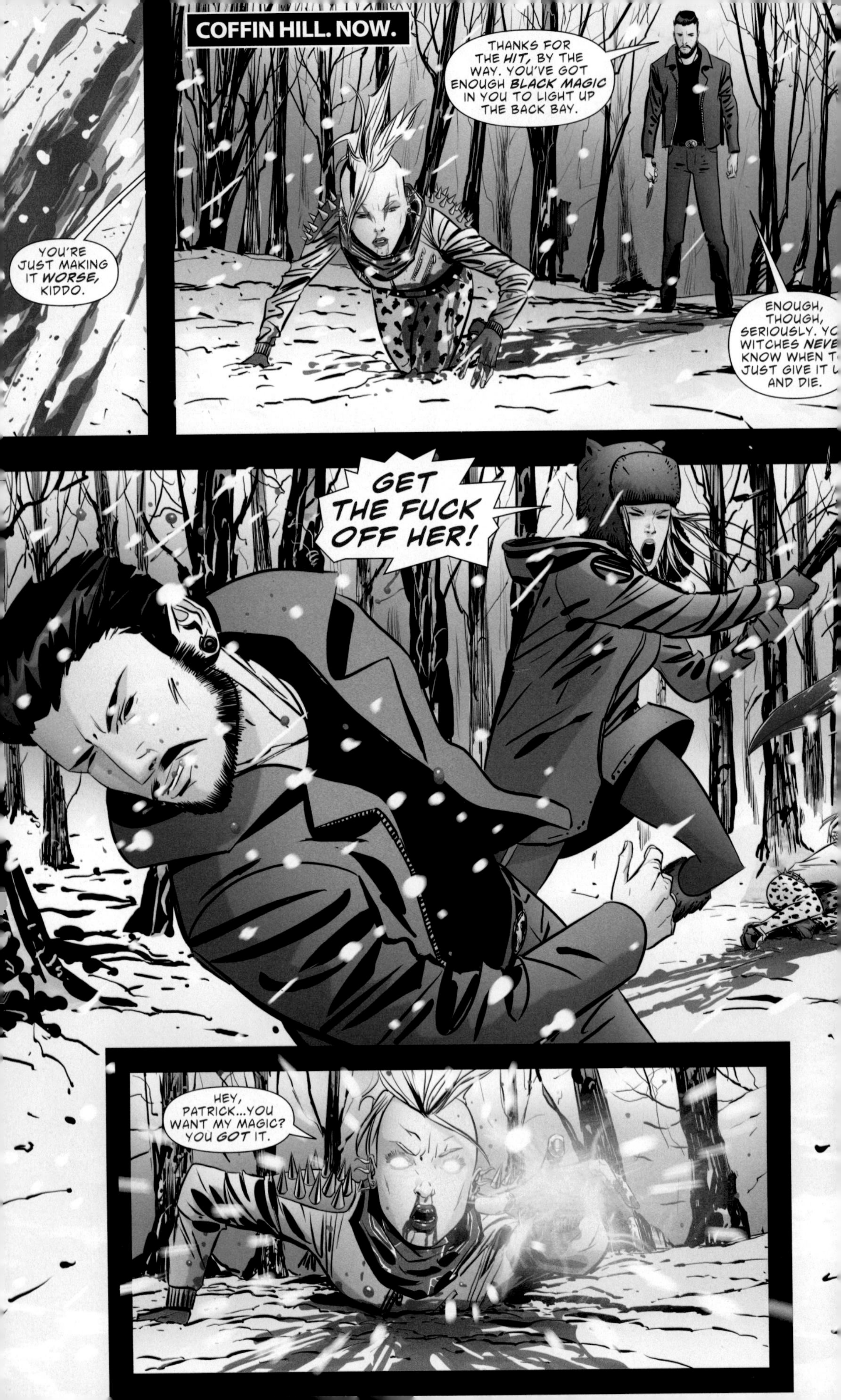
COFFIN HILL. NOW.
THANKS FOR THE HIT, BY THE WAY. YOU'VE GOT ENOUGH BLACK MAGIC IN YOU TO LIGHT UP THE BACK BAY.
YOU'RE JUST MAKING IT WORSE, KIDDO.
ENOUGH, THOUGH, SERIOUSLY. YO WITCHES NEVE KNOW WHEN T JUST GIVE IT U AND DIE.
GET THE FUCK OFF HER!
HEY, PATRICK...YOU WANT MY MAGIC? YOU GOT IT.

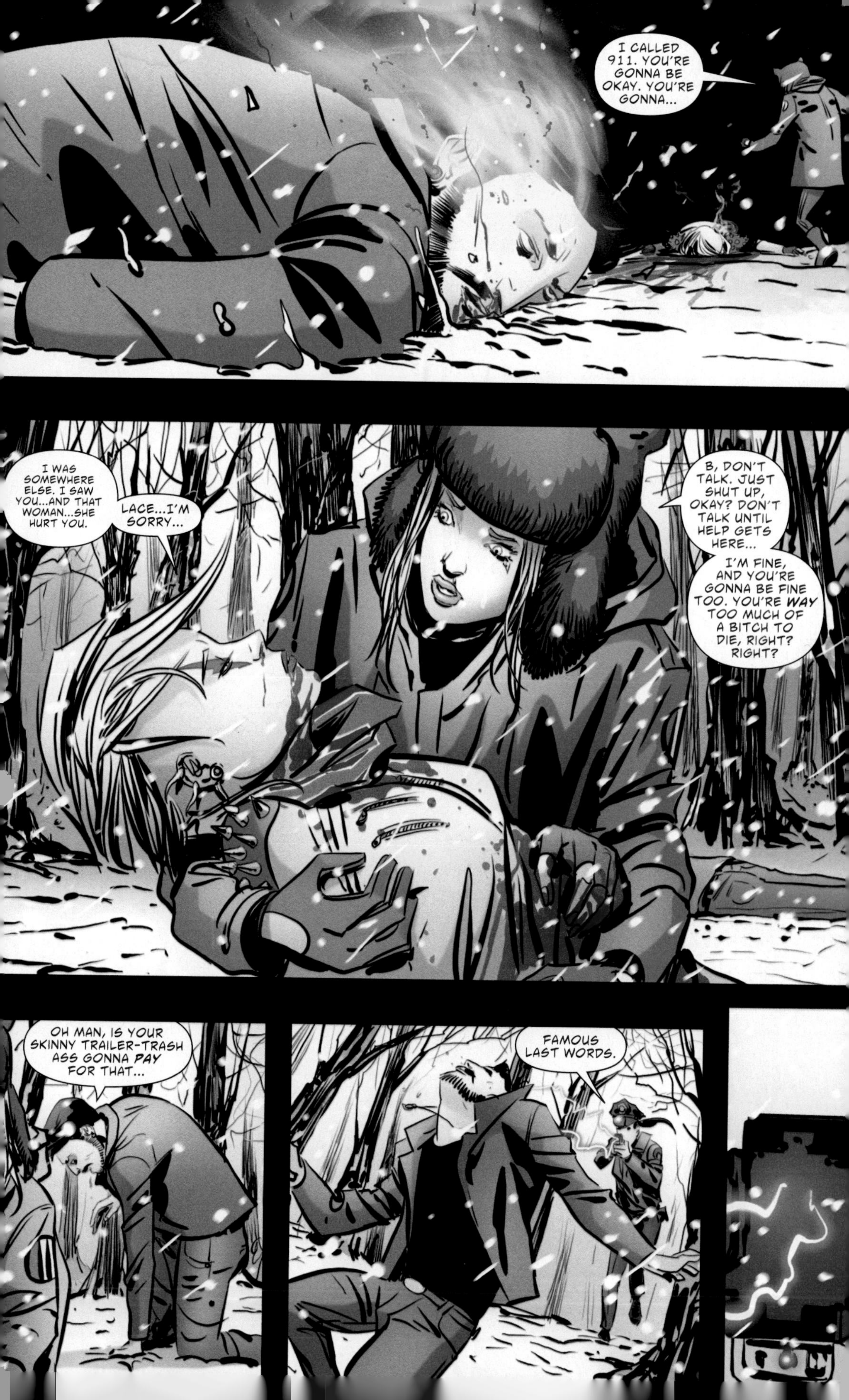
I CALLED 911. YOU'RE GONNA BE OKAY. YOU'RE GONNA...
I WAS SOMEWHERE ELSE. I SAW YOU...AND THAT WOMAN...SHE HURT YOU.
LACE...I'M SORRY...
B, DON'T TALK. JUST SHUT UP, OKAY? DON'T TALK UNTIL HELP GETS HERE...
I'M FINE, AND YOU'RE GONNA BE FINE TOO. YOU'RE WAY TOO MUCH OF A BITCH TO DIE, RIGHT? RIGHT?
OH MAN, IS YOUR SKINNY TRAILER-TRASH ASS GONNA PAY FOR THAT...
FAMOUS LAST WORDS.

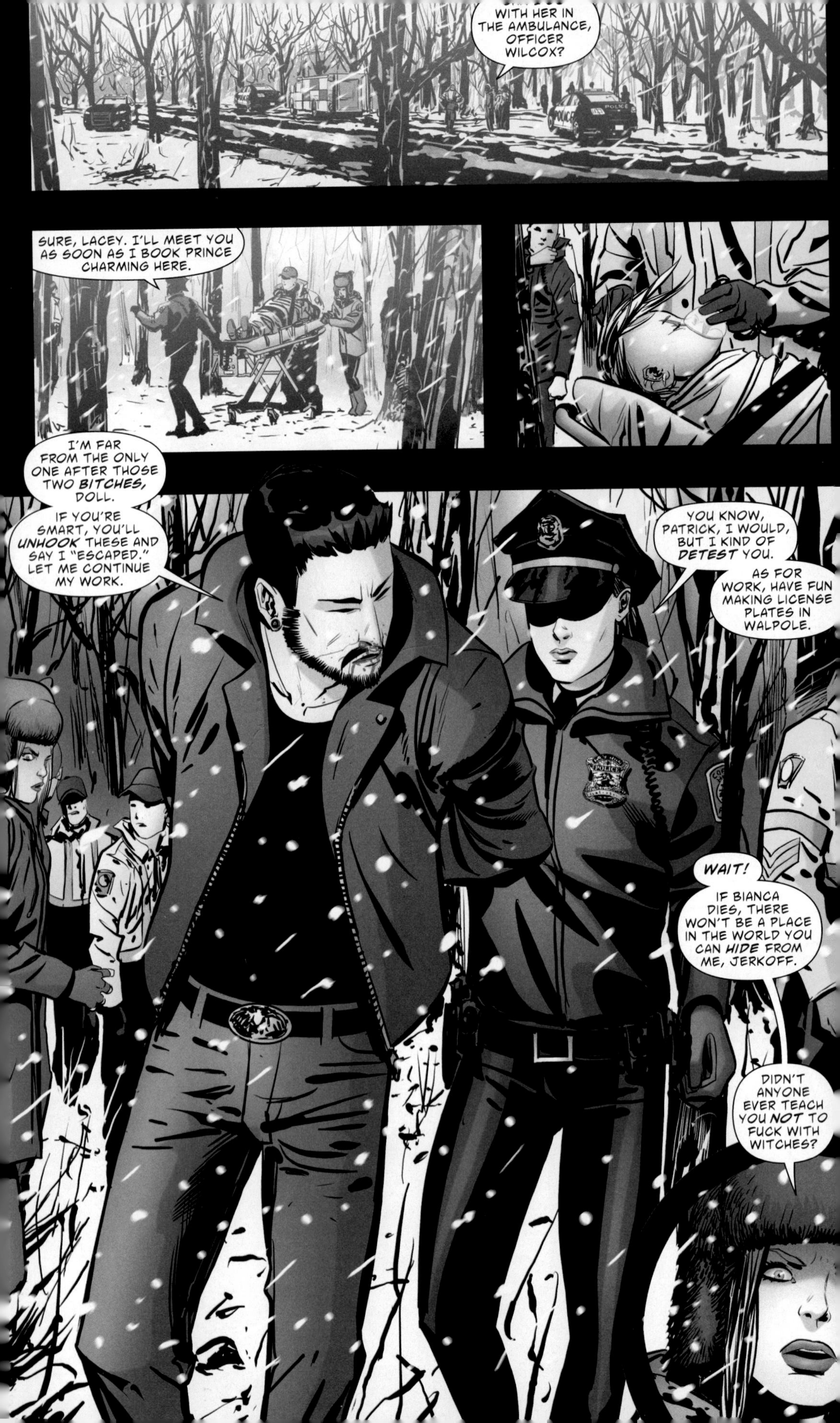

WITH HER IN THE AMBULANCE, OFFICER WILCOX?
SURE, LACEY. I'LL MEET YOU AS SOON AS I BOOK PRINCE CHARMING HERE.
I'M FAR FROM THE ONLY ONE AFTER THOSE TWO BITCHES, DOLL.
IF YOU'RE SMART, YOU'LL UNHOOK THESE AND SAY I "ESCAPED." LET ME CONTINUE MY WORK.
YOU KNOW, PATRICK, I WOULD, BUT I KIND OF DETEST YOU.
AS FOR WORK, HAVE FUN MAKING LICENSE PLATES IN WALPOLE.
WAIT!
IF BIANCA DIES, THERE WON'T BE A PLACE IN THE WORLD YOU CAN HIDE FROM ME, JERKOFF.
DIDN'T ANYONE EVER TEACH YOU NOT TO FUCK WITH WITCHES?

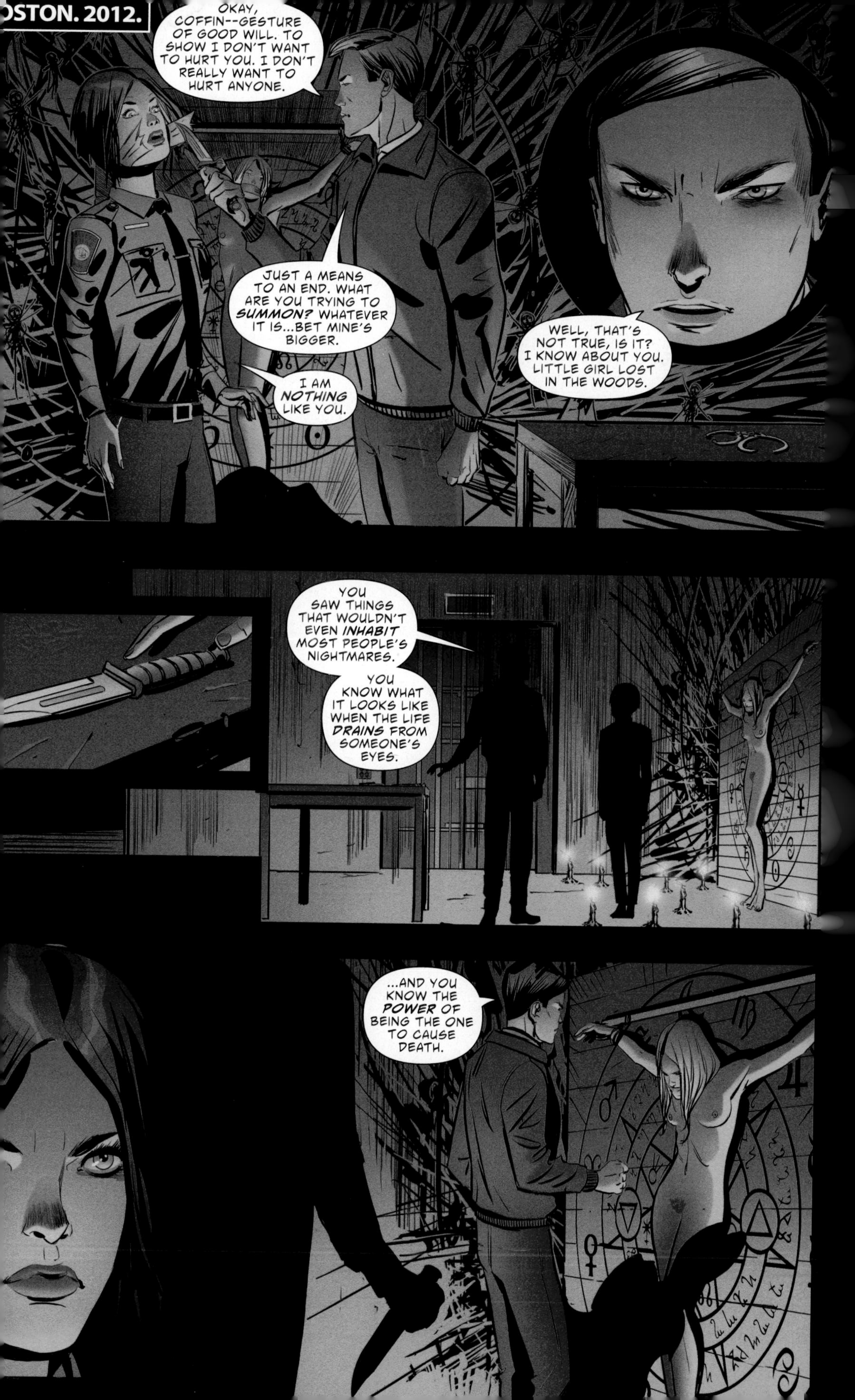
OSTON. 2012.
OKAY, COFFIN--GESTURE OF GOOD WILL. TO SHOW I DON'T WANT TO HURT YOU. I DON'T REALLY WANT TO HURT ANYONE.
JUST A MEANS TO AN END. WHAT ARE YOU TRYING TO SUMMON? WHATEVER IT IS...BET MINE'S BIGGER.
I AM NOTHING LIKE YOU.
WELL, THAT'S NOT TRUE, IS IT? I KNOW ABOUT YOU. LITTLE GIRL LOST IN THE WOODS.
YOU SAW THINGS THAT WOULDN'T EVEN INHABIT MOST PEOPLE'S NIGHTMARES.
YOU KNOW WHAT IT LOOKS LIKE WHEN THE LIFE DRAINS FROM SOMEONE'S EYES.
...AND YOU KNOW THE POWER OF BEING THE ONE TO CAUSE DEATH.

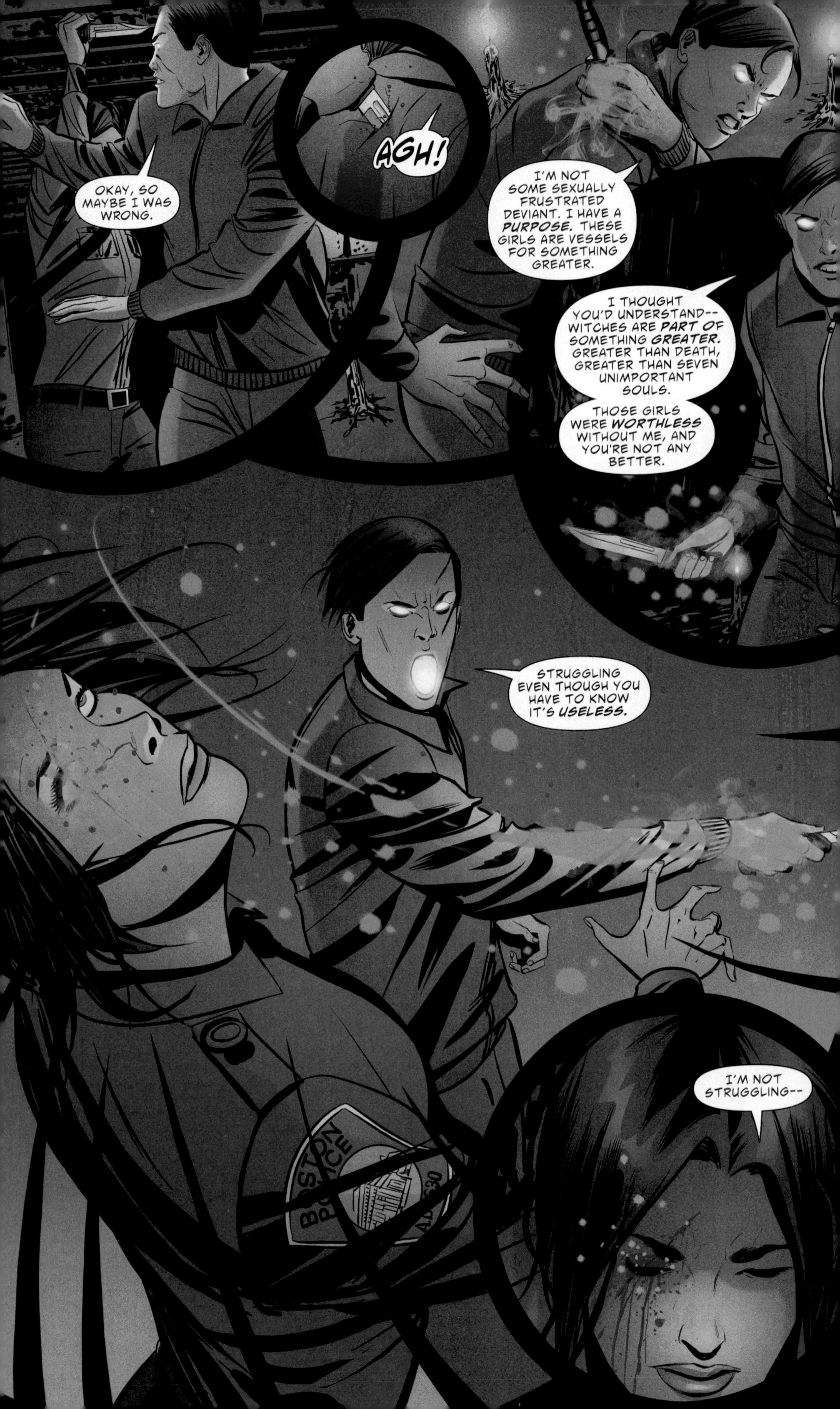
OKAY, SO MAYBE I WAS WRONG.
AGH!
I'M NOT SOME SEXUALLY FRUSTRATED DEVIANT. I HAVE A *PURPOSE.* THESE GIRLS ARE VESSELS FOR SOMETHING GREATER.
I THOUGHT YOU'D UNDERSTAND-- WITCHES ARE *PART OF* SOMETHING *GREATER.* GREATER THAN DEATH, GREATER THAN SEVEN UNIMPORTANT SOULS.
THOSE GIRLS WERE *WORTHLESS* WITHOUT ME, AND YOU'RE NOT ANY BETTER.
STRUGGLING EVEN THOUGH YOU HAVE TO KNOW IT'S *USELESS.*
I'M NOT STRUGGLING--
BOSTON POLICE

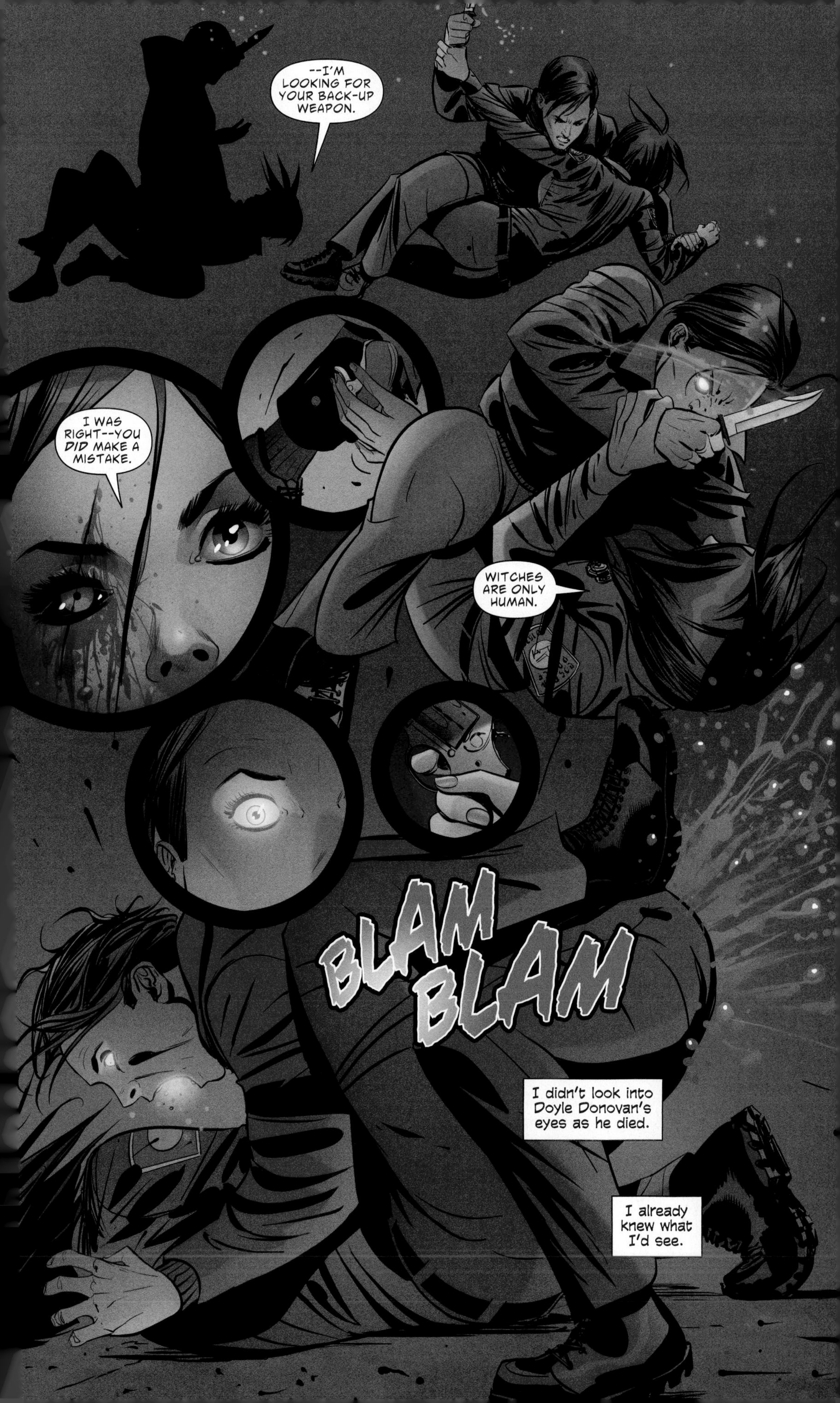
--I'M LOOKING FOR YOUR BACK-UP WEAPON.
I WAS RIGHT--YOU *DID* MAKE A MISTAKE.
WITCHES ARE ONLY HUMAN.
BLAM
BLAM
I didn't look into Doyle Donovan's eyes as he died.
I already knew what I'd see.

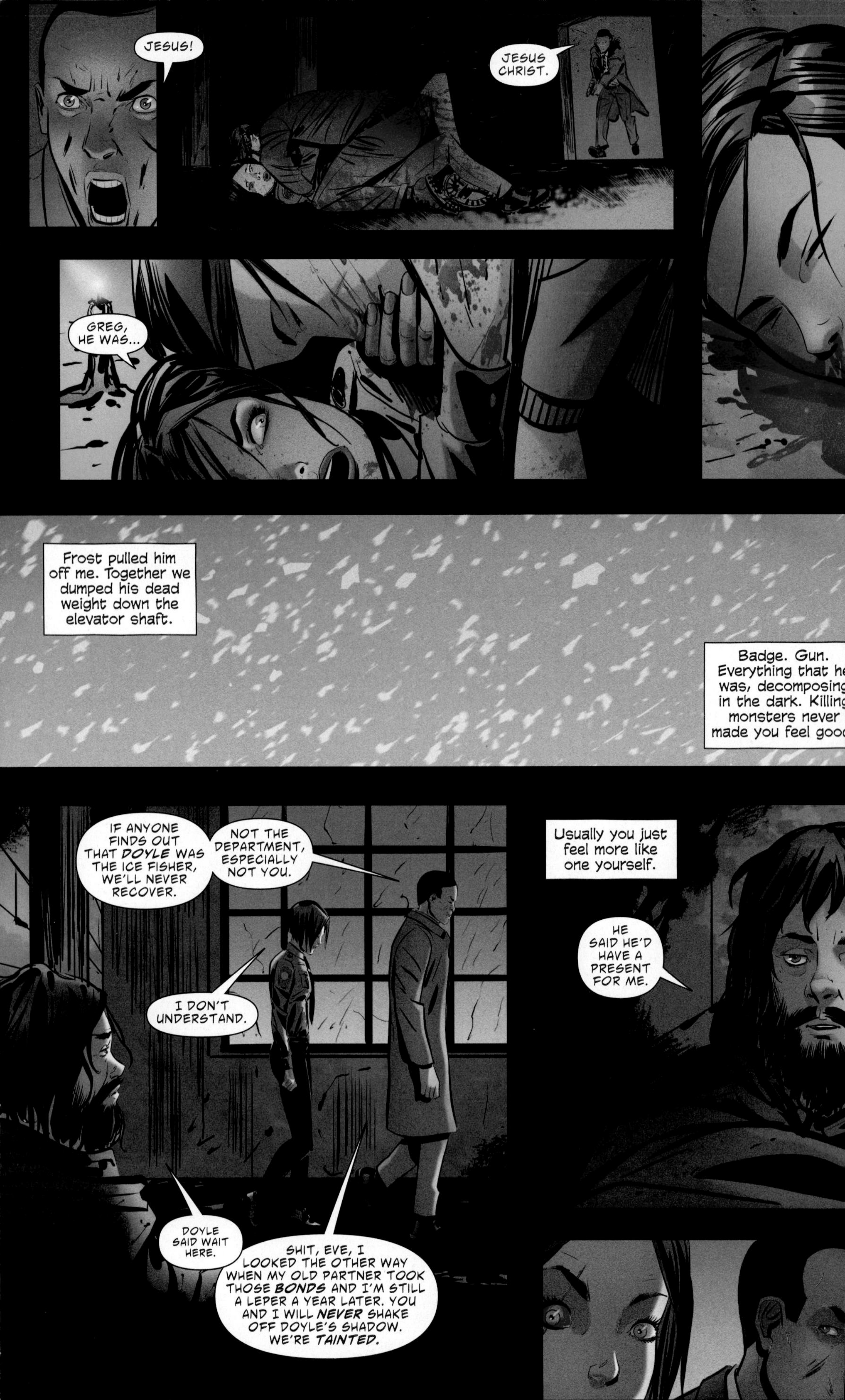
JESUS!
JESUS CHRIST.
GREG, HE WAS...
Frost pulled him off me. Together we dumped his dead weight down the elevator shaft.
Badge. Gun. Everything that he was, decomposing in the dark. Killing monsters never made you feel good.
IF ANYONE FINDS OUT THAT DOYLE WAS THE ICE FISHER, WE'LL NEVER RECOVER.
NOT THE DEPARTMENT, ESPECIALLY NOT YOU.
I DON'T UNDERSTAND.
SHIT, EVE, I LOOKED THE OTHER WAY WHEN MY OLD PARTNER TOOK THOSE BONDS AND I'M STILL A LEPER A YEAR LATER. YOU AND I WILL NEVER SHAKE OFF DOYLE'S SHADOW. WE'RE TAINTED.
Usually you just feel more like one yourself.
HE SAID HE'D HAVE A PRESENT FOR ME.
DOYLE SAID WAIT HERE.

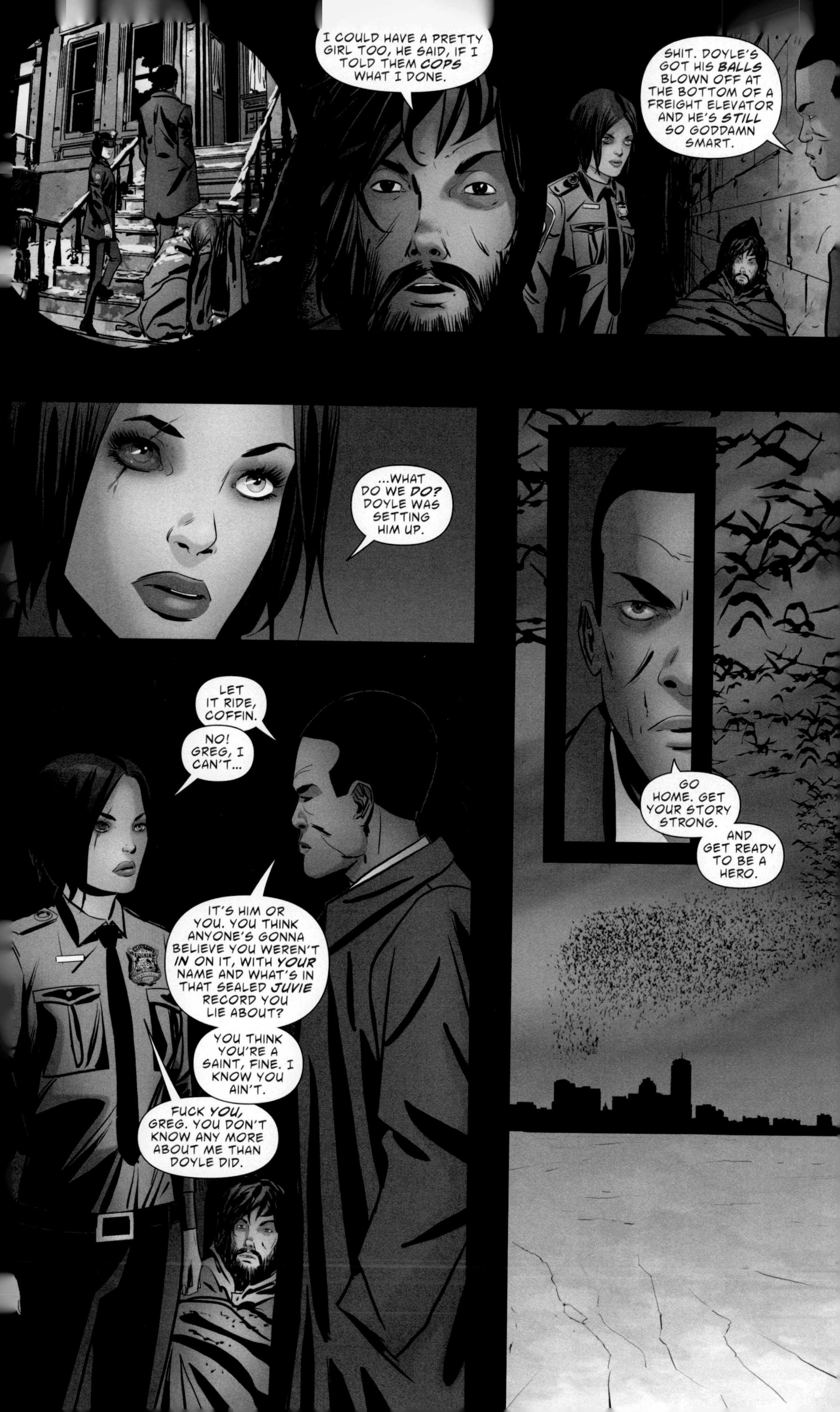
I COULD HAVE A PRETTY GIRL TOO, HE SAID, IF I TOLD THEM COPS WHAT I DONE.
SHIT. DOYLE'S GOT HIS BALLS BLOWN OFF AT THE BOTTOM OF A FREIGHT ELEVATOR AND HE'S STILL SO GODDAMN SMART.
...WHAT DO WE DO? DOYLE WAS SETTING HIM UP.
LET IT RIDE, COFFIN.
NO! GREG, I CAN'T...
IT'S HIM OR YOU. YOU THINK ANYONE'S GONNA BELIEVE YOU WEREN'T IN ON IT, WITH YOUR NAME AND WHAT'S IN THAT SEALED JUVIE RECORD YOU LIE ABOUT?
YOU THINK YOU'RE A SAINT, FINE. I KNOW YOU AIN'T.
FUCK YOU, GREG. YOU DON'T KNOW ANY MORE ABOUT ME THAN DOYLE DID.
GO HOME. GET YOUR STORY STRONG.
AND GET READY TO BE A HERO.

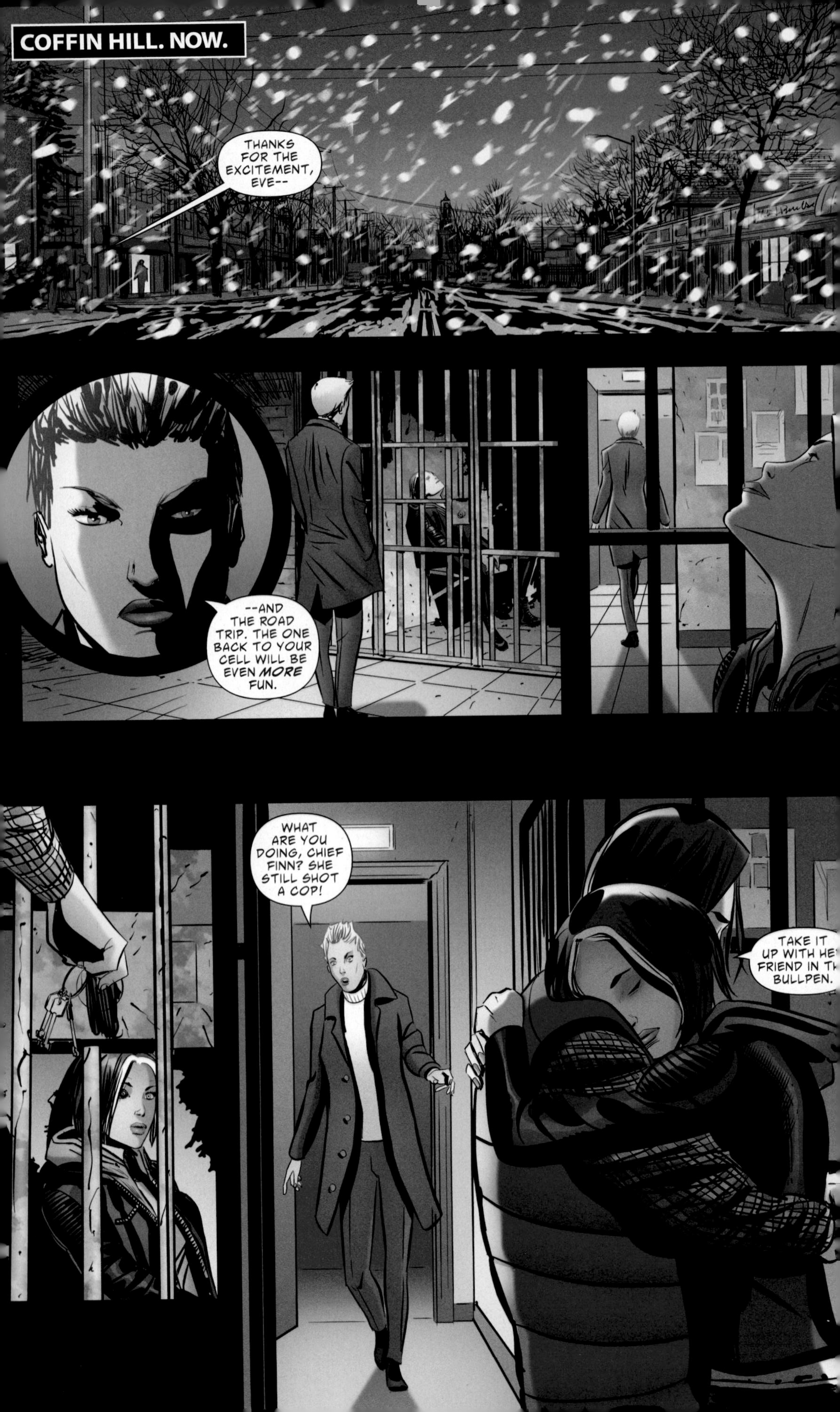
COFFIN HILL. NOW.
THANKS FOR THE EXCITEMENT, EVE--
--AND THE ROAD TRIP. THE ONE BACK TO YOUR CELL WILL BE EVEN MORE FUN.
WHAT ARE YOU DOING, CHIEF FINN? SHE STILL SHOT A COP!
TAKE IT UP WITH HE FRIEND IN TH BULLPEN.

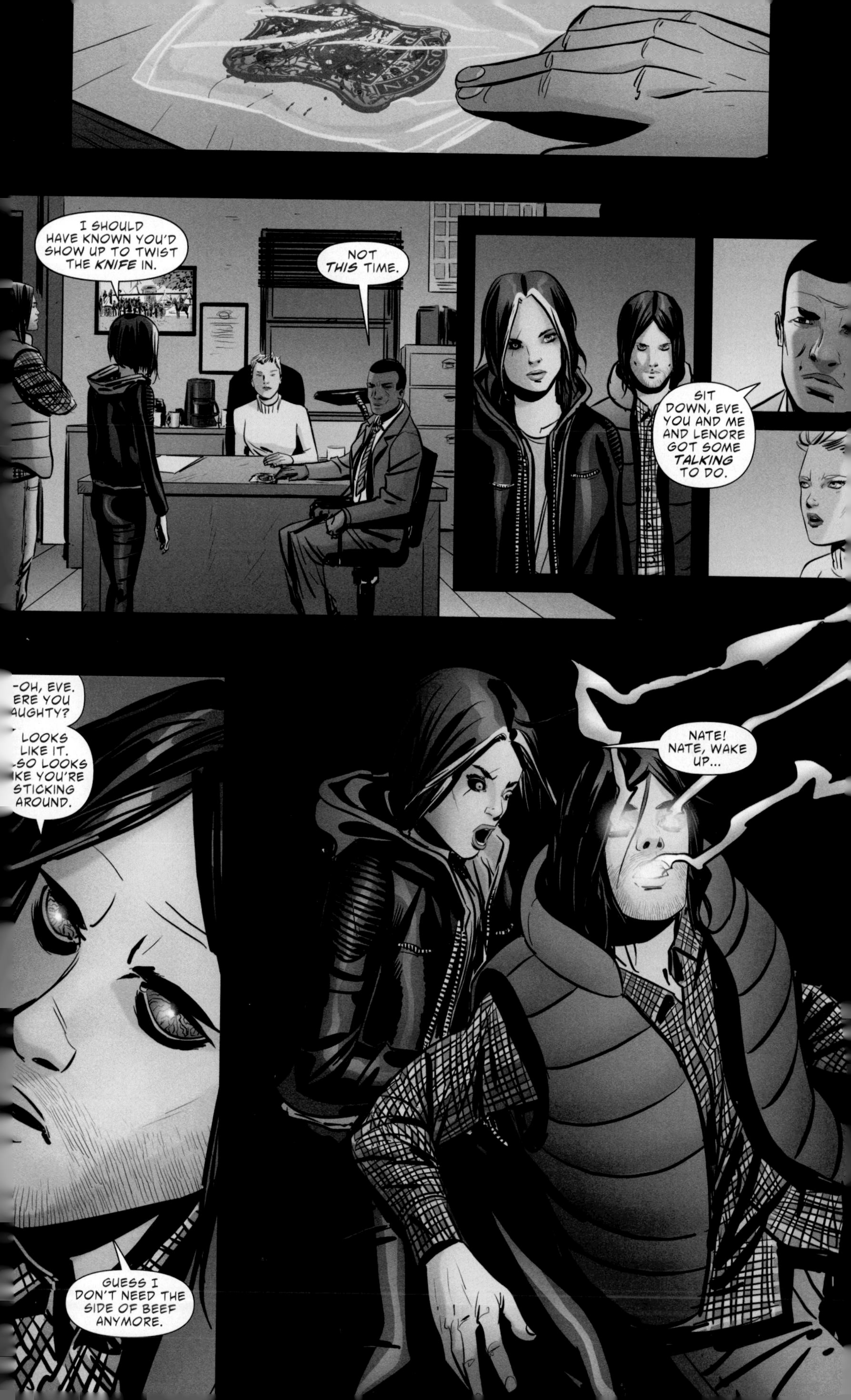
I SHOULD HAVE KNOWN YOU'D SHOW UP TO TWIST THE *KNIFE* IN.
NOT *THIS* TIME.
SIT DOWN, EVE. YOU AND ME AND LENORE GOT SOME *TALKING* TO DO.
-OH, EVE. ERE YOU AUGHTY?
LOOKS LIKE IT. SO LOOKS KE YOU'RE STICKING AROUND.
NATE! NATE, WAKE UP...
GUESS I DON'T NEED THE SIDE OF BEEF ANYMORE.

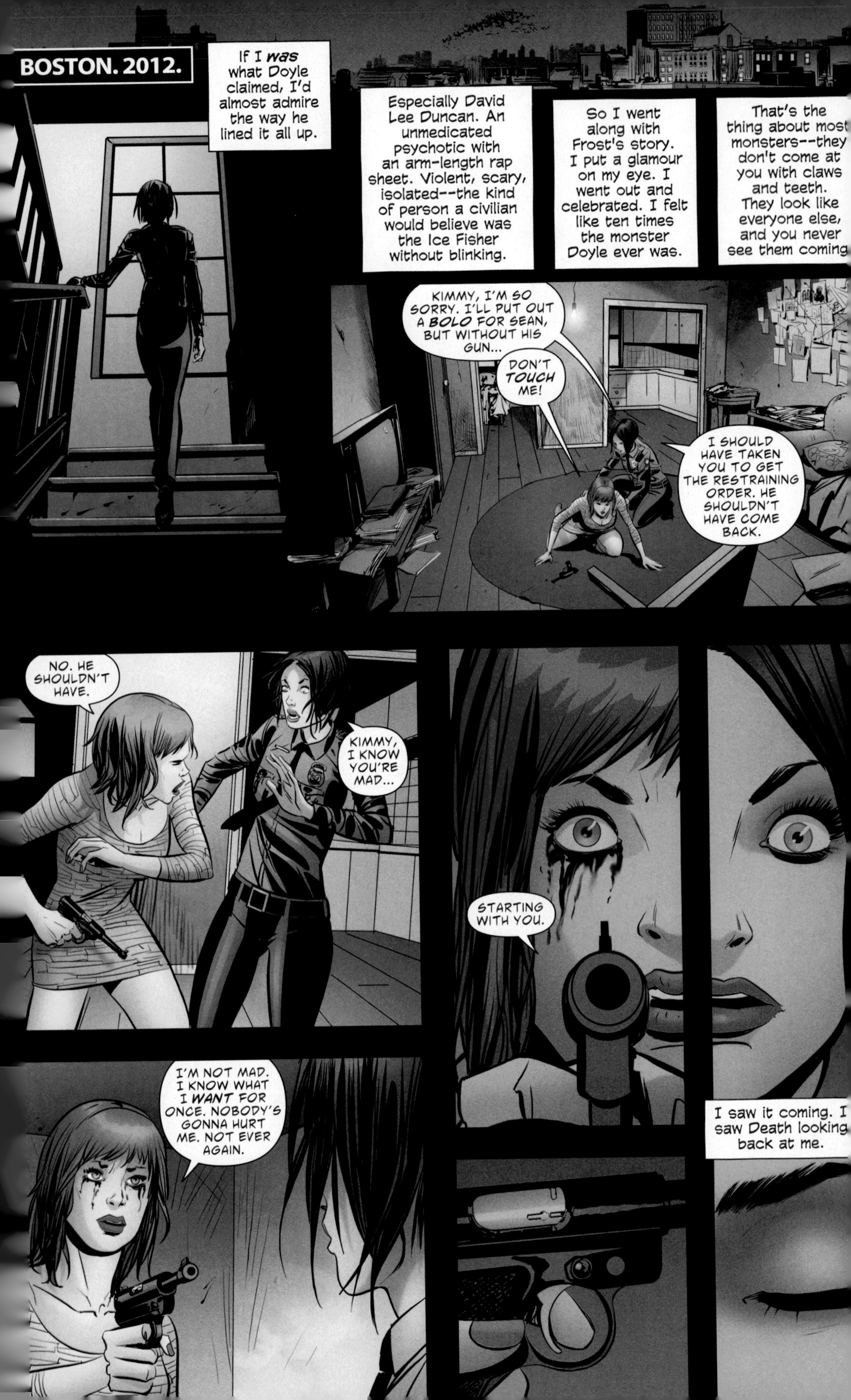
BOSTON. 2012.
If I was what Doyle claimed, I'd almost admire the way he lined it all up.
Especially David Lee Duncan. An unmedicated psychotic with an arm-length rap sheet. Violent, scary, isolated--the kind of person a civilian would believe was the Ice Fisher without blinking.
So I went along with Frost's story. I put a glamour on my eye. I went out and celebrated. I felt like ten times the monster Doyle ever was.
That's the thing about most monsters--they don't come at you with claws and teeth. They look like everyone else, and you never see them coming
KIMMY, I'M SO SORRY. I'LL PUT OUT A BOLO FOR SEAN, BUT WITHOUT HIS GUN...
DON'T TOUCH ME!
I SHOULD HAVE TAKEN YOU TO GET THE RESTRAINING ORDER. HE SHOULDN'T HAVE COME BACK.
NO. HE SHOULDN'T HAVE.
KIMMY, I KNOW YOU'RE MAD...
I'M NOT MAD. I KNOW WHAT I WANT FOR ONCE. NOBODY'S GONNA HURT ME. NOT EVER AGAIN.
STARTING WITH YOU.
I saw it coming. I saw Death looking back at me.

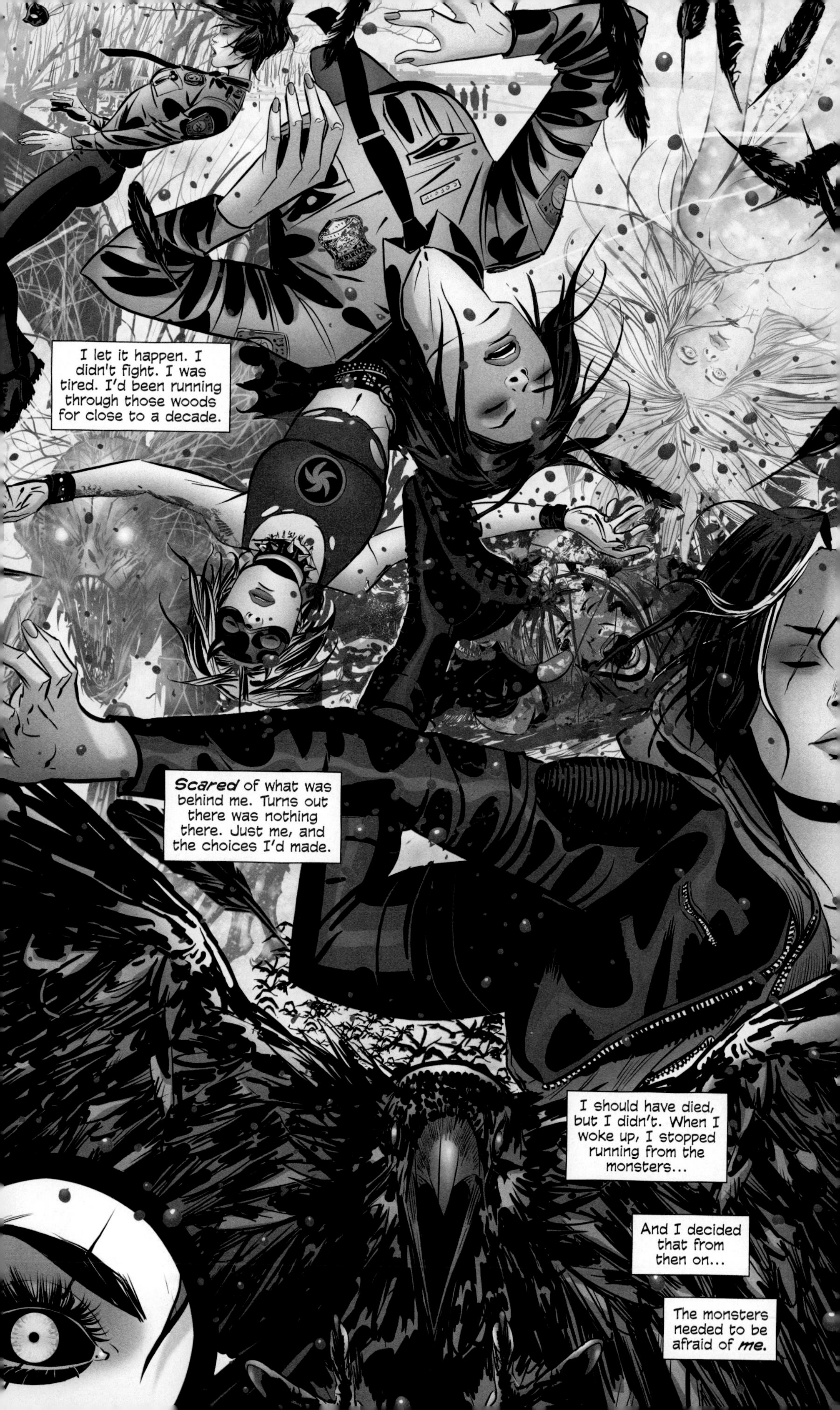

I let it happen. I didn't fight. I was tired. I'd been running through those woods for close to a decade.
Scared of what was behind me. Turns out there was nothing there. Just me, and the choices I'd made.
I should have died, but I didn't. When I woke up, I stopped running from the monsters...
And I decided that from then on...
The monsters needed to be afraid of *me.*

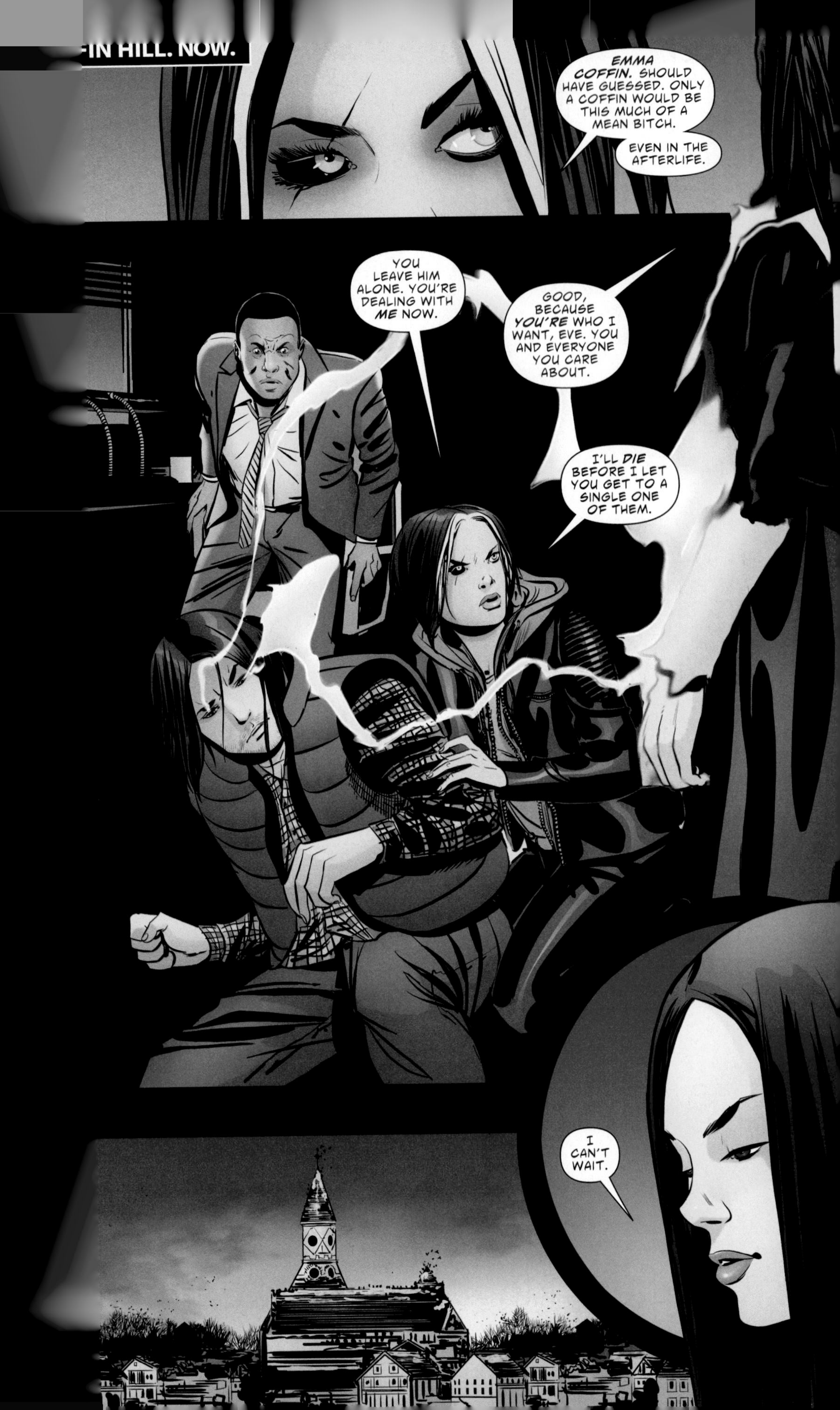

...FIN HILL. NOW.
EMMA COFFIN. SHOULD HAVE GUESSED. ONLY A COFFIN WOULD BE THIS MUCH OF A MEAN BITCH.
EVEN IN THE AFTERLIFE.
YOU LEAVE HIM ALONE. YOU'RE DEALING WITH ME NOW.
GOOD, BECAUSE YOU'RE WHO I WANT, EVE. YOU AND EVERYONE YOU CARE ABOUT.
I'LL DIE BEFORE I LET YOU GET TO A SINGLE ONE OF THEM.
I CAN'T WAIT.

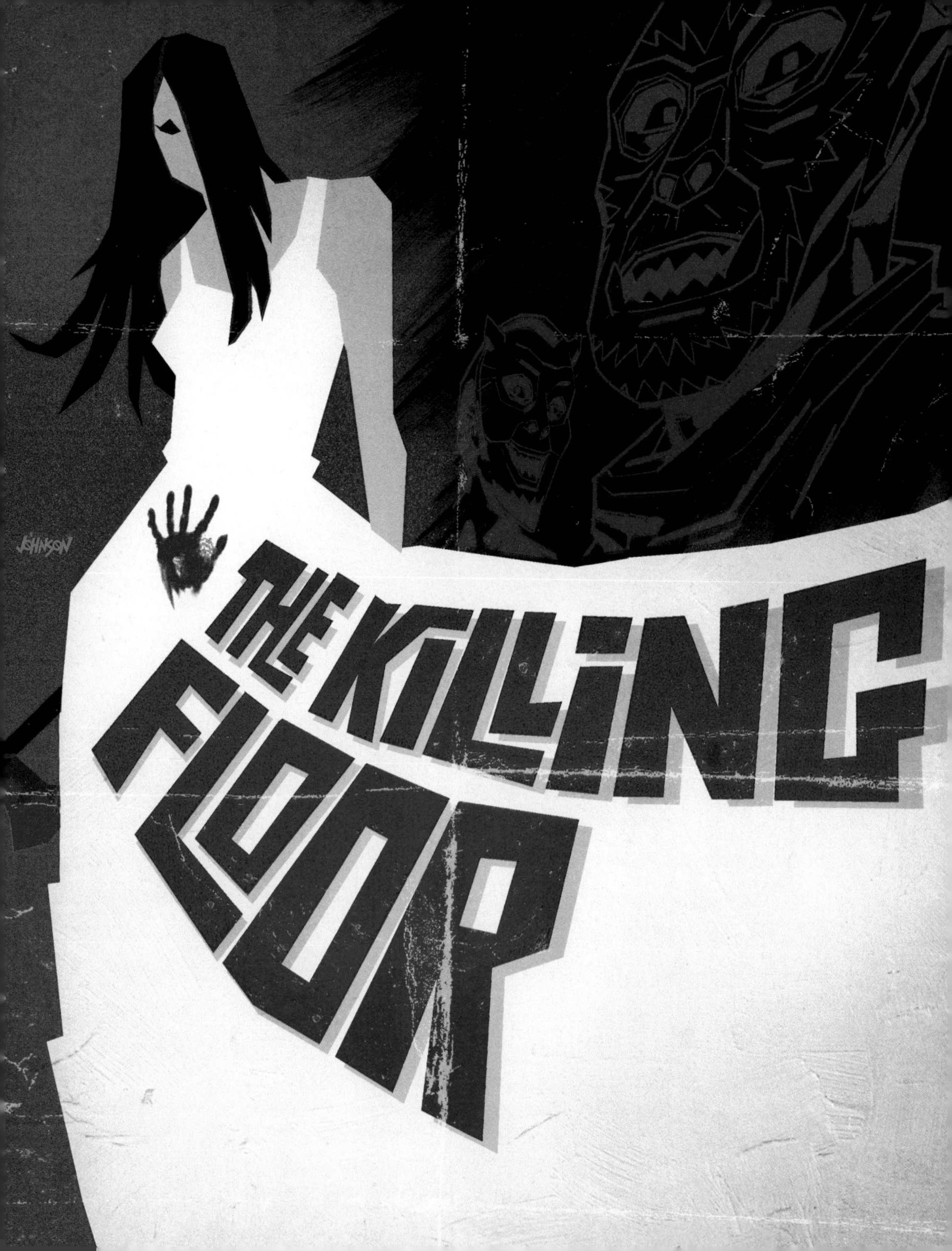

JOHNSON
THE KILLING FLOOR

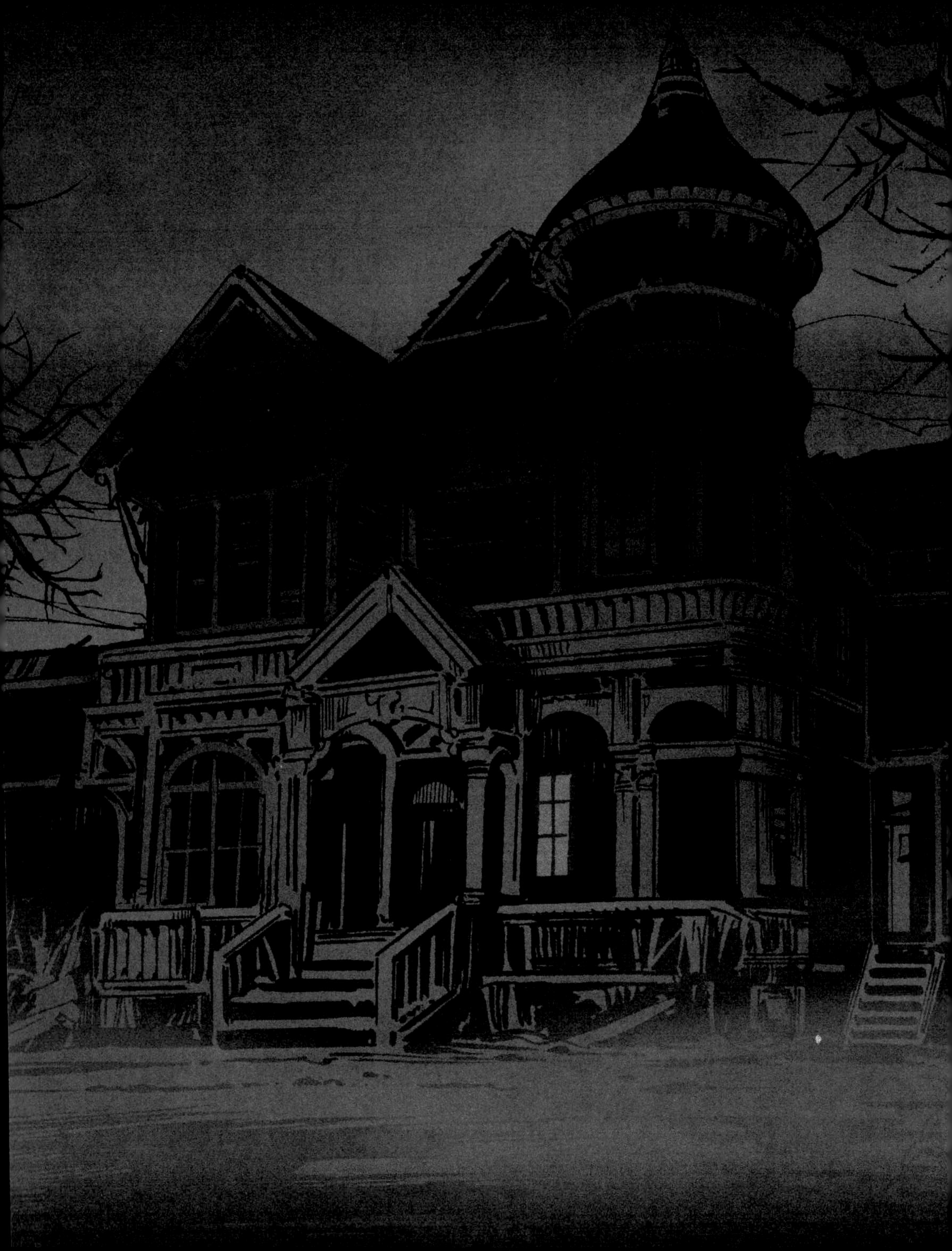

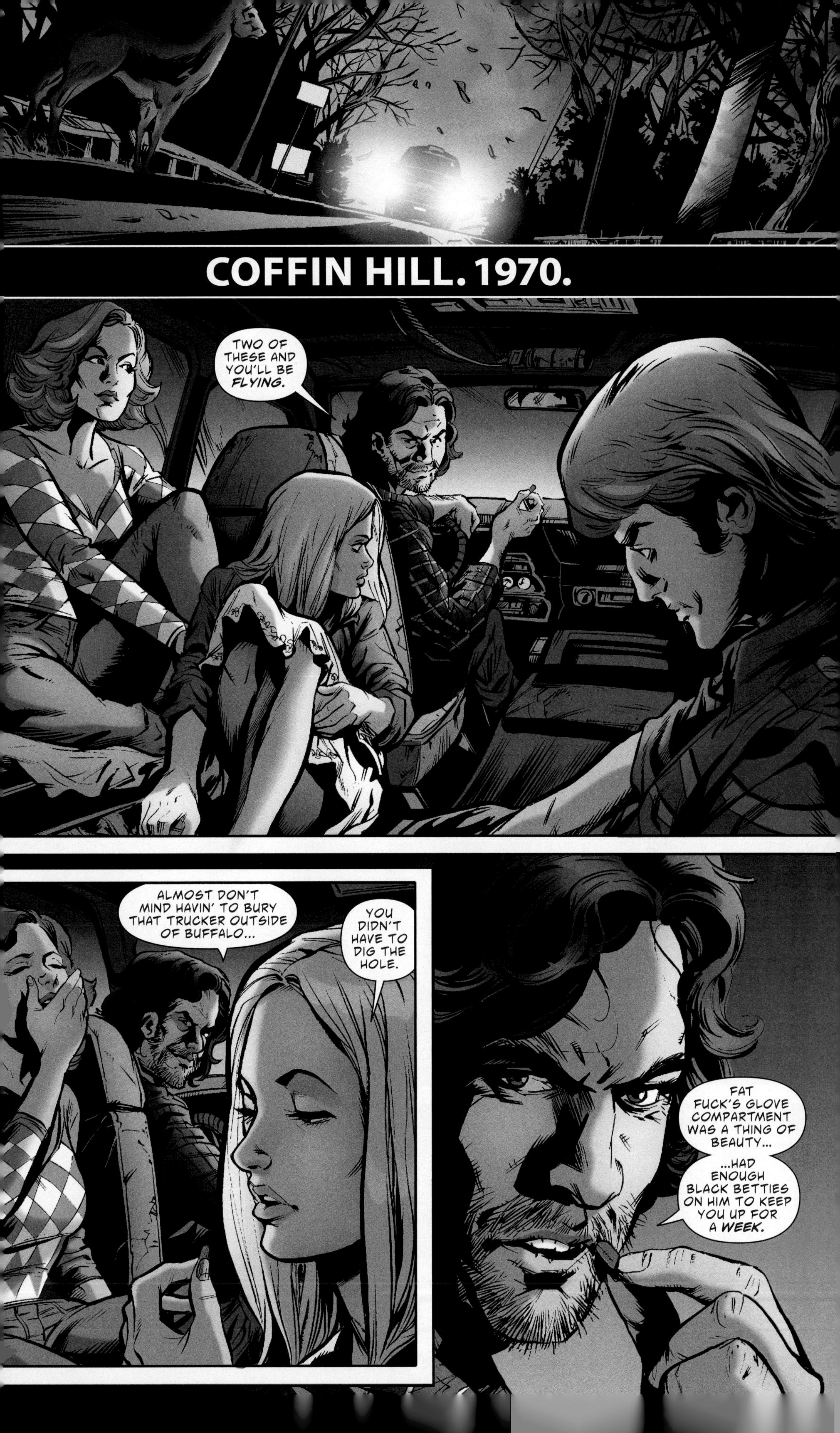
COFFIN HILL. 1970.
TWO OF THESE AND YOU'LL BE FLYING.
ALMOST DON'T MIND HAVIN' TO BURY THAT TRUCKER OUTSIDE OF BUFFALO...
YOU DIDN'T HAVE TO DIG THE HOLE.
FAT FUCK'S GLOVE COMPARTMENT WAS A THING OF BEAUTY...
...HAD ENOUGH BLACK BETTIES ON HIM TO KEEP YOU UP FOR A WEEK.

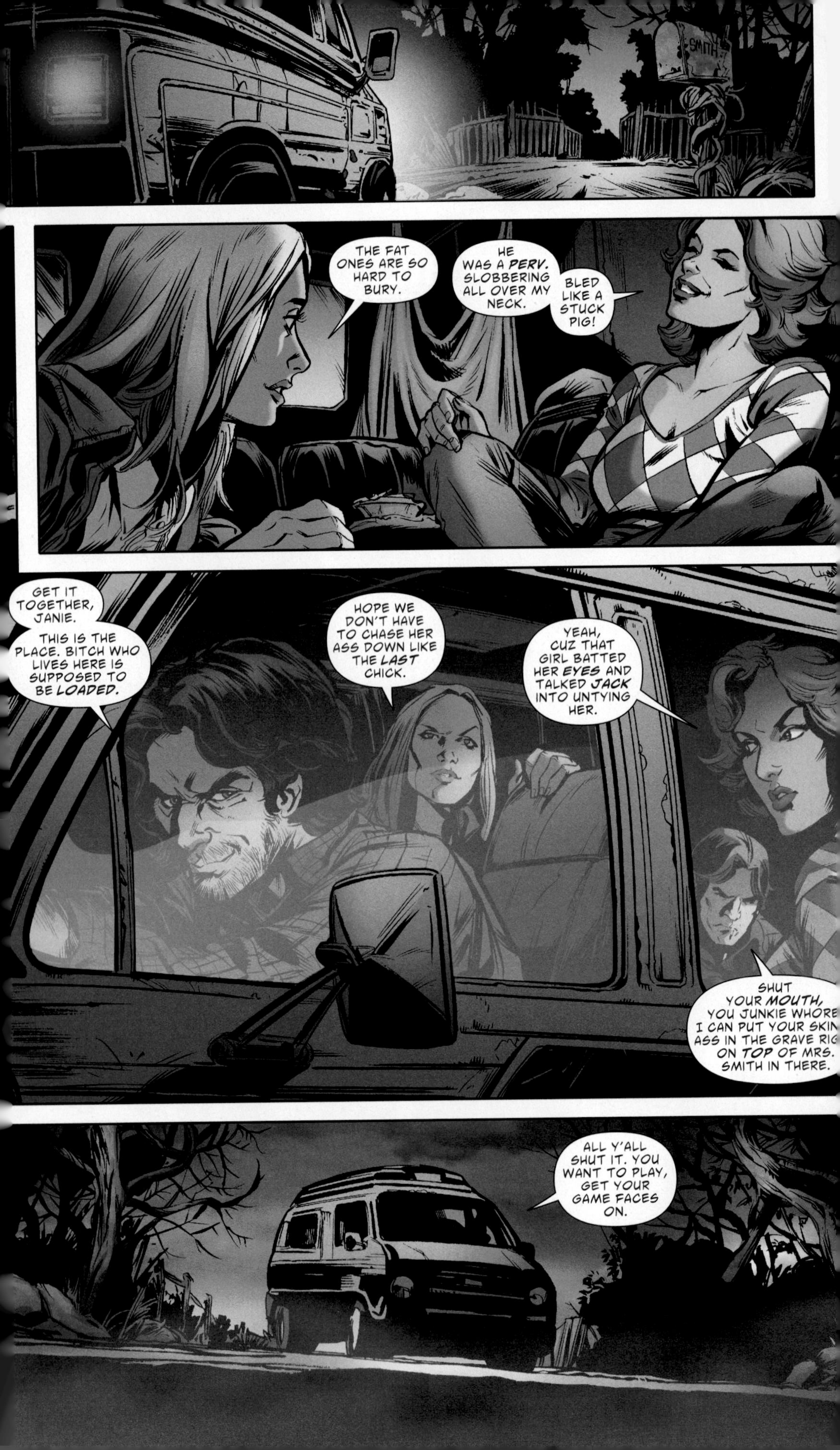
THE FAT ONES ARE SO HARD TO BURY.
HE WAS A PERV. SLOBBERING ALL OVER MY NECK.
BLED LIKE A STUCK PIG!
GET IT TOGETHER, JANIE.
THIS IS THE PLACE. BITCH WHO LIVES HERE IS SUPPOSED TO BE LOADED.
HOPE WE DON'T HAVE TO CHASE HER ASS DOWN LIKE THE LAST CHICK.
YEAH, CUZ THAT GIRL BATTED HER EYES AND TALKED JACK INTO UNTYING HER.
SHUT YOUR MOUTH, YOU JUNKIE WHORE. I CAN PUT YOUR SKIN ASS IN THE GRAVE RIG ON TOP OF MRS. SMITH IN THERE.
ALL Y'ALL SHUT IT. YOU WANT TO PLAY, GET YOUR GAME FACES ON.

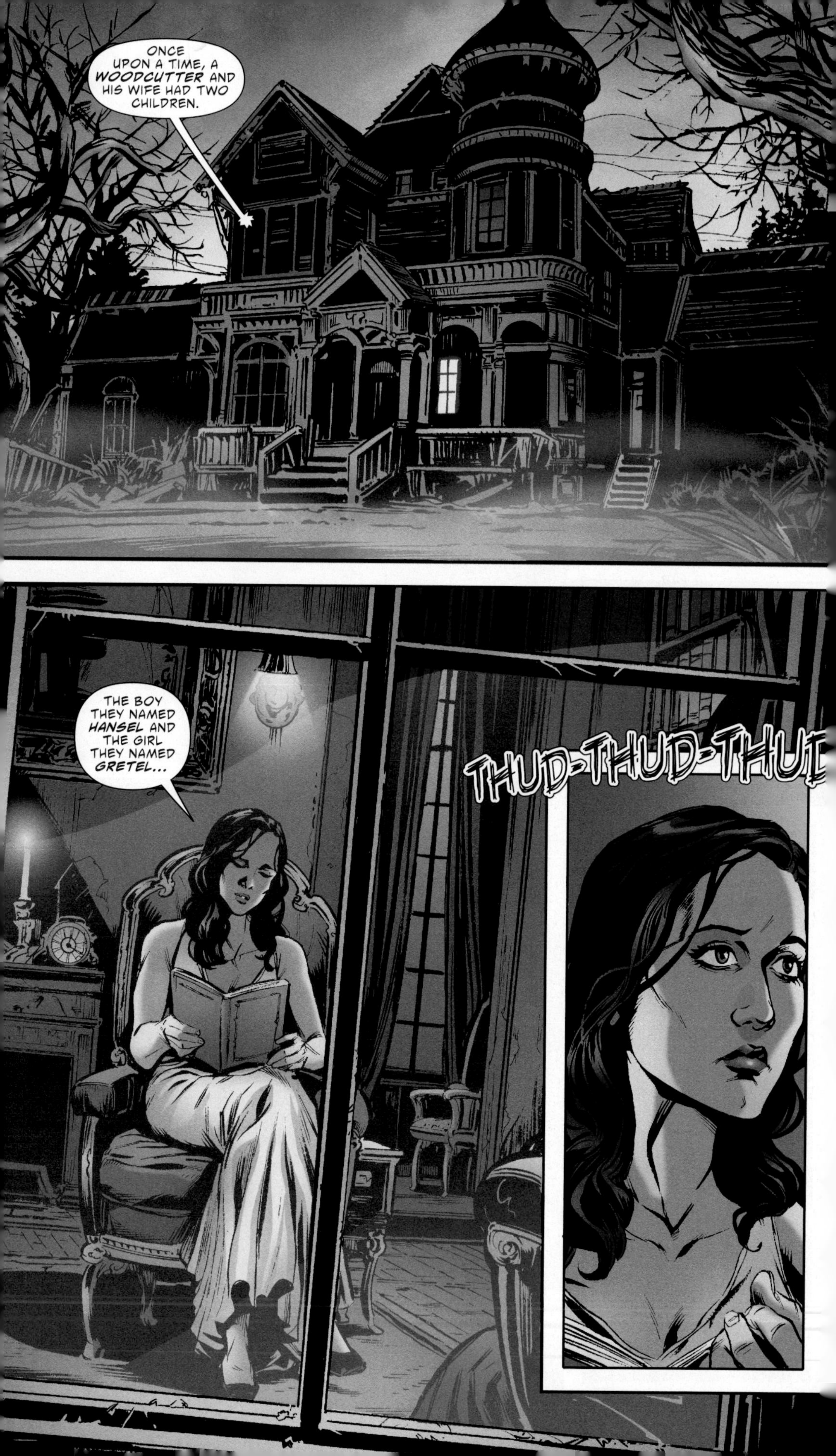
ONCE UPON A TIME, A WOODCUTTER AND HIS WIFE HAD TWO CHILDREN.
THE BOY THEY NAMED HANSEL AND THE GIRL THEY NAMED GRETEL...
THUD-THUD-THUD

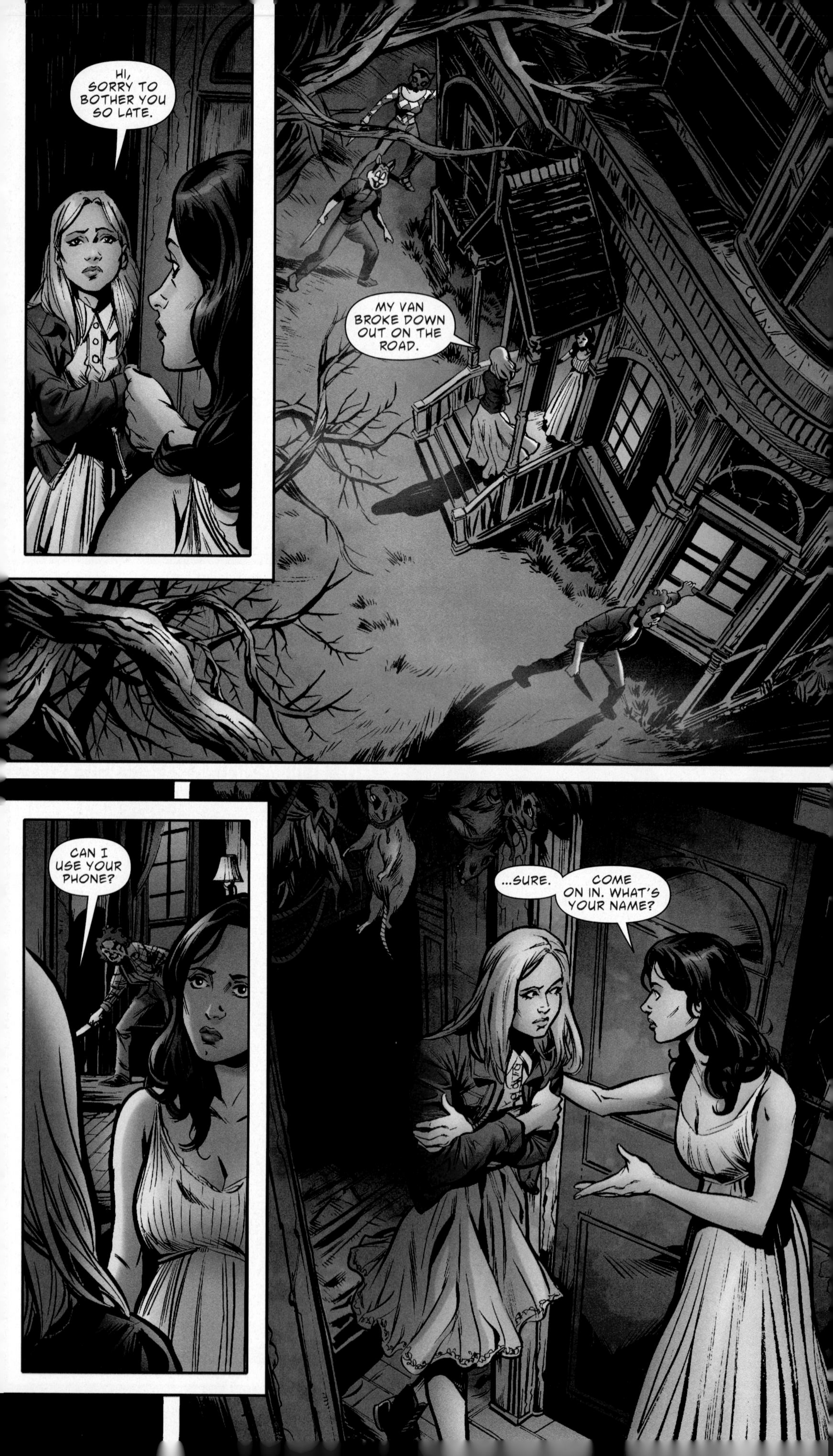
HI, SORRY TO BOTHER YOU SO LATE.
MY VAN BROKE DOWN OUT ON THE ROAD.
CAN I USE YOUR PHONE?
...SURE.
COME ON IN. WHAT'S YOUR NAME?

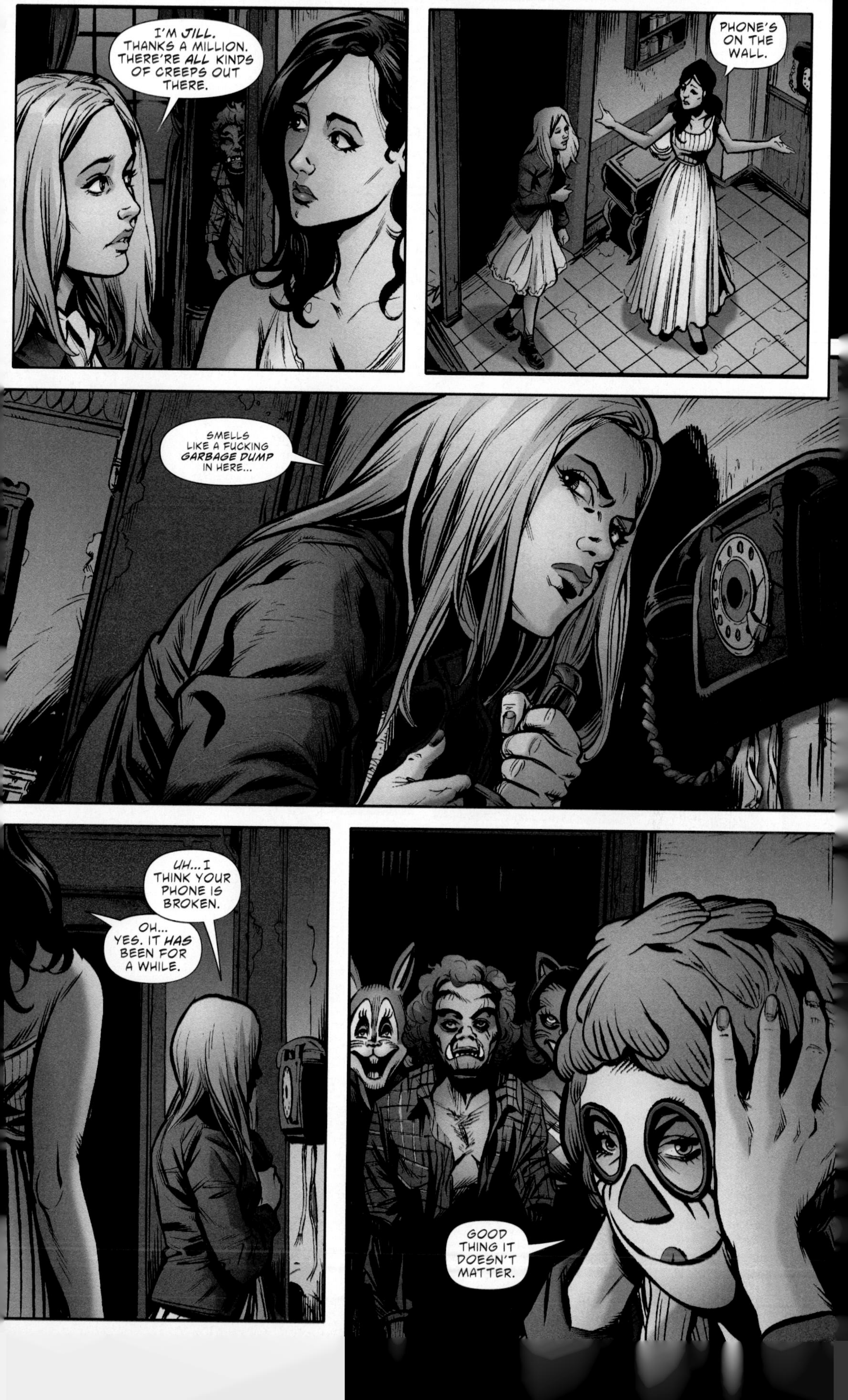
I'M JILL. THANKS A MILLION. THERE'RE ALL KINDS OF CREEPS OUT THERE.
PHONE'S ON THE WALL.
SMELLS LIKE A FUCKING GARBAGE DUMP IN HERE...
UH... I THINK YOUR PHONE IS BROKEN.
OH... YES. IT HAS BEEN FOR A WHILE.
GOOD THING IT DOESN'T MATTER.

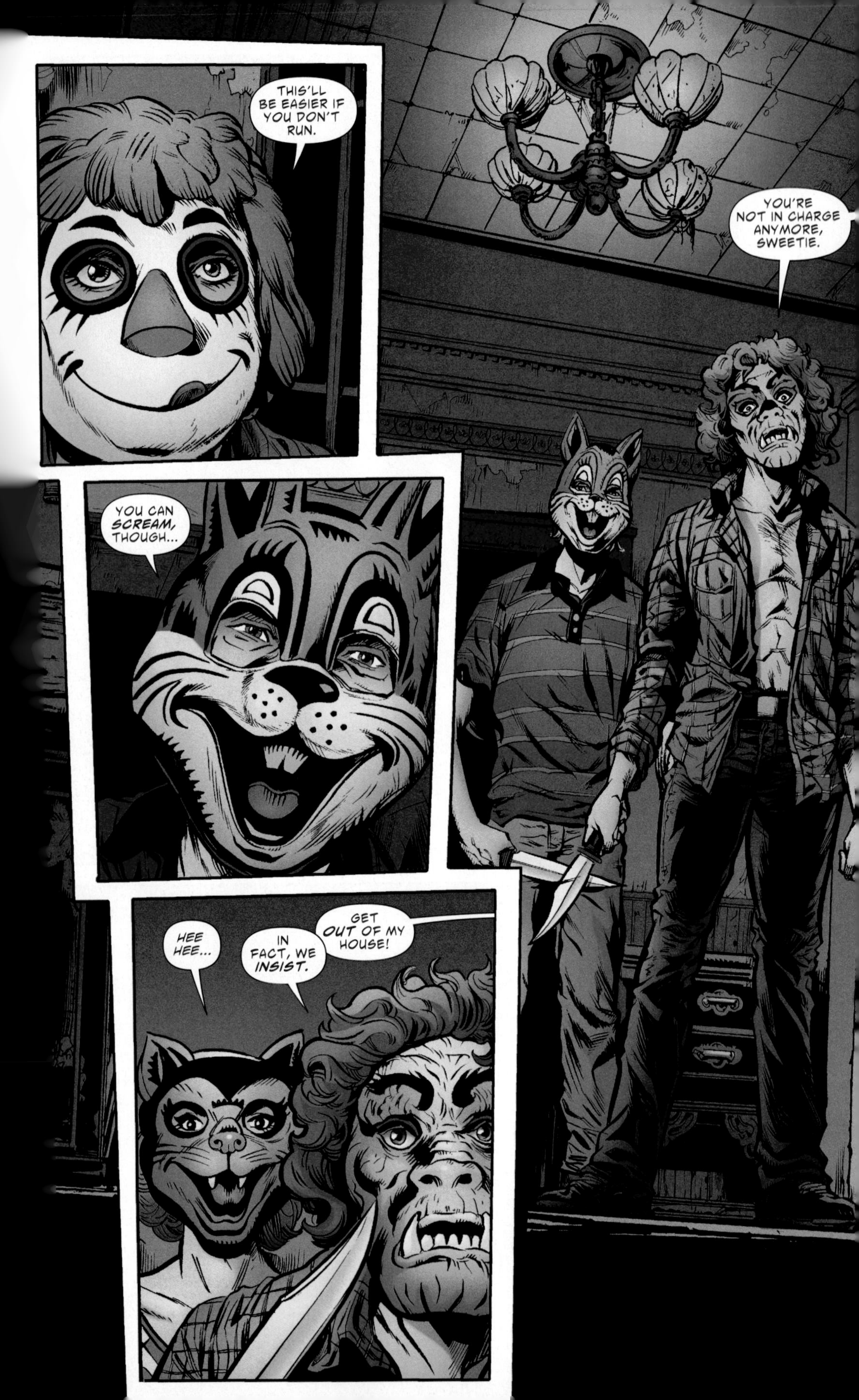
THIS'LL BE EASIER IF YOU DON'T RUN.
YOU CAN *SCREAM*, THOUGH...
HEE HEE...
IN FACT, WE *INSIST*.
GET *OUT OF MY* HOUSE!
YOU'RE NOT IN CHARGE ANYMORE, SWEETIE.

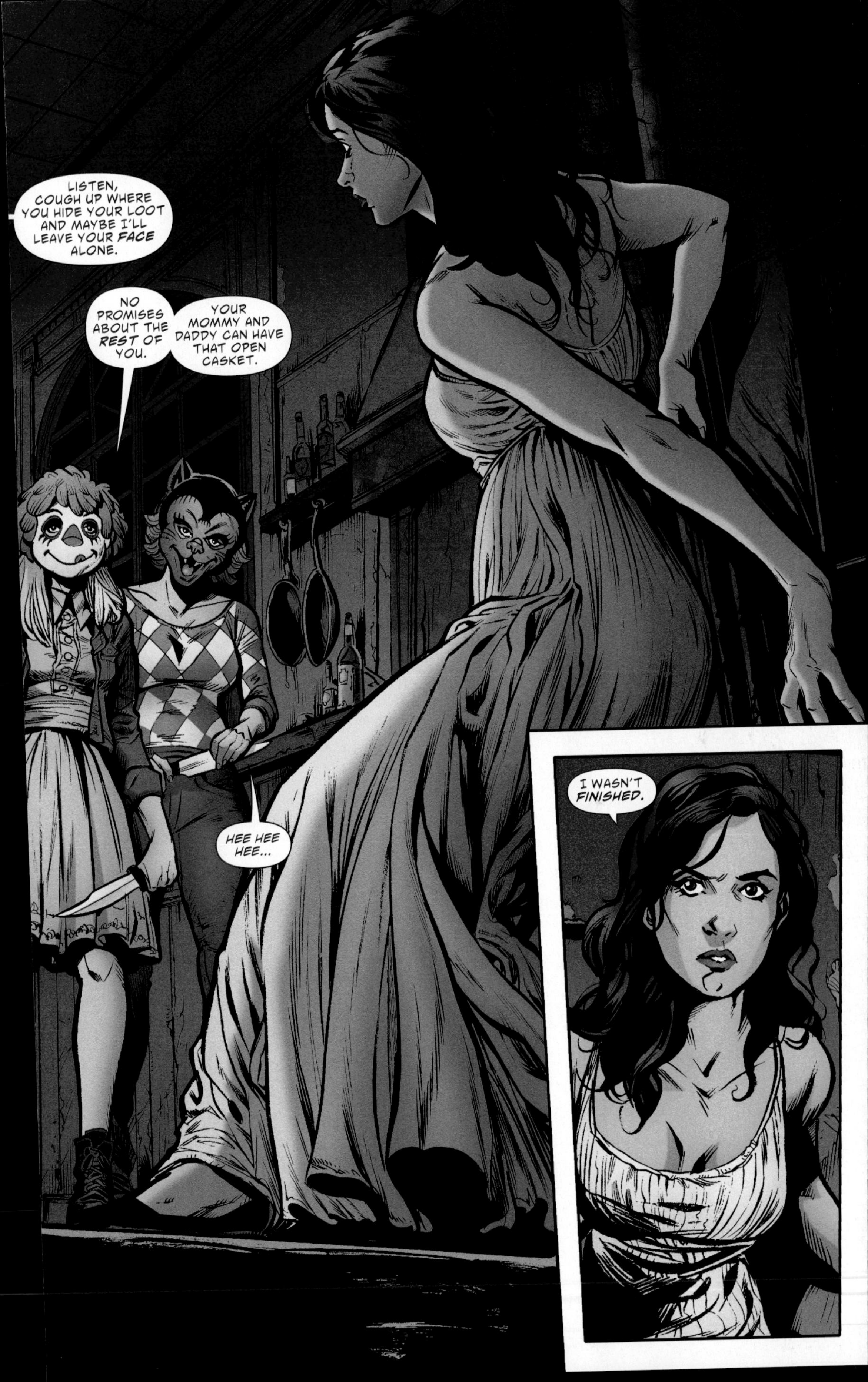
LISTEN, COUGH UP WHERE YOU HIDE YOUR LOOT AND MAYBE I'LL LEAVE YOUR *FACE* ALONE.
NO PROMISES ABOUT THE *REST* OF YOU.
YOUR MOMMY AND DADDY CAN HAVE THAT OPEN CASKET.
HEE HEE HEE...
I WASN'T *FINISHED*.

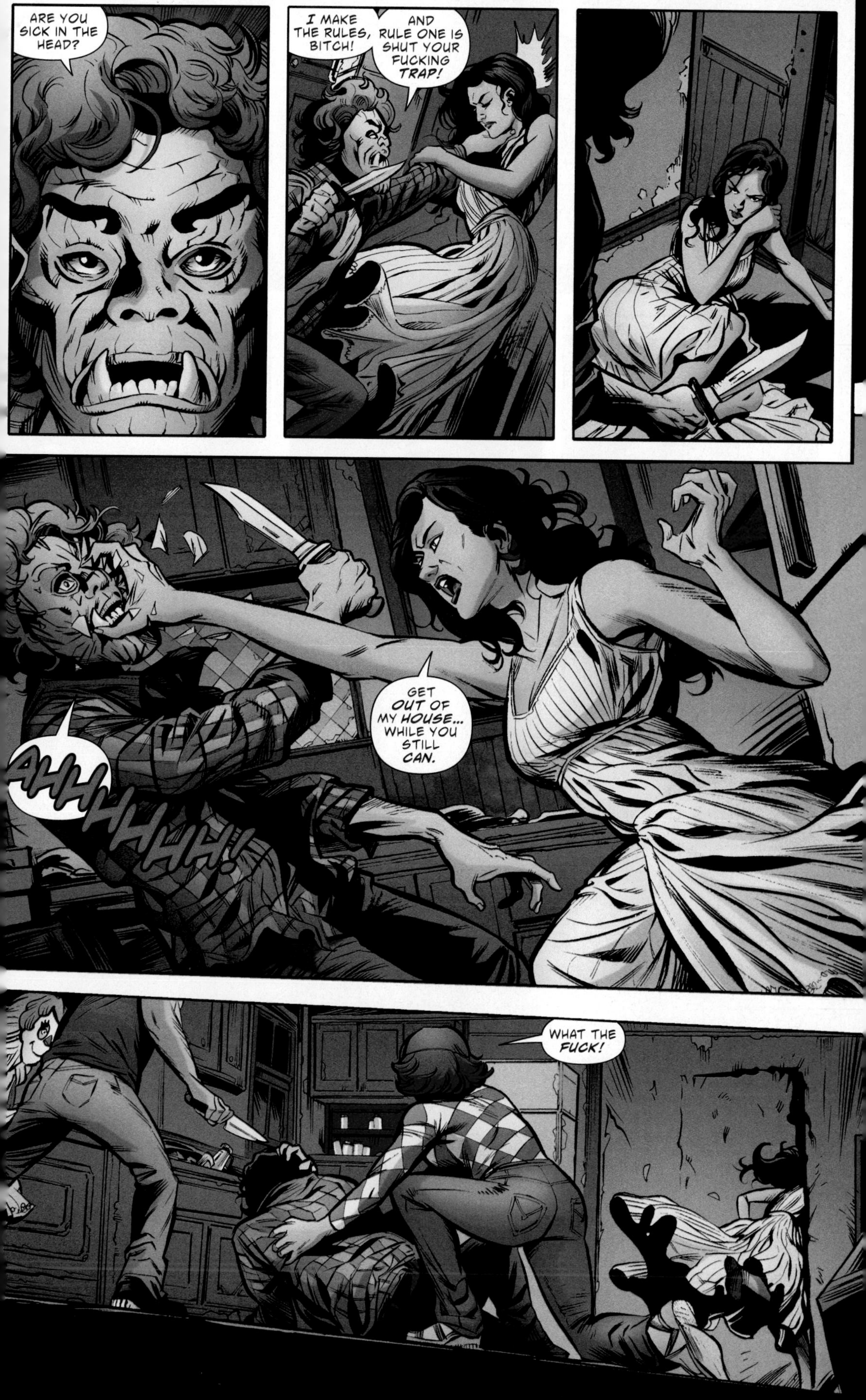

ARE YOU SICK IN THE HEAD?
I MAKE THE RULES, BITCH!
AND RULE ONE IS SHUT YOUR FUCKING TRAP!
GET OUT OF MY HOUSE... WHILE YOU STILL CAN.
AHHHHHHH!
WHAT THE FUCK!

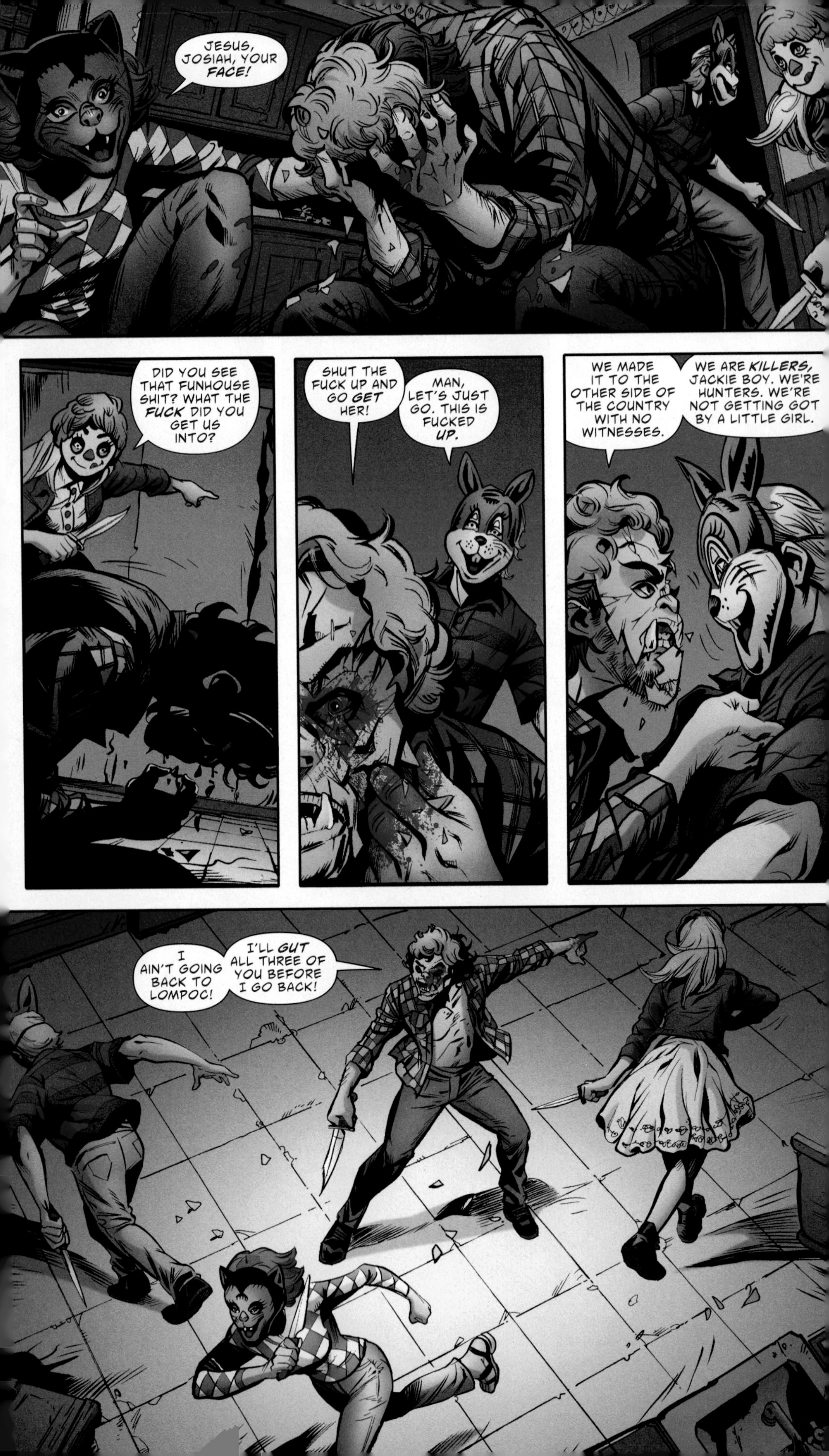
JESUS, JOSIAH, YOUR FACE!
DID YOU SEE THAT FUNHOUSE SHIT? WHAT THE FUCK DID YOU GET US INTO?
SHUT THE FUCK UP AND GO GET HER!
MAN, LET'S JUST GO. THIS IS FUCKED UP.
WE MADE IT TO THE OTHER SIDE OF THE COUNTRY WITH NO WITNESSES.
WE ARE KILLERS, JACKIE BOY. WE'RE HUNTERS. WE'RE NOT GETTING GOT BY A LITTLE GIRL.
I AIN'T GOING BACK TO LOMPOC!
I'LL GUT ALL THREE OF YOU BEFORE I GO BACK!

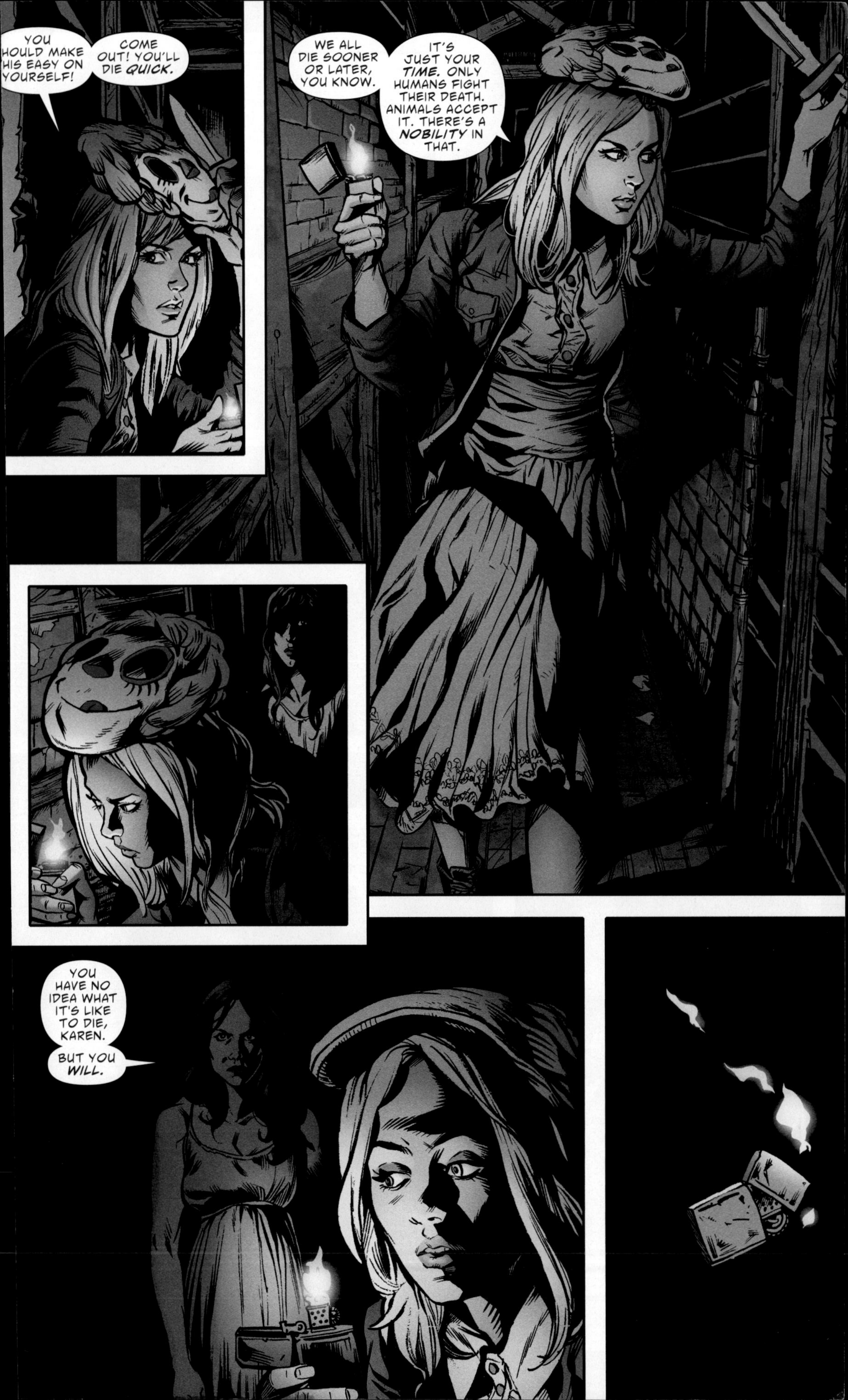
YOU HOULD MAKE HIS EASY ON YOURSELF!
COME OUT! YOU'LL DIE QUICK.
WE ALL DIE SOONER OR LATER, YOU KNOW.
IT'S JUST YOUR TIME. ONLY HUMANS FIGHT THEIR DEATH. ANIMALS ACCEPT IT. THERE'S A NOBILITY IN THAT.
YOU HAVE NO IDEA WHAT IT'S LIKE TO DIE, KAREN.
BUT YOU WILL.

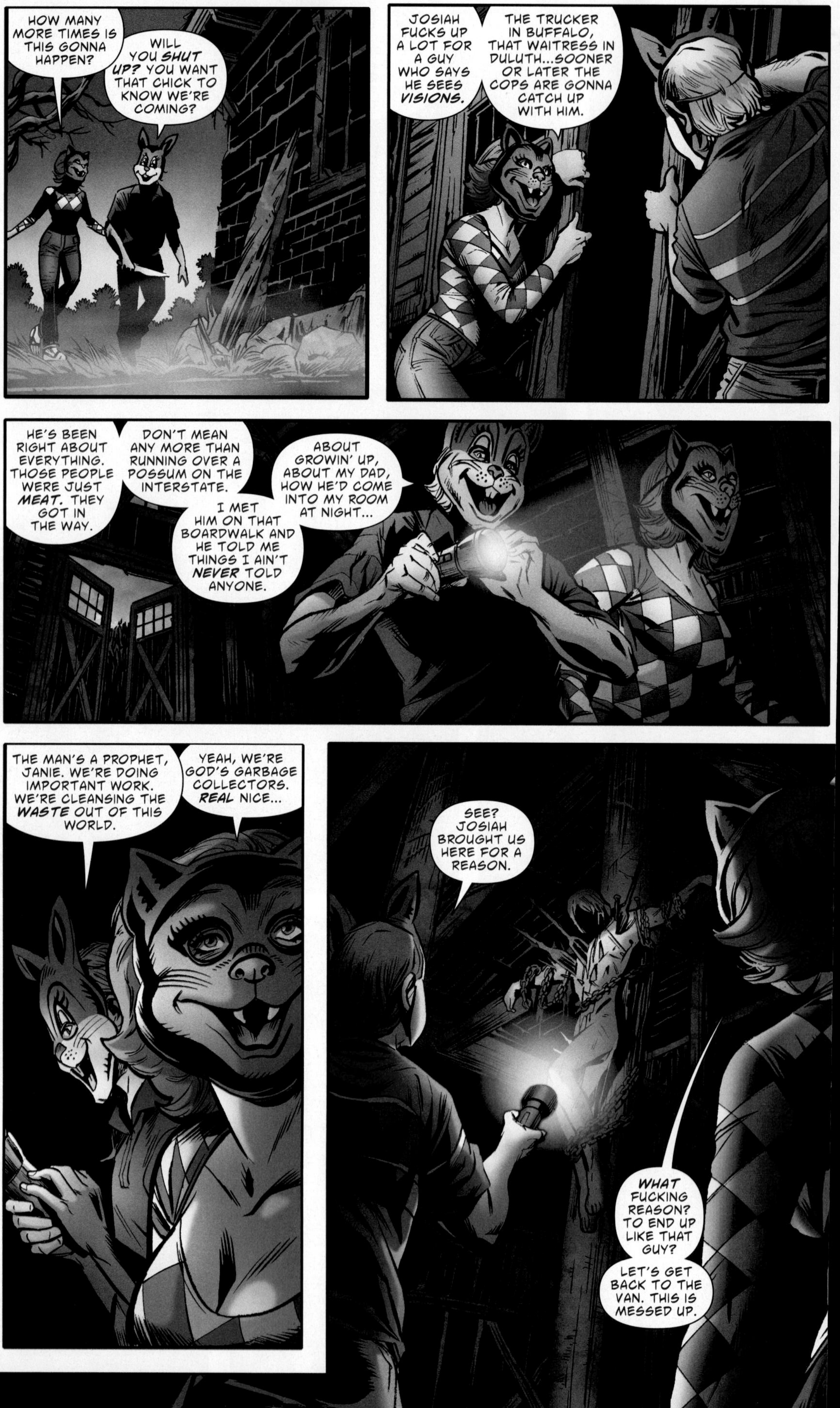
HOW MANY MORE TIMES IS THIS GONNA HAPPEN?
WILL YOU *SHUT UP?* YOU WANT THAT CHICK TO KNOW WE'RE COMING?
JOSIAH FUCKS UP A LOT FOR A GUY WHO SAYS HE SEES *VISIONS.*
THE TRUCKER IN BUFFALO, THAT WAITRESS IN DULUTH...SOONER OR LATER THE COPS ARE GONNA CATCH UP WITH HIM.
HE'S BEEN RIGHT ABOUT EVERYTHING. THOSE PEOPLE WERE JUST *MEAT.* THEY GOT IN THE WAY.
DON'T MEAN ANY MORE THAN RUNNING OVER A POSSUM ON THE INTERSTATE.
I MET HIM ON THAT BOARDWALK AND HE TOLD ME THINGS I AIN'T *NEVER* TOLD ANYONE.
ABOUT GROWIN' UP, ABOUT MY DAD, HOW HE'D COME INTO MY ROOM AT NIGHT...
THE MAN'S A PROPHET, JANIE. WE'RE DOING IMPORTANT WORK. WE'RE CLEANSING THE *WASTE* OUT OF THIS WORLD.
YEAH, WE'RE GOD'S GARBAGE COLLECTORS. *REAL* NICE...
SEE? JOSIAH BROUGHT US HERE FOR A REASON.
WHAT FUCKING REASON? TO END UP LIKE THAT GUY?
LET'S GET BACK TO THE VAN. THIS IS MESSED UP.

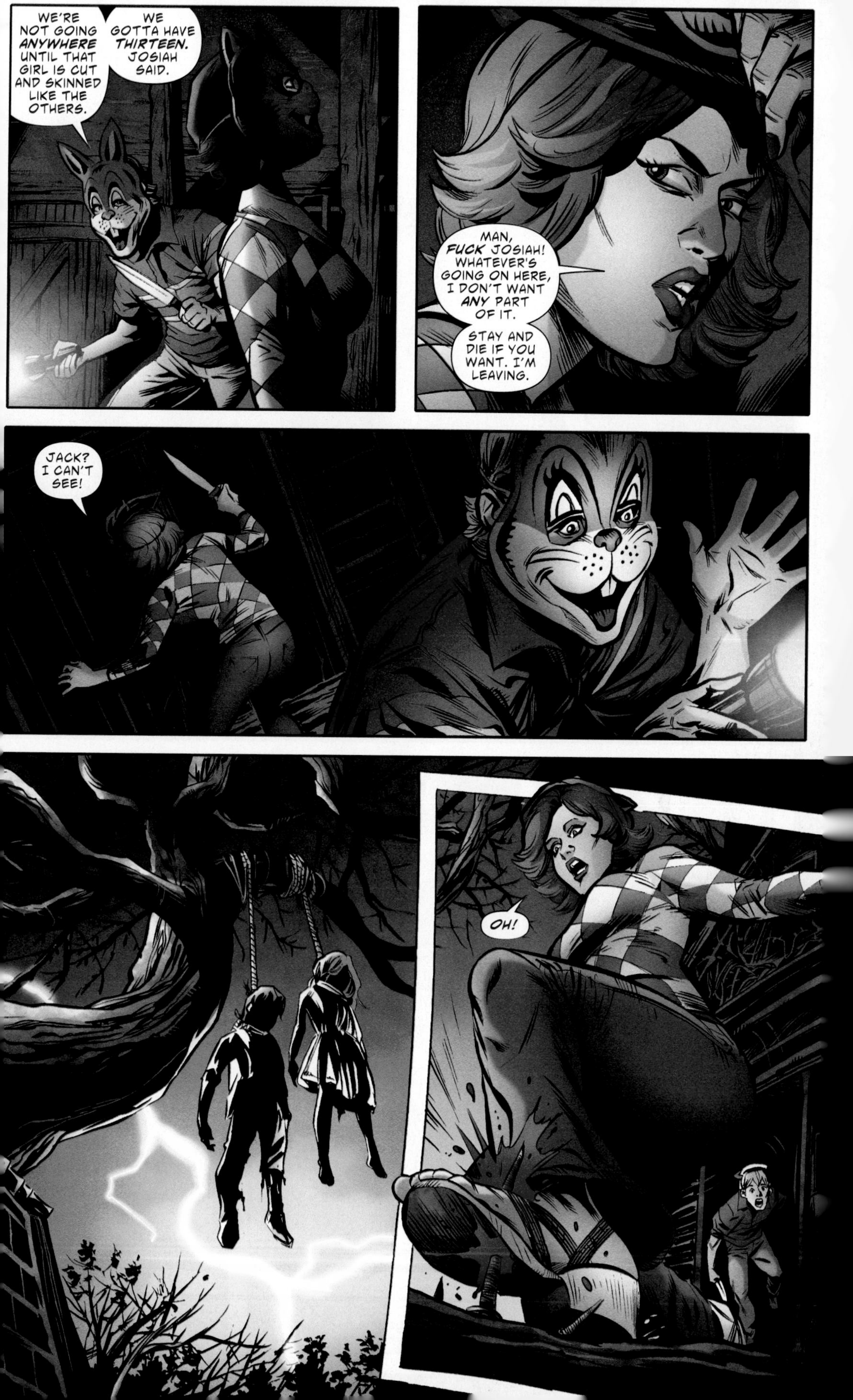

WE'RE NOT GOING ANYWHERE UNTIL THAT GIRL IS CUT AND SKINNED LIKE THE OTHERS.
WE GOTTA HAVE THIRTEEN. JOSIAH SAID.
MAN, FUCK JOSIAH! WHATEVER'S GOING ON HERE, I DON'T WANT ANY PART OF IT.
STAY AND DIE IF YOU WANT. I'M LEAVING.
JACK? I CAN'T SEE!
OH!

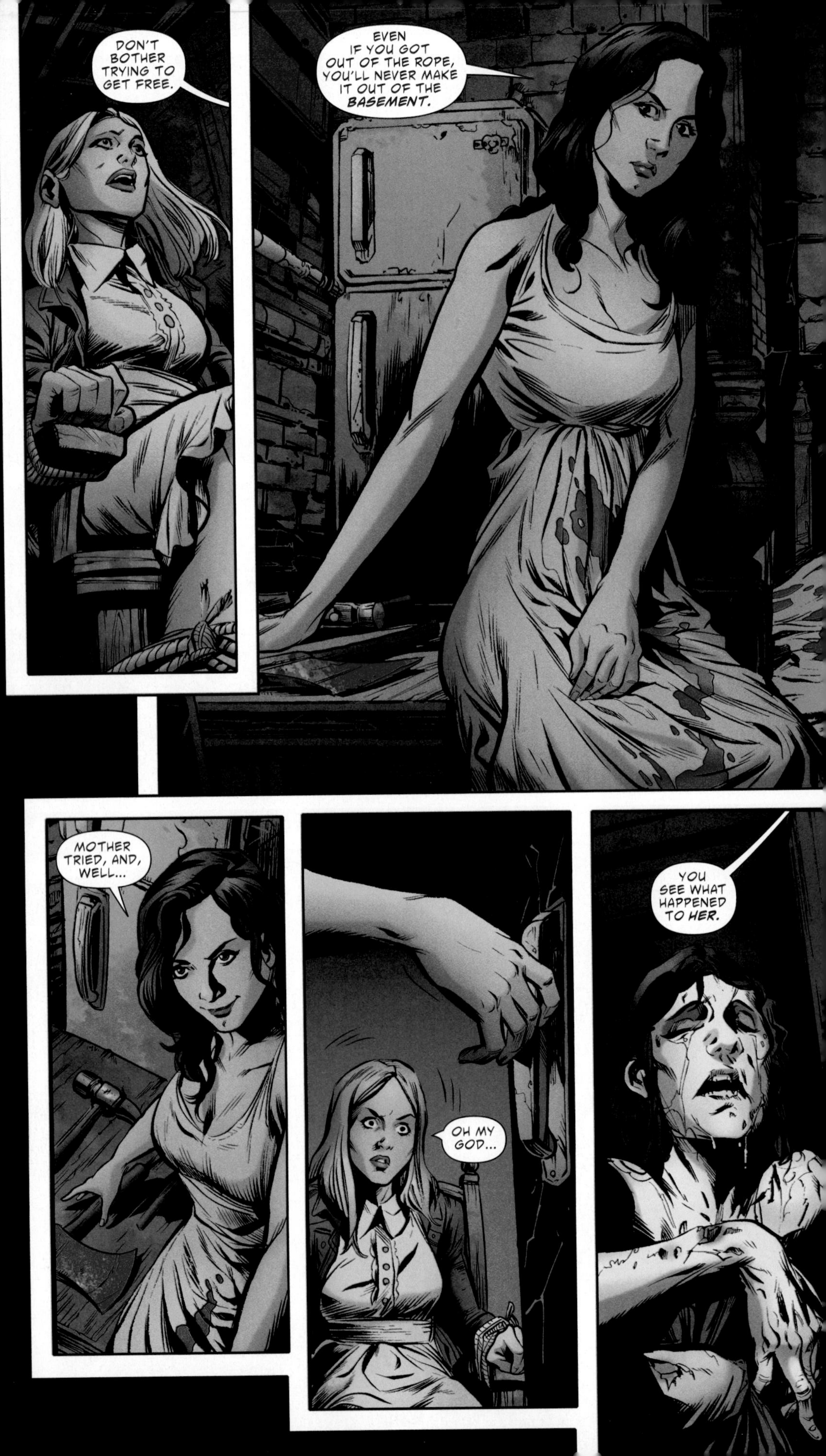
DON'T BOTHER TRYING TO GET FREE.
EVEN IF YOU GOT OUT OF THE ROPE, YOU'LL NEVER MAKE IT OUT OF THE *BASEMENT.*
MOTHER TRIED, AND, WELL...
OH MY GOD...
YOU SEE WHAT HAPPENED TO *HER.*

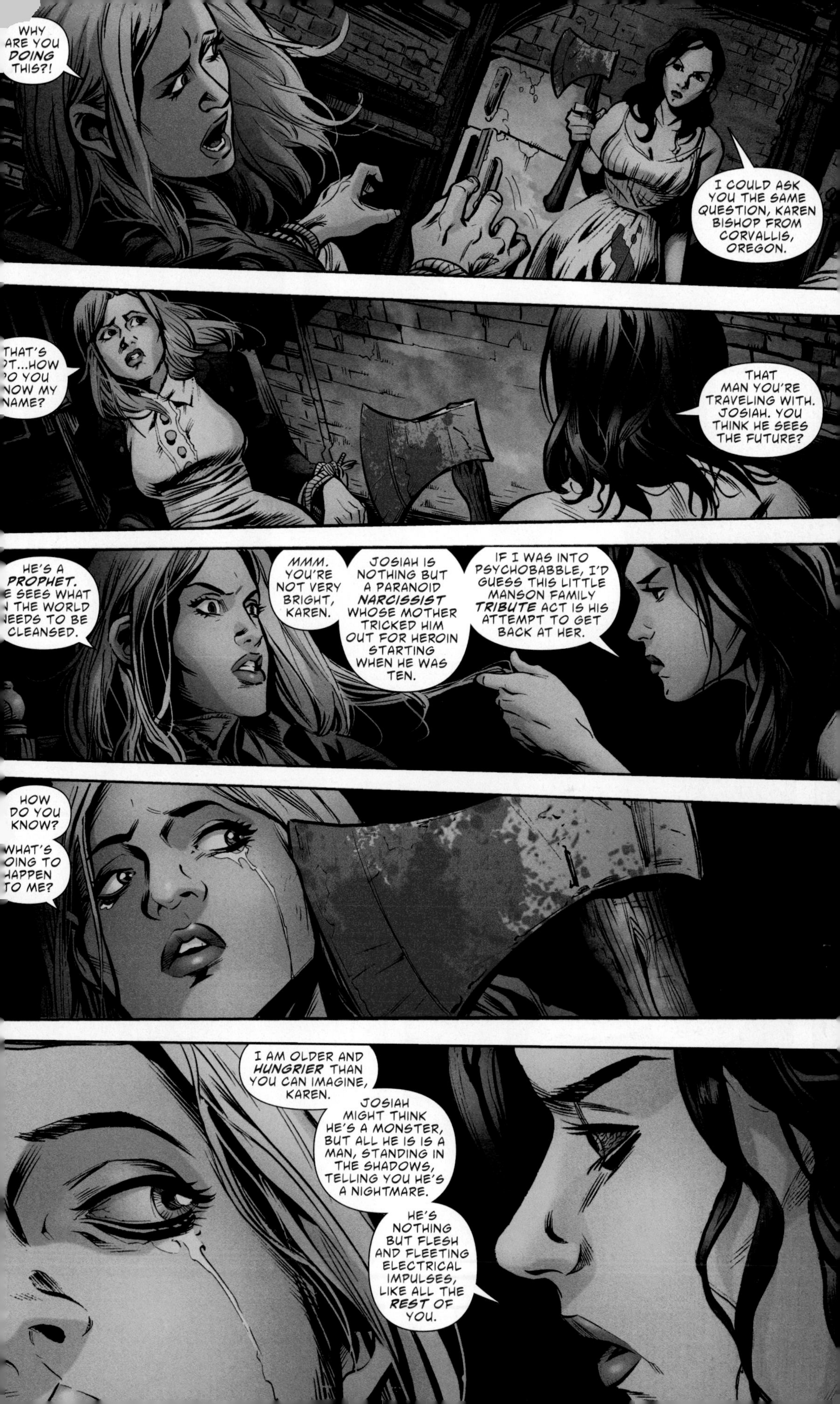

WHY ARE YOU DOING THIS?!
I COULD ASK YOU THE SAME QUESTION, KAREN BISHOP FROM CORVALLIS, OREGON.
THAT'S ...T...HOW ...O YOU ...NOW MY NAME?
THAT MAN YOU'RE TRAVELING WITH. JOSIAH. YOU THINK HE SEES THE FUTURE?
HE'S A PROPHET. ...E SEES WHAT ...N THE WORLD ...EEDS TO BE CLEANSED.
MMM. YOU'RE NOT VERY BRIGHT, KAREN.
JOSIAH IS NOTHING BUT A PARANOID NARCISSIST WHOSE MOTHER TRICKED HIM OUT FOR HEROIN STARTING WHEN HE WAS TEN.
IF I WAS INTO PSYCHOBABBLE, I'D GUESS THIS LITTLE MANSON FAMILY TRIBUTE ACT IS HIS ATTEMPT TO GET BACK AT HER.
HOW DO YOU KNOW?
WHAT'S ...OING TO ...APPEN TO ME?
I AM OLDER AND HUNGRIER THAN YOU CAN IMAGINE, KAREN.
JOSIAH MIGHT THINK HE'S A MONSTER, BUT ALL HE IS IS A MAN, STANDING IN THE SHADOWS, TELLING YOU HE'S A NIGHTMARE.
HE'S NOTHING BUT FLESH AND FLEETING ELECTRICAL IMPULSES, LIKE ALL THE REST OF YOU.

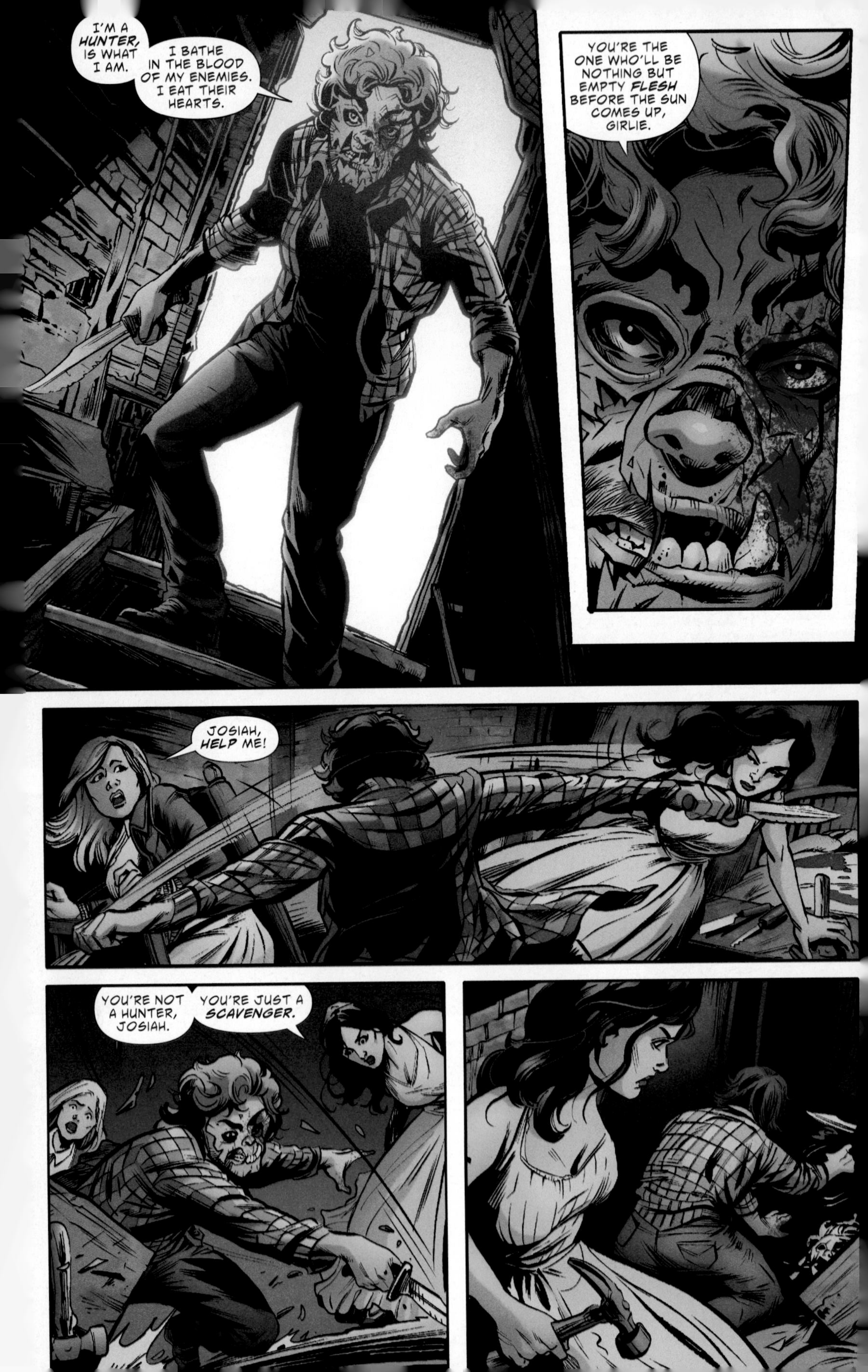
I'M A HUNTER, IS WHAT I AM.
I BATHE IN THE BLOOD OF MY ENEMIES. I EAT THEIR HEARTS.
YOU'RE THE ONE WHO'LL BE NOTHING BUT EMPTY FLESH BEFORE THE SUN COMES UP, GIRLIE.
JOSIAH, HELP ME!
YOU'RE NOT A HUNTER, JOSIAH.
YOU'RE JUST A SCAVENGER.

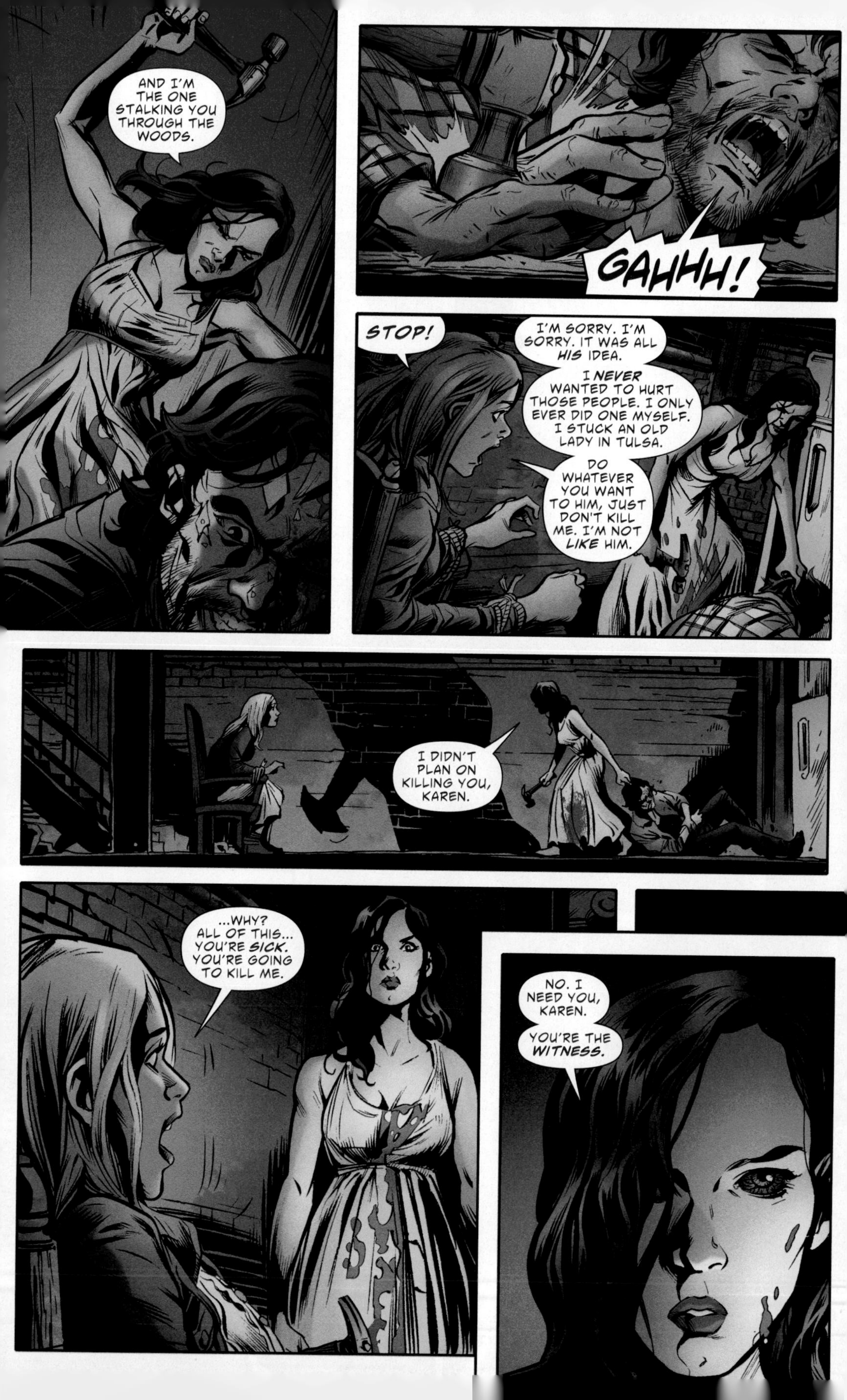
AND I'M THE ONE STALKING YOU THROUGH THE WOODS.
GAHHH!
STOP!
I'M SORRY. I'M SORRY. IT WAS ALL HIS IDEA.
I NEVER WANTED TO HURT THOSE PEOPLE. I ONLY EVER DID ONE MYSELF. I STUCK AN OLD LADY IN TULSA.
DO WHATEVER YOU WANT TO HIM, JUST DON'T KILL ME. I'M NOT LIKE HIM.
I DIDN'T PLAN ON KILLING YOU, KAREN.
...WHY? ALL OF THIS... YOU'RE SICK. YOU'RE GOING TO KILL ME.
NO. I NEED YOU, KAREN.
YOU'RE THE WITNESS.

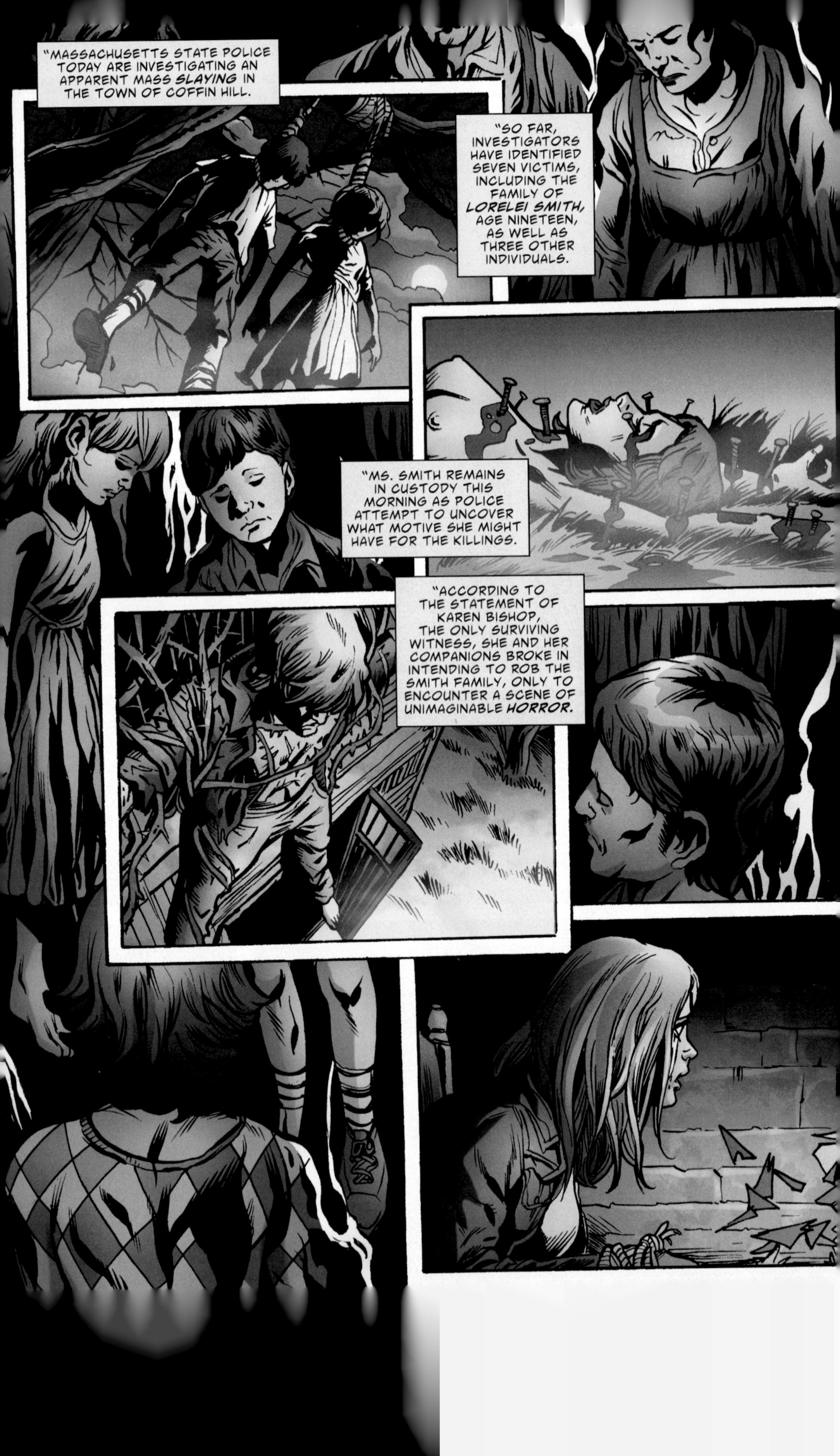
"MASSACHUSETTS STATE POLICE TODAY ARE INVESTIGATING AN APPARENT MASS *SLAYING* IN THE TOWN OF COFFIN HILL.
"SO FAR, INVESTIGATORS HAVE IDENTIFIED SEVEN VICTIMS, INCLUDING THE FAMILY OF ***LORELEI SMITH,*** AGE NINETEEN, AS WELL AS THREE OTHER INDIVIDUALS.
"MS. SMITH REMAINS IN CUSTODY THIS MORNING AS POLICE ATTEMPT TO UNCOVER WHAT MOTIVE SHE MIGHT HAVE FOR THE KILLINGS.
"ACCORDING TO THE STATEMENT OF KAREN BISHOP, THE ONLY SURVIVING WITNESS, SHE AND HER COMPANIONS BROKE IN INTENDING TO ROB THE SMITH FAMILY, ONLY TO ENCOUNTER A SCENE OF UNIMAGINABLE ***HORROR.***

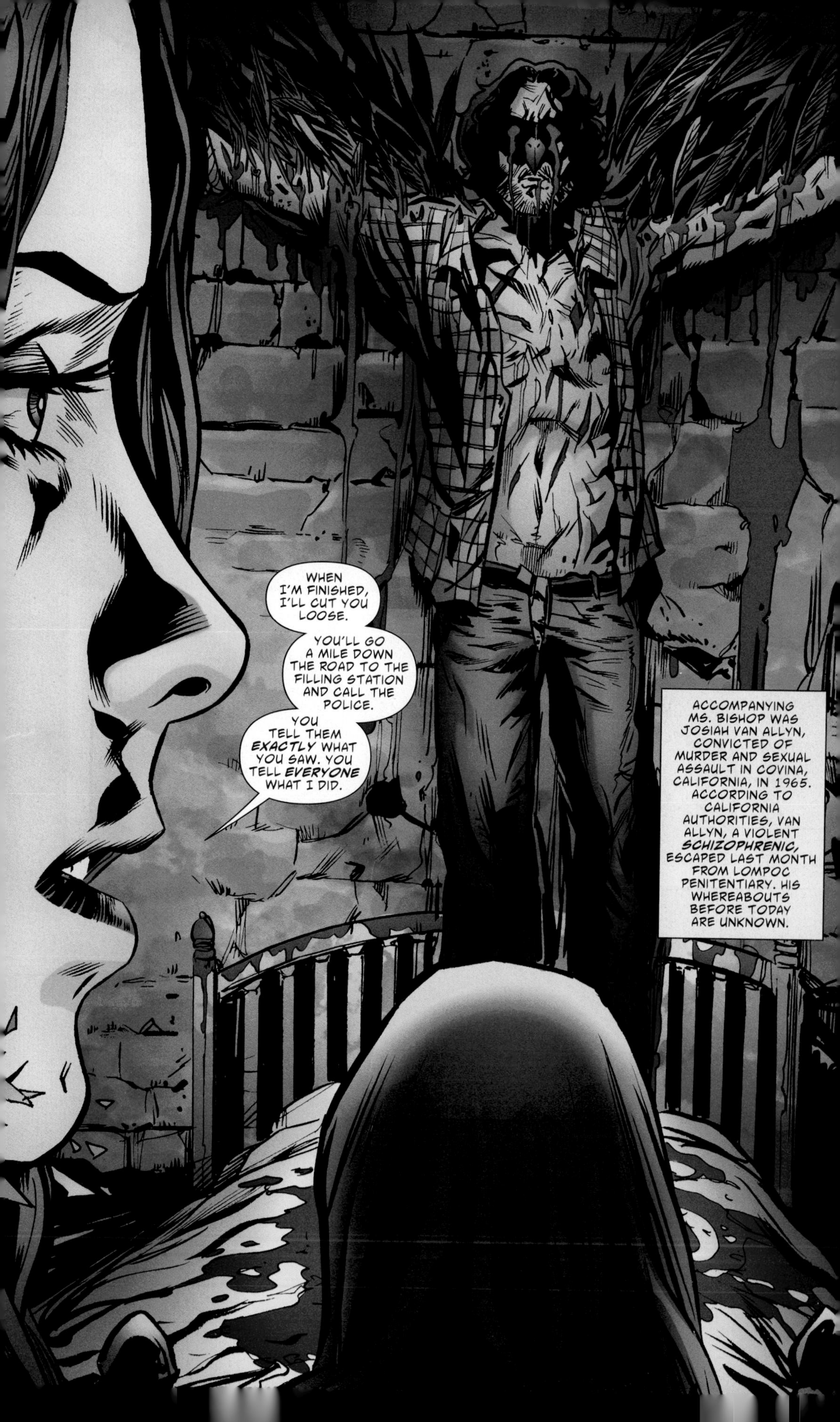
WHEN I'M FINISHED, I'LL CUT YOU LOOSE.
YOU'LL GO A MILE DOWN THE ROAD TO THE FILLING STATION AND CALL THE POLICE.
YOU TELL THEM *EXACTLY* WHAT YOU SAW. YOU TELL *EVERYONE* WHAT I DID.
ACCOMPANYING MS. BISHOP WAS JOSIAH VAN ALLYN, CONVICTED OF MURDER AND SEXUAL ASSAULT IN COVINA, CALIFORNIA, IN 1965. ACCORDING TO CALIFORNIA AUTHORITIES, VAN ALLYN, A VIOLENT *SCHIZOPHRENIC,* ESCAPED LAST MONTH FROM LOMPOC PENITENTIARY. HIS WHEREABOUTS BEFORE TODAY ARE UNKNOWN.

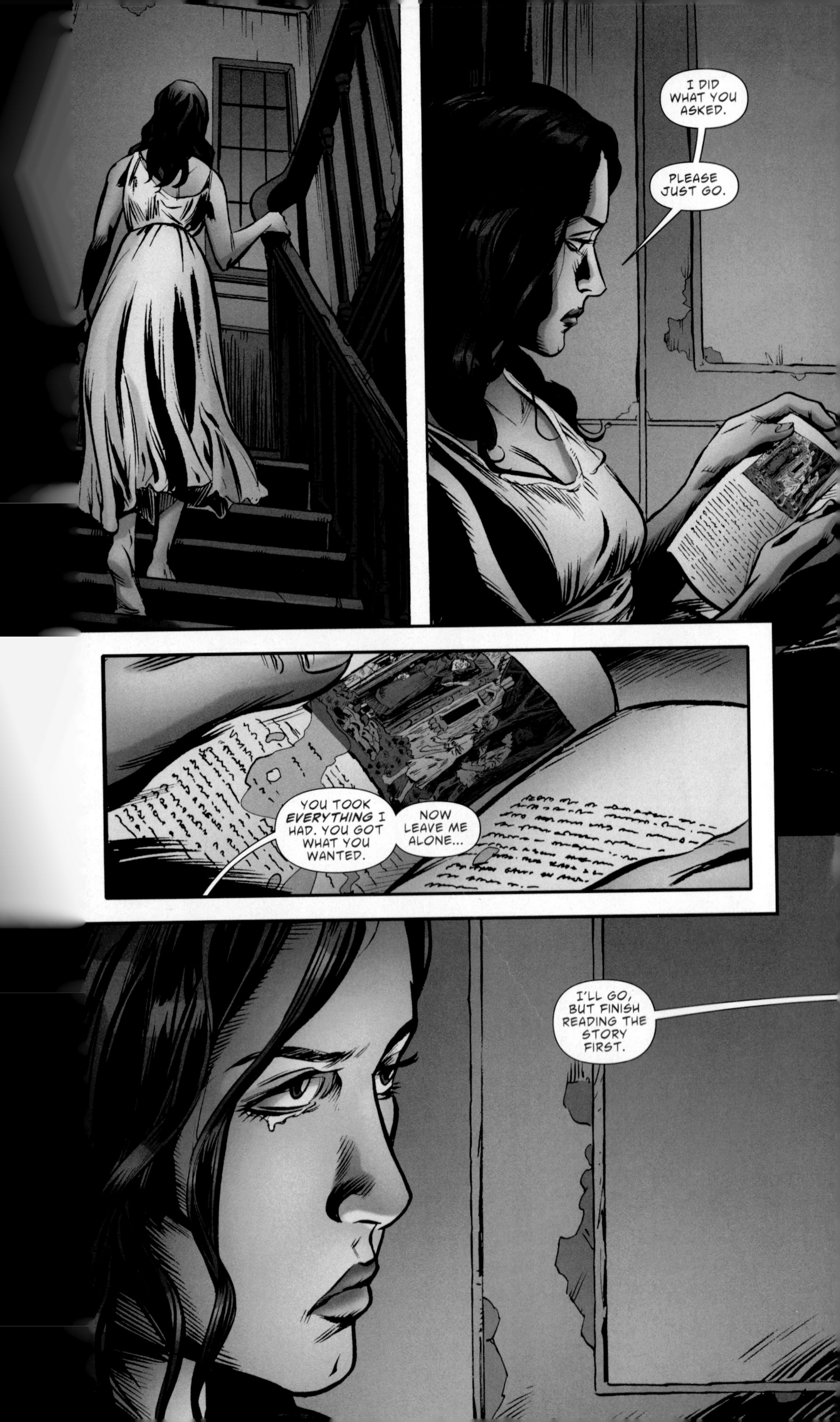
I DID WHAT YOU ASKED.
PLEASE JUST GO.
YOU TOOK EVERYTHING I HAD. YOU GOT WHAT YOU WANTED.
NOW LEAVE ME ALONE...
I'LL GO, BUT FINISH READING THE STORY FIRST.

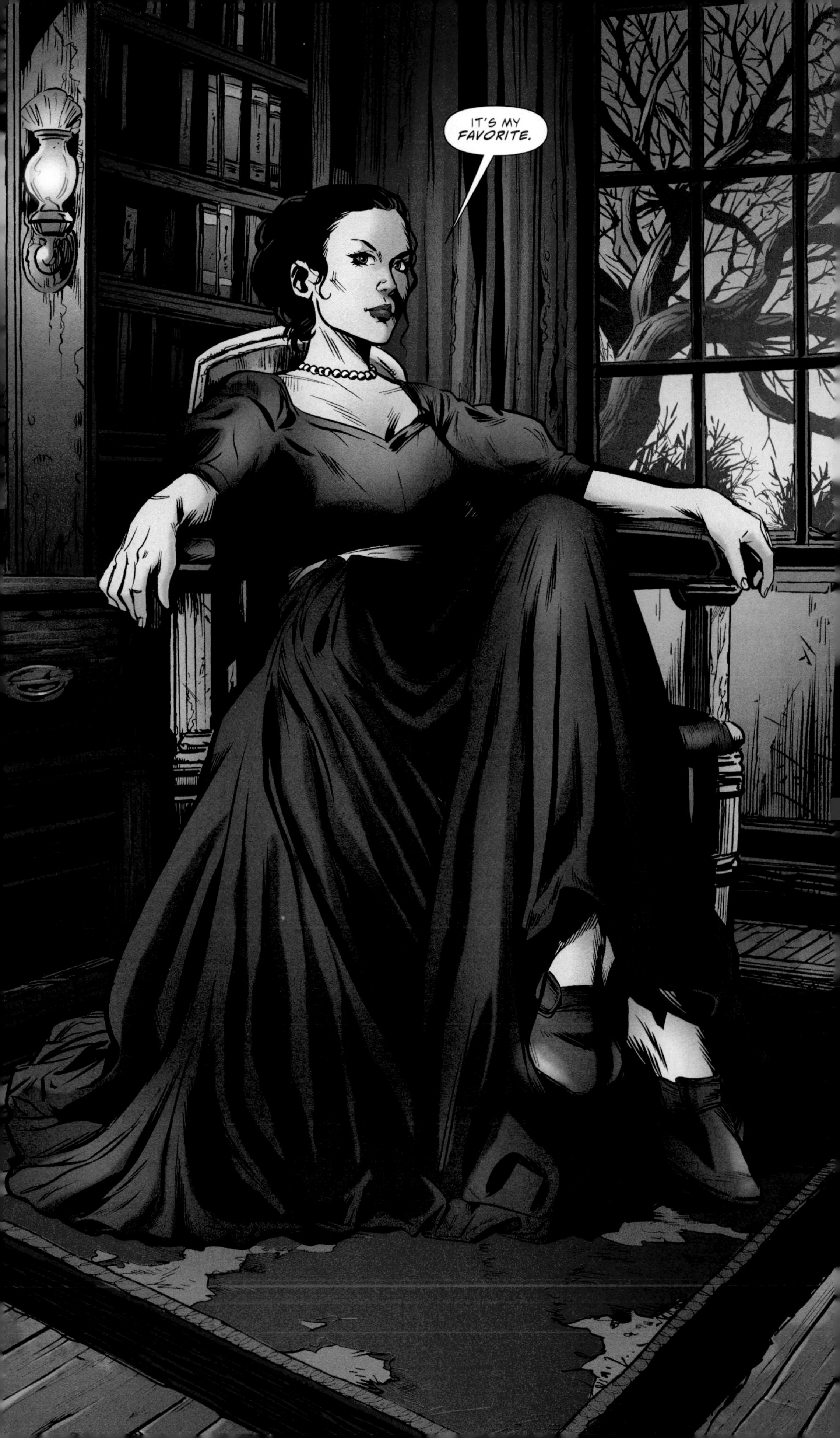
IT'S MY FAVORITE.

Lorelei sketch by **Ryan Kelly**

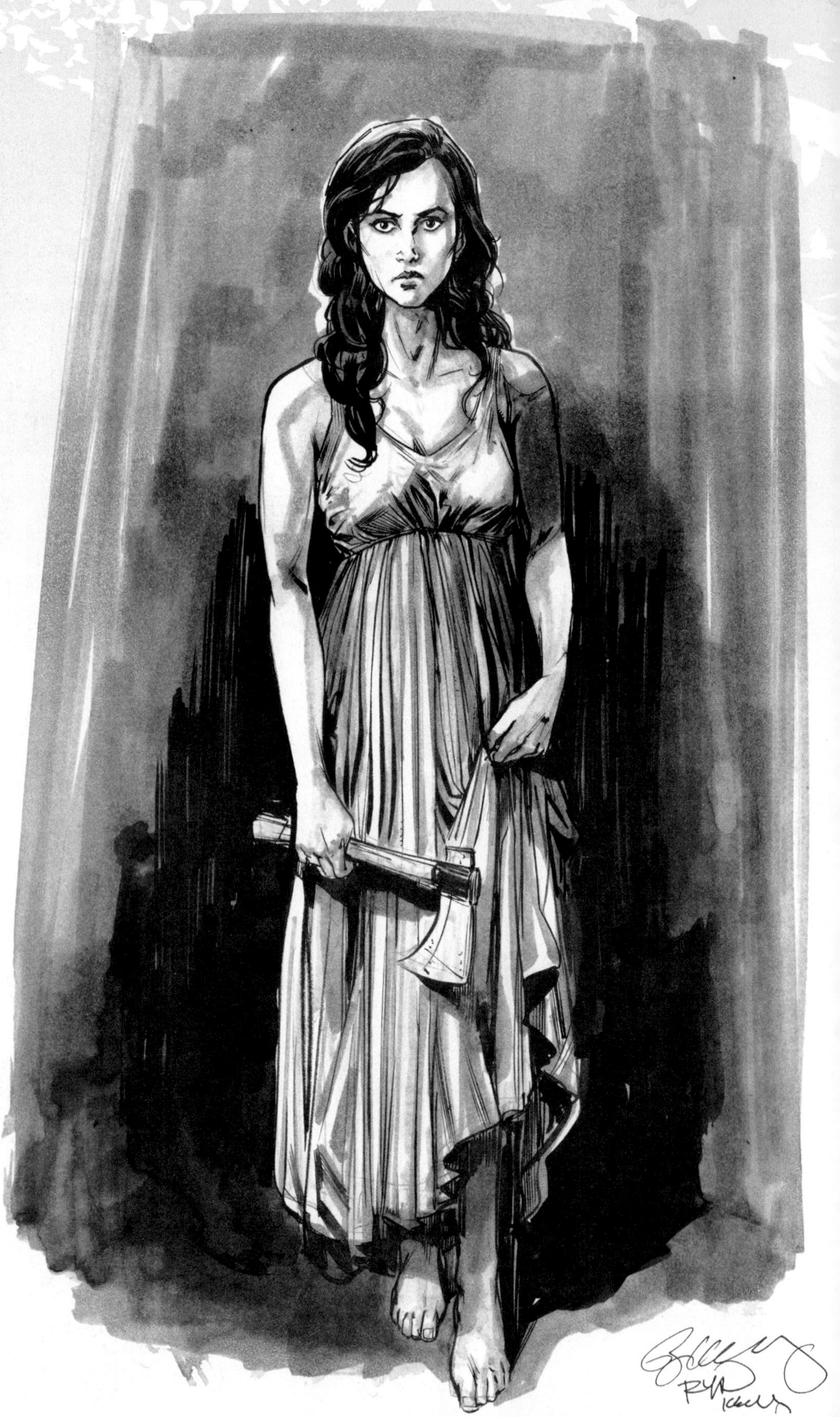

Killers sketch by **Ryan Kelly**

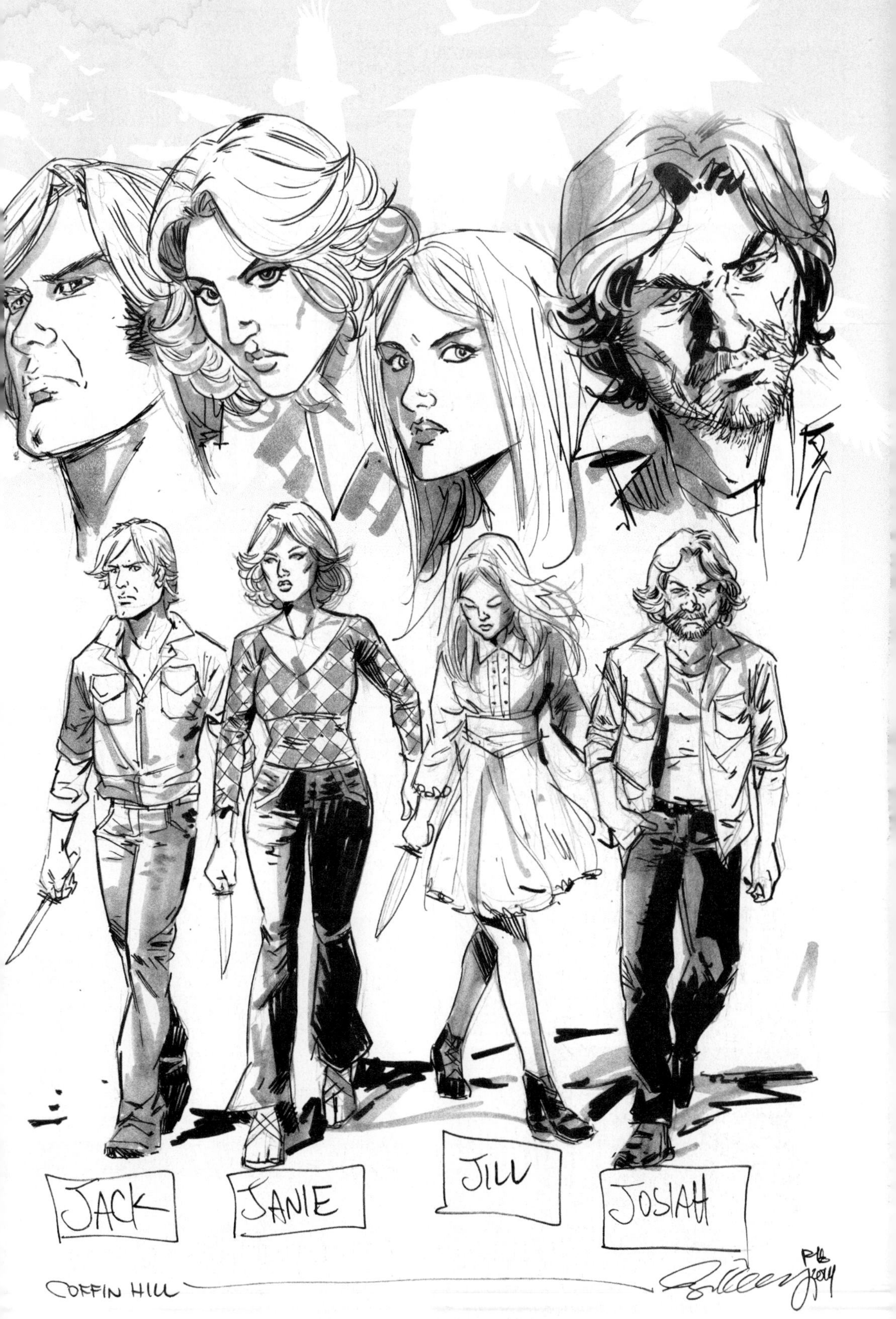
JACK
JANIE
JILL
JOSIAH
COFFIN HILL

COFFIN HILL #8 page layouts by **Inaki Miranda**

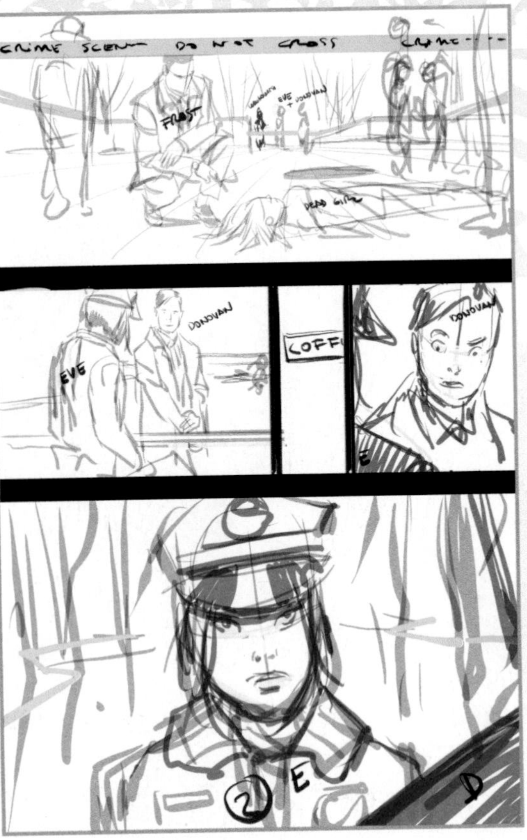
CRIME SCENE DO NOT CROSS
FROST
DEAD GIRL
EVE
DONOVAN
COFF
DONOVAN
E
E
D
2

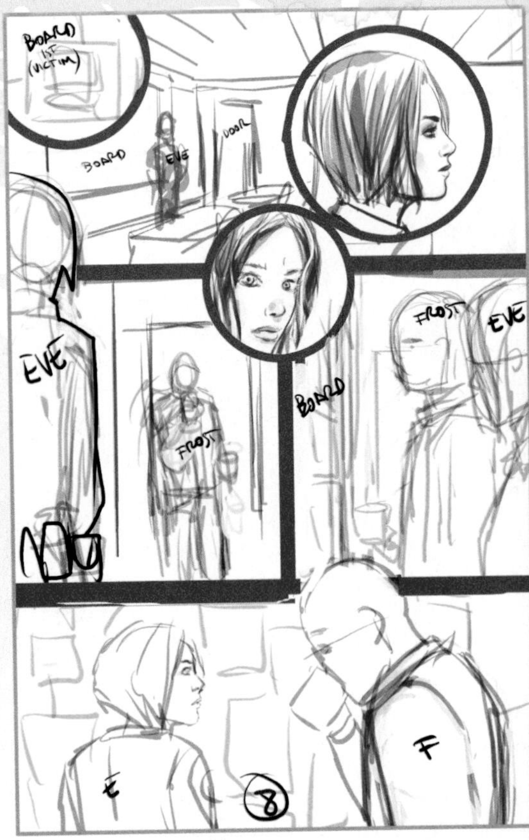
BOARD
1ST
(VICTIM)
BOARD
EVE
DOOR
EVE
FROST
BOARD
FROST
EVE
E
F
8

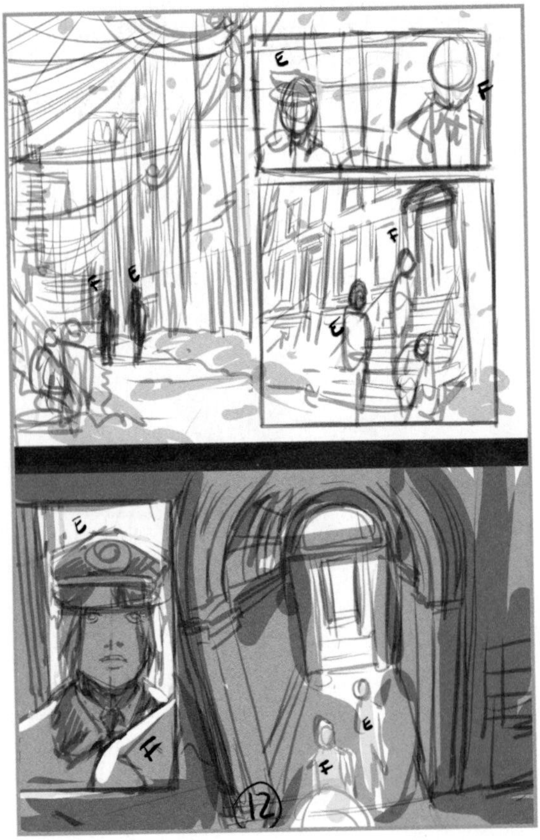
E
F
F
E
F
E
E
F
E
F
12

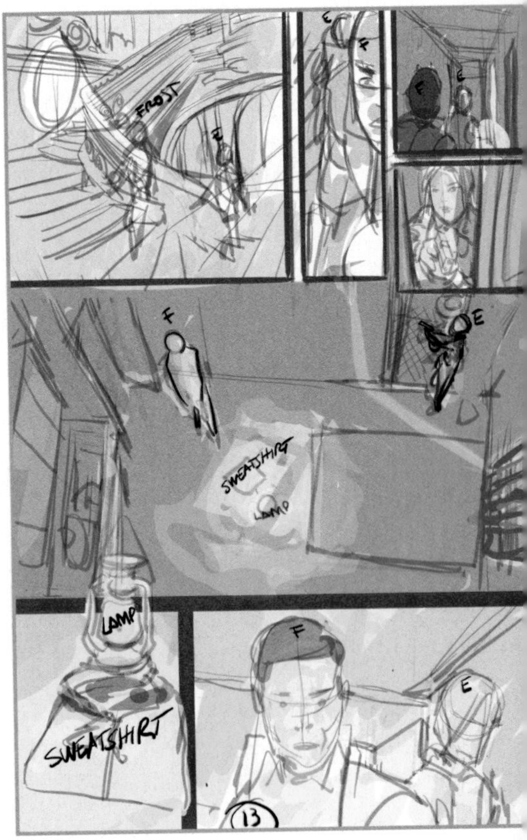
FROST
E
F
F
E
F
E
SWEATSHIRT
LAMP
LAMP
SWEATSHIRT
F
E
13

COFFIN HILL #9 page layouts by **Inaki Miranda**

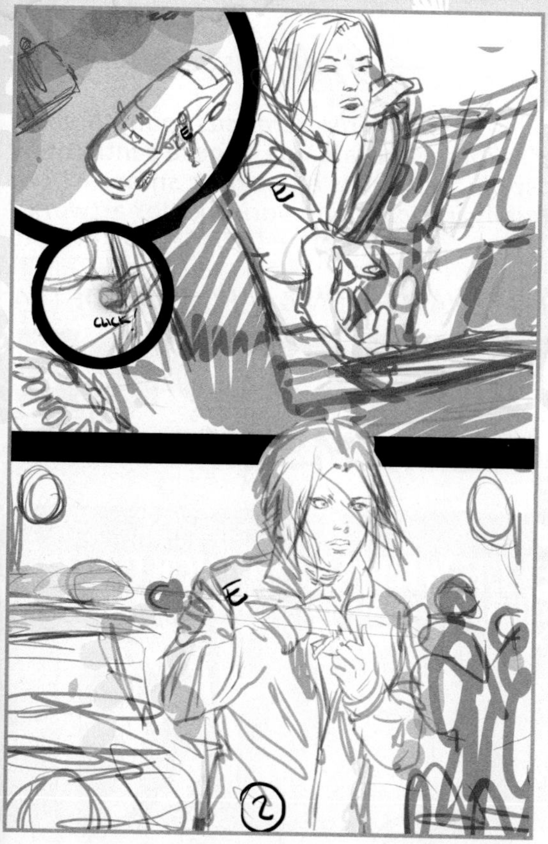
CLICK!
2

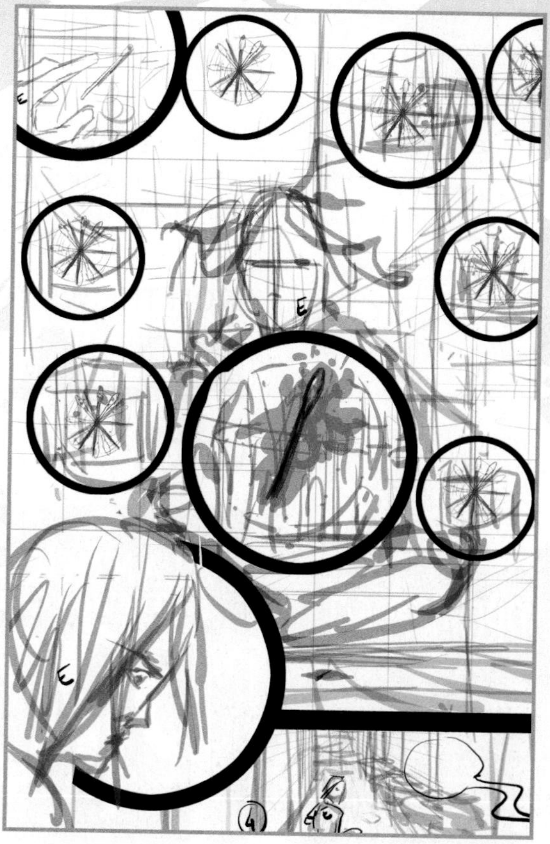
4

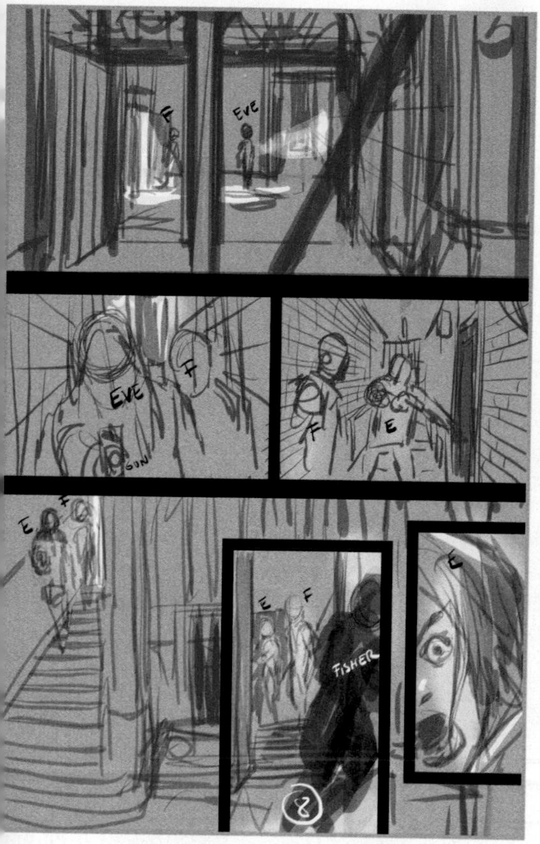
EVE
EVE
GUN
FISHER
8

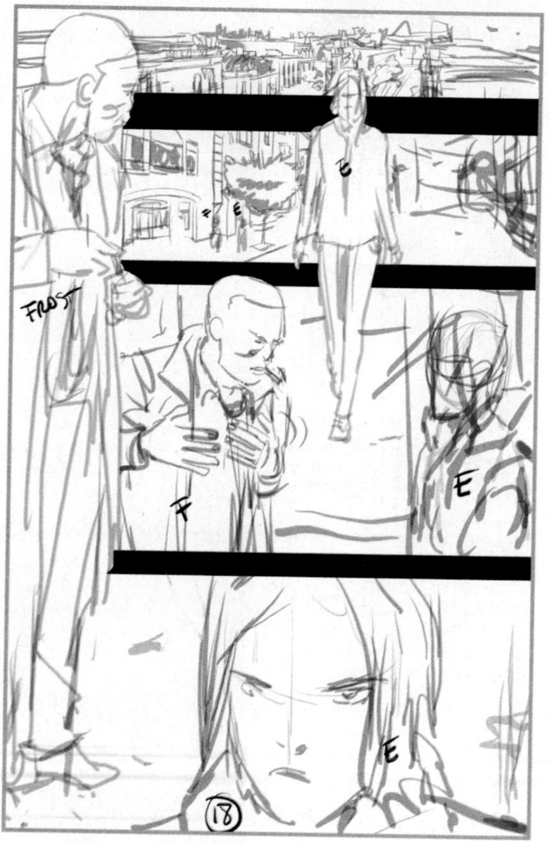
FROST
18